OXFORD

Son of Queen Elizabeth I

By Paul Streitz

Oxford Institute Press
2001

Library of Congress Cataloging-in-Publication Data

Streitz, Paul, 1943–

Oxford: Son of Queen Elizabeth I

Includes bibliographical references and index.

Library of Congress Control Number: 2001 129201

ISBN 0-9713498-0-0
hard cover
ISBN 0-9713498-1-9
paperback

1. Shakespeare, William, 1564–1616, Authorship, Oxford Theory
2. Oxford, Edward de Vere, 17th Earl of, 1550–1564,—Authorship
3. De Vere, Edward, 1548–1604, Biography
4. Tudor, Elizabeth, 1533–1603, Biography
5. Dramatists, English—Early modern, 1500–1700—Biography
6. Nobility—Great Britain—Biography.

Printed and bound in the United States of America.

Oxford Institute Press
8 William Street
Darien, CT 06820

Cover Design: Paul Streitz

For Hilda and Natasha

Table of Contents

Table of Figures

ACKNOWLEDGEMENTS

This work rests on the shoulders of many scholars and researchers who have patiently endured the derision of the established academic world to produce groundbreaking work that will be more appreciated in coming years. Among those ever-living Shakespearean scholars are Delia Bacon, George Greenwood, Mark Twain, B.M. Ward, J. Thomas Looney, Eva Turner Clark, Charles Wisner Barrell, Charlton Ogburn, Dorothy Ogburn, and Charlton Ogburn Jr. My thanks to all the patient Oxfordian scholars who have searched for the true William Shakespeare.

My special thanks to Elisabeth Sears for her pioneering work on Edward de Vere; to Pidge Sexton and Roger Stritmatter for their literary advice; to Stephanie Caruana and Elisabeth Sears for their exhaustive work on Oxford's early literary history; to Katherine Chiljan for her list of dedications to Oxford; to Robert Brazil for his work on Shakespeare's printers, to Barbara Burris for her work on the Ashbourne Portrait; to Mark Alexander for his insights on Shakespeare's legal world; to Vincent Cuenca for advice on the Spanish language; to Professor Tom Holland for his Latin translations; to Nina Greene for her Internet discussion group and to all those who participated in debates on the issues found in this book; to Blanche Parker of the Darien Library for her assistance; to Susan Harris of the Bodleian Library and Lori Johnson of the Folger Shakespeare Library; to Gretchen Haynes and Franklin Cook for their editorial and editing guidance; to Eileen Duffin, Marilyn Clarke, and Natasha Streitz for their proofing skills; to Marilyn Clarke for her perceptive comments on Edward de Vere; and to Hank Whittemore for his encouragement, his comments, and his invaluable assistance.

GENTLE READER

The British monarchy remains out of bounds, more so than other social institutions. Indeed, one could say that a conspiracy of silence surrounds the extraordinary and probably unique hierarchical system of privilege that emanates from the monarch. Why? Because those who are close enough to see what goes on behind the palace walls keep their lips buttoned in the hope that they too might be co-opted into that system via highly coveted awards. Blabbermouths are not knighted. Nor are they retained as friends or servants. Neither do they keep the affection of princes.

— Ilse Hayden

It is almost impossible to write a balanced study of Elizabeth I. The historiographical tradition is so laudatory that it is hard to avoid either floating with the current of applauding opinion or creating an unseemly splash by swimming too energetically against it. The marketing of Elizabeth began in her own reign, with the efforts of Protestants, official propagandists, and profit-seeking balladeers. Enthusiastic praise was turned into structured history by William Camden, who wrote his *Annales* in the 1610s. Camden formulated the historiographical agenda for the reign, and historians have usually followed his scheme: Elizabeth inherited chaos at home and threats from abroad, but with her own foresight and skill she imposed unifying solutions to national problems. The reign of Elizabeth was thus a golden age of progress, in which a careful queen inspired her people to greatness and checked any divisive militant tendencies. The 'Camden version' has dominated interpretations of Elizabeth over the past century: it was followed in most of the almost 90 biographies published since 1890.

— Christopher Haigh

It is inconceivable that anyone who has [encountered genius] could maintain the belief that genius is often held back by social factors. If genius is not given form by context, it will make its own. It is this aggressive reordering of context that is genius. It is simply unimaginable that context, whether the intellectual matrix facing the genius or the social and economic factors touching his life, could dissuade him.

— Steven Goldberg

A FEW DISSENTERS

DELIA BACON

[Shakespeare] carries the court influence with him, unconsciously, wherever he goes. He looks into Arden and Eastcheap from the court standpoint, not from these into the court, and he is as much a prince with Poins and Bardolph as he is when he enters and throws open to us, without awe, without consciousness, the most delicate mysteries of the royal presence.

— The Philosophy of the Plays of Shakespeare Unfolded

WILLIAM HENRY SMITH

Not one single manuscript has ever been found to identify Shakespeare (i.e., Shakspere) as the author of these productions; nor is there, among all the records and traditions handed down to us, any statement that he was ever seen writing or producing a manuscript; none that he ever claimed as his own, or repudiated (as unworthy of him) any of the worthless productions presented to the public in his name.

— Bacon and Shakespeare

SIR EDWIN DURNING LAWRENCE

There is also shown in the plays the most perfect knowledge of court etiquette, and of the manners and the methods of the greatest in the land, a knowledge which none but a courtier moving in the highest circles could by any possibility have acquired.

— Bacon is Shake-speare

MORSE JOHNSON

It is certain, therefore, that whoever wrote the works must have been known both personally and by reputation to a number of his contemporaries. Why, then, is there no reference during his lifetime by a friend or relative or a neighbor or a theatre colleague or a business associate connecting the works with the man? There has to be some rational explanation for this undeniable fact and unique mystery. The only one that makes possible sense to me is that, whoever wrote the works, every effort was for some reason made to conceal his authorship.

MARK TWAIN

Isn't it odd, when you think of it, that you may list all the celebrated Englishmen, Irishmen, and Scotchmen of modern times, clear back to the first Tudors—a list containing five hundred names, shall we say?—and you can go to the histories, biographies, and cyclopedias and learn the particulars of the lives of every one of them. Every one of them except one—the most famous, the most renowned—by far the most illustrious of them all—Shakespeare!—About him you can find nothing. Nothing of even the slightest importance. Nothing worth the trouble of storing away in your memory. Nothing that even remotely indicates that he was ever anything more than a distinctly commonplace person.

I answered as my readings of the champions of my side of the great controversy had taught me to answer: that a man can't handle glibly and easily and comfortably and successfully the *argot* of a trade at which he had not personally served. He will make mistakes; he will not, and cannot, get the trade-phrasings precisely and exactly right; and the moment he departs, even a shade, from a common trade-form, the reader who has served in that trade will know the writer *hasn't.*

For experience is an author's most valuable asset; experience is the thing that puts the muscle and the breath and the warm blood into the book he writes.

The author of the Plays was equipped, beyond every other man of his time, with wisdom, erudition, imagination, capaciousness of mind, grace, and majesty of expression. Everyone had said it, no one doubts it. Also, he had humor, in rich abundance, and always wanting to break out. We have no evidence of any kind that Shakespeare of Stratford possessed any of these gifts or any of these acquirements.

— *Is Shakespeare Dead?,* 1909

SIGMUND FREUD

I no longer believe that William Shakespeare, the actor from Stratford, was the author of the works which have so long been attributed to him. Since the publication of *Shakespeare Identified*, I am almost convinced that in fact Edward de Vere, Earl of Oxford, is concealed behind this pseudonym.

— Interpretation of Dreams, 1930 edition

The name "William Shakespeare" is most probably a pseudonym behind which there lies concealed a great unknown. Edward de Vere, Earl of Oxford, a man who has been regarded as the author of Shakespeare's works, lost a beloved and admired father while he was still a boy, and completely repudiated his mother, who contracted a new marriage soon after her husband's death.

— Abriss der Psycho-Analyse, 1940

We will have a lot to discuss about Shakespeare. I do not know what still attracts you to the man of Stratford. He seems to have nothing at all to justify his claim, whereas Oxford has almost everything. It is quite inconceivable to me that Shakespeare should have got everything secondhand: Hamlet's neurosis, Lear's madness, Macbeth's defiance and the character of Lady Macbeth, Othello's jealousy, etc. It almost irritates me that you should support the notion.

— Letter to A. Zweig, 1937

CHARLIE CHAPLIN

In the work of the greatest geniuses, humble beginnings will reveal themselves somewhere but one cannot trace the slightest sign of them in Shakespeare....Whoever wrote [Shakespeare] had an aristocratic attitude.

ANONYMOUS, 1852

How comes it that Raleigh, Spencer, and even Bacon—all with genius so thoroughly kindred to the author of *Hamlet*—have all ignored his acquaintance? Raleigh and Bacon seem not to have known of his existence; while Spencer, if he alludes to the works, takes care to avoid the name. In short, Heywood, Suckling, Hales, and all the others who are recorded to have spoken of Shakespeare "with great admiration," confine themselves to the works, and seem personally to avoid the man—always excepting "Rare Ben Johnson."

SAMUEL ADAMS

Stratford upon Avon is interesting as it is the Scaene of the Birth, Death and Sepulture of Shakespeare. Three doors from Inn, is the House where he was born, as small and mean, as you can conceive. They shew Us an old Wooden Chair in the Chimney Corner, where He sat. We cut off a Chip according to the Custom. A Mulberry Tree that he planted has been cut down, and is carefully preserved for Sale. The House where he died has been taken down and the Spot is now only Yard or Garden. The Curse upon him who should removed his Bones, which is written on his Grave Stone, alludes to a Pile of some Thousands of human Bones, which lie exposed in that Church. There is nothing preserved of this great Genius which is worth knowing—nothing which might inform Us what Educations, what Company, what Accident turned his Mind to Letters and the Drama. His name is not even on his Grave Stone. An ill sculptured Head is sett up by his Wife, by the Side of his Grave in the Church. But paintings and Sculpture would be thrown away upon his Fame. His Wit and Fancy, his Taste and Judgment, His Knowledge of Nature, of Life and Character, are immortal.

> — From a letter when Adams and Thomas Jefferson visited Stratford-upon-Avon. Jefferson wrote nothing about the occasion except a record of his expenses.

MALCOLM X

Another hot debate I remember I was in had to do with the identity of Shakespeare. No color was involved there; I just got intrigued over the Shakespearean dilemma. The King James translation of the Bible is considered the greatest piece of literature in English. They say that from 1604 to 1611, King James got poets to translate, to write the Bible. Well, if Shakespeare existed, he was then the top poet around. But Shakespeare is nowhere reported connected with the Bible. If he existed, why didn't King James use him?

HUGH R. TREVOR-ROPER

During his lifetime nobody claimed to know him. Not a single tribute was paid to him at his death. As far as the records go, he was uneducated, had no literary friends, possessed at his death no books, and could not write. It is true, six of his signatures have been found, all spelt differently; but they are so ill formed that some graphologists suppose the hand to have been guided. Except for these signatures, no syllable of writing by Shakespeare had been identified. Seven years after his death, when his works were collected and published, and other poets claimed to have known him (actually, we shall see, only one: Ben Johnson), a portrait of him was painted. The unskillful artist has presented the blank face of a country oaf.

HENRY JAMES

I am "sort of" haunted by the conviction that the divine William is the biggest and most successful fraud ever practiced on a patient world. The more I turn him round and round the more he so affects me. But that is all—I am not pretending to treat the question or to carry it any further. It bristles with difficulties, and I can only express my general sense by saying that I find it almost as impossible to conceive that Bacon wrote the plays as to conceive that the man from Stratford, as we know the man from Stratford, did.

LESLIE HOWARD

Now this [holds up Looney's book] proves conclusively that Shakspere wasn't really Shakespeare at all ... He was the Earl of Oxford. The Earl of Oxford was a very bright Elizabethan light, but this book will tell he was a good deal more than that ... "Alas poor Yorick"—the Earl of Oxford wrote that, you know.

— Scene from the movie *Pimpernel Smith*

ORSON WELLES

I think Oxford wrote Shakespeare. If you don't agree, there are some awfully funny coincidences to explain away.

WALT WHITMAN

Conceived out of the fullest heat and pulse of European feudalism—personifying in unparalleled ways the medieval aristocracy, its towering spirit of ruthless and gigantic caste, with its own peculiar air and arrogance (no mere imitation)—only one of the "wolfish earls" so plenteous in the plays themselves, or some born descendant and knower, might seem to be the true author of those amazing works, works in some respects greater than anything else in recorded literature.

— *November Boughs,* 1888

MARK RYLANCE

As an actor my training is to look for the motivation necessary for any act. I find that the unfortunately limited evidence of the Stratfordian authorship theory seems to reveal little more than monetary motivation ... I find the work of the Shakespeare Oxford Society reveals a character, in Edward de Vere, motivated to use the mask of drama to reveal the true identity and nature of his time, as only someone in his position would have known, and as was the well established habit so clearly demonstrated in *Hamlet.*

HERMAN SINSHEIMER

At a distance of four centuries, Elizabeth Tudor and William Shakespeare look like brother and sister. He too had a unique receptivity ... He assembled a thousand years around his throne. He is, as it were, a woman-man just as his sister Elizabeth is a man-woman ... To us, William's work is embedded in Elizabeth's role and William's poetry is redolent of Elizabeth's work. He is the Elizabethan poet, ... she is the Shakespearean Queen. Shakespeare the Spear-Shaker!... The plays are Elizabethan conquests, extensions of territory, expansions of privilege and power, additions of wealth to a nation that is experiencing a whole world.

— Shylock: The History of a Character

DAVID McCULLOUGH

The strange, difficult, contradictory man who emerges as the real Shakespeare, Edward de Vere, the 17th Earl of Oxford, is not just plausible but fascinating and wholly believable. It is hard to imagine anyone who reads the book with an open mind ever seeing Shakespeare or his works in the same way again.

— Foreword to *The Mysterious William Shakespeare*

Amb. PAUL H. NITZE

I believe the considerations favoring the Oxfordian hypothesis ... are overwhelming. ...It's fashionable today to declare "the death of the author"; the author's life and experience count for naught. Any consideration of the author's intention or meaning is rejected. Rejected, too, is any thought that the author was communicating ideals of value to the spectator or the reader. For those afflicted by this fashionable myopia, who Shakespeare was, how he lived and what he was trying to tell us are irrelevant. But fashions come and go, and I am told there are signs that the negation of authorial intention in academic literary criticism has peaked.

Mr. Justice LEWIS F. POWELL JR.
I have never thought that the man of Stratford-on-Avon wrote the plays of Shakespeare. I know of no admissible evidence that he ever left England or was educated in the normal sense of the term. One must wonder, for example, how he could have written *The Merchant of Venice*.

JAMES LORD
Their lives (artists) become interpenetrated by the art through which they attempt to give life to life, and such a profound interdependence is generated between what they are and what they do that ultimately the two achieve a common character.

DAVID GONTAR
What makes me nervous is the constant invitation to imagine the creator of the empire of the strange as a boring man who lived a boring life, whether noble or common. No, the violence and sexuality of the dramas and poems must mirror in some sense the flesh and blood behind them. What is most overlooked about Shakespeare is that he suffered, and somehow expressed and overcame that suffering in his art. Unless we can compose a biography, which reflects the alienation and agony of Shakespeare's poetry, we will have failed to take the measure of the man. Apparently that failure is our destiny.

CHARLES WISNER BARRELL
Ultimately the trail led to the previously disregarded and half-obliterated foot prints of Edward de Vere, Queen Elizabeth's wayward and unhappy Lord Great Chamberlain and one-time lover—a poet, court dramatist, and patron of players of outstanding contemporary fame, but a man whose consuming passion for art and scholarship made him a prey to designing machinations of politicians and courtiers; to escape whose blighting influence he turned to the companionship of common poets, dramatists, musicians and actors; one who fell afoul of the taboos of his own caste and "lost his good name" as a result; a nobleman, bearing the second oldest title in the realm, who "wasted his substance" and "squandered his patrimony on men of letters," whose bohemian mode of life seems to have attracted him.

CHARLTON OGBURN

Nothing we know about de Vere or about Shakespeare is incompatible with their having been the same; that the positive indications that they were the same are plentiful and striking and accumulate with investigation; that the facts are found to eliminate all other candidates, leaving de Vere the only one who could have been Shakespeare.

— *The Mysterious William Shakespeare*

J. THOMAS LOONEY

After all there are few joys in life like that of laying hold of some new and important truth, and carrying it to others in the full and assured faith that such truth is destined to prevail. It is in the conscious and successful propagation of constructive ideas that man attains the highest sense of self-realization, and if our "Shakespeare" beliefs do not, of themselves, belong to the highest domains of thought, they, at any rate, deal with literature which does; and, in my opinion, by giving us the personality which informs and vitalises that literature, contribute the largest factor towards its right interpretation.

— Letter to Eva Turner Clark, June 26, 1926

INTRODUCTION

When I began this book, my intention was to write a biography of Edward de Vere that focused on his personality, literary life, and creativity: a portrait of the artist. To better understand him, I felt it was important to understand aristocratic life in the Elizabethan age, which was the childhood environment of Edward de Vere. This involved reading a good number of books on the Tudors and particularly on Queen Elizabeth. The more I read, the more I realized that historians of the period were concealing more than they were revealing. This was especially true about Elizabeth's relationship with Thomas Seymour during 1548 when she was a girl of thirteen years. Practically all historians of the period claim nothing untoward happened. This is despite substantial evidence to the contrary; for them the image of the Virgin Queen remains intact.

Elizabethan history was, and still is today, an effort in damage control to protect the reputation of the Virgin Queen. The first historian might present facts A and B, the second historian might present facts C and D, and the third historian might present facts E and F, and so on. After presenting a limited number of the facts, each historian concludes that the rumors of Elizabeth having a child at age thirteen were only rumors. Yet no historian has presented all the facts from A to Z, which paint a picture not easily dismissed. For example, one historian prints one innocuous legal deposition in full but completely omits a more damaging deposition. Such a selective presentation of facts would convince a reader of only one biography that the issue had been covered and the case found unproven. Such books usually end with the historian's calming reassurances that, despite all the rumors, Elizabeth was indeed the Virgin Queen. However, the more one reads, the more the Virgin Queen becomes a myth built by the Tudor monarchy and perpetuated by noncritical historians. Each historian, in turn, attempts to quash the rumor that the princess bore a child during this period.

Historical research of the Elizabethan period is complicated by the fact that Elizabethan England was a totalitarian monarchy. The few presses that existed were controlled by the Crown, critics of the monarchy were ruthless suppressed, and the Crown had a network of spies and informers to track dissidents. Any written records of the Queen's misbehavior would be few, and it would be sheer luck if any did survive. In addition, only about five percent of the population was literate, and that percent consisted mainly of the aristocrats, the clergy, and the lawyers. These social classes were the ones that most benefited from the benevolence of the monarch and were hardly likely to commit any transgressions of the monarch to paper. Those in the lower social classes, such as servants, townspeople and midwives, were not literate and thus were unable to leave any written historical record. In short, it is a historical investigation where the historian can expect to find little, if any, direct documentation.

In addition, the events are 450 years in the past, with many letters and documents destroyed in the course of time. Often the documents that do survive are from the very sources most likely to be the key conspirators, so these documents are least likely to contain any incriminating evidence. Written historical documents are useful, but they can often be misleading or deliberately false. In the case of an unwanted childbirth by a public figure, it is unlikely there would be any such documents such as diaries or public records. To expect a substantial written historical record of events that persons in high places wanted kept secret would be to expect a historical record that never would have been created in the first place.

However, the superiority of hard historical evidence, such as letters and other documents, is somewhat overstated. For example, if a bloody knife were found with the fingerprints of the suspect on it, that could be regarded as hard evidence. On the other hand, if the victim and the knife were in the suspect's kitchen, it may well be that the fingerprints were the result of normal household use. In other words, the hard evidence is also dependent upon the circumstances; therefore, in some sense, all hard evidence is circumstantial. In the case of the trial of a Hollywood celebrity, the jury did not believe any of the hard evidence presented and instead chose to believe that it was circumstantial (that is, planted by a racist police force). J. Thomas Looney's comment on circumstantial evidence provides a useful insight:

> A few coincidences we may treat as simply interesting; a number of coincidences we regard as remarkable; a vast accumulation of extraordinary coincidences we accept as conclusive proof. And when the case has reached this stage we look upon the matter as finally settled, until, as may happen, something of a most unusual character appears to upset all our reasoning. If nothing of this kind ever appears, whilst every newly discovered fact adds but confirmation to the conclusion, that conclusion is accepted as a permanently established truth.[1]

Four criteria are suggested to examine the possibility of a hidden, secret child: The first would be if there were any rumors or gossip about the birth of such a child. While rumors and gossip are not substantive evidence, they are often part of oral folk history that has a basis in fact and merits further investigation. As we will see, even the written historical record provides substantial grounds for suspicion.

Second, was there a period of time when the proposed mother was not in public view? Human females are severely limited in activities the last month of pregnancy. When their pregnancies are publicly visible, they need seclusion, concealment, and a group of attendant women to assist in the childbirth.

Third, was there a child raised nearby the alleged mother that receives special or unusual treatment? Was the child reared as a nephew or as a child of a close friend? Further, the child might receive special consideration from the birth mother. Similarly, does the child seem to receive special consideration from those surrounding the mother?

Fourth, did the adult life of the alleged child indicate a relationship to the alleged mother or parents? In the case of an author, one can further ask if the literary works revealed themes and associations with the alleged mother and the child's hidden place in society.

The purpose of this book is to critically examine all the historical evidence to determine whether or not Elizabeth had a child in the summer of 1548 and whether or not this child was raised as Edward de Vere, 17th Earl of Oxford, better known to the world as the author "William Shakespeare."[a]

---

[a] Parentheses in original quotes are represented as ( ); those added by this author are represented by brackets [ ]. Italics added by this author are noted as [*Italics* added]; otherwise the italics are as they appear in the source.

"Shakespeare" or "Author" refers to the true author of the works, whoever that might be. The "man from Stratford-upon-Avon" or "Shakspere" refers to the person from Stratford. "Edward de Vere" or "Oxford" denotes Edward de Vere, 17th Earl of Oxford.

THE ASHBOURNE PORTRAIT

The cover of this book is a three-quarter portrait of a nobleman, known as the Ashbourne Portrait of Shakespeare. This portrait now hangs in the Folger Shakespeare Library in Washington, D.C., founded by Henry Clay Folger in 1932. It currently holds one of the largest collections of Shakespearean books, paintings, and memorabilia in the world. It also publishes a scholarly journal, *The Shakespeare Quarterly.* The Folger Shakespeare Library gives this description of Folger's first interest in Shakespeare:

> Henry Clay Folger's interest in Shakespeare was sparked by a lecture he attended when he was a student at Amherst College in 1879. The ticket he purchased for 25¢ to hear Ralph Waldo Emerson is now part of the collections housed in the library he founded—the Folger Shakespeare Library—in Washington, DC.[1]

Ironically, Emerson strongly supported Delia Bacon, and he enabled her to have her book on Shakespeare published. This was the first book that proposed that someone other than the man from Stratford was the Author known as William Shakespeare. Emerson was always skeptical of Stratfordian authorship, so Folger might have been aware of the Authorship controversy from his first introduction to Shakespeare. His purchase of both the Ashbourne Portrait and later the *Edward de Vere Geneva Bible* indicates that he may have been aware of Edward de Vere as a candidate for the true Shakespeare. At least he was open-minded about the idea as indicated by his purchases. Had Folger lived a few more years, the history of the Authorship issue might have been very different indeed.

Instead, the Folger Shakespeare Library became the bastion of Shakespearean orthodoxy. It has unabashedly maintained that the man from Stratford-upon-Avon was the Author, suppressed opposing views, and slandered its critics. If ever there were an institution similar to the Catholic Church of the Middle Ages in its insistence on faith over rational inquiry, it would be the Folger Shakespeare Library. The policies of its hierarchy have stifled academic debate on the Authorship issue and intimidated academics wanting to do work on the Authorship issue. Diversity, tolerance for dissenting viewpoints, and freedom to express contrarian opinions are not the hallmarks of the Folger Shakespeare

Library's handling of the Authorship issue.[a] The Ashbourne Portrait is a sterling example of the Folger Shakespeare Library's and the larger academic community's reaction to Authorship issues and presents an opportunity to show where the historical record has been suppressed, distorted, and perhaps even falsified to preserve the myth of the Bard of Avon.

The Ashbourne Portrait of Shakespeare emerged from obscurity in 1847 in Ashbourne, Derbyshire, when Rev. Clement U. Kingston, one of the masters of Queen Elizabeth's Free Grammar School, noticed the Hamlet-like qualities of the portrait. The portrait had been in the possession of one of the old English country families, and its origins are linked to Sir Thomas Cockayne of Ashbourne Hall, Derbyshire, who founded the school in 1585, where the painting was eventually discovered. In 1671, Sir William Boothby bought Ashbourne Hall, and the portrait remained in the family's hands until the hall's sale in April 1846, the year before the painting was "discovered."

In 1696, before another sale of Ashbourne Hall, one of the series of owners of the painting, the Earl of Wentworth, referred to a painting in his will as a three-quarter portrait of "my wife's great-grandfather, the Earl of Oxford." In 1782, an inventory of the same Wentworth heirloom paintings mentions no three-quarter portrait of the Earl of Oxford, Edward de Vere. Instead, there is mention of a three-quarter-length portrait of "Shakespeare" placed next to a portrait of Horatio Vere. This implies that in the minds of the Wentworths, this three-quarter portrait refers to Oxford and Shakespeare as if they were the same person.

At the turn of the twentieth century, the portrait was in rags, so it was rebacked to preserve the painting. Three art experts, Abraham Wivell, Samuel Timmins, and M.H. Spielmann, vouched that the picture's composition and style dated it as an Elizabethan Renaissance painting. In 1910, Dr. M.H. Spielmann did a number of studies on the portrait and reported the findings in *Connoisseur Magazine.* The suspicion that this portrait might be a fraud prompted Spielmann's work. During the mid-1800s, a number of fake Shakespeare letters and poems had emerged, and the art world was suspicious of any portrait turning up labeled "Shakespeare."

Spielmann noted several irregularities in the portrait that indicated it had been altered to fit the common conception of what William

---

[a] In due fairness to the professional staff of the Folger, they have been courteous, competent and professional in finding materials for this book. The criticism of the Folger Shakespeare Library in this book is directed at the senior management of the library and the official policies of the library, not at the professional staff.

Shakespeare looked like based on the Droeshout engraving of the *First Folio*. The most noticeable change in the portrait was to move the hairline back and to raise the crown of the skull, making the subject appear to have an unnaturally high skull, such as in the Droeshout engraving, and much more bald. This made the portrait more like the Droeshout engraving of the title page to the *First Folio*. Spielmann notes this in his 1904 article:

> At some early period, the hair seems to have been retouched, or re-varnished with a bituminous medium, perhaps at the same time as the ruff at the throat.[2]

Subsequent restorations by the Folger Shakespeare Library lowered the height of the skull and made the portrait match normal human proportions. The portrait shown on the cover of this book is after the restorations.

Other modifications noted by Spielmann include the bright gold of the thumb ring and emblem of the book which did not match the subdued colors of the remainder of the portrait. The gold inscription in the upper left corner of the portrait stated "Aetatis suae 47 Anno 1611." This links the portrait with the man from Stratford-upon-Avon who was born in 1564 and would have been forty-seven years old in 1611. Dr. Spielmann further noted that the sitter for the portrait looks much like one of the gentlemen in the wedding procession portrait of Queen Elizabeth. In this portrait, Elizabeth is on a cart covered by a canopy and surrounded by courtiers:

> We thus have the presentment of a handsome, courtly gentleman, well formed and of good bearing, and apparently of high breeding, thoughtful, and contemplative; so sincere in expression and presentation that the picture cannot be regarded in any sense a theatrical portrait. It resembles rather one of the gentlemen who accompanied Queen Elizabeth in her progress to Hunsdon House according to the tradition ...[3]

Spielmann concludes:

> The *Ashbourne Shakespeare*, then, remains a mystery, but I am not without hope of discovering a solution to the puzzle.[4]

Eustace Conway purchased the painting in 1929 and then sold it to the Folger Library. Despite the reservations about the sitter for the portrait, the Folger Shakespeare Library purchased it and displayed it as a portrait of Shakespeare, or at least as one of a series of representations of the man. There was no strenuous objections to this designation, nor were there any other candidates for the subject of the portrait.

This changed dramatically after the publication of an article in the January 1940 issue of *Scientific American*. The author of that article,

Charles Wisner Barrell, concluded that the sitter for the painting was Edward de Vere, 17th Earl of Oxford, who was in his view, the true Author, William Shakespeare. Barrell was on the public relations staff of Western Electric as director of the Motion Pictures Bureau. He had previously represented the Rotograph Company, an American branch of the Photographisce Gessellschaft of Berlin, the originator of the modern rotogravure process. In such capacities, Barrell was knowledgeable in photographic techniques and was in contact with experts in the field.

Barrell's article stated that an X-ray analysis confirmed alterations of the portrait as Spielmann had pointed out a half century before. These modifications showed an intent to make the portrait more similar to the *First Folio* engraving and the dates consistent with the life of the man from Stratford-upon-Avon. The X-rays confirmed that the hairline had been pushed back several inches to make the sitter appear balder and to have an unnaturally large head. Second, the alterations reduced the originally huge, fluted ruff around the collar to make it more appropriate for a gentleman and less appropriate for a nobleman. Further, Barrell argued that the 1611 date covered a coat of arms in the upper left portion of the painting, which Barrell concluded looked similar to those of Oxford's wife, who was of the Trentham family. Barrell also concluded that alterations to the sitter's thumb ring covered a boar's head inscribed on the ring. The boar's head was the symbol of the Earl of Oxford.

Barrell further stated that the X-ray revealed the initials "CK" in the right hand corner, identifying the painter as Cornelius Ketel (1548–1616), a Dutch portrait artist. However, in this author's opinion, the X-ray image of the initials reproduced in *Scientific American* do not match the initials of Cornelius Ketel as Barrell presents in the article. (The X-rays in the *Scientific American* article are very faint in the magazine, and they would be totally illegible in another generation of reproduction; consequently, they are not printed this book.)

The accounts of the Ketel workshop during the period mention a full-size portrait of Oxford, along with paintings of other aristocrats. Karel Van Mander, a fellow artist, made a contemporary account of Ketel's career in which he describes Ketel painting a portrait of the Earl of Oxford. If Cornelius Ketel painted the portrait, it could not have been painted in 1611 (the date of the inscription). The account of Ketel's life ascribed to Van Mander, Ketel's artist friend, dates his stay in London from 1573 to 1581:

> Ketel also made a portrait of the Duke of Oxford (Edward de Vere), the High Chancellor (Sir Christopher Hatton), and of many other important members of nobility, with their wives and children. Some of these portraits were life size and full length.[5]

To be consistent with Ketel's stay in London until 1581, the maximum age that Oxford could have been at the time of the sitting would have been thirty-three or thirty-four. Consequently, there would be only a difference of six to seven years between the portrait done of Oxford in Paris (see Figure 1) and the Ashbourne Portrait, yet the age difference between the two sitters looks greater than seven years. If one concludes that the sitter is older than thirty-three, this eliminates Ketel from being the painter; still, this does not eliminate it from having been painted by someone in the Ketel workshop.

In *Scientific American,* Barrell states that the Ashbourne Portrait is not the only case of a period painting of an unknown aristocrat being doctored to represent a portrait of Shakespeare. Referring to Oxford, Barrell writes:

> My investigation to date convinces me that a whole series of portraits of this eccentric peer who had lost caste, political reputation, and wealth for reasons that historians associate with literary and dramatic extravagances, were long since converted into representations of "Shakespeare." The two likenesses known as the Portland and the St. Albans pictures, which show Lord Oxford wearing head-coverings, could not be so easily disguised. These bear his name and titles on their surfaces. Such a situation should explain logically why eight or more antique paintings are listed by "Encyclopaedia Brittanica" as traditional portraits of the hazel-blue-eyed, auburn-haired "Bard of Avon" which depict him in the apparel of a nobleman.[6]

Despite Barrell's expertise, X-rays are by their nature murky and subject to interpretation. The whole issue of the X-rays was further complicated because the X-rays taken by Barrell were destroyed. According to those who knew Barrell, *Scientific American* put over a hundred X-rays into storage. It is unclear who removed the X-rays or who destroyed them. Apparently, Barrell thought they were permanently and safely stored and that he could always retrieve them at will, but that proved not to be the case.

Further, investigations on the Ashbourne Portrait by Barbara Burris in her paper "The Golden Book, Bound Richly Up" have uncovered a description of the book held by the sitter of the portrait. In the 1613 George Chapman play *The Revenge of Bussy D'Ambois,* a character describes Oxford:

And as the foolish Poet that still writ
All his most selfe-loved verse in paper royall,
Or Partchment rul'd with Lead, smooth'd with the Pumice;
Bound richly up, and strung with Crimson strings;
Never so blest as when hee writ and read
The Ape-lov'd issue of his braine; and never
But joying in himselfe; admiring ever.[b]

Chapman's description indicates that either he had seen the portrait or knew of such a book owned by Oxford. Chapman indicates that the book contains Oxford's own verses, "his most self-loved verse." Other Oxford supporters maintain that the sonnets were written after 1599. However, both views might be correct. Many of Oxford's plays were written, rewritten, updated, and modified. This might be the case with the sonnets. Another candidate for the small book in his hand, if it were not his own (he even could have rested his hand on a Bible), would be Castiglione's *Il Cortegiano* (*The Courtier*). Equally interesting is Chapman's comment that Oxford, "the foolish Poet still writ, All his most self-loved verse in paper *royall.*" Authors did not invoke allusions to being royal lightly or accidentally. Along the same lines, Chapman repeats the same words frequently used by Shakespeare: "never" and "ever." Oxford frequently used the words "ever/never" as an abbreviation or monogram of Edward de Vere, that is, "E-Ver" for Edward de Vere:

Never so blest as when hee writ and read
The Ape-lov'd issue of his braine; and *never*
But joying in himselfe; admiring *ever.*   [*Italics* added]

---

[b] This book keeps the original spellings and capitalizations from its sources where possible. While this might initially pose some difficulty for the reader, it will give a better understanding of the people and the language of the time. However, many secondary source documents used in this book have converted passages into modern English; unfortunately, this creates an unavoidable inconsistency. Hints in reading Elizabethan English: "I's" and "J's" are interchangeable. "Iohn" would be "John." The Roman numeral "viij" would be "viii." In addition, "y" can be an "i" as in "Wyfe" or "yt." This book changes the Elizabethan "f" as an "s" to the modern "s."

Figure 1.   Edward de Vere, Paris Portrait

Figure 2.   Ashbourne Shakespeare

Figure 3.   Sir Hugh Hamersley

The strongest evidence is what is seen by the naked eye. The face of the sitter is the ultimate litmus test, and murky X-rays of gryphons and boars and literary evidence are only secondary supporting evidence. On The preceding page is a portrait known to be of Oxford done in 1575 in Paris (Figure 1), then the Ashbourne Portrait (Figure 2) as restored by the Folger and underneath is a portrait of Sir Hugh Hamersley (Figure 3), who will be discussed shortly.

While the sitter for the Ashbourne painting is older, he nevertheless has the identical facial characteristics of the younger man. Both portraits show a thin, elongated, oval-shaped face with a somewhat pointed jaw. The brow over the eyes is not prominent, and the eyebrows are thin. The right eye of each sitter is slightly walleyed. The noses are identical. If you overlay one face upon the other, they line up perfectly. In short, a facial comparison of the Ashbourne Portrait to a known portrait of Oxford identifies the subject of the Ashbourne Portrait as Edward de Vere.

After the publication of the *Scientific American* article, the Folger Shakespeare Library reversed its position: The organization that had been content to label the portrait as the man from Stratford for over a decade had now declared the painting *picta non grata*. After several years of searching for another plausible identity for the sitter of the painting, the Folger Shakespeare Library found Sir Hugh Hamersley, mayor of London for a period in the 1600s. His most outstanding qualification as subject for this portrait was that he was born in 1565, a year after the man from Stratford-upon-Avon. The Folger Shakespeare Library needed someone to be the sitter for the portrait other than Edward de Vere. The case for Oxford's authorship of the Shakespeare works was growing, and the portrait in the Hamlet-like pose added another bit of circumstantial evidence. More damaging to the Stratford case was the fact that the painting gave a compelling physical identity to someone else as the Author. The fact that Spielmann had linked the portrait to the wedding procession portrait, in which one of the men looks like Edward de Vere, was even more reason to disassociate the portrait from Shakespeare.

Elisabeth Sears, past president of the Shakespeare-Oxford Society, describes the occasion when the Folger Shakespeare Library declared that Sir Hugh Hamersley was the sitter for the Ashbourne Portrait:

> The portrait of Hamersley was originally placed beside the Ashbourne at the Folger and was something of a joke because there was no resemblance at all. Hamersley had a heavy jowly British bulldog face. It was so unlike the Ashbourne that it was ludicrous. It was interesting that the next time I saw the Ashbourne on display there, there was no Hamersley picture, only a printed message beside the portrait that it "had been identified as Lord Mayor Hamersley.[7]

The last portrait (Figure 3) is a close-up of a portrait of Sir Hugh Hamersley, which currently hangs in the Haberdasher's Guild in London. The features of the sitter are very different from either of the other two portraits. The sitter has a pronounced brow over the eyes, his nose is longer and more tapered at the end, the eye sockets are larger, the eyebrows are heavier, the shape of the cheeks flatter, and the flesh over the eyelids is more pronounced. There is almost no resemblance to the other two faces other than they are all men with beards. However, Elisabeth Sears states that the Haberdasher's Guild portrait shown in this book is not the one that was originally displayed by the Folger. She says that the portrait displayed was very different, and it was identified at that time as belonging to descendants of Hamersley; whereas, the Haberdasher's Guild owns the portrait in this book.

In 1979, the Folger Shakespeare Library "restored" the Ashbourne Portrait. After this restoration, the library claimed that the true date on the painting was 1612. The Folger's revised date then fit the birth date of Hamersley (47 + 1565 = 1612). A comparison of the dates on the painting before and after the cleaning does not make a strong case that the 1611 date was an alteration; rather, the new date appears to be the addition of a vague tail to the last "1" of 1611 to turn it into 1612.

Whether or not the "restoration" deliberately altered the dates to make it conform to the new orthodox position on the painting remains to be seen. However, one of the good things about the restoration is that the crown of the head was given a normal proportion by moving the hairline forward and adding slight shading across the top of the sitter's bald pate. This now portrays a realistic resemblance to a human skull. Other portraits of Oxford indicate that he had a full head of hair in his later years. The Folger commissioned its own X-rays of the portrait and then declared that they showed nothing that Barrell found in the *Scientific American* article.

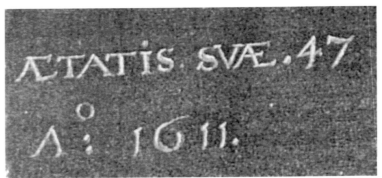

Figure 4.   1611 Date, before Restoration

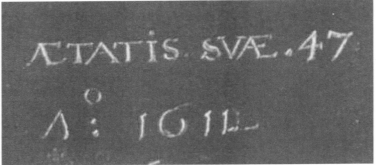

Figure 5.   1612 Date, after Folger Restoration

To reliably examine the portrait, such an examination would have to be done by some neutral body such as the Metropolitan Museum in New York City, yet this might not be enough to satisfy Oxfordian critics of the Folger. The Folger has had the opportunity and motive to alter the portrait to make it fit its view of the Authorship question. Whether it altered the portrait and destroyed what Barrell claimed to have found is a matter of conjecture, yet the Folger has long lost any claim to objective neutrality in literary matters. It has destroyed its reputation as a curator of Shakespeare artifacts in its handling of the Ashbourne Portrait controversy. When the controversy first arose, the library should have had the picture inspected and X-rayed by a neutral third party. Of course, it never wanted an objective opinion: it wanted only an opinion that fit its notion that the man from Stratford is the Author. Its open and avid support of the man from Stratford biased any results the library might have produced and cast suspicion on its restoration of the portrait. If results of any such examination by a third party no longer support the sitter as Edward de

Vere, a reasonable person might suspect that the Folger Shakespeare Library altered the portrait in ways favorable to its position on the Authorship issue.

The Folger Shakespeare Library pressed its case for Sir Hamersley in an article in 1993 by William L. Pressly, printed in *The Shakespeare Quarterly,* which is published by the Folger Shakespeare Library. The Folger continued advocating for Hamersley despite the obvious lack of any physical resemblance between the subjects of the known portrait and of portraits of Hamersley and the Ashbourne Portrait:

> Yet while Barrell's pseudo-scientific study proved less than conclusive (and less than he claimed), he did establish what Spielmann had suspected: there was more to the painting than met the eye.[8]

This is a not-so-subtle disclaimer of the years of misrepresentation when the Folger Shakespeare Library actively presented the painting as Shakespeare from Stratford-upon-Avon, despite the fact that Dr. M. H. Spielmann expressed doubt about the sitter for the portrait and even pointed toward an aristocrat in a portrait of Queen Elizabeth. The quote further slanders Barrell with the term "pseudo-scientific" even though Barrell's reputation and expertise were acknowledged and his scientific methods rigorous enough for the editors of *Scientific American.*

Pressly's article in *The Shakespeare Quarterly* is an example of the publication's bias and editorial malfeasance. The misleading article does not present a full and complete picture of the controversy surrounding the Ashbourne Portrait. Rather, it is a legal defense brief that paints its client in the most flattering light and omits any contradictory evidence. Missing from Pressly's article is any discussion of the origins of the painting, its connection to the Vere family, or any rationale of how a painting of the Lord Mayor of London was found in rural England.

Even more astounding, Pressly never describes the history of the painting or connects the origins of the painting with Hamersley of London. While it sounds plausible that a "Sir" might have had a portrait done, the whole proposition is much more dubious when we learn that Hugh Hamersley was by trade a haberdasher in London, but he was not mayor of London until 1627. The social gulf in the stratified Elizabethan society makes it virtually impossible that a tradesman would be posing (without even being knighted as yet) in such an aristocratic garb. If the date of this portrait is 1611 or 1612, this was fifteen years before Hugh Hamersley became mayor and sixteen years before his knighthood. There is no substantive reason given why Sir Hamersley would be in higher-level aristocratic apparel nor any explanation why he posed with a bare head instead of a hat.

Pressly omits any discussion of the historical record of the Ketel workshop, and he blithely dismisses the claim that Ketel painted the portrait with:

> On stylistic grounds, even though the painting is in poor condition, one can confidently state that Ketel never touched this canvas.[9]

What these stylistic grounds are he never explains, and he omits telling the reader that the journal of the Ketel workshop indicated that such a painting had been done of the Earl of Oxford. (Usually those supporting the man from Stratford-upon-Avon are most dissembling when they "can confidently state." Other such evasive words are "undoubtedly" and "assuredly.")

Pressly's article never gives a side-by-side comparison of the faces in the Ashbourne and Hamersley portrait. Instead, the Hamersley portrait in his article is a full-length, full-page illustration in which the face of Sir Hamersley is about three-quarters the size of a dime. The printing is so dark that the facial characteristics are not distinguishable. The only thing that one can see is a nose and two eyes peering out of a massive dark beard. This is another of Pressly's sleight-of-hand techniques where he is revealing information but not enough information to constitute full and complete disclosure. It is impossible for a reader of Pressly's article to make an accurate comparison of the faces. One can only imagine that, if the faces were very similar and supported his claim, he would display large, side-by-side illustrations of the respective faces.

Pressly shows his overall position on the broader issue of Authorship by invoking the prestige of Harvard University when he quotes a letter from Theodore Spencer, a university spokesman. Again, there is the tactic of slander when the Harvard representative derides those who disagree with a prevailing opinion by labeling them "cranks":

> Harvard has no "official" attitude on the subject, but I can assure you that *no member* of the *English* Department has the *slightest doubt* that the plays *were written* by William Shakespeare. The evidence is overwhelming and is not to be shaken *by cranks*.[10]

This letter is a good example of denial, wherein the unofficial policy constitutes the official policy, but nobody wants to admit it because it conflicts with the illusion of academic freedom and the expression of divergent opinions. The unofficial Harvard policy is enough to keep all aspiring graduate students and such in line. Therefore, there is no need for an official policy.

Pressly again writes about the Ashbourne Portrait in *A Catalogue of Paintings in the Folger Shakespeare Library,* published by Yale University Press. Werner Gundersheimer, director of the Folger Shakespeare Library, congratulates Pressly on his book: "The Library and its trustees are grateful to Pressly for his painstaking and imaginative scholarship."[11] This gives an official Folger Shakespeare Library endorsement of this book. One can agree that Pressly's scholarship is "imaginative," but not "painstaking." Gundersheimer gives this praise in full knowledge of the controversy surrounding the portrait and the omission of a substantial number of relevant facts.

In the description of the man from Stratford-upon-Avon as Author in this article, Pressly repeats the litany of the Bard of Avon as if it were some absolute undisputed truth. "Shakespeare studied at the free grammar school at Stratford."[12] (There is not one solitary bit of evidence that he, Shakspere, ever attended a day of school anywhere, or even evidence that he was literate.) "Shakespeare worked as an actor as a member of the Earl of Leicester's company."[13] (The only records of his being an actor occur years after the fact and that is the sum of two references.) "In 1594 he acted before Queen Elizabeth."[14] (The record of this is in great dispute.) Even if true, the evidence Pressly cites may establish him as a man involved in the theater, but it does not establish him as a writer of anything. Pressly ignores the volumes of evidence and academic critiques. For Pressly, there is no legitimate Oxfordian argument.

Amazingly, *A Catalogue of Paintings in the Folger* never once mentions who the artist might be, which is a sine qua non of an art catalogue. Nor does it give any indication of the controversy, or describe the origins of the painting. These lapses are necessary for the exclusion of information indicating that Oxford was the subject of the portrait. The article is not a full and accurate disclosure of all relevant information, but rather another instance of disregarding inconvenient facts because they point to Edward de Vere as the subject of the portrait.

In his determination to bury the Earl of Oxford, in another section of his *Catalogue*, Pressly again omits facts and shades interpretations. The library has in its possession a miniature of William Herbert, 3rd Earl of Pembroke. Pressly describes the earl:

> William Herbert, third earl of Pembroke, was born at Wilton on 8 April 1580.
>
> The editors John Heminge and Henry Condell dedicated the First Folio of 1623, the first collected edition of Shakespeare's plays, to Pembroke and his brother Philip. Pembroke certainly had known Shakespeare, and, given his earliest name, William Herbert, he has at times been identified as the

"W.H." of Shakespeare's sonnets. This association, however, is now generally discounted, as it seems highly unlikely that the two men were close friends, nor would Lord Herbert later have been addressed by his youthful name. The fact that Pembroke had been appointed Lord Chamberlain in 1615, giving him the responsibility of overseeing the production and publishing of plays, is sufficient to explain the dedication of the First Folio to him.[15]

In fact, it is insufficient. This is a repeated trick of the Stratfordian defenders, that is, to present a smattering of the relevant information and then declare that their case is proven. What is conspicuous by its absence is detailed information on the two Herbert brothers. What is not said is that William Herbert, Earl of Pembroke, was once affianced to Bridget Vere, Oxford's youngest daughter, and his brother, Philip Herbert, Earl of Montgomery, was married to Susan Vere, the second of Oxford's daughters. In other words, Oxford's son-in-law and his brother sponsored the printing of the *First Folio*, if one takes the custom of dedications into account.

Further, after James became king, there was a performance of *Measure for Measure* as part of seasonal and wedding festivities attended by the king. Several orthodox Shakespeare books mention this to show the new king's fondness for the works of William Shakespeare. Few mention that this was the wedding of Susan Vere to Philip Herbert. In addition, one of the few drawings of any female actor in costume is that of Susan Vere as Thomyris in *The Masque of Queenes* by Inigo Jones. One does not have to scratch the literary or theatrical history of the Elizabethan period very hard to run upon the Earl of Oxford and his relatives.

Pressly fabricates the Stratford man's connections to aristocrats in the little blurb "Pembroke certainly had known Shakespeare" when he is referring to the man from Stratford-upon-Avon. There is no historical evidence that William Shakspere of Stratford-upon-Avon ever met an aristocrat in his life, that he ever spent a day in an aristocratic home, or received a farthing as an author from any aristocratic patron. There is none whatsoever. Once again, we find that ubiquitous "certainly" when there is a complete lack of evidence. "Pembroke certainly had known Shakespeare" is a complete product of "unblinkered historical imagination."

Despite its claims that the Ashbourne Portrait is not of the Earl of Oxford, the Folger Library has done nothing to dispose of this painting, and it continues to display a portrait of "the mayor of London." This makes no sense until one considers the financial implications. If the portrait is of Sir Hugh Hamersley, then it has little financial value. On the other hand, if it is the Earl of Oxford but Oxford is not William

Shakespeare, the portrait has only a modest value. Finally, if it is the Earl of Oxford and the Earl of Oxford is Shakespeare, then the portrait has an almost infinite value as a stunning portrait of the greatest literary figure the world has ever known.

The Folger Shakespeare Library claims the portrait not to be of Shakespeare, yet it acts as if the painting is of Oxford-Shakespeare, or at least that this is a reasonable possibility. To put this proposition to the test, this author made the Folger Shakespeare Library an offer of $55,000 for the portrait of Sir Hugh Hamersley. This is a generous offer for a portrait of an obscure ex-mayor of Elizabethan London. Gundersheimer, director of the library, refused the offer. While the library has been very irresponsible in literary matters, one can only admire, with a certain amount of bemused irony, its prudence and good judgment concerning this work of art, which could be one of the most valuable portraits on the planet.

Ironically, the portrait now hangs in the Founders Room, which was the original office of the founders, Henry Clay Folger and his wife, Emily Jordan Folger. This is a very odd place to hang the portrait of a haberdasher and former mayor of Elizabethan London. The portrait is shown to those taking the tour of the Folger Library, but it is not on full public display. For further irony, the Folger Library keeps the call number of the portrait "S1" for Shakespeare, and its title remains "Ashbourne Portrait of Shakespeare."

The Folger Library has gone further than simply stifling dissent by ignoring the critics of the man from Stratford-upon-Avon. Barrell's identification of the Ashbourne Portrait as the Earl of Oxford was profoundly threatening to the claim of the man from Stratford-upon-Avon as the Author. The Folger Shakespeare Library began a misleading and deceptive campaign to discredit Barrell's identification. This included conjuring up an obscure gentleman of the Elizabethan period who looks nothing like the figure of the Ashbourne Portrait and beyond all reason claimed it was the sitter for the portrait. In its *Shakespeare Quarterly* and *A Catalogue of Paintings in the Folger Shakespeare Library,* it published articles that are incomplete, dissembling, and misleading. If such misinformation and omissions had occurred in any financial document, it would constitute fraud. As it is, it is academic misconduct of the most flagrant and odious nature. It remains, however, an unanswered question whether the Folger Shakespeare Library engaged in the most pernicious sabotage and altered the Ashbourne Portrait to obscure its identity as Edward de Vere.

The Shakespeare Quarterly, published by the Folger Shakespeare Library, printed Pressly's article. To this author's knowledge, it has not had an article on Shakespeare from an Oxfordian point of view, which is not surprising. This is despite fifty years of scholarship on Edward de Vere, 17th Earl of Oxford, a substantive number of biographies on Oxford, and a growing Oxfordian movement. The editor's staunch defense of the man from Stratford-upon-Avon shows the partisan nature of the publication. Gail Kern Paster in *Harper's Magazine,* in the most amazing statement imaginable by an academic, writes that those supporting the man from Stratford-upon-Avon have no obligation to the historical truth.

> Yet, Shakespeare's [Shakspere's] defenders, as opposed to his biographers, have a narrower obligation to historical truth. All we need to prove is that such a man from Stratford could have written the plays, not that he did so. And for such a task, even the dullest biographical facts, aided by the unblinkered historical imagination, prove suggestive indeed.[16]

In the history of the Shakespeare Authorship controversy, there has never been a clearer statement that the case for the man from Stratford is nothing less than a religion. For Paster, the unsupported historical claims for the Stratford man's authorship "aided by unblinkered historical imagination" (that is, pure conjecture), is the basis for her conclusions for his authorship and rigorous scrutiny is simply not necessary. Despite her claims, about the "dullest facts;" they suggest just the opposite. They suggest that the man from Stratford-upon-Avon never wrote anything in his life. Yet "unblinkered historical imagination" has launched a thousand biographies and a million scholarly papers lauding him as the Author.

Such rabid partisanship on the part of its editor indicates why *The Shakespeare Quarterly* is a journal confined to the narrowest definitions when it comes to the Authorship question and why it must avoid any articles, or even faint whisperings, that might question the Stratford man's authenticity as the Author. The entire process of "peer review" of academic journals works well to ensure quality when the area of discussion is not under dispute. However, when an area is under dispute, such as with the Authorship controversy, the editors can shut out the dissenting voices. By claiming that articles with a contrary opinion do not meet their scholastic standards, they can institute rigorous censorship. The challengers are powerless because they have no editors associated with the publication who can express a contrary opinion.

If the purpose of an academic journal is to present a wide range of diverse and sometimes conflicting opinions in the search for truth, then *The Shakespeare Quarterly* has failed miserably. It has also failed the mandate of the founders of the Folger Shakespeare Library. The founders dedicated the library to the study of "Shakespeare." The library was not dedicated to the study of the man from Stratford-upon-Avon, nor was it dedicated to the founding of an academic quasi-religion. To accurately define its editorial content, the journal should be named *The Stratfordian Quarterly*.

The Stratfordian perspective on Authorship is at odds with the study of every other known figure of literature and art. Practically every anthology of any known writer contains a detailed description of the author's life and then makes connections between the author's life and his work. In marked contrast, the Stratfordian perspective is to disconnect the Author from the works by claiming that the works reflect an imaginary world created by a man far removed from the courts and kings. For them, the works are simply the product of a genius's imagination and have no connection to a biographical human being.

In order to understand the Folger Shakespeare Library's rabid defense of the man from Stratford-upon-Avon as Author, it is useful to look at parallels in the scientific world. Scientific revolutions have occurred and the reaction to them has been studied. In contrast, the literary world is far more staid. With the exception of the Shakespeare Authorship controversy, there are not the majestic intellectual wars that frequently occur in the sciences. Frank J. Sulloway explores the reaction to innovation in his book *Born to Rebel*. He makes several observations that are relevant to the current literary authorship debate:

> These and other contemporary reactions to Darwin's evidence for evolution tell us something important: No matter how compelling this evidence was in *Darwin's* mind, it was not convincing to others. This circumstance underscores the deep-seated ideological commitments that most naturalists were unwilling to abandon. Such commitments included a belief in a constant world, the theory of Design, and the presumption of man's unique status in the Creation. The diverse reactions to Darwin's evidence for evolution underscore an important principle about science. "Facts" in science do not speak for themselves but assume their meaning based on theoretical and ideological commitments. The practice and the beliefs of scientists are embedded in a greater social context. [17]

> As some historians of science have pointed out, anomalous evidence—the stuff that supposedly spawns most scientific revolutions—is usually recognized as anomalous only after the fact. The human mind finds it much easier to assimilate facts into existing cognitive structures than to accommodate these structures to anomalous findings. The history of science is replete with evidence that confirms the observation that *most scientists resist innovation.* [18]

In an identical fashion, literary scholars and historians of the Elizabethan period have been simply blind to the most obvious of facts. When one reads histories of the period concerning the man from Stratford-upon-Avon, it becomes apparent that a most implausible story is exaggerated beyond any rational bounds and the most obvious flaws in the story totally ignored.

English literature resists innovation even more strongly than the sciences do. English literature is simply not supposed to be reinventing itself after 400 years of studying the man from Stratford as Author. It may be some consolation, or perhaps concern, to Oxfordians to know that it took more than a century for Copernicus's claim that the Earth revolves around the sun to be accepted. Alfred Wegener's theory of continental drift was not accepted for fifty years—and for that matter, among religious fundamentalists, Darwin is still not accepted. Creationism lives on in some communities, and Stratfordianism will probably never die out altogether. In a similar fashion, the myth of the Virgin Queen has turned Elizabethan history into a religious liturgy that ignores any heretical notions.

Thomas S. Kuhn, in *The Structure of Scientific Revolutions,* comments on how a strongly held paradigm of beliefs can preclude the observation of the most obvious of phenomena:

> The Chinese, whose cosmological beliefs did not preclude celestial change, had recorded the appearance of many new stars in the heavens at a much earlier date. Also, even without the aid of a telescope, the Chinese had systematically recorded the appearance of sunspots centuries before these were seen by Galileo and his contemporaries.[19]

While it might be unknown to the public, there has been skepticism for over a century that the man from Stratford-upon-Avon was the author of the works attributed to "William Shakespeare." In 1856, Delia Bacon, an American woman, not related to Sir Francis Bacon, began a controversy that has continued for over a century when she proposed that the man from Stratford-upon-Avon was not the author of the works attributed to William Shakespeare. In her book *The Philosophy of Shakespeare Unfolded,* she argued that the works had the markings of a man of extended knowledge and familiarity with the court of Elizabethan England. She proposed that Sir Francis Bacon, along with others, were the collective Author of the works. This was the first large cannon fired in a literary war that has only grown in intensity. She based her conclusions on the similarities between Francis Bacon's philosophies and the philosophies revealed in the plays of William Shakespeare. She never conducted any biographical or historical research to support her conclusions. *The Philosophy of Shakespeare Unfolded* is often turgid, rambling, moralizing, philosophical, and pedantic. It is very often difficult to penetrate, but sometimes extremely insightful and worth quoting at length:

> Yes, when that Royal Injunction, which rested alike upon the Play-house, the Press, the Pulpit, and *Parliament* itself, was still throttling everywhere the free voice of the nation—when a single individual could still assume to himself, or to herself, the exclusive privilege of deliberating on all those questions which men are most concerned in—questions which involved all their welfare, for this life and the life to come, certainly *'the Play, the Play was the thing.'* It was a vehicle of expression which offered incalculable facilities for evading these restrictions. It was the only one then invented which offered then any facilities whatever for the discussion of that question in particular—which was already for that age the question. And to the genius of that age, with its new *historical, experimental,* practical determination—with its transcendent poetic power, nothing could be easier than to get possession of this instrument, and to exhaust its capabilities.
>
> For instance, if a Roman Play were to be brought out at all,—and with that mania for classical subjects which then prevailed, what could be more natural?—How could one object to that which, by the supposition, was involved in it? And what but the most boundless freedoms and audacities, on this very question, could one look for here? What, by the supposition, could it be but one mine of poetic treason? If Brutus and Cassius were to be allowed to come upon the stage, and discuss their views of government, deliberately and confidentially, in the presence of an English audience, certainly no one could ask to hear from their lips the political doctrine then predominant in England. It would have been a flat anachronism, to request them to keep an eye upon the Tower in their remarks, inasmuch as all the world knew that the corner-stone of that ancient and venerable institution had only then just been laid by the same distinguished individual whom these patriots were about to call to an account for his military usurpation of a constitutional government at home.[20]

Delia Bacon was followed by Mark Twain, who titled part of his autobiography *Is Shakespeare Dead?* He noted that no one in Stratford-upon-Avon ever identified the man born William Shakspere as the Author. Twain stated there were no references to the man as the Author while he was alive. His relatives never made any claim that he was the famous Author while he was alive nor after he was dead. Twain further questioned how the Author could have such an extensive and precise use of legal terms, while the man from Stratford-upon-Avon had no legal training. He maintained that each profession has language and terms that are used only without fault by someone who is in the profession. Mark Twain never gave any strong opinion for another candidate as Author, but he was certain the man from Stratford-upon-Avon was not the Author.

Sir George Greenwood's book *The Shakespeare Problem Reconsidered* heavily influenced Mark Twain. Sir Greenwood, a lawyer, was also not sure who Shakespeare was, but he was stinging in his criticism of the supporters of the man from Stratford-upon-Avon. Greenwood showed that the biographers of the man had failed to show how their candidate could have had such precise knowledge in complex areas of the law. Mark Twain used the thinking of Greenwood and gave examples of precise knowledge and language that one might gain in a trade and that cannot be feigned. For both Greenwood and Mark Twain, whoever Shakespeare was, he was not the man from Stratford-upon-Avon.

Sigmund Freud asked how the works drenched in blood, incest, and neurosis was so removed from the known history of the man from Stratford-upon-Avon. Also included in this list of skeptics are Walt Whitman, Ralph Waldo Emerson, Malcolm X, Charlie Chaplin, Henry James, Otto Von Bismarck, and Leslie Howard, among others. Recently, we might add the distinguished Shakespearean actors Sir John Gielgud, Sir Derek Jacobi, and Michael York.

J. Thomas Looney (pronounced Loh-ney), an English schoolteacher, published his landmark work *Shakespeare Identified in Edward de Vere, The Seventeenth Earl of Oxford* in 1920. This changed the Authorship controversy from a general dissatisfaction with the man from Stratford-upon-Avon to one with a plausible candidate. While Sir Francis Bacon had many intellectual qualities and was contemporary with the period, he never demonstrated any strong theatrical interests or had any poetical writings deemed similar to Shakespeare's works. By this time, most scholars of the time had abandoned Sir Francis Bacon as a serious candidate for the Author although they were uncertain who might be a better candidate. Thomas Looney changed all that because his book began the search for the true Shakespeare in a completely different way than his literary predecessors begun. Rather than start with the premise that the man from Stratford-upon-Avon, or anyone else, wrote the works, Looney began by first examining the works and determining the personal, literary, and biographical characteristics of the Author. As he succinctly puts it:

> What then is the usual common-sense method of searching for an unknown man who has performed some particular piece of work? It is simply to examine closely the work itself, to draw from the examination as definite a conception as possible of the man who did it, to form some idea of where he would be likely to be found, and then to go and look for a man who answers to the supposed description.[21]

For example, what would one know about the author of *The Great Gatsby* if the novel were anonymous? Reading the text, the author would appear to be someone from the Midwest who went to an Ivy League university. While familiar with the life of the wealthy, the author is somewhat an outsider to this life. In addition, the author was familiar with both Wall Street and the life of the wealthy on the North Shore of Long Island. The novel is also very short, more a long short story than a novel. Using these clues, a person might start looking for an author of short stories from the Midwest who went to an Ivy League school, and it would not be long before he would run across the name of F. Scott Fitzgerald, who was one of the most prominent short story writers of his day.

Literary scholars point to the relation between authors and their works in virtually all introductions describing any author, with one glaring exception. In introductions to works of William Shakespeare, nothing remotely connects the man from Stratford with the works or as the Author as one could imagine him from reading the works. The biography of the man from Stratford-upon-Avon and the biography of the Author known as William Shakespeare *as revealed in the works* are simply leagues apart.

Using a biographical approach, J. Thomas Looney identified the characteristics of Shakespeare as knowledge of classics, estrangement from conventional society, improvidence with money, strong artistic sensibility, support of the Tudor monarchy, and familiar with Italy. Looney then looked for a man possessing these characteristics and found the half-buried history of Edward de Vere, 17th Earl of Oxford. As might be expected, orthodox scholars roundly denounced his book. Nevertheless, a small group of literary researchers believed Thomas Looney had found the Author.

The Seventeenth Earl of Oxford, a detailed biography of the life of Edward de Vere written by B.M. Ward and was published in 1928. It showed that Oxford was not a "renegade" nobleman, but was deeply involved in the life of the Elizabethan court. Ward gave many examples of Oxford's acknowledged involvement in the arts both as a writer and as a supporter of other literary efforts. Ward further detailed Oxford's relationship with Lord Burghley, his travels to Italy, and his life at court.

Another seminal work was Eva Turner Clark's book *Shakespeare's Plays in the Order of Their Writing, A Study Based on Records of the Court Revels and Historic Allusions,* published in 1931. Eva Turner Clark addressed the subject of the dating of the plays by first looking at the records of the Master of the Revels, a court functionary who disbursed and recorded the funds for entertainment. In addition, she looked at all the plays from the point of view that they were written starting in the 1570s rather than the 1590s. She then searched for topical and historical allusions of these times. This required knowledge of the text of the plays,

European history, and knowledge of the English court and its personalities.

Traditional, orthodox Shakespearean scholars almost completely ignore the nearly 200 productions that occurred at court during Elizabeth's reign. To understand the scale of these productions, one should consider that Elizabeth had a choir of about forty singers and about thirty musicians at court. When we think of performances put on at the White House in modern times, we tend to think of a visiting soloist or small ensemble. This was not the case for court productions of the Elizabethan era. They were large productions presented for the monarch in the large halls of the castle. Orthodox scholars act as if Elizabethan theater and Shakespearean theater began with the building of the Globe in 1599. However, records indicate that London had a number of theaters north of the Thames built long before 1599. Many inn-tavern theaters gave productions and were rehearsal sites for plays later performed at court.

The reasons orthodox scholars ignore these theatrical activities becomes obvious when one examines Eva Turner Clark's work. Her work indicates that someone produced "Shakespeare-like" plays starting no later than 1571, when the Bard from Stratford-upon-Avon was but seven years old. The writer or writers of these plays is never identified by any orthodox scholars because there is no other playwright but Edward de Vere who could possibly be the Author.

For example, according to the records there was a play, *The Historie of Error*, shown at Hampton Court on January 1, 1577, which sounds very much like *The Comedy of Errors.* Another, *Portio and Demonrates*, was played at court on February 2, 1580. "Portio" gives us the strong clue that this might be similar to *The Merchant of Venice* with the main female character "Portia." The author or authors go unexamined by orthodox Stratfordian scholars because the orthodox view is that Shakespearean productions began with the public theater at the Globe—*but the court productions predated these by almost two decades.* The man from Stratford-upon-Avon could not have authored these works, and the titles and literary allusions within the works are strong evidence for Oxford's authorship.

Charlton and Dorothy Ogburn followed Eva Turner Clark with their massive book *This Star of England* in 1952. This book gave many examples of the life of Edward de Vere as reflected in the works of William Shakespeare. Their son Charlton Ogburn Jr. followed this with *The Mysterious William Shakespeare* in 1984. This work has become the standard Oxfordian textbook, and it provides copious information and detailed scholarship that proves beyond any reasonable doubt that Oxford was the Author. As expected, these new theories met fierce resistance by those committed to the previous outdated model of thinking. Max Planck's remark about physics teachers, "A new scientific truth does not triumph by convincing its opponents and making them see the light, but rather because its opponents eventually die, and a new generation grows up that is familiar with it," is equally applicable to teachers of literature.[c]

One response of the Folger Shakespeare Library to this outpouring of academic investigation was a review in the *Shakespeare Quarterly* by Giles Dawson. It did not attempt to refute the arguments presented by the Ogburns in *This Star of England*. Instead, the review pointedly avoids the evidence they presented while raising methodological concerns to the point of pedantic lunacy:

> It is a dangerous book, written with a specious plausibility likely to mislead the nonspecialist reader. This review therefore will examine not so much the conclusions of the book as its method. For in my opinion it is the basic unsoundness of method in this and other works of similar subject matter that explains how sincere and intelligent men arrive at such wild conclusions as those contained in *This Star of England*.[22]

Dawson's main complaint is that the Ogburns have not used the established literary historians. This would hardly seem surprising considering that all the established literary historians support the man from Stratford:

> And in a study much concerned with the early publication of Shakespeare and the relations between author, actor, and publisher, it is surprising to find in the bibliography no mention of any of the most eminent authorities in this field, such as Pollard, Plomer, McKerrow, Greg, and Willoughby.[23]

---

[c] Ideas once established, no matter how wrongheaded or intuitively absurd, have the longevity of the myth of alligators in the New York City sewer system. One such wrongheaded idea is that planes fly based on the Bernoulli principle of air rushing over the top of a curved wing creating a vacuum and hence lift. This is despite the problem that planes would not be able to fly upside down if the Bernoulli principle were operative (they would be sucked down according to Bernoulli), all wings are not curved on the top side, parasails and kites don't have such wings, etc., etc.

Planes, in fact, fly by the same principle as water skis: the force of being pulled or pushed through a medium (air or water) creates a push up and backward against the upwardly angled wing surface, either water ski or wing. (The Wright Brothers did experiments with kites, but none with blowing air over glass jars.) Despite this logic and the reality that planes fly upside down, practically every known text book on the subject recites the Bernoulli principle as the method of "lift" to fly planes. Pilots and engineers will also defend the "air over wings causing the lift" theory.

Academics give much lip service to "paradigm shifts," but in fact, the much ballyhooed paradigm shift is seldom first seen on campus. The longer one is committed to a certain line of reasoning, the more difficult it is to change one's mind. It is simply very difficult to abandon a long-held belief confirmed by prevailing wisdom and dogma. Old dogs can learn new paradigms, but it takes a long, long time and they have to be forced to do so.

Dawson then goes on to give an excellent description of academic research, which is entirely out of context and a de facto Freudian slip:

> Scholarship implies an attitude toward truth and a method of working toward the establishment of truth—whether of historical events or of the meaning and significance of a literary work or of the nature of the world about us. The scholar has no axes to grind. He is not eager to prove his own hypotheses correct, but rather to find out whether they are correct or not. He is ever ready to reevaluate and reinterpret his evidence and to discard one hypothesis in favor of a better. When he uncovers a fact which does not square with his hypothesis he neither shuts his eyes to it nor tries to explain it away nor trims it to fit his own preconceptions, but rather adjusts the hypothesis to fit the facts. The ability to evaluate and reevaluate evidence in any field comes with training and experience in that field.[24]

Sigmund Freud would have a wonderful time with statements such as these. Out of repressed guilt, they are transparent projections of the major faults of Stratfordian scholars onto the authors of this Oxfordian work. The Stratfordian scholars have constantly revised their hypothesis to make it fit with the emerging facts and make it consistent with the man from Stratford-upon-Avon's authorship. If the Author knew Italian and the man from Stratford-upon-Avon was unlikely to have learned Italian, then the Author borrowed his knowledge of Italian from others. If the Author had an extensive knowledge of law and the man from Stratford-upon-Avon had no connection to law, then the Author's knowledge of law must be faulty, etc. The Stratfordian position has constantly been to downgrade one of the most exquisite intellects the world has ever known. Current Shakespearean literary fashion is simply to ignore the Authorship issue altogether. The orthodox establishment is so frightened by the Authorship issue that one can read many issues of the *Shakespeare Quarterly* before finding a reference, any reference at all, to the actual human Author of the works.

Instead of concentrating on the issues raised by the Ogburns, Dawson concentrates on the most pedantic issues and admonishes the Ogburns to scrupulously check all quotations and references. "And finally in publishing he will scrupulously check all quotations and references."[25] Dawson is apparently a close student of trees but obliviously has never seen a forest. He was also the individual who saw nothing when shown the X-rays taken by Barrell.

In fairness to Dawson, he does ask a question that has bedeviled Oxfordians, "And I cannot believe that with scores of men and women privy to the secret—many of them Oxford's enemies—it could have remained hid till our own century."[26] This a very valid question and has historically been answered by supporters of the Earl of Oxford by saying that aristocratic taboos prevented Oxford's name from being connected to his works. However, other noblemen's names were attached to their works after their deaths, but when the *First Folio* was published in 1623, nineteen years after Oxford's disappearance, it remained under the pen name of William Shakespeare. The answer to this intriguing question should be apparent by the time the reader is finished with this book.

The support for the man from Stratford is bedeviled by the complete lack of any literary record of the man. There are no letters in his hand, no stage directions, no correspondence from him, and only one letter to him, which apparently was never delivered. The only writings about him as a person by the literary lights of the day mark him as a clown and buffoon. For a man to write over thirty plays, major poems, and numerous sonnets, there is no personal record of any writings whatsoever. There is not one document written in the hand of the man from Stratford-upon Avon "William Shakespeare." This is curious indeed. There is no evidence that the man from Stratford went to school or could read or write. This amazing lack of any record of any literary activities of the man from Stratford is filled in with amazing fabrications. One imaginative Shakespearean scholar puts forth conjecture as fact in S. Schoenbaum's *Shakespeare's Lives*:

> "Patient investigation has yielded some information about the masters of the Stratford grammar school in Shakespeare's time, but records for pupils at the school during the sixteenth century have long since vanished. Scholarship has instead had to content itself with reconstructing the curriculum, about which a good deal may be inferred from the analogy of other Elizabethan grammar schools."[27]

No, it cannot be inferred. There is no record of Shakspere's attendance at any school in Stratford-upon-Avon, and there is no evidence of personal correspondence or other such evidence that indicates the man could either read or write. Inferences, conjectures, and suppositions fill in the lack of literary record for the man from Stratford. Strangely, while there are abundant records that indicate the birth, children, death, and legal dealings of the man, there is not one record of any literary dealings.

The few facts surrounding the man from Stratford have been magnified to support his authorship, and the facts that contradict his authorship have been ignored: Conjecture about his life has replaced facts. Conjecture fills in the many biographical holes in the Stratford man's biography. The conjecture then hardens over time into facts of his existence. "Shakespeare knew Latin" changes to "the Stratford man learned Latin at the local Stratford school," then changes again to the Stratford man was a "scholar in Latin and the classics." G.P.V. Akrigg condones the use of conjecture in his book *Shakespeare & the Earl of Southampton.* In short, he admits that he is making it up:

> In this second part of our book, as we seek to trace the relationship between Shakespeare and his patron, we shall often lack evidence and be forced back upon conjecture. But we offer our readers this double assurance: we will endeavor to limit ourselves to those conjectures, which seem to have some real likelihood, and we will keep before us Johnson's warning that conjecture must never be 'wantonly nor licentiously indulged.' [28]

As others do with their "facts" about the man from Stratford's life, Akrigg hardens conjecture into fact. He subtly slips in "Shakespeare and his patron," as if he, or anyone else, ever proved any relationship. He never has shown in his book, nor has anyone else, that the man from Stratford ever knew the Earl of Southampton, or that there was any relationship whatsoever. This is the general approach to filling in the numerous holes in the biography of the Stratford man. Talk about it long enough, write enough conjectures, and then accept the conjecture as fact; this is the method of these historians.

The Stratfordian world is a comforting and reassuring one to those who refuse to dig deeper into the characters and the period. Hundreds if not thousands of books tell of the genius of the man from Stratford. Can a thousand Ph.D.s be wrong? Can all those learned dons in flowing robes from Cambridge, Harvard, and other fine institutions be so wrong? Could all those conferences on the Bard from Stratford-upon-Avon, with all those learned professors droning away on abstruse minutiae simply have it all wrong? Nay, 'tis impossible. The legend is further backed by a rural temple in the heart of England, turned into some theme park re-creation of the Middle Ages, creating a prosperous industry of several million pounds a year flowing into the coffers of Stratford-upon-Avon. Yet, if the legend of the man from Stratford is not quite dead, Stratfordian scholarship is a dead man walking.

There is also an ideological bias to the whole defense of the man from Stratford-upon-Avon as Author. For the defenders of the man from Stratford, it is not simply a literary mystery or an exercise in presentation. Rather, it is also a defense of what the figure of the man from Stratford-upon-Avon represents to them as a political-ideological-religious totem. If someone could find a candidate from the lower-middle classes, perhaps a Bard of Woolwich, he would receive a much warmer reception than would an Earl of Anything. The notion that an aristocrat of the first rank, or any rank for that matter, is the Author of the works attributed to that sterling example of the English common man raises the hackles on the neck of orthodox Shakspere defenders throughout the world.

It little matters that the actual man from Stratford-upon-Avon was a rather successful businessman who accumulated a considerable fortune. Neither does it matter that this paragon of English decency sued at the drop of a pound note, avoided taxes, let his daughter be raised illiterate, and, in an endearing show of marital affection, left his wife his "second best bed." By English law, she had the right to live in the dwelling of her marriage but because of Shakspere's will, she did not have the right to ownership or to leave it to whomever she wished upon her death. What matters for this point of view is not so much the actual facts of the biography of the man from Stratford, but the ability to label the man from Stratford as a common man, a good bloke, a genial fellow, and a man of the people. He is not much different from anyone else, except he happened to be god-gifted with this touch of literary genius.

Academics studiously avoid Shakespeare's political and social positions in his writings or pass them off with benign comments that he took a Tudor or aristocratic viewpoint. Here the argument is not whether these social views are correct or incorrect; it is rather that the literati and academics studiously avoid the Author's views. There is far more likely to be some article in an academic journal titled "The Semeiotics of Shakespeare in a Post-Feminist World" than an article titled "The Aristocratic World View of William Shakespeare":

> O, when degree is shak'd,
> Which is the ladder to all high designs,
> The enterprise is sick. How could communities,
> Degrees in schools, and brotherhoods in cities,
> Peaceful commerce from dividable shores,
> The primogenitive and due of birth,
> Prerogative of age, crown, sceptres, laurels,
> But by degree stand in authentic place?
> Take but degree away, untune that string,
> And hark what discord follows! Each thing meets
> In mere oppugnancy [opposition]. The bounded waters
> Should lift their bosoms higher than the shores
> And make a sop of all this solid globe.
> Strength should be lord of imbecility,
> And the rude son should strike his father dead;
> Force should be right, or rather right and wrong,
> Between whose endless jar justice resides,
> Should lose her names, and so should justice too.
> Then everything includes itself in power,
> Power into will, will into appetite,
> And appetite, an universal wolf,
> So doubly seconded with will and power,
> Must make perforce an universal prey

And last eat up himself. Great Agamemnon,
This chaos, when degree is suffocate,
Follows the choking;
And this neglection of degrees is it
That by a pace goes backward in a purpose
It hath to climb. The general's disdain'd
By him one step below, he by the next,
That next by him beneath; so every step,
Exampled by the first pace that is sick
Of his superior, grows to an envious fever
Of pale and bloodless emulation.
And 'tis this fever that keeps Troy on foot,
Not her own sinews. To end a tale of length,
Troy in our weakness lives, not in her strength.
Troilus and Cressida, Act 1, Scene 3

Much to the annoyance of the liberal, egalitarian academic world, this is pretty much Shakespeare's worldview. To get around this difficulty, academics then give up the Author's voice. For them, Shakespeare does not believe these words; he only put words in the mouths of characters, which express ideas he does not believe. Jonathan Bate, a noted classical and Shakespearean scholar and with distinctly left-wing political views has this to say about the Author's political views.

Shakespeare put some persuasive political rhetoric into the mouths of Ulysses in *Troilus and Cressida*, but this is not to say that Ulysses' argument is the argument is the argument of the whole play, let alone an expression of the personal political beliefs of its author.[29]

Now the distance between the Author and the works enlarges even more. Points of view and authorial comment by Shakespeare are completely disregarded. Notables such as Charlie Chaplin and Walt Whitman differed with this newfound egalitarian Shakespeare and found the Bard anti-democratic, anti-egalitarian, and, to use that awful word, "aristocratic." Here is Whitman on Shakespeare:

Conceiv'd out of the fullest heat and pulse of European feudalism—personifying in unparallel'd ways the medieval aristocracy, its towering spirit of ruthless and gigantic caste, with its own peculiar air and arrogance (no mere imitation) only one of the "wolfish earls" so plenteous in the plays themselves, or some born descendant and knower, might seem to be the true author of those amazing works—works in some respects greater than anything else in recorded literature.[30]

Whitman concludes:

Think, not of growths as forests primeval, or Yellowstone geysers, or Colorado ravines, but of costly marble palaces, and palace rooms, and the noblest fixings and furniture, and noble owners and occupants to correspond—think of carefully built gardens form beautiful but sophisticated gardening art at its best, with walks and bowers and artificial lakes, and appropriate statue-groups and the finest cultivated roses and lilies and japonicas in plenty—and you have the tally of Shakspere. The low characters, mechanics, even the loyal henchmen—all in themselves nothing—serve as capital foils to the aristocracy. The comedies (exquisite as they certainly are) bringing in admirably portray'd common characters, have the unmistakable hue of plays, portraits, made for the diverstisement only of the élite of the castle, and from its point of view. The comedies are altogether non-acceptable to America and Democracy.[31]

The legend of the man from Stratford metamorphosed to fit the emotional and historical needs of the English nation and then metamorphosed further to fit the needs of the academic class of historians and literature professors. Established academics have not questioned the rather thin strands of evidence that connect the man from Stratford to the works, and those who do question them meet with a barrage of criticism for proposing such heresy. If this were Elizabethan times, dissenters would be flogged, thrown in prison, and tortured until they changed their views. John Stubbs (appropriately named) had his right hand cut off for opposing the Queen's marriage to a Frenchman. The penalties in American and British academia are not so violent. Ostracism, opprobrium within the academic community, denial of tenure, exclusion from prestigious publications, and loss of job opportunities for those with a controversial viewpoint are all means that the academic community uses to maintain its static version of established truth.

If the situation were reversed, a man of the people was hiding his identity behind an aristocrat, there would probably be a posse of liberal academics pursuing this unsung proletarian genius. Class warfare and class politics are very much a part of the agenda of many current defenders of the man from Stratford-upon-Avon. Beyond all reason or evidence, they continue to defend his authorship, not because they believe it to be true, but because they cannot tolerate the thought of a man from the upper social classes of Elizabethan England replacing their beloved Bard. The sword of ignorant prejudice cuts both ways, and in this case, their refusal to recognize Oxford is simply class bigotry.

It is not surprising, then, that the major contributions to the Authorship issues (as with many other disciplines) come from those outside the established, prestigious academic community. Newton, Einstein, Darwin, and others would fall under this definition of men making substantial contributions to a subject without the accreditation of a Ph.D. In a similar fashion, it has largely been the independent thinkers, unaffiliated with any academic organization, unburdened by the weight of "established truths," and unhampered by that weighty certificate of orthodox thinking, the Ph.D., who have made the major contributions to the Authorship controversy.

College teachers and high school teachers are intimidated from exploring the subject by the constant stream of invectives poured out by the Folger Shakespeare Library and its minions. The Folger Shakespeare Library has effectively poisoned the well of Shakespeare scholarship and made legitimate questions of Authorship into heresy against the religion of Bardolatry. Teachers cannot encourage their students to explore the subject unless they are willing to take on their faculties and the entire academic Shakespeare establishment. It is one thing to be an advocate of a cause or even question current dogma when one has little at stake; it is another thing to be intellectually adventurous when one's salary, promotions, and livelihood can be threatened. Consequently, students writing on the subject of Edward de Vere have received failing grades for their efforts, and one book agent related the tale that she received an F-minus for writing on the subject. The F from the teacher was for broaching the subject and the minus, probably sheer vindictiveness.

In addition, such academic intimidation tends to make even Oxfordian scholars timid. In the battles over evolution, not all those converted to evolution through natural selection were complete converts. There were many quasi-evolutionists who accepted evolution but with the divine still having a role at key junctures, especially as it concerns the evolution of man. In the same sense, many Oxfordians accept the Earl of Oxford as the Author, but they are unwilling to accept the difficult biographical baggage and rewriting of Elizabethan history that goes along with him. Academics are by nature a conservative lot, charged with teaching established truth and wisdom to their young charges. They cannot swim with every new fashion or responsibly teach unproven ideas and theories. As a result, even Oxfordian scholars attempt to retain as much of the previous knowledge and thinking as possible and make gradual changes to their intellectual curriculum about Shakespeare. For many, it is simply changing the name of Shakespeare to Oxford and accepting an aristocrat as the Author—and that it is the end of it. As this book hopes to show, accepting Oxford as the Author is much more difficult and complex than that.

At the extremes of the Stratfordian adherents are the Bardolaters (that is, those who worship Shakespeare as a demigod), and as in all religions, they are impervious to contradictory facts or logic. In Darwin's case, those with doubts about creationism were slandered as atheists; today, those with doubts about the man from Stratford-upon-Avon are slandered as aristocrats. With the slander in place, the defenders attempt to change the nature of the argument from one of facts and implications to one of motives. Those who are on the Stratfordian side are true and holy, while those who doubt are aristocrats with only the vilest of motives. It would take some extended work in psychology to fully understand these "true believers," which is beyond the scope of this work.

At minimum, it appears that the most rabid defenders of the man from Stratford-upon-Avon use the Bard as an emotional prop to resolve their own anxieties. Defining an out-group that is worthy of contempt allows them to project their anger and feelings of personal inadequacy into the now despised group of nonbelievers. Denial is the mechanism used to avoid the most basic questions about the Stratford man's authorship and delusion is the mechanism used to create a superhero who can perform the most amazing literary feats without the seeming requisite education, knowledge, or even point of view. Creationists, religious fanatics, conspiracy theorists, and extreme Stratfordians have much in common as to methods, anti-intellectualism, and intensity of beliefs. These are methods to reduce personal anxieties. As someone once said, it may be only a psychological defense, but people have psychological defenses for reasons.

Academic resistance and inertia means that acceptance of Oxford and teaching Oxford as the Author known as William Shakespeare will not occur because of changes in academic acceptance. Those at the very top of the Shakespearean hierarchy are the most resistant because they have the most to lose. The scholarship they have been doing for the past hundred years has been bogus, and they have failed to have any one scintilla of academic courage to explore the Authorship issues. The strategy of the academics has been to stifle the Authorship issue and hope that it does not surface until after they reach retirement.

The Authorship issue is over 150 years old, but despite massive evidence of Oxford's authorship contained in the books of Looney, Clark, Ward and the Ogburns, acceptance has been nil. While this book may make some advances, it is not reasonable to assume that it is going to change the minds of unchangeable academics. Most likely, what will happen is that someone in the movie industry will realize that Oxford's story is intriguing, dramatic, and worthy of a film presentation. When this *Oxford in Love* movie hits the proverbial theater near you, students will be walking into their college and high school Shakespeare classes asking questions about Oxford. The success of the movie *Shakespeare in Love* showed the willingness of audiences to accept or want to believe that the Author was in some way personally connected to the works he wrote, which has always been the Oxfordian position. This future movie will be decisive in precipitating a sudden change in mass consciousness that will force academia to acknowledge Oxford's authorship. In other words, it will not be a slow, trickle-down change but rather a sudden change in perceptions. One year, it will be the man from Stratford who wrote the works, and the next year, it will be that Oxford was the Author. Popular culture could be the catalyst for change of the highbrow culture of aristocratic academics cloistered in ivy-covered fortresses.

The English Literature departments of the elite institutions of Harvard University and Yale University have been those who have been craven in their responsibilities to simply honesty and truth. This is despite the fact that their professors are instituted from the competitive pressures of the job market by the practice of tenure, which is suppose to give their academics intellectual freedom to explore what they will. Nevertheless, they have avoided the Authorship issue and produced the most ridiculous explanations in defense of the man from Stratford. In the same *Harper's Magazine*, esteemed Shakespeare professor at Yale University, Harold Bloom says:

> Oxfordians are the sub-literary equivalent of the sub-religious Scientologists. You don't want to argue with them, as they are dogmatic and abusive.[32]

After starting with that slander, Bloom states how he artfully dodges the questions that Oxfordians have raised:

> A decade ago, I would introduce my Graduate Shakespeare seminar (never my Undergraduate) by solemnly assuring the somewhat resentful students that *all* of Shakespeare, and not just the Sonnets, had been written by Lucy Negro, Elizabethan England's most celebrate East Indian whore. [33]

He goes on:

> In fact, we don't know for sure who this narcissistic young nobleman was, though Southampton will do, and there are many candidates for the Dark Lady, though none so exuberant as Lucy Negro. All we actually do know, quite certainly, is that the frequently unhappy (though remarkably restrained) poet indeed was Will Shakespeare. These are "his sugared sonnets among his private friends," doubtless a socially varied group extending all the way from lowlife actors (and Lucy Negro!) to the petulant Southampton, patron and (perhaps) sometime lover. [34]

Again, this is stating conjecture as fact. In this literary debate, Bloom chooses to say the poet "indeed was Will Shakespeare" while not adding a single fact to support such a statement. In fact, "his sugared sonnets among his private friends" was a statement a literary figure of the time, Francis Meres, applied to the writings of the Earl of Oxford! Is this comment of Bloom's a Freudian slip of repressed guilt or a deliberate clue as to true Author? Bloom, as other scholars, states that Southampton was the patron and sometime lover of the man from Stratford. Yet, no scholar has ever shown one letter between the two, shown one account that Southampton ever gave a farthing to the man, that they ever met or that the man from Stratford ever set foot in an aristocratic household.

The Yale University Press recently published *Shakespeare, The King's Playwright, Theater in the Stuart Court.* This imaginary exercise in scholarship purports to show how Will Shakspere was King James' playwright without ever showing that the playwright spent a single, solitary day at court. The Yale University Press also published *Shakespeare's Brain,* in which the author (a Harvard graduate) goes on for two hundred pages in the most turgid academic prose, without once addressing the problem of whose skull the brain might be lodged in.

When the earth-centered concept of the universe began to break apart as new findings arose, the concept of the earth-centered world was not simply abandoned; rather more and more complicated theories evolved. More obfuscation was created to explain away the discrepancies and avoid abandoning the theory. In an opposite fashion, the Shakespearean world of Gail Kern Paster and Jonathan Bate and other such scholars has become one of reducing the level of Shakespeare to fit what might be possible with a man from Stratford-upon-Avon. One of the two greatest minds of humankind is reduced to a petty playwright who purloins others works and whose knowledge of anything is not particularly impressive. The current defense of the man from Stratford's authorship is one of delusion, fantasy and denial. Aided and abetted by their vivid "historical imagination" any Shakespearean scenario can be considered valid. There is simply no standard of historical truth because as Gail Kern Paster so eloquently states the position:

> All we need to prove is that such a man from Stratford could have written the plays, not that he did so. [35]

The Authorship issue is not simply a literary quarrel in a literary teapot. Millions of students in the past five decades have been taught a scenario of the creation of the works of William Shakespeare that has been dubious at best and subject to criticism for over a century. Moreover, there is a moral lesson that has been wrongly applied. In all teachings to our children and in other areas of school, we stress the virtues of study, perseverance and hard work as the most important contributing factors to success. This is true whether it be academics, sports or the professions. Genius we are taught is not inspired, but the result of ninety-nine percent perspiration as Thomas Edison remarked. To all this there is one singular exception: "William Shakespeare"—the greatest genius of them all.

This author, as opposed to all others, in the conventional view, did not suffer for his art. He did not apprentice himself to the craft of literature and theater with long hours of painstaking study. He did not write because he felt a strong moral imperative to express his viewpoint. He did not face strong opposition to staging his works. In the conventional view, he simply appeared out of nowhere, was relatively uneducated, seemingly unafflicted by any personal traumas, wrote for financial gain about a world he did not know or care about, and then disappeared back into the obscurity of a small town. The was able to do this simply because he had some incredible gift of "genius." Substitute the word "magic" for "genius" and the true implication of the intellectual position becomes clearer.

Further, this myth of untutored, unstudied, magical genius is is simply not true. The Author spent years of arduous study to accumulate the knowledge that is evidenced in the works; he faced immense opposition to his plays; he faced financial ruin; his personal history is so traumatic that it is a wonder that he retained the ability to function, much less turn out masterpieces of literature. This is all lost with the conventional viewpoint of Shakespeare, much to impoverishment of the students who have studied the orthodox biography of his life and the rest of the world as well.

In *Shakespeare the Invention of the Human,* Harold Bloom captures the magnitude of Oxford's achievement:

> ...he went beyond all precedents (even Chaucer) and invented the human as we continue to know it. A more conservative way of stating this would seem to me a weak misreading of Shakespeare: it might contend that Shakespeare's originality was in the *representation* of cognition, personality, character. But there is an overflowing element in the plays, an excess beyond representation, that is closer to the metaphor we call "creation." The dominant Shakespearean characters—Falstaff, Hamlet, Rosalind, Iago, Lear, Macbeth, Cleopatra among them—are extraordinary instances not only of how meaning gets started, rather than repeated, but also of how modes of consciousness come into being.[36]

It is unfortunate that Bloom has not been more open-minded in his forty years of scholarship and unfortunate that he has not taken a closer look at the life of Edward de Vere. If he had, he would have found a life and a personality that was as full, complex and fascinating as any of the characters ever put on the stage. It is literature's loss that such a fine intellect as Bloom's was not able to apply itself to the mind that was Oxford's. Oxford was able to do what Bloom describes because he had created his own intellect, his own cognition and done it under the circumstances that are simply unimaginable. In Bloom's sense, Edward de Vere, 17th Earl of Oxford was the first human. A more conservative way of saying this would be a weak misreading of the Author and his life.

Many teachers may simply believe that institutions such as the Folger Shakespeare Library and prestigious universities have thoroughly investigated the matter in a fair and impartial manner. Therefore, they rely with confidence on the orthodox interpretation. Relying on the elite institutions, for them the matter has been investigated and the case against the man from Stratford is totally unproven. Most would be shocked at the deliberate cover-up, suppression of information, and distortions that have been perpetrated by the Folger Library and leading Stratfordian scholars. The only bright spot in this sordid academic scandal has been the University of Massachusetts at Amherst's recent doctorate award to Roger Stritmatter for his work on Edward de Vere's Geneva Bible. This Bible was purchased for Edward de Vere and has the family crest on it. It contains footnotes and markings that can be directly linked to the works of William Shakespeare.

The award of this dissertation was a landmark event in Shakespearean studies and marks the first time the academic world has awarded a doctorate under the assumption that someone other than the man from Stratford was the Author of the Shakespeare canon. Dr. Stritmatter's dissertation committee, William Moebius, James Freeman, Edwin Gentler, Elizabeth Petrify, and Daniel Wright, should be congratulated and commended on their search for truth and their courage in the face of adversity in bringing this doctorate into fruition. One can only hope that this will encourage other academic institutions to engage in a wider range of scholarship on the Authorship issue. In 1992, Charles Vere informed Herman Gundersheimer of the importance of the de Vere Bible. Gundersheimer and the Folger Shakespeare Library pointedly ignored the importance of the de Vere Geneva Bible because it is a direct link between the Author and Edward de Vere.

The point of this lengthy introductory screed is to illustrate for the reader that the suppression of the truth about the authorship of the works of William Shakespeare and, likewise, the perpetuation of the myth of the Virgin Queen have involved a deliberate strategy of intimidating academics. Those in high academic positions have suppressed a full investigation into the Authorship issues, prevented alternative view-points from being aired, and slandered those who dissented from the orthodox Shakespearean theory. Some of those who fly the flag of academic freedom are also those who are most systematic and ruthless in maintaining the status quo. The case for the man from Stratford-upon-

Avon has remained around so long not because of the strength of the case but because those in positions of academic power have been able to stifle dissent and prevent the opposite side from being heard in the halls of academia. One can only expect that the findings of this book will meet the most severe derision because it turns Elizabethan, Shakespearean, and Oxfordian history upside down. Nevertheless, the viewpoint presented here will eventually prevail because truth has the hardness of diamonds.

Trustees of Amherst College oversee the Folger Shakespeare Library, and public and private organizations contribute heavily to its funding. Perhaps it is time that these organizations and individuals reevaluate the administration and policies of the Folger Shakespeare Library. After the death of its visionary founder, Henry Clay Folger, the Folger Shakespeare Library began to engage in deliberate policies of suppression of information, distortion of facts, and silencing of diverse points of view that have continued to this day. Its behavior for five decades has been egregious, despicable, and at odds with any standard of civilized intellectual discourse and intellectual inquiry. Perhaps it is time that changed.

In contrast to a Stratfordian world of an undying certainty, the Oxfordian world is unsettling, unstable, and unsure. Oxfordian scholarship leads us down an unstable, frightening path. But then again, so did the theory of relativity. In the subatomic world, quantum mechanics led us to a world of quarks and leptons, particles without mass or charge, and other such phenomena. In the world of astronomy, relativity led us to black holes, cosmic strings, and the big bang theory of the universe. There are mysteries inside mysteries inside enigmas.

The Oxfordian quest is not for those who rely on tradition as evidence. The Oxfordian world is not for those who yearn for tradition over knowledge, scholarship over the search for truth. There are many disagreements among the Oxfordians themselves. Was Southampton the child of Elizabeth and Oxford? What was the order of writing of the plays? Why were the plays published in the *First Folio*? Under what circumstances were they published? A dozen questions yield a hundred questions. What was the historical period like? How must British history be revised if the Oxfordian theories are true? What does it mean when it is said that Thomas Seymour "woke the fifteen year old Elizabeth each morning?" A hard look, a skeptical eye, and a strong stomach are required to understand the nasty, brutal world of the Elizabethans.

✳ ✳ ✳ ✳

Oxford's heart beats strong under the floorboards of the Folger. It will not be exorcised until the Ashbourne Portrait becomes the centerpiece of the Folger and acknowledged as the portrait of the true Author: Edward de Vere, 17th Earl of Oxford. The Ashbourne Portrait derives its name from the village of Ashbourne, five miles from Rocester Abbey, home of the Trentham family. The Countess Elizabeth Trentham-Vere was the second wife of Edward de Vere, 17th Earl of Oxford.

SEX, MURDER, INCEST, AND TUDORS

INCEST AND BASTARDS

Henry VIII was second in line to throne, behind his older brother Arthur. In 1500, Arthur married the Spain's Princess Catherine of Aragon, and then he died two years later. Henry was subject to the same ruthless, sadistic treatment given other children of his era. A disobedient child had to crawl across the room to beg forgiveness of a parent. An ambassador reported that Henry VIII was so afraid of his father that he could only mumble in his presence. The ambassador further reported that the king had nearly beaten the young Henry to death.[1] Terrified children grow up to be terrifying rulers as they displace their fears and angers on their helpless subjects.

Arthur was ill throughout the two years of his marriage, and Catherine maintained that their union was never consummated. After Arthur's death, Henry received a Papal dispensation to marry his sister-in-law even though no one questioned at the time Catherine's assertion that she was a virgin. Henry and Catherine were married for fifteen years before Henry started proceedings to divorce using the previous marriage to his brother as grounds for annulment.

Incest for the Elizabethans did not mean only sexual relations between biologically related individuals. For example, if a man had sexual relations with a woman and then had sexual relations with her sister, the second relationship would be incestuous. This was the doctrine of carnal contagion. Incest was the fundamental personal-political-legal-religious issue of the Tudor dynasty, affecting all claims to the throne. If Arthur had sexual relations with Catherine, then the marriage would have been valid. Consequently, Henry's marriage with Catherine would have been incestuous and, therefore, grounds for an annulment.

Henry VIII began proceedings to divorce Catherine based on incest by disputing Catherine's assertion that she had been a virgin when she married him. He claimed that she had relations with his brother and, therefore, the marriage was invalid despite the dispensation he had obtained to marry her. Catherine maintained stoutly that she was a virgin when she married Henry. This dispute resulted in the long, rancorous legal and papal wrangling over Henry's divorce from Catherine. Despite Henry's attempts to coerce Catherine into granting him a divorce, she maintained until her death that she was the legitimate Queen of England. All of Catholic England and Europe supported her claim. Incest was the raison d'être for Henry's divorce, yet the more fundamental cause was Catherine had not brought forth a male heir. Henry had gone further than his usual dalliances by falling madly in love, lust, or infatuation with Anne Boleyn.

The incest issue emerged again when Henry VIII wanted Anne Boleyn executed when she too had failed to produce the desired male heir to the throne. Mary Boleyn, Anne's sister, was acknowledged to have been Henry's mistress before his marriage to Anne. According to Elizabethan thinking, the marriage between Henry and Anne would have been incestuous because of Henry's relations with her sister. However, Henry did not proceed along these lines when he sought to divorce Anne Boleyn. Instead, he claimed that Anne had been unfaithful with Mark Smeaton, a musician of the court, and further that she had incestuous sexual relations with her brother, George Boleyn, and previous relations with two other men, who were wealthy political supporters of Anne. Henry and his supporters included Anne's brother in the charges to reduce the influence of the Boleyn faction and, at the same time, to gain the properties that a conviction would cause to be forfeited to the Crown. Under Tudor law, someone convicted of treason would forfeit his or her property to the Crown. This was a device that Henry used several times to rid himself of troublesome nobles and enrich himself at the same time.

The charges against her brother and the other men were patently false, and they went to the block claiming they were innocent. The charges against Mark Smeaton were more clearly corroborated than the charges against any of the others. He was seen leaving the Queen's apartment late one evening. She insisted that he was there to play music, but Mark Smeaton confessed that he was guilty of carnal relations with the Queen. In a day when a man thought his last confession on Earth could mean eternal salvation or damnation, he may have been speaking the truth.

Anne may have seen Mark Smeaton as a necessary and desperate means to produce a male heir for the aging king. Henry VIII had four or more illegitimate children, three of whom were males, so Henry was confident that his wife was at fault for failing to produce a male. Henry's eldest illegitimate son was Henry Fitzroy, by his mistress Elizabeth Blount. The king married the mother to Gilbert Tailboys of Lincolnshire and sent her off to the country. The son was openly acknowledged as the king's, but his surname was not Tudor. Neither did he carry the name of his foster father or his mother's maiden name; rather, he carried a surname that had been created for him, Fitzroy, which meant "son of king." This buttresses the argument that the custom of raising children under another name and in another household was familiar to the Elizabethans. Later, the young man became the Duke of Buckingham, and at one time, he was in line to inherit the throne, but he died when he was eighteen.

Henry's second son was Henry Cary, later Lord Hunsdon, by his mistress Mary Boleyn, the aforementioned older sister of the king's wife Anne Boleyn. More than once, Henry married ex-mistresses to one of his senior ministers. This procedure was a retirement plan of sorts for the mistress. For the minister, it generally meant the good graces of the king and financial rewards. For the boy, it meant that he had a nominal father, but that did not seem to matter very much. When Elizabeth was born in 1533, Henry Cary was nine and he blurted out one day that he was the son of his lord, the sovereign king. Apparently his mother had told him this, but it is doubtful whether he committed such an indiscretion again. Henry Cary was made Lord Hunsdon decades later when Elizabeth became queen. Ironically, he became Lord Chamberlain (but not Lord Great Chamberlain) and the supposed head of a theater company. The third alleged son was Sir John Perrot, whose mother was Mary Berkeley. When in the Tower, Sir John asked how Elizabeth could treat her own brother so badly.

There was also alleged to have been a daughter, Etheireda, whose mother was Joan Dobson. There may have been other children by other lower-born women of the court, but these go unrecorded. To summarize, Henry VIII had a variety of children who were raised in a variety of homes with a variety of males as foster fathers. Although known to be sons of the king, they nevertheless had various surnames. This practice can then be described as a normal Tudor practice of dealing with unwanted children of royalty. We might think of this as a very abnormal family practice in the twenty-first century, but it was a very normal family practice among the Tudor royalty. Unwanted children were given to other aristocrats to be raised by a variety of foster parents, under a variety of foster parent names, or in the case of one son, a name was created for him. The handling of Henry's illegitimate children foreshadows the same methods used to handle Elizabeth's illegitimate children.

These questions directly influenced Princess Elizabeth's legitimacy in several ways. First, there was the argument of the Catholics that Henry VIII's marriage to Catherine of Aragon was legitimate. Therefore, the argument was that the marriage of Henry to Anne Boleyn was invalid and Elizabeth was a bastard. Second, Parliament declared her a bastard in 1536 after her mother was convicted of adultery and incest and Anne was beheaded. Third, another allegation not brought forth by Henry VIII was that Anne Boleyn's sister Mary had been his mistress and, therefore, his marriage to Anne had been an incestuous one through the doctrine of carnal contagion. An act of Parliament in 1536 declared that to sleep with the sister of one's mistress was to commit incest, further reconfirming Elizabeth's status as a bastard.

The issue of incest was not an abstract one to the young Elizabeth. It was at the center of the various Tudor claims to the throne of England and of Elizabeth's right to be the sovereign of England. The Catholic opponents of Elizabeth were those most vocal that Elizabeth was the illegitimate daughter of a whore with no right to be monarch.

PSYCHOLOGY OF THE TUDORS

Historians are reluctant to discuss the psychological motivation of groups or individuals. The field known as psychohistory has made little headway over the past twenty years in producing an understanding of the behavior of leaders or the groups they lead. History, for those lacking such psychological orientation, is a parade of events, dates, and personalities with little understanding of the motivations, backgrounds, childhoods, or psychological history of the participants. Such historians seem to regard the behavior of any ruler or historical personage as a matter of personal intellectual choice no matter how bizarre, cruel, avaricious, or psychotic. If any individual of contemporary society tortures and murders twenty people, it is both criminal and psychotic. However, if a monarch tortures and burns a thousand heretics for having the wrong faith, it is not considered as psychotic behavior, but as an accepted, even if unenlightened, practice of the times.

Conventional historians, in addition, are unable to make any judgments or give any psychological explanations of the behavior of groups, either current or historical; that is, why do groups and their leaders act at times as if they are in a psychotic trance? For example, how did perfectly law abiding, Bible carrying Americans during the 1930s often gather and on the slightest provocation lynch Negro men? Alternatively, how did one of the enlightened Western countries that had produced such notable men as Goethe and Albert Einstein engage in the systematic destruction of millions of humans? If conventional historians are reluctant to make psychological examinations of the rulers of nations, they are even more reluctant to examine the psychology of nations, epochs, or societies. There is some politically correct inhibition against regarding any society as psychologically dysfunctional, no matter how reprehensible the behavior. Nevertheless, neurotic, sociopathic, psychotic behavior is what it is. Saying it is another century or another culture cannot ameliorate that. Human sacrifices are psychotic human reactions to psychological trauma whether it is the sacrifice of Aztec virgins, martyrs of the Christian era, lynchings in the United States, millions to gas chambers, or millions to Gulags.

In contemporary society, we expect that a child that is beaten, tortured, denigrated, and abused will have a difficult, if not psychotic, adulthood. We are not surprised that a sizeable number of criminals and psychotics have such childhoods. However, what happens when an entire society beats, tortures, and terrifies its children? Such a society will act out its fears and aggressions in open sociopathic behavior such as the murder and torture of despised groups and individuals. Thus, Tudor society was fundamentally more psychologically primitive than modern Western society. The paranoid fears and aggressive psychotic behavior openly manifested itself in Elizabethan custom and law. The skulls of executed criminals were placed on posts to line the roadway. Torture was used to extract "confessions" from the accused. Poisoning of opponents was considered a viable option for removing political enemies. The press was censored and controlled by the monarchy. Dissenting writers were punished by floggings. John Stubbs lost his right hand. Anthony Babbington, a conspirator against Elizabeth, was hanged, cut down, and while still alive, had his genitals cut off, was split open, and then cut into quarters. A quick death by the executioner's axe was seen as a form of mercy.

Disease and death came early and regularly to the Elizabethan population. Peasants were threatened by famines caused by too much or too little rain. Plagues were endemic to cities in the summer because animal and human sewage ran in the streets. Crowds cheered as bears, chained to posts, were ripped apart by savage dogs. Pit bulls are so named because they were set upon bulls to tear them apart for the amusement of crowds. These manifestations of sadistic, psychotic behavior were not limited to the criminal class but were expressed as the social norm through church permissions and secular law. Death and cruelty marked this period in a way that we can barely imagine as twentieth century human beings. There were never any feelings of guilt or remorse that this was not a proper standard of human behavior. The ability to emphasize with another's feelings, emotions, or pain was a quite undeveloped quality in the Elizabethan personality.

The Tudor monarchs were a family of terrified children who grew into terrified rulers. As children, they were all subject to the abuse and neglect that produces terrified children in any society; these children simply happened to be born in royal families. At birth, they were taken from their mothers and wrapped in swaddling. Swaddling was strips of cloth

43

wrapped around the child, binding it like a mummy. The child was immobilized for months. The children were nursed by a series of wet nurses and cared for by servants of the Crown. While not physically beaten because of their royalty (unless by their royal parents), the children were constantly terrified by warnings of hell and damnation for their evil natures. They were isolated from their parents, whom they were taught to worship from afar. The close warmth of physical comfort and nurturing was a foreign notion to Elizabethans. The idea that parents should do what was best for the welfare of the child was a foreign concept to an Elizabethan. The child was meant to do whatever was best for the parent, not the other way around. In the landed aristocracy, the wishes of the young adult meant little when it came to marriage. The marriages were arranged to ensure the best property arrangement for the parents, and the wishes of the child were not relevant. Female children, if they were thought of at all, were largely seen as breeding stock for the male hereditary lines.

The upbringing of the royal children was almost a perfect prescription for developing neurotic or psychotic adults. If not the direct recipients of violence, they saw others murdered and executed around them. These children were in chronically stressful situations from the moment of their birth, not only because of the absence of meaningful parenting by their mothers and fathers, but also because they were often in fear for their very lives. Both Princess Mary and Princess Elizabeth were threatened with death by their next of kin. When Princess Mary refused to take the oath of supremacy recognizing Henry as head of the church, Henry wanted to execute her. It was Sir Thomas Cranmer, then bishop of Winchester, who saved her life by urging the king not to execute his own daughter. Cranmer organized the compromise whereby Mary Tudor signed a humiliating document that forced her to recognize "that the marriage heretofore had between His Majesty and my mother the late Princess Dowager was by God's law, and man's law, incestuous and unlawful."[2] In the case of Elizabeth, her mother was legally murdered by her father. Elizabeth was later threatened with death by her sister Mary for her alleged participation in the Wyatt rebellion, an uprising against Mary's Catholic policies.

Children brought up in such environments have distinct emotional characteristics and patterns of behavior as adults. As adults, they simply cannot form meaningful bonds of love and attachment with other human beings. Their relationships with others are distrustful and erratic. Often great passion is followed by complete abandonment and murder. Intimacy produces the fear of being overwhelmed, which is followed by an equally strong rejection. However, the Tudor children, as opposed to non-royal children, became kings and queens and in such exalted positions they could act out their infantile aggressions on the national and world scene. Tudor monarchs did not have to torture small animals when at a whim they could pass a new law or send human sacrifices to the stake to appease their inner torments. The term "whipping boy" comes from the punishment of young princes. When a royal prince committed some infraction of the rules, he was not whipped. Instead, a fellow student or child in the royal court received the thrashing. The custom taught a valuable lesson to the young princes; that is, when you are a royal, others will pay for your sins.

The Tudors as adults were manipulative and cruel. They wreaked personal vengeance on others beyond all comprehension. In an instant, a loyal and loving wife could become a villainous traitor headed for the block. Henry VIII could blithely walk away from the legal murder of his second wife, Anne Boleyn, and marry his new wife the next day. Henry would consider executing his daughter Mary for refusing to bow to his wishes, and he was only dissuaded from doing so by his councilors. The young Edward VI could be convinced to sign the death warrants of his two uncles. Bloody Mary would send hundreds to painful, fiery deaths for their religious beliefs. Elizabeth was willing to condone murder to have the man she loved for a husband. The Tudors trusted no one, and no one trusted them.

The ability to form affectionate and lasting relationships and to have a conscience and a standard of behavior toward others that was more than an immediate gratification of needs was almost totally beyond the Elizabethan personality. Even into modern times, the ability of royal families to form affectionate bonds between members of the family is limited. Movies and videos show royal families moving around a garden with each member several feet distant from the others. Physical touching between child and parent or parent and child was limited. It was not until Princess Diana that one could see a royal family member actually showing affection and warmth toward her own children. There are revealing photographs of the young princes on a ship running to greet their mother as she stands there with open arms. Simply put, Princess Diana was operating at a higher psychological level than the family she joined. She was better able to form attachments and both give and receive affection; her royal husband could only look on baffled.

Despite these limitations of and generalizations about the Tudor monarchs, Elizabeth functioned at a higher level of affection and responsibility. While her ability to form relationships was impaired and she was capable of great personal cruelty, she did not act out her personal traumas on the English nation. During her reign, there was nothing like her sister's burning of heretics or her father's twisted religious policies.

Elizabeth addresses the dissolving of Parliament in 1593 and acknowledges the obligation of the ruler for the protection of the ruled:

> Many wiser princes than my selfe you have had, but one onely excepted (whom in the dutie of a child I must regard, and to whom I must acknowledge my selfe farre shallow) I may truly say, none whose love and care can bee greater, or whose desire can be more to fathome deeper for preventions of danger to come, or resisting of dangers, if attempted towardes you, shall ever be found to exceed my self.[3]

Hers was a quantum leap in realization that the ruler had obligations and responsibilities to the ruled. One cannot imagine such a speech by Henry VIII or Queen Mary. For them, the obligations flowed one way and one way only, and that was the obligation of the subjects to the monarch with no corresponding obligation of the monarch to the subject. From one point of view, Elizabeth's speech and her actions during her reign show a ruler capable of having a personal attachment to those she ruled: put another way, with the state being synonymous with the extended family, that the parent had obligations and responsibilities to the child. Therefore, Elizabeth's reign was a watershed in human history, and much of it was due to her unique personal intelligence and strength that enabled her to transcend much of her childhood history.

From an opposite point of view, Elizabeth was caught between conflicting domestic and international forces. She constantly vacillated and refused to give any firm directions to the country's foreign or domestic policies, except to keep her own power and prerogatives as queen. She was parsimonious with the nation's budget and abhorred spending for military purposes. The result of her indecisions was a rule of prudence dictated as much by circumstances as by the Queen's wisdom and personal good judgment.

THE NOBILITY'S REASON FOR EXISTENCE

In contrast to popular belief, the aristocrats of Elizabethan society were not absolute owners of great names, great wealth, land, and titles. Rather, they were proprietors of these benefits in return for absolute fealty to the state. They could be asked to give up any properties at any time, and they were required to do whatever the monarch desired. A nobleman could not refuse the request of the Queen to go and live in Ireland for twenty years or assume a foreign diplomatic assignment. The Queen's physician was quickly at the doorstep of those nobles who claimed ill health to avoid an unpleasant duty. Aristocrats could not marry, travel abroad, or engage in any commercial enterprises without the permission of the monarch. Elizabeth was quick to vent her wrath on any of her ladies-in-waiting who married and threw several of them in prison for marrying without her permission, a permission she was often loathe to give, especially as she got older.

Elizabeth marked her reign by many progresses or tours of the countryside where she and the entourage of her court visited the country homes of the aristocrats. The aristocrats were expected to pay the entire costs of the Queen's visit plus give the Queen gifts of gold plate. The Queen would not be reticent to express her displeasure if such gifts were inadequate. Such visits impoverished many an aristocrat.

It was service to the state, or service to the state as represented by the monarch, that justified the existence of the aristocratic class. In exchange for their duties, they expected to be rewarded with lands and commercial privileges commensurate with their rank and efforts on behalf of the Queen. The aristocrats agreed with a caste system wherein privilege was a payment for service; what they generally disagreed with was that the rewards were often promised but not given. They did not object to their servitude per se, nor did they have any vision of any other social system that did not involve such servitude; what they objected to was lack of appropriate reward for their servitude.

The Elizabethan notions of property were still very much feudal in both concept and execution. The Crown owned all the property; the aristocrats were "tenants of the Crown" for the property they controlled. In turn there were "tenants of the lord," and in turn subtenants of those. No one really owned any real property free and clear of these mutual obligations. As Sir Thomas Smith (later a tutor of Edward de Vere) puts it, "No man holdeth land simply free in England, but he or she that holdeth the crown of

England: all others hold their land in fee,"[4] that is, they were all tenants of the Crown and none owned land outright.

If an aristocrat (tenant of the Crown) died without a male heir of twenty-one years of age, the underage heir became a ward of the Crown, which then controlled the properties and marriage rights in an elaborate wardship system. The lands and properties did not automatically return to the heir upon him reaching his majority, but instead the heir had to sue for his livery to gain these back. Often these properties were in a reduced state after exploitation by the guardians. The annual average revenue to the Crown for the administration of these wardships during Elizabeth's reign was £14,700,[5] which was a considerable sum.[a] This feudal system led to chronic abuses of the heirs and could be seen as an indirect method of taxation, extortion, or theft by the Crown from the underage heirs.

From one point of view, Elizabethan England can be imagined as a very large corporate state in which everyone was employed by the state, the state owned all the property, and the monarch was the head of the state. None could object to or refuse the dictates of the monarch, no more than one can object to or refuse the dictates of a modern corporate hierarchy. Of course, in a modern society, one can actually resign a corporate position, but a nobleman of the Elizabethan era could neither refuse an order of the monarch nor resign his aristocratic title. The nobleman was bound for life to the system and to the monarch.

For an Elizabethan, the thought of social change or of a flexible social order would be anathema. This would be true for both for the upper classes and for the lower classes of society. While the fixed structure of the class system prevented (or at least allowed very little) social mobility, it did provide a haven of psychological safety. The class system was sanctified by religion and regarded as part of the natural order of life. It could only be at one's utmost peril to rebel against the social order of the aristocrats, but even more importantly, there was no concept of any social order other than one that was determined by birth into a fixed station of life.

The major duty of all the aristocrats, both males and females, was to give birth to as many legitimate heirs to their title as possible. The

---

[a] There is no agreed-upon manner of computing what an Elizabethan pound would be worth in today's currency. Some items that we would consider commonplace might be extremely costly, such as books, while other staples of existence might not be as expensive. One manner of reckoning is that Shakspere's house in Stratford-upon-Avon, which seems a solid middle-class dwelling, was purchased for about £60. If we assume that such a dwelling today would be £150,000 or $225,000, then an Elizabethan pound is equivalent to £2,500. These comparisons are very rough. Oxford was later to receive a yearly stipend of £1,000 or roughly £2,500,000 per year in current money,or $4,000,000.

continuance of their rank and position depended upon this. The Seymour family rose to power because Jane Seymour was able to give Henry VIII a legitimate male heir to the throne. No matter how educated, how beautiful, or how high in the social structure a woman might be, she had nothing unless she could produce legitimate heirs. In a day of high infant mortality and short life spans, the more heirs produced, the better. Sudden death by disease was an ever-present threat to the aristocratic stability. Queen Elizabeth at the height of her youth and beauty was stricken by smallpox, and she came close to death. The facial scars of this disease marked her beautiful, pale complexion, and from the time of her smallpox onward, she wore a white make-up composed in part of crushed eggshells to hide the ravages of the disease.

The Elizabethan period was a crossroads of the heritage of the Middle Ages and the emergence of a new social class that was less dependent on conformity to religion and to the state. A ruling female monarch in and of itself shattered old notions of the social system. Aristocrats began to pride themselves on their learning and knowledge, their use of foreign languages, and their worldliness. Part of this was a social veneer, but even so, in the process, the classical, timeless outlook of Elizabethan England was a world away from the medieval, feudal, Catholic view of Henry VIII, only a little more than a decade earlier. The Elizabethans translated and absorbed the ancients into their culture and looked abroad to the Italian Renaissance for the latest plays and dramas.

The universities of Cambridge and Oxford were centers of the English Renaissance. The scholars at these universities looked back beyond the Biblical teaching of the Catholic Church to the literary and philosophical works of the Greeks and Romans. Professors of Greek and Roman were important positions at these universities. Today, we would regard such professors as quaint scholars of long-dead languages, but in Elizabethan society these positions opened a door to reflections on man and society that were not possible in the dogma ridden world of Catholic authority. Soon, the universities began to create the educated class of commoners that entered government service and later trained at London's Inns of Court. They became the emergent class of lawyers and administrators that occupied the lower rungs of government and, from there, the more talented individuals rose in power and status.

A confluence of forces paved the way for the Elizabethan Renaissance. The importance of the ladies of the court should not be underestimated, especially women such as Queen Anne Boleyn and Queen Katherine Parr. Their influence soon extended to the monarchy itself, and especially to Princess Elizabeth Tudor who was the daughter of Anne Boleyn and was educated by her stepmother, Katherine Parr. While the male aristocrats might disappear with the changing political winds of the court, the women of the court tended to remain as a more or less cohesive group. Women who were ladies-in-waiting to Anne Boleyn were in turn ladies-in-waiting to the following queens: Jane Seymour, Katherine Parr and Mary Tudor. There has probably never been such a group of educated women who had so much influence on the policy of state as the aristocratic women of the Elizabethan Court; most prominent among these would be Queen Anne Boleyn, Queen Katherine Parr and, eventually, Queen Elizabeth.

Ultimately, Edward de Vere, 17th Earl of Oxford, brought the Elizabethan Renaissance into its full fruition. Oxford brought back from his trips to Italy everything from the knowledge of Italian literature, art, and music, to a pair of embroidered gloves for the Queen and a perfume that was from then on known as the Oxford perfume. However, Oxford's efforts did not occur in isolation. There was a religious and intellectual awakening in England before Oxford's birth. The universities were caldrons of intellectual turmoil that produced a new humanism, and Shake-speare/Oxford became its greatest exponent.

ANNE BOLEYN

Anne Boleyn, Elizabeth's mother, came from the prominent Howard family. The Howards were descendants of Edward I and, thus, in some ways had greater claim to the throne than did the Tudors who usurped the throne on Bosworth Field with the death of Richard III. Thomas Boleyn, her father, was an official of Henry VIII's who was frequently on diplomatic missions abroad. As a consequence of these missions, Anne Boleyn moved at an early age from the Boleyn family home in England to the Low Countries and was raised by Duchess Margaret at the royal court at Mechelen as one the children

Figure 6.   Queen Anne Boleyn

of her family. When Henry VIII's sister, Mary Tudor, married Louis XII of France, she moved her entourage to Paris to live with her husband. A member of this entourage was Mary Boleyn, Anne's sister. Anne Boleyn went from the Netherlands to Paris to join her sister and live at the royal court of the King of France.

Mary Boleyn was reported by King Francois I to be the most promiscuous lady at his court. Upon Mary Boleyn's return from the French court, she soon became the mistress of Henry VIII, and continued in that capacity after she married Thomas Cary and became Lady Cary. One historian reports a rumor that Mary's and Anne's mother had also been a mistress of Henry VIII's, but Henry denied that. When Henry maneuvered to have a bill passed through Parliament that would prevent his wife, Catherine of Aragon, from appealing the divorce decree to Rome, Sir George Throckmorton told Henry that it would not be wise for him to marry Anne "for it is thought ye have meddled both with the mother and the sister." Henry replied, "Never with the mother."[6] Despite Henry's denials, Catholic propaganda maintained that Anne was his daughter as well as his wife.

Anne Boleyn arrived at the court of Henry VIII in her twenties, by that time an experienced woman by Elizabethan standards during a time when women customarily married at fourteen. Anne Boleyn was well educated, spoke fluent French, and was versed in the charms and manners of the French court. She was reported to be an excellent dancer. Henry VIII made her the same offer he had made to so many others: to make her his exclusive mistress. From Henry's point of view, this appears to have been a more or less semi-official position within his court. She refused him; this but whetted Henry's desire. He was soon love-struck by the elegant and intelligent Anne Boleyn, and her refusals made her only more desirable.

Anne Boleyn knew that Henry VIII was no more likely to keep only one mistress than he was to sprout wings and fly. She knew the fate of women who had taken the position. They would be Henry's favorite for a

> For I must of necessity obtain this answer of you, having been above a whole year struck with the dart of love, and not yet sure whether I shall fail, or find a place in your heart and affection. This uncertainty has hindered me of late from naming you my mistress, since you only love me with an ordinary affection; but if you please to do the duty of a true and loyal mistress, and give up yourself, body and heart, to me, who will be, as I have been your most loyal servant (if your rigour does not forbid me) I promise you that not only the name shall be given you, but also that I will take you for my mistress, casting off all others that are in competition with you, out of my thoughts, affections and serving you only.[7]
>
> Henry VIII to Anne Boleyn

while, be showered with jewels and money, and then Henry would grow weary and find another. If during the course of the affair, the mistress had to bear the king's child, the child would be raised in a foster family. Anne Boleyn would have no part of it. She rebuffed Henry's advances. She had no wish to eventually be put in the dustbin with Henry's ex-mistresses, a very crowded place indeed.

As time passed, it became more obvious that his first wife, Catherine of Aragon, was not going to bear Henry a son. She had suffered through several stillbirths, and her advancing age made another child more unlikely with each passing year. The longer Anne held out, the more she was seen as a young woman, who if married to Henry, might bear him the long-sought-after legitimate son. Her position grew stronger each year, while Catherine of Aragon's grew weaker. Her steadfast refusals to become Henry's mistress were what made her so attractive to Henry because another illegitimate son would not answer his need for an undisputed male heir.

In addition to the personal attraction the king had for her, Anne provided a powerful intellectual and religious stimulus for Henry to break with the Catholic Church. Only the clergy were allowed to read the Bible at this time. All subjects of England were proscribed from reading the Bible, except the ladies of the court. Anne was one of the most dynamic of this church reform group and read the Bible in French. She had discussed theology while at the French court and she was not to be stifled in England. She was the one who provided intellectual and theological reasons to support Henry's divorce, more so than any of the clergy surrounding Henry, who were more motivated by their desire to please the king rather than a desire for fundamental religious change. Henry's move toward becoming the head of the church in England was not simply a matter of changing the constitutional religious leadership of Rome. It was a profound change in the relationship of God, the church and the state, and Anne Boleyn was at the center of this change

The later confiscation of the Catholic Church's properties was enabled by Henry's shift in religious positions. This confiscation of the church lands was accomplished by a variety of means, one of which was to accuse the monks and nuns of a monastery of sins of the flesh, which as often as not was true, or of other types of corruption. The property and goods were then confiscated by the Crown and immediately sold at a discount price to the aristocracy. This turned the church properties into ready cash. As time went by, the supporters of Henry's religious policies were often those aristocrats and other wealthy individuals who benefited from the confiscation policies.

Historians portray the confiscation of the Catholic Church properties as simply a transfer of wealth from religious control to the Crown's control. However, there was a great social and personal cost paid by the English citizenry, especially the poorest elements of society most dependent on the church's welfare. A considerable number of those in the monasteries were either poor workers or those receiving charity. They were put off the property and made to wander the countryside as vagrants, begging for a living or stealing bread to survive. Sometimes monks or nuns were given small pensions, but these were at the level of the most common laborer.

The towns of the era had strict laws against vagrancy and minor theft, and hanging was among the punishments for minor criminals and vagrants. Roads leading into towns were often festively decked with hanging bodies or heads of vagrants. A law passed in 1536 provided that if someone was a vagabond, that is, without a means of support, he was to be whipped; the second offense entailed being whipped and part of the ear cut off, and the third offense met with hanging:

> Many letters have survived from judges and government officials that give the number of malefactors executed after a recent assize or quarter sessions —some of them for high treason or murder, but the great majority for theft. The figures usually vary from six or eight to twelve or fourteen per session. If an average of ten persons were hanged at every session, this means that forty a year would be hanged in every county, which means 1,600 a year in the forty counties of England, even if we disregard Wales, where different circumstances prevailed. This would amount to about 60,000 during the thirty-eight years of Henry's reign. It is over 2 per cent of the 2,800,000 inhabitants of Tudor England, equals the proportion of the 6,000,000 Jews exterminated by Hitler, who constituted 2 per cent of the population of occupied Europe; though it falls short of 10,000,000 Russians who are said to have been put to death under Stalin's regime, more than 5 per cent of the population of the U.S.S.R.[8]

The wealth collected by Henry VIII provided upkeep for the expensive English occupation of portions of France and several military encounters on French soil. In addition, Henry went on a substantial building campaign, enlarging or refurbishing old palaces and building completely new ones. Nonesuch Palace was a seven-year building effort and produced a uniquely beautiful structure so that there was "none such like" this marvel. Many of the major palaces of the English royalty were built and improved from the wealth confiscated from the churches and the displacement of the poor.

The Catholics passionately hated Anne Boleyn for engineering the break from Rome and introducing heresy (that is, Protestant thinking) into England, and for Henry's confiscation of church properties. They were right on all counts. Anne Boleyn was both a personal and intellectual force that forever changed England and thus the world. Her influence over the subsequent religious events of the times has been generally underestimated, as historians and popular biographers have focused more on the melodrama of her marriage and execution than on her political influence.

The most important way that Anne had political power was through her direct access to the King. Causes brought to the Queen's attention were often granted by virtue of her support. Anne also had direct influence on the emerging Anglican Church by securing appointments of men who, as evangelical bishops, favored a direct interpretation of the Bible by the laity. She was influential in securing appointments of both high-level bishops and lower-level clergy. These men lasted in their positions after the death of Anne and through the reign of Mary. They were a continuing influence on religious policies long after Anne Boleyn was dead.

Anne's role in having English translations of the Bible printed in Europe and imported to England is difficult to ascertain. Although it is certain that Anne herself read and talked about the Bible, she usually read it in the language most familiar to her, French. The very act of reading the Bible, exercising her judgment, and expressing her opinions about it indicates how far Anne was from the tradition of interpretations of the Bible coming only from Catholic priests. Anne was a self-made woman both in deed and in thought. Continental reform of the Catholic Church and the Protestant ideas of direct reading of the Holy Scriptures by the laity were ideas that came to England by many means; one of those means was at the highest level of government, Queen Anne Boleyn.

In the summer of 1531, Henry turned his wife, Catherine of Aragon, out of the court. Before this, both Catherine and Anne Boleyn had often lived at court together. Catherine regarded Anne as another one of Henry's paramours whom he would eventually abandon, even though this was at least four years after Henry had begun his divorce. It was not to be so. From this point on, Henry lived openly with Anne Boleyn as his wife. He increased his pressure on his wife and daughter, Mary, to agree to a divorce, but they continued to refuse.

In January 1533, Anne was pregnant, and she married Henry around January 25, 1533, in a secret ceremony. Anne was crowned queen on June 1, 1533, at Westminster Abbey a week after Bishop Cranmer declared Henry's marriage to Catherine to have been unlawful. The coronation was not a huge success with Londoners, who were rather sullen for such an occasion. Elizabeth was born three months later, on September 7, 1533, at Greenwich Court. The astrologers and others had predicted a son for Henry. He had arranged for a tournament to be held when his male heir arrived, but he canceled the tournament when the child was announced to be female.

Elizabeth was christened at the Church of the Franciscan Friars in Greenwich with all the appropriate ceremony. She was then moved to Hatfield with a large retinue of servants and attendants. There is no record of Anne Boleyn ever mentioning or seeing her infant daughter, and there was no record of Elizabeth ever commenting about her mother. In 1534, Parliament passed the Act of Succession, which required every subject to swear that the children of Henry and Anne Boleyn were the lawful heirs to the English throne. Sir Thomas More and Bishop Fuller were among those who refused to take the oath; they were executed along with a number of Catholic monks. However, to balance the scales, Henry also burned several Anabaptists as heretics for denying the Real Presence of Christ in the Eucharist. Henry continued to humiliate Catherine of Aragon because she refused to recognize the Act of Succession. He took her daughter, Princess Mary, from Catherine and made her live at Elizabeth's residence as a virtual prisoner. Mary was often humiliated in the presence of her younger sister and not allowed to send or receive letters from her mother. Henry had now bastardized his first daughter.

Anne Boleyn had two miscarriages and then gave birth to a stillborn son. Henry slowly turned against her and began to carry on his extramarital affairs without hiding them from Anne. As Anne's relationship with Henry deteriorated, her enemies began to plot her downfall. Archbishop Cranmer moved against Anne and placed a series of spies to watch her movements. Late one night, a court musician, Mark Smeaton, was seen coming from her chambers. He claimed that he was there to play music for the Queen, but his excuse held little weight with the vengeful Cranmer. In May 1536, Anne was arrested and charged with adultery with four men, including her brother and Mark Smeaton. The first three maintained their innocence until death, but Mark Smeaton immediately confessed and maintained his guilt until death.

Only with Smeaton was there any direct testimony of a possible liaison with Anne, for he had been seen leaving her chambers. The other three were charged to remove Anne's most ardent political supporters and for Henry's monetary gain. It was a foregone conclusion that anyone brought to trial by the king would be found guilty. The only question was whether the king would show mercy and permit death by beheading rather than the more gruesome hanging, disemboweling, and quartering. Many aristocrats quietly accepted their death sentences to try to avoid having the Crown inflict greater damage on their surviving families. In addition, a quick death by the axe was preferably to hanging and disembowelment. Few, if any, aristocrats blamed the king for their unjust end even though he was the one directly responsible.

Henry VIII legally murdered Anne Boleyn by use of the English judicial system. His wife could not see the charges before the trial, know what witnesses might be called against her, call witnesses in her own defense, nor employ effective counsel. The jury was there to give the verdict that was desired by the king. It was inconceivable that they would find any other verdict but guilty. Anne Boleyn was executed on May 19, 1536. Henry married Jane Seymour the next day.

PRINCESS ELIZABETH

Princess Elizabeth was thirty-three months old when her father executed her mother. History books do not reveal any thoughts or reflections Elizabeth might have had on her mother's execution. She must have been aware of it as a child at some age and obviously, as an adult, she became aware of the circumstances. There must be a significance of some sort that Elizabeth adopted the motto of Anne Boleyn, "Ever the Same." There appears to be no written record that Anne Boleyn ever made any comment about the welfare of her daughter.

Jane Seymour gave Henry VIII what he had so longed for, a healthy, legitimate baby boy, although Jane died of septicemia several days after the birth. The child was the legitimate male heir and would become Edward VI upon the death of his father. His two uncles were Edward Seymour and Thomas Seymour, brothers to Jane Seymour, and two men who played a central role in Elizabeth's life. Edward was born in October 1537 when Elizabeth was four years old. Elizabeth and her sister Mary attended the christening ceremony.

While Elizabeth must have been too young to realize the full implications of all the court politics, her older sister Mary at twenty-one was aware of the implications of Edward's birth. Mary and Elizabeth had been declared bastards by the Act of Succession of July 1536. Although Elizabeth was given the title "the King's daughter, the Lady Elizabeth," she was by an act of Parliament a royal bastard. Both girls had households of over thirty servants and were treated as quasi-royal, as long as they accepted that they had no claim to the throne and recognized Henry's other child, Edward VI, to be his only legitimate offspring.

Elizabeth was brought up mainly at the Hatfield residence under the care of Lady Bryan and more directly under the care of her nurse and governess Katherine Champernowne, who would later marry and become Katherine Ashley. This was the beginning of a lifelong relationship for Elizabeth, and it was the most consistent and loving relationship she would know. Even if she did not always have the best judgment, Katherine Ashley was devoted to Elizabeth's welfare. She would be with Elizabeth through many different households and eventually became a lady-in-waiting when Elizabeth became queen; she died in her old age still in the service of her Queen.

Historians have always agreed that Elizabeth I was the daughter of Henry VIII. However, the actions of her half-sister, Mary, throw this assumption into question. When Queen Mary came to the throne, the easiest course of action would have been to marry Elizabeth to some foreign prince and send her to the far reaches of Christendom, possibly by marrying her to some obscure German prince. This would effectively remove her

> ### Dr. John Dee
>
> Was a doctor, scholar, astrologer and advisor to Elizabeth: He was influential in having her explore the New World. As a diplomat from Poland, his code name was 007.
>
> There is a fondness in England for naming series of numbers. The telephone number 777-4422 would be said as "triple-seven, double four, double two." Hence, 007 is "double oh seven;" not "zero-zero-seven," or "oh, oh, seven."

as a locus of dissent and hope for the English Protestants. Without any action on Elizabeth's part, she was always a potential threat to the Catholic regime of her sister. Yet Mary did not act to betroth and marry her to a foreign prince because to do so would have validated Elizabeth as daughter of Henry VIII. Up to her dying days, Mary refused to acknowledge Elizabeth as her sister, and only under pressure from her councilors to avoid a civil war after her death did she agree to Elizabeth as an heir to the throne.

Mary's doubts revolved around the circumstances of Anne Boleyn and Henry VIII's marriage. They were married hurriedly and secretly after waiting for almost five years. Anne then gave birth to an Elizabeth less than nine months later. The first possibility was that Anne and Henry had premarital sexual relations and that Elizabeth was the product of these relations.

However, the second possibility was more troubling: that is, that Anne was impregnated by someone else, and Anne had to marry Henry in a hurry because she was with child. The candidate for another father falls on the musician, Mark Smeaton, who was later executed for having relations with the Queen. The handsome musician was Anne's court musician before and after she married Henry. Was Elizabeth the daughter of an illicit relationship between Mark Smeaton and Anne Boleyn? Her half-sister, Mary, seemed to think so.

Henry VIII's medical history indicates that he most probably was afflicted with syphilis, and some of his children may have inherited congenital syphilis. Henry was eighteen and his first wife, Catherine of Aragon, was twenty-four when they married in 1509. Catherine had a stillborn daughter two years later, then a son who died after two months, another child who died shortly after birth, a premature delivery, and finally a daughter Mary, who survived into adulthood. Anne Boleyn delivered Elizabeth, had a miscarriage, and then had a dead boy delivered prematurely. The fact that there were nine pregnancies but only two surviving children is strong presumptive evidence that Henry VIII suffered from syphilis.[b] In his later years, Henry suffered from a sore leg that apparently had a gummatous tumor in the muscle and bone. This would also be a symptom of syphilis at a developed stage. In addition, his oldest surviving daughter, Mary, had a sickly disposition, an overly large head and thinning hair and was unable to conceive. These symptoms point to her suffering from congenital syphilis. In contrast, Elizabeth was a healthy child and adult, and her physical health may have been an indication she was not the daughter of Henry VIII. Whether or not Elizabeth was the actual child of Henry is open to question, but it was clear that her sister, Mary, thought she was the child of Mark Smeaton.

After the birth of her half-brother, Elizabeth spent the next several years in various residences, always attended by Kat Ashley. When Elizabeth was nine years old, Henry VIII married his last wife, Katherine Parr. Elizabeth spent five years with Queen Katherine. Katherine was responsible for Elizabeth's formidable education from nine to fourteen, and Kat Ashley was responsible for her earlier education. Elizabeth by all accounts had a precocious intellect. She was able to write and speak perfectly in French and Italian, less well in Latin, and had moderate capabilities in Spanish and Greek. She read the New Testament in Greek, and was familiar with the orations of Socrates and the tragedies of Sophocles. In her later years, she greeted a Polish ambassador speaking in Latin and congratulated herself that she was still fluent, but somewhat out of practice. When as queen she attended plays in Cambridge and Oxford, the plays were often in Latin, as were the sermons. The Queen gave

---

[b] Syphilis arrived in Europe shortly after 1492 and proceeded its devastating course of infection. The English called it the "French disease," and the French called it the "Italian disease," and the Italians called it the "Spanish disease." The Spanish in turn called it the "French disease" from a Latin poem called "Infirmitatem Gallorum" or "French Sickness."

speeches in Latin at the graduations she attended at the universities. By any standard, her knowledge and intellectual capacities were prodigious. In December 1544, Elizabeth presented to Katherine Parr a translation of a French work. Elizabeth had titled her translation *A Godly Meditacyon on the Cristen Sowle, concernynge a love towardes God and hys Christe, coplyed in French by Lady margarete Quene of Navar and aptly translated into Englysh by the ryght vertuouse Lady Elyzabeth daughter of our late souverayne, Kyng Henri VIII.* It was published in Germany in the later years of her reign as *A Godly Medytacyon of the Christen Sowle,* with an introduction and afterward by John Bale, a noted Protestant reformer, scholar, and theologian. This work is generally referred to as *The Mirror of the Sinful Soul.* It was a translation of *Le Miroir of de l'âme pécheresse,* by Marguerite Angoulême, Queen of Navarre, who was sister to the king of France. Marguerite's most famous work was *The Heptameron*, which was a collection of stories of romance, love, and sex, some of it incestuous. The work Elizabeth translated had been sent to Anne Boleyn, probably about 1534, and then to Katherine Parr. This was a translation of some twenty-seven pages. In it, Elizabeth exercised editorial judgment and changed words or phrases to fit her own meaning. It was a prayerful reflection on sin and the need for God's grace to achieve salvation. In her letter to Katherine Parr, Elizabeth writes:

> And therefore have I as for an essay or beginning (so following the right noble saying of the proverb aforesaid) translated this little book out of French rhyme into English prose, joining the sentences together as well as the capacity of my simple wit and small learning could extend themselves.[9]

One would imagine that historians would prominently mention the fact that Elizabeth translated a work from French when she was eleven as evidence of her intellect, but they do not. The problem is the subject matter of the book, which is incest or at least a multifaceted relationship with God that may be interpreted as incestuous. At a minimum, the translation connects Elizabeth to the books of Marguerite of Navarre, whose works were controversial and not in keeping with what a proper young princess should have on her reading list. Elizabeth describes her translation as follows:

> The which book is entitled, or named, *The Mirror or Glass of the Sinful Soul*, wherein is contained how she (beholding and contemplating what she is) doth perceive how of herself and her own strength she can do nothing that good is, or prevaileth for her salvation, unless it be through the grace of god, whose mother, daughter, sister, and wife by the scriptures she proveth herself to be.[10]

Christopher Haigh makes this comment on Elizabeth's translation:

When she was eleven, she prepared a translation from French for presentation to her current stepmother, with some intriguing errors: she rendered "père" as "mother," omitted a line on a father's forgiveness of his child, and had wives executing adulterous husbands instead of vice versa. Her mother and a stepmother were executed for alleged adultery and treason, two stepmothers died in childbirth, and a German stepmother was married for diplomatic convenience and divorced for lack of interest. Elizabeth did not get a good impression of the fortunes of royal wives.[11]

It is difficult to understand this complex and enigmatic translation of Elizabeth's. On one hand, to ignore it would seem to leave out an essential piece of intellectual evidence that indicates what influenced Elizabeth. On the other hand, to simplify its complex and barely understandable implications with a few quick sentences would be to exaggerate its importance without the detailed analysis required. Given the later involvement of Elizabeth, Katherine Parr, and Sir Thomas Seymour, biographers have stayed clear of any routes leading to Marguerite of Navarre and her unorthodox beliefs. Whether or not Marguerite's bawdy tales were an influence on the proper and religious Katherine Parr and precipitated events for Elizabeth remains to be examined and much on the topic will forever be only speculation.

Sir John Cheke was the supervisor of education of the royal children. Roger Ascham was Edward's first tutor, and William Grindall was Elizabeth's tutor. All were silent Protestants during the reign of Queen Mary. Roger Ascham gave much credit to Elizabeth's intellectual capabilities. His method of tutoring often involved double translations, where his pupil would first translate from Latin into English and then back into Latin. He also taught penmanship in the Italian style, and Elizabeth wrote in the florid Italian script. At this time, there were two methods of penmanship: there was the older script, based on German and medieval English, which still had the German "f" for "s" and is difficult if not impossible to decipher by a modern reader. This was being replaced by the Italian script taught to Elizabeth. The change in handwriting was thus an external manifestation of the new humanism and the new teachings in the universities and in the reform churches. Elizabeth's handwriting in the Italian script is very clear to current sensibilities. When she became queen, she continued to write in the Italian script and her courtiers and counselors soon adopted the style. One of the reasons we write the way we do today is that Elizabeth established this as a standard of handwriting in the English-speaking world.

> There are many honourable ladies now who surpass Thomas More's daughters in all kinds of learning; but among all of them the brightest star is my illustrious Lady Elizabeth, the king's sister; so that I have no difficulty in finding subject for writing in her praise, but only in setting bounds to what I write. I will write nothing however which I have not myself witnessed. She had me for her tutor in Greek and Latin two years, but the foundations of her knowledge in both languages were laid by the diligent instruction of William Grindall, my late beloved friend, and seven years my pupil in classical learning at Cambridge. From this university he was summoned by John Cheke to court, where he soon received the appointment of tutor to this lady.
>
> After some years when through her native genius, aided by the efforts of so excellent a master, she had made a great progress in learning, and Grindall, by his merit and the favour of his mistress, might have aspired to high dignities, he was snatched away by a sudden illness. I was appointed to succeed him in his office, and the work which he had so happily begun, without my assistance, indeed, but not without some counsels of mine, I diligently laboured to complete. Now, however, released from the Court and restored to my old literary leisure here, where by her beneficence I hold an honest place in this University. It is difficult to say whether the gifts of nature or of fortune are most to be admired in that illustrious lady. The qualities praised by Aristotle meet altogether in her—beauty of person, greatness of mind, prudence and industry, all in the highest degree. She has just passed her sixteenth birthday, and exhibits such seriousness and gentility as are unheard of in one of her age and rank. Her study of true religion and learning is most energetic. Her mind has no womanly weakness, her perseverance is equal to that of a man, and her memory long retains that which it readily grasps. She talks French and Italian as well as English: she has often talked to me readily and well in Latin, and moderately so in Greek. When she writes Greek and Latin, nothing is more beautiful than her handwriting. She is as much delighted with music as she is skillful in that art.[12]
>
> Roger Ascham

Ascham was a Cambridge scholar and a member of the reform, humanist movement, as Protestants were called. This movement was dedicated to go beyond the Bible and study the Greek and Latin classics. They also emphasized the reading of the Bible by individuals, not just clerics, but they did not go so far as to contradict the king. While understanding the natural tendency to flatter the monarch or anyone of royal blood, Ascham's comments about his pupil strike a true note as to Elizabeth's intellect. Interestingly, Ascham wrote that Mildred Cook was the best student of Greek and could read and write it as well as she could read English. Mildred Cook would later become the wife of William Cecil, Lord Burghley, Elizabeth's Principal Secretary of the Council and her lifelong advisor. Elizabeth also learned the other skills of a well-born lady of the time: the ability to sew, embroider, dance, ride, sing, and play a musical instrument or two. Elizabeth was especially proficient at the virginals, the Elizabethan equivalent of the piano.

Katherine Parr, Elizabeth's stepmother, was the last wife of Henry VIII, and she wrote three books of religious devotionals, which while not great works of art or philosophy, nevertheless reflected aspects of her thinking. Her father, Henry, was a fine musician, composed several songs and wrote a book on religion which while not original, did show his capacity for sustained intellectual accomplishment. Little was recorded of Queen Mary's intellect or literary works. In brief, the education and the religious and cultural environment of the court were stimulating, and the kings and queens of England of the time were perhaps the most educated of English history. Latin was the official language of law and the unofficial language of the educated. The plays, masques, and music performed at court were seen by a highly educated audience. Many in the court were multilingual, and plays were performed in Latin as well as in English.

Roger Ascham had written an earlier book on the subject of teaching children, *Schoolmaster, a plain and profit way of teaching children to understand and write and speak in Latin tong.* His methods were not the usual birch whipping method of forcing students to pay attention. Ascham felt that students should be encouraged, not threatened, a very novel idea for the time. In some respects, Elizabeth was raised in a somewhat tolerant and understanding manner, at least as far as her tutors were concerned. At least Ascham considered that the child's best interest would be better served in a less punishing environment. The education of Elizabeth was at the forefront of the Protestant Reformation, when education and tolerance for the individual were stressed and practiced. Some of these characteristics transferred into Elizabeth's personality and then into her political viewpoint and leadership.

The upbringing of Elizabeth was in marked contrast to the upbringing of her half-sister. Spanish tutors instructed the young Princess Mary, and one named Vives recommended that the whipping rod never be removed from a boy's back. He wrote, "The daughter especially shall be handled without cherishing. Cherishing marreth sons, but it utterly destroyeth daughters."[13] If the number of religious burnings is a rough gauge of the relative degree of psychological stability of the rulers, Henry VIII burned eighty-one heretics in thirty-eight years, Queen Mary burned about three hundred in five years, and Elizabeth burned five people in forty-five years.

It is also worth noting that both Henry VIII and Elizabeth were later-born children, who were not first in line for the throne. In contrast, Mary was the firstborn, and Edward VI was the firstborn male son, which puts him in a unique category. Firstborn children in a family tend to adopt the authority of the parents and be more authoritarian in their personality.

They tend to align themselves with the established culture of their parents. Mary was the firstborn child of the Tudors, and she was the ruler who most stubbornly tried to maintain the Catholicism of her mother. Religion was an absolute and not simply a tactic of rule for Mary. She stubbornly tried to turn back the religious clock to a Catholicism that was no longer possible for a sizeable number of her subjects. In a similar manner, the young Edward VI showed the same signs of rigidity as a devout Protestant who wished to convert his oldest sister, Mary, to the new faith of his father.

In contrast, Elizabeth and Henry VIII were more flexible in their approach to politics and religion. Religion for Henry and Elizabeth was a method of rule for their personal and political ends. It was not an end in and of itself for which they would sacrifice political power. Elizabeth's flexibility and pragmatic rule made her able to walk the difficult middle road between the warring religious factions of her era. A good part of this may be due to her unique upbringing as a child, and part of it may be due to her position in the family as a later-born child.

Whatever Elizabeth's personal frailties, whatever her personal history, whatever her personal failings, whatever her sins, omissions, vanities or misjudgments, without her, there would be no William Shakespeare. There would be no *Hamlet* or *Richard III*. There would have been nothing like the Elizabethan Renaissance without Elizabeth. It is very difficult to conceive that Shakespeare would have been performed at all, much less that his work would have flourished, during the rule of Henry VIII. Whatever the entanglements between Oxford and Elizabeth in their multilevel relationship, Elizabeth was the Queen. It was her desire for theatrical performances that allowed Oxford to write, and the highest levels of English society saw his plays. Someone once said that it takes talent to recognize genius. Based on this remark, Elizabeth was very talented indeed. Shakespeare flourished in the Elizabethan age, not the other way around. At some high level of understanding, Elizabeth must have understood the artistic significance of the works that were coming from Oxford's pen, even though the topics were often those that might offend an authoritarian monarch.

QUEEN KATHERINE PARR

Katherine Parr was Henry VIII's last wife. She was first married at the age of twelve to Edward Borough, Lord Gainsborough, in Lincolnshire, who was in his late fifties or sixties. It was unlikely that she had to fulfill her marriage vows at such a tender age, and she remained with her mother for another year or two after being wed. Her husband died three years after the marriage, and Katherine was a widow at the age of fifteen. Her next marriage was to John Neville, Baron Latimer, in 1534. He was approximately forty-two, and she was nineteen. He was a wealthy man; the match assured that Katherine would be a wealthy woman

Figure 7.   Queen Katherine Parr

if she survived him. She did not have any children by either husband.

In 1536, Henry and Thomas Cromwell had the dissolution of the monasteries in full swing. The result of this dissolution was to place thousands of monks and nuns on the street along with sizeable numbers of beggars who had no other means of support. The Crown then sold the confiscated lands, and the moneys went to the royal treasury. There was considerable corruption involved in the sale of these valuable properties. This—combined with the large number of people formerly supported by the monasteries now in need of shelter by the local parishes—put the country on the brink of rebellion.

The first armed resistance to the dissolution of the monasteries was on September 28, 1536, when the monks and people of Hexam in Northumberland took up arms and threw Cromwell's ministers out of the town in an uprising known as the Pilgrimage of Grace. Thousands in the North took up arms. They were loyal to the king, but wanted Lord Cromwell and Sir Richard Riche, Chancellor of Augmentations, deposed. These men were the instruments of Henry's policies. Lord Latimer, Katherine's husband, was besieged by thousands of rebels. He faced either losing his life and property or joining the rebels. If he joined the rebels, he could hope for the best in case the rebels were defeated. If he opposed the rebels, he and his family might be dead. His best hope was a future pardon from the king. Lord Latimer was an unlikely and reluctant rebel.

The rebellion was eventually put down and the leadership of the rebellion executed. Lord Latimer and Katherine Parr were in danger of losing their lives, even though they had been unwilling participants in this show of force against Henry. Katherine and her husband traveled to London, where Katherine explained that her husband had only acted as he did because of the threats to them. She said that while they might have chosen an honorable death, this would have meant that they could not act in Henry's best interest while in the rebel camp and they would only have been useless martyrs. Henry accepted this, and the two were spared their lives. Katherine was confident and courageous in dealing with the king and her even-tempered, thoughtful intelligence became a force to be reckoned with in court politics.

Katherine Parr again became a widow in February 1543 after the death of her second husband, Lord Latimer. Shortly thereafter, Henry VIII also became a widower after the execution of his fifth wife Katherine Howard. After the execution, Henry quickly looked toward the young widow Katherine Parr for a bride. She married the aging Henry VIII on July 12, 1543, against the advice of several ladies of the court who were concerned by Henry's fitful disposition and his marriage record of having executed two of his five previous wives. Nevertheless, the levelheaded Katherine married Henry

> "I, Henry, take thee, Katherine, to my wedded wife, to have and to hold from this day forward, for better for worse, for richer for poorer, in sickness and in health, till death us depart, and thereto I plight my troth."
>
> "I, Katherine, take thee, Henry, to my wedded husband, to have and to hold from this day forward, for better for worse, for richer for poorer, in sickness and in health, to be bonair and buxom in bed and at board, till death us depart, and thereto I plight my troth."[14]

with the aplomb of a corporate executive taking on a new assignment. The difference was that this assignment was marriage to an aging king of unreliable disposition, ill health, and little tolerance for personal confrontation.

Katherine was the first queen who attempted to mend the relationship between Henry and his three children: Mary, his daughter by Catherine of Aragon; Elizabeth, his daughter by Anne Boleyn; and Edward, his son by Jane Seymour. They were all present in Henry's household in August 1543 and later at Christmas festivities. Edward and later Elizabeth began calling her "mother." Elizabeth, the most ostracized of the Tudor children, showed a great affection for Katherine. Elizabeth had tutors and caretakers for whom she had a great regard, such as Katherine Ashley, but these were ladies-in-waiting to her and not her royal equals. They could not receive the same admiring affection due a queen and stepmother; Queen Katherine Parr was the only woman the young Princess Elizabeth ever called "mother."

The great trust and reliance Henry placed in Katherine Parr was indicated when he went to France to wage war in 1543. Five days before departing, he gave a writ making her regent to act in his stead while he was in France. This was a powerful position indeed:

First, touching the Queen's Highness and my Lord Prince:

The king has resolved that the Queen shall be Regent in his absence and that his process shall pass and bear *teste* in her name, as in like cases heretofore; and that a commission for this be delivered to her before his departure. She shall use the advice and Counsel of the Archbishop of Canterbury, Lord Chancellor Wriothesley, the Earl of Hertford, the Bishop of Westminster (Thirlby), and Sir William Petre, secretary.[15]

As the Queen gained in political strength, she garnered more enemies. The ostensible issue was religion, and her principal enemies were the Duke of Norfolk, a Catholic, and Stephen Gardiner, archbishop of Canterbury. These men wished to move the English Church toward a more Catholic conformity. This meant the Bible was to be taught only by the church, which would interpret it for the masses. To do this, they would need to reduce the influence and ideas of Katherine Parr and her ladies of the court who favored and supported a broad, humanistic religion. Humanism includes the idea of study of the ancient classics of Greece and Rome and a direct reading and personal interpretation of the Bible. Without going into detail, the conservatives' plot was to charge several ministers and aristocrats with heresy, which meant they had questioned the king's wisdom in a religious matter. The plan was to torture the ministers and aristocrats, obtain confessions, and implicate the Queen. In short, the conservatives were intent on using the legal system to murder Queen Katherine.

Henry, paranoid that he was, would always be quick to believe that someone was plotting against him: He trusted no one, and treason consisted of nothing more than disagreeing with the king's religious policies. A heretic was thereby also a traitor. If he had suspicions that Katherine Parr was a secret heretic, he was probably right. Katherine had published three devotional tracts outlining her religious views, and she had frequently debated Henry on matters of faith to the point of dangerous confrontations. In 1543, Henry had issued a book of faith known as the

King's Book, which sharply directed religion back toward Catholic orthodoxy. The book, along with restrictive laws, drastically limited the reading and discussion of the English Bible, stating that such reading and discussion encouraged arrogance and dissension among the people.

As part of this move back toward the Catholic faith, for example, Anne Askew was tortured and burned for denying the Real Presence (that is, the idea that Christ actually was in the Eucharist and that communion was not simply a symbolic ceremony). Anne Askew was tortured in an attempt to implicate women close to the Queen and burned as a heretic on July 16, 1546. She had to be carried to her burning on a chair because her legs were bent and useless after torture on the rack. She was burned along with two other heretics, but she never implicated the Queen or other women of the court. Anne Askew had been a childhood friend of the Queen, which further connected Katherine to this Protestant heretic. The danger was very real for the Queen and the ladies of the court who were of a Protestant persuasion. Most likely, they had heretical books, and Katherine's discussions with the king could be interpreted as challenges, if not open heresy.

The Queen's enemies moved to have her and her ladies arrested and sent to the Tower for interrogation. Once there, Katherine would probably suffer the same fate as two of Henry's other wives, death by the executioner's axe. Doctor Thomas Wendy, Henry's physician, informed Katherine of the plot against her and, in fear for her life, she quickly took action. She realized that if she were imprisoned in the Tower without direct access to Henry, she would be doomed. She approached the king in his bedchamber, attended by a few peers. She said that if she had spoken of religion, it was to learn from the king's wisdom. She maintained that it was preposterous for a woman's views to prevail over her husband's and said she was only a humble woman ready to be taught by her husband and wise king. Further, she said, her conversations with him were to provide him diversion and distraction from his ailing leg. She said she had encouraged discussion:

> ... that I, hearing your Majesty's learned discourse, might myself receive profit thereby; wherein, I assure your Majesty, I have not missed any desire in that behalf, always ferring [deferring] myself in all such matters to your Majesty, as by ordinance of nature it is convenient [correct] for me to do.[16]

Katherine Parr's charm, humbleness, flattery, and sincerity had wooed the king. He replied:

> And is it even so, sweetheart? And tended your arguments to no worse end?
> Then perfect friends we are now again, as ever at any time heretofore.[17]

The king was present in the garden when Lord Chancellor Thomas Wriothesley entered with forty of the king's guards to take the Queen and her ladies for interrogation in the Tower—and certain death. The king rudely turned them around with his full fury.

Katherine's intelligence, logic, sincerity, and non-threatening behavior had saved her life. At a supper party a year or so before his death, Henry announced that he was considering reversing the doctrine of the Real Presence and adopting a Protestant communion service. This is, of course, after the torture and death of Anne Askew, among others, for their denials of conscience.

Henry died on January 28, 1547. After his death, and according to his generous will, Katherine Parr received extensive gold plate and money. She had a life interest in land bestowed upon her by Parliament and was the owner of the palace at Chelsea and the manors of Wimbledon and Hanworth. Her staff for her establishments was probably in the neighborhood of 200 people. After the king's death, Elizabeth resided with Katherine at Chelsea. It was through Katherine Parr that Elizabeth came to know Thomas Seymour.

KATHERINE PARR AND THE LORD ADMIRAL

Henry VIII stipulated in his will the order of succession to the throne and the conditions of guardianship of his son, Edward, because his son would become king while still a minor. The stipulations provided that a council of sixteen men should rule England during Edward's minority. These were all men who were loyal to Henry and accepted the doctrine of royal supremacy over the church. Henry clearly foresaw the dire consequences that could arise if one man held too much power in the young king's name. Despite the precautions of Henry VIII, Edward Seymour, the young king's uncle, quickly developed influence over the young king, pushed aside others on the council, and assumed almost total control over England. He assumed the role of Lord Protector and made himself Duke of Somerset.

Figure 8.   Thomas Seymour

With the death of Henry VIII, those in power were now dedicated Protestants both because of their religious beliefs and because many of these nobles had profited handsomely by Henry's confiscation of church property. This group was even more tolerant of Protestantism than Henry, and several of Henry VIII's religious restrictions were repealed. These Protestant views were inculcated into the young King Edward VI, who had firm Protestant tutors, and even though young, he often revealed his strong Protestant education. Despite this strong Protestantism, Edward Seymour had a tolerant religious streak in him and refused to let anyone be tortured or burned for religious views, which was seen as a sign of weakness by many. Bishops Gardiner and Bonner, for instance, were not executed, but simply confined in the Tower with the required creature comforts.

Thomas Seymour, Edward's brother, was a man equally dedicated to his own advancement and power, and he was intensely jealous of his brother's new position as Lord Protector. Thomas Seymour was a rogue, a bounder, and a man of apparently infinite energy, unlimited schemes, and blind ambition. These qualities, combined with an almost complete lack of discretion and political sense, doomed him for a quick and bloody end in the world of high court intrigue. As Lord Admiral of England, Thomas Seymour had the responsibility to protect English shipping interests in the English Channel from pirates. As a fox in charge of the chicken coop, he arranged with the pirates to use his property in the Scilly Isles as a haven in return for a percentage of the booty.

After the death of the Henry VIII, Thomas Seymour proposed marriage to the young Princess Elizabeth, who was twelve years old at the time. This was a brash attempt to enter the royal line of succession through marriage. In an era of sudden and untimely deaths, Elizabeth had only her sister, Mary, before her in order of succession. In addition, Mary was a fervent Catholic whose standing was adamantly opposed by the Protestant faction ruling the country through the young king. If for any reason both Edward VI and then Mary died, then Thomas Seymour would be the de facto king by controlling his young bride. It is very doubtful that the council would ever have approved a marriage between Princess Elizabeth and Thomas Seymour, but if Elizabeth married him secretly or without the permission of the council, the deed would be fait accompli, and the council and his brother would be helpless.

Elizabeth promptly rejected Seymour's proposal with a letter that indicates maturity beyond her years, but Katherine Parr may have edited it, as Elizabeth was a part of the Dowager Queen's household at Chelsea and Hatfield:

> Therefore, my lord Admiral, permit me to say frankly that since there is no one in the world who holds your merit in higher esteem than I do, nor finds greater pleasure in your society while I may regard you as a disinterested friend—I shall continue to preserve the satisfaction of looking upon you as such, apart from that closer intimacy of marriage, which often causes the possession of personal merits to be forgotten. Let your lordship be persuaded that if I refuse the good fortune of being your wife, I shall never cease to interest myself in all which may add greater glory to yourself, and that I shall make it my greatest pleasure to remain,
>
> Your servitor and good friend, ELIZABETH[1]

Quickly recovering from Princess Elizabeth's rejection, Thomas Seymour rekindled the old embers of his aborted romance with Katherine Parr and produced a conflagration. There had been a romance brewing between Katherine Parr and Thomas Seymour after the death of her second husband while Henry VIII was alive. However, the king must have developed a fascination for Katherine Parr while still married to Katherine

Howard, and he appointed Thomas Seymour to various positions that required him to be out of the country or at sea, far away from the comely young widow Katherine Parr.

Often true rogues and scoundrels can make otherwise stable, virtuous, intelligent, and wise women completely lose their heads, fall deeply in love, and behave in ways that completely contradict their previously stable behavior. At any rate, Katherine Parr had clearly fallen in love with Thomas Seymour when she first met him and later wrote:

> I would not have you think that this mine honest good will toward you to proceed of any sudden motion or passion for as truly as God is god, my mind was fully bent the other time I was at liberty to marry you before any man I knew.[2]

The expression "love is blind" derives from the mythological representation of a blind Cupid flying about shooting his arrows willy-nilly into the most inappropriate couples. Nowhere did the dart of love produce a more tragic passion or strike a more vulnerable target than it did with Katherine Parr.

MARY SEYMOUR DISAPPEARS

Thomas Seymour proposed to Katherine Parr and she accepted. Thomas then moved to obtain permission to marry from his nephew, the young king. He needed this permission because Katherine Parr was Queen Dowager, an important personage within the aristocratic hierarchy. Thomas Seymour was the favorite of the young king, who often resented the stern rule of his other uncle. Periodically, Thomas gave gifts of several pounds in gold to the young king. His generosity was contrasted by his brother's niggardly policies in keeping the young king completely financially dependent upon him. The little boy king noted the events in his journal with a certain sense of satisfaction when he crossed his stern protector. His notes reveal the tensions between Thomas and his brother, the Lord Protector:

> The lord Seimour of Sudley maried the quene whose nam was Katarine, with which maring the lord Protectour was much offended.[3]

Thomas Seymour and Katherine Parr were married during May 1547 in a private ceremony. His marriage to Elizabeth's stepmother made Thomas Seymour the stepfather to Elizabeth. He was already her stepuncle because he was the uncle of her stepbrother Edward VI. Perhaps the irrepressible Thomas Seymour provided some necessary élan vital to Katherine's life that had been missing in her previous three marriages. Her balance and good judgment had been replaced by a marriage of passion, but she had chosen an impossible bounder who was to bring much grief to all concerned. Katherine Parr, Thomas Seymour, and Elizabeth lived at the household in Chelsea. Also living in the household at various periods was Lady Jane Grey, who had a claim to the throne as granddaughter of Henry VII. Lady Jane Grey was the daughter of Mary Tudor, Henry VIII's youngest sister. She was close enough to the throne to be of great interest to Thomas Seymour's schemes.

In the spring of 1548, Katherine Parr found herself pregnant with Thomas Seymour's child, expected in late August or September of that year:

> On Wednesday, 13 June 1548, Seymour accompanied his wife, who was now six months pregnant, and his young ward, Lady Jane Grey, from Hanworth to Sudeley Castle in Gloucestershire.[4]

Now one would expect that Elizabeth would accompany the Queen to Sudeley Castle to be present at the birth of the child, but inexplicably Princess Elizabeth was sent to Cheshunt a few weeks before Katherine moved to Sudeley Castle. At Cheshunt, Elizabeth was under the watchful eye of Sir Anthony Denny. Sir Denny was married to Mary Champernowne, the sister of Elizabeth's governess, Katherine Champernowne-Ashley. This movement was "in the week after Whitsun in 1548,"[5] which fell on May 20, 1548, so the date would be the week of May 27, 1548. This was the last week that Elizabeth saw her beloved stepmother alive. Princess Elizabeth would stay at Sir Anthony Denny's household from May 1548 until October of that year.

On August 3, 1548, Mary Seymour was born to Katherine Parr and Thomas Seymour at Sudeley Castle. Katherine was in her thirty-sixth year. Shortly thereafter, she was on her deathbed due to complications from the birth. She developed a puerperal fever, from an infection of the placental site that can spread from the uterine wall and into the bloodstream. These infections are generally the result of handling of the mother with unclean hands during the delivery. The death scene of Katherine Parr with her husband Thomas Seymour was poignant yet strangely ambivalent. It is possible that Katherine died of an infection, which was common to childbirth given the midwife practices of the day. Nevertheless, Katherine was reported to have had a disturbing interchange with her husband on her deathbed, as reported by Elizabeth Tyrwhitt, her stepdaughter by her first marriage:

> Two days before the death of the Queen, at my coming to her in the morning, she asked me where I had been so long, and said unto me that she

did fear such things in herself that she was sure she could not live. I answered, as I thought, that I saw no likelihood of death in her. She then, having my Lord Admiral by the hand, and divers others standing by, spake these words, partly, as I took, idly (in delirium): 'My Lady Tyrwhitt, I am not well handled, for those that be about me careth not for me, but stand laughing at my grief. And the more I will to them, the less good they will to me.' Whereunto my Lord Admiral answered, 'Why, sweetheart, I would you not hurt.' And she said to him again, aloud, 'No, my Lord, I think so'; and immediately said him in his ear, 'but my Lord you have given me many shrewd taunts.' These words I perceived she spake with good memory, and very sharply and earnestly; for her mind was sore disquieted. My Lord Admiral, perceiving that I heard it, called me aside, and asked what she said, and I declared it plainly to him. Then he consulted with me that he would lie down on the bed with her, to look if he could pacify her unquietness with gentle communication, whereunto I agreed; and by the time that he had spoken three or four words to her she answered him roundly and sharply, saying, 'My Lord, I would have given a thousand marks to have had my full talk with Huick (her doctor) the first day I was delivered, but I durst not for displeasing you.' And I, hearing that, perceived her trouble to be so great that my heart would serve me to hear no more. Such like communications, she had with him in the space of an hour, which they did hear that sat by her bedside.[6]

Queen Katherine Parr died on the morning of September 5, 1548. Her deathbed scene raises two important questions. First, was Thomas Seymour either a contributor to Katherine's death or negligent in her welfare? Second, why was a stepdaughter by a first marriage long since past (Lady Jane Grey was also there) present at the birth, but Elizabeth was not. When first arriving at Cheshunt, Elizabeth wrote Katherine Parr and the letter indicates the depth of feeling Elizabeth had for her stepmother:

Although I could not be plentiful in giving thanks for the manifold kindness received at your Highness' hand at my departure, yet I am something to be borne withal, for truly I was replete with sorrow to depart from your Highness, especially leaving you undoubtful of health: and, albeit I answered little, I weighed it more deeper, when you said you would warn me of all evils that you should hear of me; for if your Grace had not a good opinion of me, you would not have offered friendship to me that way, that all men judge the contrary. But what may I more say, than thank God for providing such friends to me; desiring God to enrich me with their long life, and me grace to be in heart no less thankful to receive it than I now am glad in writing to show it; and although I have plenty of matter, here I will stay, for I know you are not quiet to read. From Cheston [Cheshunt], this present Saturday.

Your Highness's humble daughter, Elizabeth.[7]

Despite these deep feelings toward Katherine Parr, she did not attend the delivery of the birth of Katherine Parr's child. This was strange, indeed, and there must have been some pressing reason to keep her from Katherine's bedside.

Katherine left her property and fortune to her husband in a will dictated to her doctor and chaplain. Her will indicates that she died loving her husband when she gives all to him and wishes only that it would have been more:

> That she, then lying on her death-bed, sick of body, but of good mind and perfect memory and discretion, being persuaded, and perceiving the extremity of death to approach her, gives all to her married spouse and husband, wishing them to be a thousand times more in value than they were or [had] been.[8]

English and world history may have been very different if this good woman had survived this childbirth. In an Elizabethan world of treacherous scoundrels, neurotics, and sociopaths, Queen Katherine Parr stands as a fortress of resolve, virtue, good judgment, and intellectual acumen, which makes events at Chelsea between her, her husband, and Elizabeth that much more inexplicable. While it is only speculation, it would seem that Elizabeth's early life, relations with her sister, and early reign as monarch would have been different if Queen Katherine Parr had been present to provide her wisdom and be a moderating influence.

After Katherine's funeral, Thomas Seymour went to gather his followers in the west of England. He intended to marry Elizabeth and win over the king and council. His plan was to gather his thousands of tenants and servants and stage a rebellion to overthrow his brother and make himself Lord Protector. Thomas Seymour was not successful in his attempts to raise an armed following, but he did have access to the young king. He had induced the young king to give him a key to his chamber, which he had copied. Thus, history rewards us with one of its more amusing vignettes in this aborted coup d'etat.

On January 18, 1549, Thomas Seymour went to the king's chamber with his duplicate key to kidnap his nephew, and he managed to reach the king's chambers. His plan might have been successful except for the king's pet spaniel. The dog barked, a gun went off, the guards were alerted, the plot was foiled, Thomas Seymour was arrested, and the Tower acquired a new prisoner. Later interrogations revealed that part of this plot involved blackmailing one of the directors of the mint to coin money to be used for raising a private army. A bill of attainder was quickly passed on Thomas Seymour. A bill of attainder was an act of Parliament that by majority vote condemned a man to death without benefit of trial. The bill had to be signed by the king, but required no legal confrontation between the accused and his accusers. Henry VIII had sent many men to their deaths using the bill of attainder. (This gruesome legal practice was eventually repudiated.)

Edward Seymour, Lord Protector and Duke of Somerset, was now in a difficult situation. If he forced the young king to sign the bill, clearing the way for execution of his brother, he could be accused of being too weak to protect his own brother and therefore unable to protect other aristocrats who pledged loyalty to him. He would be accused of having a despicable lack of compassion for his own brother and disregarding important family loyalty. On the other hand, if Edward did not have the king sign the bill, he would leave his notorious, hotheaded, and treasonous brother as an ever-present locus of dissent, and he would be accused of not punishing acts of treason. Edward Seymour decided after some delay to have the young king sign the death warrant. After some pressure, the young king signed the bill of attainder, sending his favorite uncle to the block. Thomas Seymour was executed in the spring of 1549. He had so many transparent schemes that he hardly constituted any real danger to the realm. He was executed more for his sheer audacious stupidity than anything else, but dead is dead, and dead he was. Elizabeth was to say of the event, "This day died a man with much wit and very little judgment."[9]

At Thomas's death, his daughter, Mary Seymour, was less than a year old. At first, she was taken in by her aunt, the wife of her uncle, Edward Seymour, but these duties were soon to be passed to the Duchess of Suffolk, Frances Brandon, who took the baby with her to Grimsthorpe. The costs of maintaining the child were considerable given the number of servants and other expensive goods and services involved with raising an almost royal child. The Duchess of Suffolk wrote to William Cecil who was then an administrator on the Lord Protector's staff. Her first letter reveals the lack of concern of her aunt and uncle, Edward Seymour, for the child:

> I have so wearied myself with letters (to the duke and duchess of Somerset) that I have none for you. Another time you will have letters when they have none. I reminded my lady of her promise of some pension for maintaining the late queen's child who, with a dozen others, lies at my chamber. The continuation of this will keep me in debt this year. The marquess of Northampton [Queen Katherine Parr's brother] to whom I should deliver her, has as weak a back for such a burden as I, and would receive her, but more willingly with appurtenances. Never a word that I ask you.

> July 24 [1549] Grimsthorpe
> Katherine [Brandon], Duchess of Suffolk [10]

She followed the letter with another that gives a more detailed description of her plight:

It is said that the best means of remedy to the sick is first plainly to confess and disclose the disease wherefore lieth for remedy; and again, for that my disease is so strong that it will not be hidden, I will disclose me unto you. First, I will (as it were under *benedicite* and in high secrecy) declare unto you that all the world knoweth, though I go never so covertly in my net, what a very beggar I am. This sickness, as I have said, I promise you, increaseth mightily upon me. Amongst other causes whereof is, you will understand not the least, the Queen's child hath lain, and yet doth lie at my house, with her company about her, wholly at my charges. I have written to my Lady Somerset at large; which was the letter I wrote (note this) with mine own hand unto you; and among other things for the child, that there may be some pension allotted unto her according to my Lord Grace's promise.

Now, good Cecil, help at a pinch all that you may help. My Lady also sent me word at Whitsuntide last by Bartue (Richard Bertie, the Duchess of Suffolk's steward, whom she later married) that my Lord's Grace, at her suit, had granted certain nursery plate and stuff as was there in the nursery. I send you here enclosed (a list) of all parcels as were Appointed out for the child's use; and that ye may the better understand that I cry not before I am pricked, I send you Mistress Eglonby's letter unto me, who, with the maids, nurses, and others, daily call on me for their wages, whose voices mine ears may hardly bear, but my coffers much worse. Wherefore I cease, and commit me and my sickness to your diligent care, with my hearty commendations to your wife.

At my manor of Grimsthorpe, the 27th August.
Your assured loving friend,
K. Suffolk[11]

This letter was dated August 27 but no year put on the letter; most likely, it was the year following the child's birth, that is, 1549. A few months later, Parliament restored the lands of her father to the young Mary, but not her appropriate titles. Susan E. James in *Kateryn Parr: The Making of a Queen* reports on it thus:

Restored in blood on 22 January 1550, Mary Seymour was made legally eligible to inherit any family property to which she might subsequently fall heir. Lands formerly owned by her parents, forfeited at her father's death, had already been snapped up by new owners. Mary Seymour disappears from the records shortly after this. As her maintenance grant was not renewed on 17 September 1550, when the original 18-month grant would have expired, Kateryn Parr's 'so pretty a daughter', almost certainly died at Grimsthorpe sometime around her second birthday, and she is probably buried somewhere in the church at Edenham, which still contains memorials to the family of her guardian, the Duchess of Suffolk.[12]

When historians use words such as "almost certainly," they should be interpreted as "we have absolutely no idea, and this is a guess." Rather than have an uncomfortable mystery, historians prefer to ignore the anomalies of history with a soothing denial or conjecture presented as fact. Historians tend to identify with the subjects of their biographies and unconsciously become their advocates. Thus, Henry VIII was not a paranoid sociopath (and his daughter Mary even more so), he was just someone who put people to the stake and executed wives. Even known scandalous behaviors of Elizabeth were muted as historians polished and maintain unblemished images of those they study.

Mary Seymour was not an important person in the Elizabethan hierarchy, nor was she an important person in English history. She was the infant daughter of the deceased Dowager Queen, and she was not in line for the throne. The property of her father had been confiscated by the Crown and later sold. She would not have been wealthy; yet, Mary Seymour's disappearance has pro-found implications for Elizabethan history and the history of William

Figure 9.   William Cecil

Shakespeare. This was a concrete example of how a child could be made to "disappear." Furthermore, the disappearance of Mary Seymour was incontrovertibly linked to William Cecil while he was serving under Edward Seymour, the Lord Protector.

William Cecil was the son of a landowner who had small holdings and who profited through land transactions connected with Henry VIII's confiscation of church properties. He attended Cambridge and was attracted to the Protestant teachings of the university, and he became part of the newly emerging Protestant class of scholars and politicians. He took legal training at Gray's Inn and then entered government service under Edward Seymour, Lord Protector to Edward VI. He became Master of the Court of Request, a member of Parliament for Stamford, secretary to the Lord Protector Somerset, a member of the Privy Council, and Secretary of State. In 1551, he was knighted, but it was not until

Elizabeth's reign and his daughter's marriage to the Earl of Oxford that he became Lord Burghley. He was obviously well connected to Katherine Parr, and he provided an introduction for her second book, *The Lamentations of a Sinner*. He was the crafty and intelligent man who could provide help to Katherine in a difficult situation. It is likely and logical that Katherine Parr would later turn to William Cecil for help in a distressful situation that needed discreetly handled at the highest level of government.

William Cecil survived the eventual fall and execution of Edward Seymour and then served in the government of his successor, John Dudley (Duke of Northumberland). He was saved from going to the block when Princess Mary became queen only because he had been a useful informant to Mary. His early warning to Mary thwarted the plans to capture her and put Lady Jane Grey on the throne. If there was ever a political animal that had the ability to always land on his feet, no matter who might be in power, it was William Cecil. Historians describe William Cecil as a sage advisor and Tudor loyalist. They credit his council with England's moderate path in religion, fiscal responsibility in government, and avoidance of foreign conflicts. This is all true. He had two goals: the welfare of England and the welfare of the Cecil family within England. He succeeded admirably at both goals.

William Cecil and his son Robert were the most influential ministers of the Elizabethan era, and a great deal of credit must be given to them. Yet a more objective look at their influence reveals that their methods were not always so pleasant. Both were masters of intrigue and experts at the arts of spying, counterfeiting evidence, and using torture to gain needed confessions as well as other methods of a tyrannical, authoritarian state. As William Cecil so wonderfully put it, he was a master of "throwing the stone without that the hand be seen."[13]

Perhaps William Cecil was Shakespeare's model for the wily, old Antigonus of *The Winter's Tale,* who leaves the changeling babe on the shore of Bohemia:

ANTIGONUS
Come, poor babe:
I have heard, but not believed, the spirits o' the dead
May walk again: if such thing be, thy mother
Appear'd to me last night, for ne'er was dream
So like a waking. To me comes a creature,
Sometimes her head on one side, some another;
I never saw a vessel of like sorrow,
So fill'd and so becoming: in pure white robes,
Like very sanctity, she did approach

My cabin where I lay; thrice bow'd before me,
And gasping to begin some speech, her eyes
Became two spouts: the fury spent, anon
Did this break-from her: "Good Antigonus,
Since fate, against thy better disposition,
Hath made thy person for the thrower-out
Of my poor babe, according to thine oath,
Places remote enough are in Bohemia,
There weep and leave it crying; and, for the babe
Is counted lost for ever, Perdita,
I prithee, call't. For this ungentle business
Put on thee by my lord, thou ne'er shalt see
Thy wife Paulina more." And so, with shrieks
She melted into air. Affrighted much,
I did in time collect myself and thought
This was so and no slumber. Dreams are toys:
Yet for this once, yea, superstitiously,
I will be squared by this. I do believe
Hermione hath suffer'd death, and that
Apollo would, this being indeed the issue
Of King Polixenes, it should here be laid,
Either for life or death, upon the earth
Of its right father. Blossom, speed thee well!   (Laying down babe.)
There lie, and there thy character: there these;   (Laying down bundle.)
Which may, if fortune please, both breed thee, pretty,
And still rest thine. The storm begins; poor wretch,
That for thy mother's fault art thus exposed
To loss and what may follow! Weep I cannot,
But my heart bleeds; and most accursed am I
To be by oath enjoin'd to this. Farewell!
The day frowns more and more: thou'rt like to have
A lullaby too rough: I never saw
The heavens so dim by day. A savage clamour!
Well may I get aboard! This is the chase:
I am gone for ever. (Exit pursued by a bear.)
                    The Winter's Tale, Act 3, Scene 3

Mary Seymour disappeared into a vast fog of English history.

ELIZABETH UNDER SUSPICION

Elizabeth was at Cheshunt with Sir Anthony Denny and his wife, Joan Champernowne, when Katherine Parr gave birth in late August 1548 at Sudeley Castle. Joan was the sister of Elizabeth's governess, Kat Champernowne Ashley, and a childhood friend of Katherine Parr. She was a part of the Protestant-humanist alignment of Queen Katherine Parr. When Anne Boleyn became queen, Anne Parr (Katherine Parr's sister), Joan Guildford, and Joan Champernowne became maids of honor. When Henry VIII was married to Anne of Cleves in 1539, Joan Champernowne (Lady Denny) was one of her ladies-in-waiting. Later, Joan Champernowne became one of Katherine Parr's ladies-in-waiting.

Sir Anthony Denny was an intellectual companion of Henry VIII, a gentleman of the Privy Chamber, a religious sparring partner for the king, a confidant, and a touchstone for the king's new ideas. He also was a confidential agent for many of the king's affairs. He was the second son of a Chief Baron of the Exchequer. He attended St. Paul's School under William Lily, and through his education and close association with Cambridge became a strong supporter of the Protestants and the humanist cause. He received Waltham Abbey in Essex for his home and an abbey at St. Albans, plus thousands of acres of land for income. He had control in the last years of Henry's life of over £200,000 of the king's money. He was a man trusted by those who desired to protect Henry VIII's Protestant daughter.

Elizabeth did not leave the Denny's until the fall of 1548, when she left Cheshunt for Hatfield accompanied by Edward Seymour's eldest son, John Seymour. She sent a note to the Lord Protector, thanking him for his concern about her health and for sending physicians to see to her health. Historians of the period agree that Elizabeth was "sick" during the summer of 1548, even if no one can accurately define the sickness, yet there are no records of any physician seeing her until the fall of 1548, when Doctor Thomas Bill visited her on orders of the Lord Protector. Elizabeth writes thanking the Lord Protector on October 15, 1548:

> Many lines will not serve to render the least part of the thanks that your Grace hath deserved of me, most especially for that you have been careful of my health; and sending unto me not only your comfortable letters, but also physicians, as Doctor Bill whose diligence and pain has been a great part of my recovery.[14]

Several medical accounts allude to the fact that Elizabeth would be fifteen in September of 1548 and her sickness related to the onset of menarche, but other than that, the record remains silent as to what might have caused this illness. It was indeed strange that the second in line to the throne should be sick for such a period and yet there would be no medical record of any doctor visiting her until the Lord Protector sends one long after the supposed illness was over. While there is a detailed record of Elizabeth's health throughout her reign, there is only speculation about this sickness. Whatever it was, it had to be serious enough to incapacitate her so she could not be with her stepmother's lying in and childbirth, a life-threatening situation for any Elizabethan woman.

On August 2, 1548, Kat Ashley wrote to William Cecil to intervene with Edward Seymour, the Lord Protector, to obtain the exchange of an English prisoner in Scotland. Elizabeth added a postscript that began "I pray you further this poor man's suit," and signed it "your friend Elizabeth." This was the first recorded connection between Elizabeth and William Cecil. There seem to be no prior meetings or correspondence between Elizabeth and William Cecil before this note, though it was, of course, possible that she had met him on one of her infrequent visits to her brother at court. Many historians have commented that this letter was the beginning of a lifelong relationship between William Cecil and Elizabeth, which is true, but few have thought to even consider what might have started this friendship. Nor has anyone questioned the extraordinary salutation and closing to this letter:

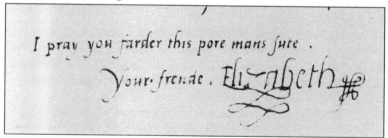

Figure 10. Elizabeth's Signature

Why was a princess of royal blood, heir to the throne, addressing William Cecil, a commoner, in such familiar terms and signing "your frende Elizabeth"? This implies that a level of admiration and mutual trust had developed between them, but what did William Cecil do that encouraged such familiarity and gratitude on the part of the future queen? Elizabeth was going beyond all bounds of Elizabethan formality, putting their relationship on a very personal basis with "your frende Elizabeth."

How did William Cecil all of a sudden become a "frende"? A year or two later, he became her surveyor at a salary of £20 per year during Mary's reign. During this period, Elizabeth instructed Thomas Parry to include a note to Cecil:

> Write my commendations in your letter to Mr. Cecil, that I am well assured, though I send not daily to him, that he doth not, for all that, daily forget me.[15]

One can understand Elizabeth being friendly all her life with those who had been loyal and trustworthy (Ashley and Parry), or ones she found as congenial, such as Roger Ascham; there was no reason for her to be so friendly to Cecil unless he had done an extraordinary deed for her. This greeting and closing implies that William Cecil had done something extraordinary to gain the trust of the young woman who said she was not won with trifles.

By the late fall of 1548, Katherine Parr was dead and Elizabeth had left the Denny family to resume her residence at Hatfield. Thomas Seymour was in the west of England fomenting dissent with his plans to usurp his brother. His unsuccessful attempt to kidnap his nephew, Edward VI, led him to the Tower, and interrogations were begun to determine the extent of his activities. Kat Ashley and Thomas Parry were arrested and sent to the Tower, where they subsequently signed confessions or statements. The council was especially concerned about whether Elizabeth received a proposal of marriage, or whether Thomas had in fact married Elizabeth after the death of his wife in the fall of 1548. Marriage was not a personal event but rather a matter of state.

These interrogations would uncover Elizabeth's improprieties with Thomas Seymour, and they cast more suspicion on her and the events of the previous spring. They reveal what caused Katherine Parr to send Princess Elizabeth from the household at Chelsea to the household of Sir Anthony Denny at Cheshunt. The examinations of Kat Ashley and Thomas Seymour taken at face value reveal an indiscretion by the young princess and an irate Katherine Parr sending Elizabeth off to be more closely chaperoned. Katherine, in this view, was acting prudently and getting Elizabeth out of the clutches of her husband, Thomas Seymour. This story is sufficient for orthodox historians to explain the events and end any further questioning.

Viewed with a more suspicious, less tolerant eye, the interrogations reveal gross improprieties being taken with the young Princess Elizabeth. The relations between Thomas Seymour, as later described by Elizabeth's governess Katherine Ashley were, in the euphemism of our day, "inappropriate." The full deposition or confession of Kat Ashley follows:

The Confession of Katharine Aschyly.
What familiaritie she hath knowen betwixt the Lord Admirall, and the Lady
Elizabeth's *Grace?*

She saith at *Chelsy*, incontinent after he was maried to the Queene, he wold come many Mornyngs into the said Lady *Elizabeth's* Chamber, before she were redy, and sometyme before she did rise. And if she were up, he wold bid hir good Morrow, and ax how she did, and strike her upon the Bak or on the Buttocks famylearly, and so go forth through his Lodgings; and sometyme go through to the Maydens, and play with them, and so go forth: And if she were in hir Bed, he wold put open the Curteyns, and bid hir good Morrow, and make as though he wold come at hir: And she wold go further in the Bed, so that he could not come at hir.

And one Mornying he strave to have kissed hir in hir Bed: And this Examinate was there, and bad hym go away for shame. She knoweth not whither this were at *Chelsy,* or *Hanworth.*

At *Hanworth,* he wold likewise come in the Mornying unto hir Grace; but, as she remembreth, at all Tymes, she was up before, savying two Mornyngs, the which two Mornyngs, the Quene came with hym: And this Examinate lay with hir Grace; and ther thei tytled [tickeled] my Lady *Elizabeth* in the Bed, the Quene and my Lord Admyrall.

An other Tyme at *Hanworth,* in the Garden, he wrated with hir, and cut hir Gown in an hundred Pieces, beyng black Cloth; and when she came up, this Examinant chid with hir; and her Grace answerid, She could not do with all, for the Quene held hir, while the Lord Admiral cut it up.

An other Tyme at *Chelsey,* the Lady *Elizabeth* herying the Pryvie-Lock undo, knowyng that he wold come in, ran out of hir Bed to hir Maydens, and then went behynd the Curteyn of the Bed, the Maydens beyng there; and my Lord tarried to have hyr com out, she can not till how long. This Examinate hard of the Gentlewomen. She thinks Mr. *Power* told it her. And then in the Galery this Examinate told my Lord that thes Things were complayned of, and that my Lady was evill spoken of: The Lord Admiral swore, God's precious Soule! He wold tell my Lord Protector how yt slawnderid hym, and he wold not leave it, for he ment no Evill.

At *Seymour-Place,* when the Quene lay there, he did use a while to come up every Mornying in his Nyght-Gown, barelegged in his Slippers, where he found commonly the Lady *Elizabeth* up at her Boke: And then he wold loke in at the Gallery-Dore, and bid my Lady *Elizabeth* good Morrow, and so go his way. Then this Examinate told my Lord it was unsemly Sight to come so bare leggid to a Maydens Chambre; with which he was angry, but he left it.

At *Hanworth,* the Quene told this Examinate that my Lord Admirall loked in at the Galery-Wyndow, and se my Lady *Elizabeth* cast hir Armes about a Man's neck. The which Heryng, this Examinate enquyred for it of my Lady's Grace, who denyed it weepyng, and bad ax all hir Women: Thei all denyed it: And she knew it could not be so, for there came no Man, but *Gryndall,* the Lady *Elizabeth's* Scholemaster. Howbeit, thereby this Examinate did suspect, that the Quene was gelows betwixt them, and did but feyne this, to thentent that this Examinate shuld take more hede, and be, as it were in watche betwixt hir and my Lord Admirall.

She saith also, that Mr. *Ashley*, hir Husband, hath diverse Tymes given this Examinate warnyng to take hede, for he did fere that the Lady *Elizabeth* did bere som Affection to my Lord Admirall, she semyd to be well please therewith, and somtyme she wold blush when he were spoken of: And one other told hir so also, but she cannot tell who it was.

Kateryn Aschyly[16] [a]

The cofferer, Thomas Parry, gives his account of hearsay evidence about Queen Katherine Parr which gives very explicit reasons for Elizabeth's departure from Hatfield. He was recalling the conversations he had with Kat Ashley:

I do remember also she told me, that the Admirall loved her but to well and hadd so done a good while; and that the Queen was jealous on hir and him, in so moche that one Tyme the Quene, suspecting the often Accesse of the Admirall to the Lady *Elizabeth's* Grace came sodenly upon them, wher they were all alone, (*he having her in his arms:*); wherefore the Quene fell out, bothe with the Lord Admirall and with her Grace also.

And hereupon the Quene called Mrs. *Ashley* to her, and told her Fansy [wish] in that Matier [matter], and of this was moch Displesure. And it was not long, before they partid asondre their Famylies, and, as I remembre, this was the Cause why she was sent from the Quene; or ells that her Grace partid from the Quene; I do not perfectly remembre whether she said, she went of herself, or was sent awaye.

Why quoth I hath ther been such familiaritie in dede betwene them? And with that, she sighed, and said, as I remembre, I will tell you more another Tyme; and all this, as I remember, was on Twelfth Eve last [around Christmas], that she told me these Thyngs. And at the same Tyme she told me, that he myght compass the Cownsell [council] if he wold, I remember she said more: "That if the King's Majestie, that Dede is, had "lived a littel longer, she [Elizabeth] shuld have been his Wief." But after she hadd told me the Tale of the fynding of her Grace in his Armes, she semed to repent, that she had gone so farre with me, as she did; and prayed me in any wise that I wold not disclose thes Matters; And I said I wold not. And agayn she prayed me not to open yt, for her Grace shuld be dishonored for ever, and she likewise undone. And I said I wold not; and said I had rather be pulled with Horses thene I wold, or such like Words.[17]

The statements of Kat Ashley and Thomas Parry are incriminating but not terribly revealing if taken at face value. Apparently under threats, they reveal Elizabeth had overly familiar relations with Thomas Seymour but not that she agreed to marry him, nor do they mention anything other than

---

[a] In a side note to the page in Haynes, it says, "From the Original, writen by Sir *Tho. Smith,* and sign'd *Kateryn Aschyly.*" Sir Thomas Smith was Principal Secretary to the Lord Protector, and he was associated with the younger William Cecil at Cambridge. Later Sir Thomas, would be a tutor for Edward de Vere, 17th Earl of Oxford.

what can be interpreted as good natured, but improper behavior toward the young princess. Nevertheless, does "he having her in his Armes: wherefore the queen fell out, both with her Lord Admiral and with her Grace also" imply a greater level of sexual involvement?

The completeness and truthfulness of these depositions has to be considered with the knowledge of who was taking the depositions. That person was Sir Thomas Smith, reporting directly to Edward Seymour, the Lord Protector. Smith was also a friend of William Cecil, who was serving as secretary for Edward Seymour, so it is unlikely that Cecil could not have known of the depositions. The objective would seem to be to put enough on the record to incriminate Thomas Seymour, but it is doubtful that any truly damaging information about Princess Elizabeth would be recorded. The depositions may record information that was damaging to Princess Elizabeth, but how thorough do they want to be if Sir Thomas Smith, William Cecil, and Edward Seymour are already privy to a secret?

Lord Robert Tyrwhit, who was interrogating Elizabeth, was sure that all the participants (Elizabeth, Kat Ashley, and Thomas Parry) were covering something, as is obvious in his report to the Lord Protector. His comments are more pointed and skeptical and lead one to believe that he was unaware of any cover-up of the events during the summer of 1548:

> They all synge onne Songe, and so I thynke they wuld not unless they had sett the Nott befor ... or ells they could not so well agree.[18]

Tyrwhit further writes to the Lord Protector:

> I do verily believe that there hath been some secret promise between my Lady, Mistress Ashley and the cofferer, never to confess till death; and if it be so, it will never be gotten of her, but either by the King's Majesty, or else by your Grace.[19]

It hardly seems that the behavior Parry and Ashley have described was something they will "never confess till death." Tyrwhit thinks Elizabeth was lying to him, but he cannot prove it or get her to confess. He says:

> But in no way she will not confess any practice by Mistress Ashley or the coffer concerning my Lord Admiral; and yet I do see it in her face that she is guilty, and do perceive as yet she will abide more storms ere she accuse Mistress Ashley.[20]

To summarize the information to this point, Elizabeth was inexplicably absent from her stepmother's lying in and was not present when she died from complications from childbirth. Ostensibly, the reason was that she was sick, although she was not visited by a doctor, nor was the sickness ever defined. The depositions of Kat Ashley and Thomas Parry revealed that there was some inappropriate behavior between her and her stepfather. While this was all rather strange, it cannot be said that it was overwhelmingly suspicious. All of Elizabeth's biographers have issued mild rebukes for the princess's behavior and explained it away as the indiscretions of a very young woman.

However, Elizabeth revealed that something far more important may have happened at Cheshunt. With her governess and cofferer in prison, Elizabeth wrote a letter to the Lord Protector at the beginning of 1549. She realized the danger she was in if she had compromised herself with Thomas Seymour. The letter was a masterful piece of diplomacy, evasion, guile, and challenge, written when she was fifteen years old without any apparent guidance of any other adult. Katherine Parr was dead, and her two trusted servants were in the Tower. Further, she knew nothing of what Kat Ashley or Thomas Parry had revealed or been forced to admit to under the threat of torture.

This was the first mention of rumors of Elizabeth being pregnant, and it was from Elizabeth herself:

> Master Tyrwhit and others have told me that there goeth rumours abroad, which be greatly both against my Honour and Honestie (which, above all things I esteem), which be these; that I am in the Tower, and with Child by my Lord Admiral. My Lord, these are shameful Schandlers [slanders], for the which, besides the great Desire I have to see the King's Majestie, I shall most heartily desire your Lordship that I may come to the Court after your first Determination; that I may show myself there as I am. Written in haste from Hatfield this 28th of January. [1549]
>
> Your assured Friend to my little power.
> Elizabeth[21]

In her letter, Elizabeth denied she was pregnant, of which no one had accused her, and she denied that she was in the Tower, which was true; she was not in the Tower. This indicates that either there were rumors of her being pregnant or that she wanted to forestall any thoughts in that direction. Yet, the wording of the letter is crafty. She denies that she was "with child," but she does not deny that she "had a child." This is a small but important distinction. Elizabeth at this point had little knowledge of what Edward Seymour, the Lord Protector, knows, believes, or does not know about her behavior with the Lord Admiral. This key sentence may have been an attempt to ferret out from the Lord Protector's reaction what he knows or does not know about the summer of 1548.

Further, Elizabeth confronts Edward Seymour with the thought of her coming to court. There, she would have been a direct threat to Edward Seymour's control and influence over the young king. Elizabeth was a precociously intelligent person and one who had the overwhelming advantage of being in line to the throne. Elizabeth wrote this letter when she was under a great cloud of suspicion and she had no adults to guide her. Katherine Parr was dead, and her trusted governess, Kat Ashley, was in the Tower for interrogation. Elizabeth did not know what she might reveal under torture or threat of torture. The maturity in this letter was far beyond her years; she managed both to be contrite and to put the Lord Protector in a difficult situation. If she came to Court, courtiers and politicians would curry favor with her, just in case she succeeded to the throne.

In a second communication to the Lord Protector and the council, Elizabeth continues to defend her virtue and asks that the council send messengers into the counties to stop the rumors of her having a child:

> And, surely, the cause why that I was sorry that there should be any such about me, was because that I thought the people will say that I deserved, through my lewd demeanor, *to have such a one* and not that I mislike anything that your lordship, or the council, shall think good, for I know that you and the council are charged with me, or that I take upon me to rule myself for I know that they are most deceived that trusteth most in themselves, wherefore I trust that you shall never find that fault in me, to the which thing I do not see that your Grace has made any direct answer at this time, and seeing they make so *evil reports already* shall be but an increasing of these evil tongues. Howbeit, you did write 'that if I would bring forth any that had reported it, you and the council would see it redressed,' which thing, though I can easily do it, I would be loathe to do, because it is mine own cause; and, again, that it should be but abridging of an evil name of me that am glad to punish them, and so get the evil will of the people, which thing I would be loth to have. But if it might seem good to your lordship, and the rest of the council, to send forth a proclamation into the countries that they refrain their tongues, declaring how the tales be but lies, it should make both the people think that you and the council have great regard *that no such rumors should be spread of any of the king's majesty's sisters.*[22]
> [*Italics* added]

The letter indicates previous correspondence on the subject, and in this letter, Elizabeth protests that she "deserved through her lewd demeanor, to have such a one." Here, the lady does protest too much and is giving away the circumstances of her relation with Thomas Seymour (that is, that she was a willing party to her involvement). Further, Elizabeth does not clearly say that she did not have such a "one." She confronts the issue of whether her "lewd demeanor" was the cause of it, but there is no clear denial of having any such child. She does not say the rumors are false; rather, she says the rumors are damaging to the "king's majesty's sisters."

Elizabeth goes on to say that she will not name those who are spreading such rumors, even though the council has agreed to redress the issue if she would report such persons. She says she feels that this is not a good idea because the blame will fall back on her. Instead, she asks that the council put forth a proclamation to stop the gossip, which, would have only fanned the flames.

Perhaps Elizabeth was discreetly told to drop the subject, and this appears to be the last letter on the subject of a child. There was further correspondence about the return of her governess, and after much negotiation in which Elizabeth again showed courage, diplomacy and fortitude, Katherine Ashley and Thomas Parry returned to her household. A year or so later, William Cecil became an overseer of Elizabeth's estates and she paid him £20 a year. William Cecil was one of the first men appointed to her council when she became queen, and he was forever after a power within the English government.

A third hand account of Elizabeth raises further suspicions about the summer of 1548. Lady Jane Dormer was one of Queen Mary's ladies-in-waiting. She married the Duke of Feria, a Spaniard who was attached to Prince Philip of Spain when he came to wed Mary. The duchess gave the account below, not recorded until many years later, to a household servant. It can only be described as rumor, but it does reveal what might have been believed in the court about the Catholic Mary, and its detailed description gives it credibility. The account gives a description of a girl that fits young Princess Elizabeth, "very fair young lady," and it shows how a midwife might have been brought into the household to attend the princess. It was possible, even probable, that the midwife would have gossiped about such an event to her neighbors, and the rumors that Elizabeth mentions in her letter to the Lord Protector could have spread from there:

> In King Edward's time what passed between the Lord Admiral, Sir Thomas Seymour and her Doctor Latimer preached in a sermon, and was a chief cause that the parliament condemned the Admiral. There was a bruit of a child born and miserably destroyed, but could not be discovered whose it was; only the report of the mid-wife, who was brought from her house blindfold thither, and so returned, saw nothing in the house while she was there, but candle light; only, she said, it was the child of a very fair young lady. There was muttering of the Admiral and this lady, who was then between fifteen and sixteen years of age. If it were so, it was the judgment of God upon the Admiral; and upon her, to make her ever after incapable of children ... The reason why I write this is to answer the voice of my countrymen in so strangely exalting the lady Elizabeth, and so basely depressing Queen Mary.[23]

Was there a child by Elizabeth that was "miserably destroyed"? On the other hand, did this child, like Mary Seymour, disappear into the fog of English history?

A CHANGELING CHILD?

The ambiguities, uncertainties, distinctions, and contradictions of Elizabethan history dissolve into a great gray mist. Out of this mist emerge simple-minded, one-dimensional characters and simple-minded renderings of complex issues. The Virgin Queen was a myth created by the Tudor propaganda machine that was copied uncritically by the vast majority of historians in the following centuries. Despite substantive evidence to the contrary, Elizabeth emerges as the dedicated public servant whose devotion to the emerging English nation knew no bounds. While Elizabeth had her virtues, her life and character are much more complex and involved than portrayed by conventional historians. To characterize Elizabeth as the Virgin Queen is to read her press releases, not the historical record. Moreover, to think such happenings did not occur simply because they were not fully recorded is to ignore the politics of what is recorded and not recorded as history. To think that Elizabeth did not have children simply because they were not documented is to contradict the culture she lived in, contradict what is known of her personally, and contradict the ability of a society to both cover up and ignore unwanted information

In over four hundred years, there have been no critical investigations of whether or not Elizabeth had children. This question has remained strictly out of bounds as a subject of historical investigation. Some historians take the Virgin Queen route wherein Elizabeth was a Puritan virgin devoted only to her country. Others are a little more candid and admit that Elizabeth engaged in some flirtatious behavior with the opposite sex but always conclude that she remained chaste throughout her life. None have investigated the rumors concerning Queen Elizabeth with any historical diligence or accuracy.

A more suspicious and suspecting mind could interpret the events of 1548 unfolding at the time like this: Katherine is either unaware of what is transpiring between Elizabeth and her husband, or in the libertine spirit of Marguerite of Navarre, she is encouraging or condoning the relationship. Whatever the situation, in April of 1548, Elizabeth can no longer hide the fact that she is five months pregnant by Thomas Seymour. Katherine Parr removes Elizabeth from the household at Hatfield and sends her to Sir Anthony Denny. She does this with the assistance and knowledge of

Edward Seymour (the Lord Protector), Sir Thomas Smith, and William Cecil. In this smaller household of close confidants, Elizabeth does not see any doctors that summer, even though reported as "sick," because any examination would have revealed she was pregnant. Elizabeth gives birth to a child (or perhaps twins) during July 1548. William Cecil removes the child to the foster care of another noble family. This completely conceals the situation, and the secret birth and placement of the child are a success.

Months later, the plan unravels when the rash and foolish actions of Thomas Seymour cause the arrest of Elizabeth's servants. They are interrogated about his behavior with Elizabeth. Kat Ashley and Thomas Parry reveal indiscretions between Elizabeth and Thomas, but nothing is said that indicates Elizabeth intended to marry him or indicates Elizabeth has been pregnant. They agree on a story before they give their depositions, and this is why they seem to "sing together" as Lord Tyrwhit put it. Sir Thomas Smith records the depositions of Kat Ashley and Thomas Parry so nothing truly damaging to the princess is recorded for posterity. It is not until Elizabeth tries to clear her name that the idea of a pregnancy is broached by anyone. Elizabeth does not know how much Kat Ashley and Thomas Parry have revealed, and she may be trying to ascertain if the Lord Protector knows or is suspicious of her, or to deny the truth in advance. After two incriminating letters, she never mentions the issue again.

In addition, the interrogations of Elizabeth, Thomas Parry, or Katherine Ashley may not have been as intensive as the history books record them as being. Lord Tyrwhit and Sir Thomas Smith may have reported to the Lord Protector through William Cecil. This would have given Cecil the power to edit the historical record of any comments that were too damaging to Elizabeth. The most damaging comments of the whole affair came not from the interrogations, but rather from the pen of Elizabeth. Only Elizabeth ever mentioned the possibility of a child.

It is a debatable question whether Edward Seymour knew of Elizabeth's pregnancy. On one hand, one could argue that William Cecil would keep a foot in all political camps and inform Edward Seymour (Lord Protector) of any private information revealed to him by Queen Katherine Parr. On the other hand, it may have been that William Cecil orchestrated the entire deception, and that is why Elizabeth is so grateful. In either case, it is unlikely that either William Cecil or Edward Seymour would inform the father, Thomas Seymour, that Elizabeth had given birth to his child. The historical record gives no indication that he was aware of such an event and, given his explosive personality, he probably would have done something about Elizabeth if he had known. The child, even though illegitimate, would have had some claim to the throne, especially if he was a male. This would have been an unthinkable position—Thomas Seymour running amuck as father of a royal child—for Edward Seymour or William Cecil. Therefore, it is realistic to think that Thomas Seymour never knew of the pregnancy of Elizabeth or the birth of his own child.

Was there a child by Elizabeth in the summer of 1548? The evidence is not conclusive nor beyond a reasonable doubt, but there are definitely grounds for suspicions. If there was a birth, what happened to that child? Was it destroyed as reported? This appears doubtful because it was a child of royal blood and had a claim on the throne. Elizabeth was the only other strong Protestant with a solid claim on the throne in a time when death by disease was often sudden. Even though she had been made a bastard at one time by act of Parliament in 1544, Henry VIII had confirmed the line of succession as Edward, Mary, and then Elizabeth. If the child king Edward VI died unexpectedly, the next in line to the throne would be the Catholic Mary. The Protestant faction would safeguard any Protestant heir to the throne, legitimate or illegitimate.

In the introduction to this book, four criteria were mentioned for determining if a child might have been born to Elizabeth. The first criterion was if there were suspicious circumstances or rumors of a child. This criterion is fulfilled by Elizabeth writing about the rumors of her bearing a child. These statements of Elizabeth are supported by the interrogations of her servants that indicate improprieties in the relationship between Elizabeth and her stepfather, Thomas Seymour. The later comments of the Duchess of Feria further corroborate the existence of rumors of Elizabeth having a child. The detailed account of the midwife's going to the house blindfolded further lends credence to their accounts by painting a very detailed picture of possible events at Cheshunt. The conclusion that the child was destroyed appears to be conjecture with little detailed description, in contrast to the birth.

In addition, there is the disappearance of Mary Seymour, another child of high status, whose last known whereabouts was connected to someone who became one of Elizabeth's most trusted councilors. This gives a *modus operandi* that an unwanted child might have been made to disappear by those in authority. William Cecil then emerged out of nowhere and for some inexplicable reason became the "friend" of the young princess forevermore.

The second criterion is having a window of opportunity to give birth to such a child. This criterion is more than fulfilled by Elizabeth being semi-isolated from the world in the company and care of supporters loyal to the Protestants and personally loyal to Elizabeth. This seclusion is even more striking because it occurred at a time when, by both custom and close emotional relationship, Elizabeth should have been present at the lying-in of her stepmother, Queen Katherine Parr. While there are claims that Elizabeth was sick during this period, she was not visited by any doctor, nor is there any account of what her illness might have been. There is no reason left for the seclusion of Elizabeth except that she was at Cheshunt to have a child in secret. In conclusion, there is the known disappearance of one child and there are grave suspicions of the birth of a second child to Princess Elizabeth.

The third criterion for evaluation was the presence of a child in close proximity to the mother who had a special relation with the mother beyond what might be expected. In the scenario created to this point, the child would also have been closely attended by William Cecil, who was the apparent mastermind behind this deception. In the next chapter, this criterion will be resolved.

The question now arises, "Where were the children hidden?"

A HASTY MARRIAGE AND THREE MURDERS

AN EARL IN A VISE

In the months after becoming Lord Protector in 1547, Edward Seymour directed his attention to John de Vere,[a] 16th Earl of Oxford, with the aim of extorting money and property from him. Apparently, he was able to force John de Vere into signing bonds that obligated the Earl to pay approximately £6,000. Since it was not possible that Edward Seymour could have loaned John de Vere such a staggering sum, there must be another explanation. It is possible that he had information on John de Vere that he could use as a pretext for criminal charges against the earl. One possibility is that John de Vere had engaged in a bigamous marriage with a Joan Jockey, much to the displeasure of his first wife, Dorothy Neville, and her relatives. Edward Seymour might have used this as grounds for his blackmail. No records indicate John de Vere paid anything to Edward Seymour, but such records might be incomplete, never closely examined, or missing.

On February 26, 1548, Edward Seymour forced the 16th Earl of Oxford to post a bond that required a marriage contract for John de Vere's daughter if the Earl did not repay the amount due. The contract would have married the Earl's daughter, Katherine de Vere, to Seymour's son, Henry. The son was seven at the time and Katherine de Vere about twelve. Part of this arrangement was a penalty that took away any collateral heirs' rights to inherit the majority of the de Vere land holdings. As there was little realistic hope that John de Vere could pay the enormous amount due, Edward Seymour had in effect forced a marriage contract on John de Vere, plus he had forced de Vere to give up other important rights. On the same day that Oxford signed away his daughter and agreed to the fine, he made a new will, witnessed by Thomas Golding, who was the brother of Margery Golding and the half-brother of Arthur Golding.

The records are not very good and the matter is not completely clear. What is clear is that after the execution of Edward Seymour, Parliament released John de Vere from this bond. This lends credibility to the idea that Edward was extorting money from John de Vere. Further, the contract for the marriage of his daughter was never enforced. Philip Morant gives this version of the Earl's predicament:

---

[a] The Earls of Oxford of the Vere family use the name de Vere, while the rest of the family simply uses Vere. Why this peculiarity exists is unexplained.

The account we have of it is as follows: Edward Seymour, Duke of Somerset, Protector of the Realm, out of his extreme avarice and greedy appetite did under color of justice convent before himself for certain criminal causes John Earl of Oxford and so terrify him that to save his life he was obliged to alienate to the said Duke by deed all his estates, lordships, castles, manores &c."[1]

In January 1548, John de Vere's first wife, Dorothy Neville, died. John and Dorothy Neville had one daughter, Katherine, who appears to have been born between 1536 and 1537, and another child who died as an infant "in the swaddling clouts." Dorothy Neville was the daughter of Ralph Neville, 4th Earl of Buckingham, and Catherine Stafford, second daughter of Edward Stafford, 3rd Duke of Buckingham. Henry VIII executed Catherine's grandfather in 1521, possibly because Buckingham was descended from Thomas of Woodstock, who was of royal blood. His marriage to Dorothy Neville allied John de Vere with much of the old aristocracy, mistrusted by Henry VIII, and the men that came to power after Henry's death. Henry never trusted the northern families such as the Nevilles (Earls of Westmoreland) and the Percys (Earls of Northumberland). It was in these regions that the rebellions against Henry took place. Henry VII and Henry VIII had pursued policies to reduce the power of the old noble families and create an aristocratic caste that was loyal to the Tudors. John de Vere was from one of the oldest titles in England, going back to 1142, and was never in the circles of the king's advisors and confidants. Throughout Henry VIII's reign, John de Vere, 16th Earl of Oxford, remained out of the political limelight.

John de Vere was free to marry in January of 1548, and he set his sights on Dorothy Fosser, who was formerly the governess of John's daughter. At the time, Dorothy was living with Sir Edward Greene. Edward Seymour and others were opposing the intentions of John de Vere to marry Dorothy Fosser. It may have been that Seymour wanted to prevent John de Vere, probably a Catholic, from marrying Dorothy Fosser because of her family's Catholic leanings, or there may have been reasons that are more complicated.

In June of 1548, Edward Seymour and William Cecil took a great deal of interest in the romantic affairs of the 16th Earl of Oxford. This was shortly after Elizabeth moved to Cheshunt. A retainer reports to them in a letter from Castle Hedingham, home of John de Vere:[b]

---

[b] Louis Thorn Golding states that the letter was addressed to William Cecil and the date of the letter 1547. The date of 1547 cannot be correct because John de Vere's wife did not die until January 1548 and then he proceeded to pursue Dorothy Fosser. There is no firm addressee on the letter, and it may have been to William Cecil or to Edward Seymour. However, in either case, the letter confirms the interest in the marriage status of John de Vere by those at court.

Sir Thomas Darcy to Wm. Cecil, June 27

After right hearty commendations these shall be to advertise you that according to my late conversation had with you in my lord's graces gallery at Westminster, I have by all means that I can inquired of the matter between my Lord of Oxenford and the gentlewoman with whom he is in love namely Mrs. Dorothy late woman to my lady Katherine his daughter. And upon conversation had with them both, I have found and do perceive them to be in the same case that they were in when my said Lord of Oxenford was before his lord's grace and no other, saving that the *banns of matrimony between them were twice proclaimed in one day.* Other treaties or solemn conversation hath not been before witness but only been in secret between them twin. Sir if it shall stand with my lord graces pleasure to have this matter further stayed, as my lord of Oxenford's honor wealth and preservations considered, I think it very expedient and may right well be, then I beseech you I may be thereof advertised. And yet, you will move his grace to direct his letters to Mr Edward Green of Sampford in whose house the said Dorothy doth now continue, commanding him by the same neither *to suffer my said lord of Oxenford to have access to her nor she unto him.* And that no privy messengers may go between them, which as I suppose will be the surest way to stay them. And upon further advertisement to be had from his grace, if it shall so stand with his pleasure, I will enter in conversations with my lord Wentworth for a marriage between my said Lord of Oxenford and one of his daughters and as they, upon sight, what other treaty may agree, so to proceed in the same. Sir upon your motion to be made unto my lord's grace concerning the premises I pray you I may be advertised by this bearer of his pleasure in the same, which knowing I shall right gladly endeavor myself to accomplish by the aid of the Blessed Trinity who have you in his continual preservation. [*Italics* added]

From Heddingham Castle the xxvij day of June
By your loving friend
Thomas Darcy
Endorsed
From Sir Thomas Darcy Knight

[Hedingham was the home of John de Vere]
Note: "i" = "j" in these Roman numerals, so xvij is 27.

State Papers (Domestic) Edward VI Vol. 1. No. 4.

This letter indicates that John de Vere had twice announced the banns of marriage to Dorothy Fosser and that access to Dorothy Fosser by John de Vere was denied. Despite the opposition of the Lord Protector, John de Vere continued to pursue Dorothy Fosser and succeeded in getting her away from the house of Sir Edward Greene, with the intent of marrying her. Yet, after all his successful effort and having had the banns of marriage announced, there was the most inexplicable twist to the story. John de Vere departed for his marriage, but instead of going to Sampford and Dorothy Fosser, he went in the opposite direction to Belchamp—there he married Margery Golding.

Margery Golding was a very unlikely bride for the Earl of Oxford. She was the sister of Arthur and Thomas Golding, who had witnessed the will forced on him by the Lord Protector. Either Margery Golding had overwhelming feminine charms that overpowered John de Vere or the Lord Protector coerced de Vere into marrying her. It is hard to imagine that de Vere would voluntarily marry into a family (the Goldings) that was not aristocratic and was firmly allied with the Lord Protector, his arch-tormentor. The banns of marriage were witnessed on August 1, 1548, and the formality in the church at Belchamp St. Paul completed with an official entry in the parish register:

> Ao. Domini 1548. The wedding of my Lord John de Vere, Earl of Oxenford, and Margery, the daughter of John Goulding Esquire, the first of August.[3]

Dorothy Fosser, jilted at the altar, complained to the council of her treatment. The council and Lord Protector, Edward Seymour, ordered the 16th Earl to pay Dorothy Fosser £10 annually during her lifetime. Dorothy Fosser thereafter married John Anson, a clerk of Sir Edward Greene, that same year. This marriage seems legitimate, or at least it never was legally challenged. This would indicate there was no binding pre-contract of marriage between Dorothy Fosser and the 16th Earl of Oxford. If there was such a contract, it would have invalidated the marriages between Dorothy and John Anson and between John de Vere and Margery Golding. A precontract of marriage was a legal, binding contract, executed before the actual contract or marriage ceremony.

In the following decades, there were two lawsuits concerning the marriage of John de Vere to Margery Golding. The first was in 1563, and the plaintiff was Katherine de Vere, the oldest daughter of John de Vere. That lawsuit will be described shortly. It was a later lawsuit, in 1585, thirty-seven years after the marriage of John de Vere and Margery Golding, that gives an intimate glimpse of the personal history of the 16th Earl of Oxford and his marriage to Margery Golding. Neither lawsuit challenged the paternity-maternity of Edward de Vere as the son of John de Vere; instead, each lawsuit questioned whether John de Vere had been legally married to Margery Golding. If his marriage was not legal because he had contracted to marry someone else, or if he had married someone else, then Edward de Vere would not have been the legal heir of John de Vere.

The legal action in 1585 was over a property that had belonged to the 16th Earl of Oxford and leased to Hugh Key. Richard Masterson had entered onto the property before the expiration of the lease. In the course of the lawsuit, there were a number of interrogatories conducted concerning the marriages of the 16th Earl of Oxford. If John de Vere had been married to a certain Joan Jockey after the death of his first wife, it would be a valid marriage and the marriage to Margery Golding would be invalid. However, the testimony proved otherwise, and the de Vere–Golding marriage was therefore lawful.

The interrogations in 1585 are by John Popham, the Queen's Attorney General, and Thomas Egerton, her Solicitor General. This high-level involvement of the Queen's legal staff in what was a routine legal matter over a piece of property of John de Vere's indicates the Queen had a direct interest in the outcome of the events. That is, the depositions might reveal something to the Queen's detriment that went beyond the issues under consideration. It was extraordinary that the Queen or her representatives would become involved in such a petty matter, unless the fundamental question of John de Vere's marriage and Edward de Vere's paternity-maternity was very important to her.

Richard Enews of Earls Colne (the home of the 16th Earl of Oxford) was deposed. He was about 92 years of age in 1585 and therefore had been alive and present throughout the life of John de Vere. He was a witness who provided accurate descriptions of the marital affairs of the 16th Earl of Oxford and a good deal about his first wife's opinion of him:

> To the vjth, he saith that the same Earle of Oxford was never divorced from the same lady Dorothie by any law, although they lyved not together somewhat before her death, through the unkind dealinge of the same Earle. But the duke of Norfolke caused this examinant to move the same ladie Dorothie to come to the Earle agayn, but she said she would never goe home agayne amongst such a bad company as were about the Earl of Oxford at that tyme.[4]

He further said that John de Vere had married Joan Jockey, but this marriage was while the Earl's first wife was still alive:

> To the ixth, he saith that the same Earl maryed with the said Johan Jockey about Corpus Christi tyde at Whit Colne Churche in the lyef tyme of the said ladie Dorothie, the which the said ladie Dorothie tooke very grevously. And it was about half a yeare after the ladie Dorothie departed from the said Earle.

> To the xth, (he saith) that Johan Jockey did knowe that the said Dorothie was lyving at the time of her marriage with the Earle, for she dwelled in the Earles Colne, and after that mariage, the lady Dorothie wrott to Mr. Tyrrell, then the same Earles Comptroller, to know yf it were true, that the said Johan were marryed to the same Earle.

To the xjth, he saith that the woman that the same Earle kept at Tilbury Hall was never maryed to the same Earle of Oxforde, but that womans name this Examinant remembreth not.

To the xijth, he saith the same Earle of Oxforde never marryed any other woman than the said lady Dorothie and Margerie, save the said Joane Jockey, whom he maryed in the life tyme of the said lady Dorothie, as is aforesaide.[5]

The meaning of all this is that John de Vere's marriage to Joan Jockey was bigamous because his wife was alive until January 1548 and, therefore, this marriage was not lawful and would not be an impediment to any future marriage if his first wife died. When his first wife died, his marriage to Joan Jockey remained null and void, and he was then free to marry lawfully.

Richard Enews further testified as to the disfigurement of Joan Jockey by those opposed to this bigamous marriage:

To the xiijth, he saith that both the said Johan Jockey, and also the woman that the same Earle of Oxforde kept at Tilburie Hall were put from the said Earle in the life tyme of the said lady Dorothie. And for the said Johan Jockey, in the absence of the Earle, the Lord Darcye and Lord Sheffielde came to the Earles Colne, and this examinant & two more with him brake open the dore where the same Joan was, and spoyled her, and this examinantes fellow, John Smyth, cutt her nose. And thereupon she was put away.[6]

This is a gruesome piece of testimony, which provides a window on the casual violence of daily life at the time. Apparently, the enemies of John de Vere were opposed to this bigamous marriage. These appear to be the relatives of his wife, Dorothy Neville. With the aid of the Earl's own men, they disfigured Joan Jockey. Cutting off the nose of a woman accused of being a prostitute was a practice of the times. The record was unclear as to what was meant by "she was put away." Whether this means she was murdered or simply sent from the Earl's estates to some other place is unclear.

The twentieth question went right to the crux of the matter and allowed the respondent to give any other information touching on the issues raised in this book:

What other matter or think have you heard, knowen, or can you saie touching the premises, or any part thereof, or touching the lawfulnes or unlawfulness of the birth of the saide Edward, now Earle of Oxforde?[7]

Richard Enews answers the Queen's lawyers:

To the xxth, he can saie no more than he hath deposed alreadie.[8]

In other words, he neither confirmed nor denied any of the circumstances of Edward de Vere's birth, or that Edward was in fact the true son of John de Vere. This man had lived at the Earl's estate all his life and had given testimony as to the Earl's first marriage and to the circumstances surrounding the Earl's second marriage. It was probable that he would have been at Earls Colne during the period of Edward's birth. Why he did not testify to more details of Edward's birth, presuming it had occurred there, remains an unanswered question. Perhaps he wanted to avoid charges of perjury or simply did not want to testify on the matter, fearing undue complications with the Queen's representatives.

Rooke Greene was another witness deposed. He had knowledge of the events because Dorothy Fosser was living at his father's home during the period in question, along with the Earl's daughter, Katherine. His depositions give a complete, firsthand account of the situation:

Examinations taken the 19th day of Jannuarie in the xxxvijth yeare of the Raeign of our soveraeign lady Queene Elizabeth, by John Popham, esquier, her majesties attorney generall and Thomas Egerton, esquier her Majestyies Solicitor-General, by virtue of her highnes commission unto them in that behalfe directed, and hereunto annexed. Rooke Greene of little Sampford in the County of Essex esquier aged about lxij years, being sworn & examined upon his othe to all the Interrogatories to him mynystered, saith:

To the xvjth he saith, that by the appoyntment of the said Earle, the same Dorothie ffosser was at this Examinantes fathers house attending on the said Katherene [John de Vere's daughter], now lady Wyndsor, about the second yeare of Kinge Edwarde after which they were both sent for awaie by the appoyntment of the duke of Sommersett [Edward Seymour], after which the same Dorothie Fosser retorned to this Examinantes father's house. And the duke of Sommersett [Edward Seymour], understandinge that the said Earle had good likinge unto the same Dorothie, gave order to this Examinantes father, that the Earle shold not be suffred to have access to the same Dorothie at his house, who tooke as much care therunto as he might; and yet nevertheles the same Earle, by his servants, gott her to be taken awaie thentent that that the said Earle might have married the same Dorothie. But in the meane tyme before the said Earle mett with the said Dorothie, the same Earle in his waie toward the place where the same Dorothie was, went to the house of the saide margerie Gouldings brother, where seing the same Margie, he grew into such a present lyking of her as he presently married her. Whereupon the same Dorothie ffosser retorned to this examinents fathers house, and founde her self greatlie greeved with the said Earle; in that he had married the said Margerie & not her self the same Dorithie, and saith, that the same Dorothie did never to this examinats knowledge affirme that she was eyther married or contracted to the same Earle, but that he had deceyved her in not maryinge with her as he had promysed, wheruppon she had had her baynes once asked in the Churche, and saith heruppon the same Dorothie complayned to the Counsell of the Earles abuse towardes here, who theruppon was awarded to paie here tenne pounde yearly during her lief, and theuppon the same Dorothie after retorned & within a yeare or therabout after married with one John Ansonne then this examinates fathers Clerke, and more saith not that Interrogatorie.[9]

He further testified:

To the xxth, he can saie noe more than he hath saide. But that the now Earle [Edward de Vere, 17th Earl of Oxford] is the lawfull yssue of the said late Earle of Oxford for any thinge that this Examinant ever knewe or heard of.[10]

This testimony gives direct evidence that Edward de Vere was the "lawful issue" of the 16th Earl and Margery Golding "for anything that this examinant ever knew or heard of." However, Rooke Green was not living at Earls Colne and would have less knowledge of the affairs of the 16th Earl of Oxford than did Richard Enews, whose testimony appears somewhat incomplete. It is interesting why this question was asked at all.

Another respondent was John Anson, to whom Dorothy Fosser was later married. His deposition gives very explicit details of the hasty marriage of John de Vere:

John Anson clerk Parson of West Turville in the Countie of Buckingham, aged about threescore yeares & somewhat upward sworne and examined to all the Interrogatories, saith.

To the xiiijth, he saith that the said Earle of Oxford was maryed unto the said Margerie Gouldinge about St. James tyde next after the death of the said ladie Dorothie, as this examinant understood it commonly reported at that tyme. And the said Dorithie ffosser tould this Examinant, that the same Earle was maryed to the same Margerie on a tuesdaie in the mornynge at Bellcham hall in the house late Sir Thomas Goulding. And that the same Earle had appoynted with the same Dorothie ffosser to have maryed with her the same Dorothie the next day being Wednesdaie following, at Haverell. And saith he hath heard that the vicar of Clare, being Chapleyne & Aumer [almoner] to the same Earle of Oxforde, did marye the same Earle and Margerie as aforesaid.

To the xvj[th] he saith that as this examinant hath hearde the same Dorothie ffosser was contracted unto the said Earle of Oxforde at Sir Edwarde Greenes at Samford hall, but saith that there followed noe marriage upon that contract, for that after the baynes asked, and a lycence for the marriage obtayned, the day before the mariage should have ben accomplished, the same Earle married with the said Margery Goulding.[11]

The only plausible explanation for this bizarre marriage is that John de Vere was forced by very powerful forces to marry Margery Golding for some unknown reason. Nevertheless, why would Edward Seymour, the Lord Protector, want to force Margery Golding on John de Vere? He had already made the main grab earlier in the year for the Earl's properties by the contract of marriage between his son and the Earl's daughter. Was the Earl's marriage forced to provide a haven, a suitable foster home, and a cover identity for a changeling boy?

ENTER EDWARD DE VERE

There are no christening records to indicate the birth of Edward de Vere. There are also no historical records of the birth or christening of his older sister, Katherine, so this may not be as suspicious as it appears. However, the hereditary titles are passed to the males of the line, so this would be a more serious omission in Edward's case. Further, John de Vere's marriage to Margery Golding was recorded in the parish register. The first mention of Edward de Vere's existence was in the will of John de Vere in 1552, where he listed his son Edward and his first daughter, Katherine.

The first mention of a specific birth date for Edward de Vere's was April 12, 1550, but this was not until William Cecil recorded it in 1576, in a memorandum concerning the marriage of Cecil's daughter in 1571. If Lord Burghley was a party to the placement of the changeling child, Edward de Vere, it was hardly likely that he was going to record a date that did not fit with the notion that Edward was the legitimate son of John de Vere and Margery Golding. A date that was two years after their marriage would be convenient and would fit the historical record of the marriage of John de Vere and Margery Golding. Percival Golding, a cousin of Arthur Golding, wrote the following after the 17th Earl of Oxford's presumed death:

> Edward de Vere, only son of John, borne the twelfthe day of April Anno 1550 Earle of Oxenford, High Chamberlayne, Lord Bolbec, Sandford and Badlesmere, Steward of the Forrest in Essex, and of the Privy Council to the King's Majesty that now is. Of whom I will only speak what all mens voyces confirm; He was a man in mind and body absolutely accomplished with honourable endowments. He died at his house in Hackney in the monthe of June Anno 1604 and leieth buryed at Westminster.[12]

This was written in a rather laudatory book on the Vere family, and it remains to be seen whether Oxford's body was later moved to Westminster. The book may be drawing on the date recorded by William Cecil.

The first legal suit concerning Edward de Vere's right to the inheritance from John de Vere was in 1563. Katherine Vere, the first daughter of John de Vere and Dorothy Neville, brought suit with her husband, Lord

Windsor, who was a relative of Northumberland, against her nominal half-brother, then the 17th Earl of Oxford. The suit challenged the legality of the marriage of John de Vere to Margery Golding on the grounds that John had been married to Joan Jockey at the time of his marriage to Margery. The suit did not question that Edward was the child of John de Vere and Margery Golding; in fact, it assumed this to be true. If successful, the suit would have meant that Edward de Vere would not have been recognized as the *legitimate* son of John de Vere and, therefore, would not have any claim to the properties of the 16th Earl of Oxford, and instead, they would go to Katherine Vere, Lady Windsor.

The merits of this were never examined in court because the suit was quickly dismissed on the grounds it infringed on matters pertaining to the Queen. The Crown maintained that Edward de Vere was a ward of the Crown upon the death of John de Vere, and therefore, the suit had no legal standing. This is an expression of extraordinary interest on the part of the Crown (that is, the Queen), who stepped in so quickly. One reason the Crown could have wanted this suit quashed is that it wanted no investigations of any matter pertaining to the affairs the 16th Earl of Oxford that might bring forth evidence relevant to the legitimacy of Edward de Vere. A second reason might be strictly financial; that is, there was a sizeable source of revenue to be gained managing the estates of orphaned aristocrats, and the Crown would lose that revenue if Oxford were declared a bastard through this lawsuit, but this is a less pressing reason for the state to be involved.

This suit was answered by Arthur Golding, brother-in-law to the 16th Earl of Oxford, who by then worked for William Cecil as a receiver in charge of accounting for income from estates. Golding's involvement and his position with William Cecil was another indication of the suit's importance to both Cecil and the Crown. The letter, which was written in Latin, follows:

> Arthur Golding alleges and to the effect of all right alleges the petition of the said lady Catherine to contain grave prejudice of the lady the Queen and to touch the legitimacy of the blood and right of hereditary possession of the said Earl and his sister and **alleges the aforesaid Earl to have been and to be a minor of fourteen years** and known and of record to be under the ward, tutelage and care of the said lady the Queen with all and singular his lands, tenements and hereditaments which of right are and ought to be in the possession and rule of the said lady the Queen during his minority. And for the same reason by the common law as by the statutes of the realm, and also by the privileges of the Court of Wards and Liveries no plea or controversy may be moved or any other be recited, set in motion or proposed before any ecclesiastical or secular judge, which touches directly or indirectly the person, state, things, goods, lands, possessions, tenements or hereditaments

of the same in any way or in any manner during his minority in the Court of Wards and Liveries of the said lady the Queen save before the master and council for the same Court to this deputed by the strength of the law of this realm. And further he alleges *that the said lady mary the sister of the said Earl was and is a minor of fourteen years* and her right and interest to depend directly on the right and title of the aforenamed Earl. Therefore he asks that the most Reverend to decree by reason of the premises that it be superseded, until special licence in this part be obtained, according to the laws and customs in like causes in the said Court of Wards and Liveries lawfully used. [*Italics* added]

28 June 1563[13]

This letter is extraordinary in two respects. First, the letter states that Edward de Vere was fourteen years old, which would make his birthday 1549. Note that the letter is dated 28 June 1563. This only adds more confusion and uncertainty to the actual birthday of Edward de Vere.

Even more extraordinary, the letter states that Edward de Vere has a sister! Arthur Golding states that both Edward de Vere and his sister are the same age, fourteen. Here he is alluding to a date that was a year after the marriage of John de Vere and Margery Golding in 1548. They could hardly both have been born in the same year unless they were twins, but there was no indication in any other records of the birth of Edward or his "sister." Also, in John de Vere's will of 1552, there was mention of Edward and his older sister, Katherine, but there was no mention of a younger sister. Of course, her name can be none other than Mary.

The circumstantial evidence and logic of the situation indicate that William Cecil placed the missing Mary Seymour and the alleged child of Princess Elizabeth in the household of John de Vere. Edward was probably placed there first, and he was followed by his half-sister a year or so later when she disappeared from the historical record. If this was so, then it would be logical that both the Queen and William Cecil would pay a good deal of attention to the welfare of these changeling children. As the story unfolds, it will be shown that William Cecil and the Queen had a great deal to do with John de Vere's nominal son.

THE FALL OF EDWARD SEYMOUR AND THE REIGN OF MARY TUDOR

In October 1551, Edward Seymour (Lord Protector, Duke of Somerset) began to lose his grip on the council by ignoring the succinct advice given to him a few months earlier by Sir Thomas Paget:

But of late your Grace is grown in great choleric fashions whensoever you are contraried in that which you have conceived in your head. A king which shall give men occasion of discourage to say their opinions frankly, receiveth thereby great hurt and peril to his realm. But a subject in great authority, as your Grace is, using such fashion is like to fall into great danger and peril of his own person.[14]

He ignored this advice and like others before him, he drastically overreached himself. His greed and manner had alienated his friends, and his enemies were very happy to seize the moment. When he sent letters to Sir Henry Seymour, John de Vere, and John Russell requesting that they send troops to assist him against the other members of the council. John de Vere, not unexpectedly, failed to go to his aid.

On October 16, 1551, Edward Seymour came late to a council meeting, and before he could take his chair, the Lord Treasurer accused him of treason. John Dudley (later Duke of Northumberland) summoned the guard and had Seymour arrested and sent to the Tower; his wife joined him shortly thereafter. On January 22, 1552, Edward followed his brother to the block. His nephew, Edward VI, was reluctant to sign his death warrant but after some pressure did so. The young king had now signed the death warrants for both his uncles. When John Dudley reorganized the council, he appointed William Cecil as his secretary. Thus Cecil, with his adroit political timing, had moved seamlessly from one regime to another.

Many thought that the young king would not survive the protection of the new Lord Protector, John Dudley, and they were right. Edward VI had always been portrayed as a sickly youth, but closer examination of the records does not reveal this to be the case. He was not the robust, hearty athlete that his father was, but he was far from being a sickly youth. The young king had suffered a bout of the measles and perhaps smallpox in the spring of 1552, but he was otherwise in robust health. He rode in a summer progress and engaged in games such as riding, shooting, and wrestling. It was only after the death of his uncle, Edward Seymour, and the installation of John Dudley as the chief power behind the throne that the young king's health began to fail. The diagnosis of the doctors was not any specific disease, but rather an overall weakening of his health. His particular symptom was a strong, persistent cough that has lead some to think that the king had tuberculosis. There are reports that he would spit up matter that was a greenish yellow-black and sometimes pink like blood. Elizabeth tried to visit the king on two occasions, but Northumberland prevented her from seeing her brother. There were rumors that the young king was being given a slow-acting poison. The actions of John Dudley did little to allay these suspicions. According to the *British Medical Journal of 1910,* which reported on the death of Edward VI under the title "Some Royal Death-Beds":

> eruptions on his skin came out; his hair fell off, and then his nails, and afterwards the joints of his toes and fingers.[15]

Edward was a precocious youth with an independent mind and a good understanding of both religion and politics. The young king kept a journal, and its entries reveal a young man who had acquired the high intellect of the Tudors. This may have made the ever-scheming John Dudley anxious as Edward VI approached the age of majority. Whatever the relationship was, Dudley would only lose influence as time passed and especially when Edward VI became king in his own right. Poisoning the young king was a method to ensure that this did not happen. A likely suspect for poisoning the young king was his son, Robert Dudley, as is reported by John Nichols in *Progresses of Queen Elizabeth*:

> The 15th of August 1551, he [Robert Dudley] was sworn one of the six Gentlemen of the Bedchamber to King Edward VI.; and Sir John Hayward, in his Life of this King, says, that after his entertainment into a place of so near service, the King enjoyed his health not long. But this is too severe an accusation of him, as he was then only nineteen, and could not at that early age be suspected, with the least probability, of so horrid a crime as the poisoning of his Royal Master.[16]

John Nichols later reports on the death of the husband of Robert Dudley's second wife:

> When he [Robert Dudley] was disposed to marry the Countess of Essex, whose husband he had procured to be poisoned in his journey from Ireland, he caused some ill potions to be given Lady Douglas, his second wife, so that with the loss of her hair and nails she hardly escaped death.[17]

From the similarity in symptoms between this incident and the death of King Edward VI, one would suspect that the same poison was used. The rumors that Robert Dudley disposed of his enemies through poisoning seem well founded, and the similarity of symptoms revealed here points toward Robert Dudley as the murderer of the young king, Edward VI.

Whatever the personal or political animosities were among its members, the Council of Edward VI was firm in its desire to keep Edward's sister, Princess Mary, from reaching the throne. Mary was a staunch, almost fanatical Catholic, and visions of her on the throne must have given nightmares to the Protestant faction. Protestants looking ahead even further than this realized that Mary was unmarried and unlikely to bear any children. These Protestants would have been looking to Elizabeth as a possible Protestant savior in the event of Mary's death.

Another route to keeping the throne in Protestant hands would have been to block Mary's ascension by putting Lady Jane Grey on the throne. She was great-granddaughter of Henry VII by his granddaughter Lady Frances Brandon and the niece of Henry VIII, which gave her considerable popular support over the Catholic Mary.

On May 21, 1553, Lord Guildford Dudley, John Dudley's son, married Lady Jane Grey. She protested vehemently against the marriage, but her protestations did little against the power of her parents. She was a reluctant bride, and she would later be a reluctant queen. John Dudley had a way of directly controlling the throne through his son if the young, "sickly" king were to die. John Dudley's plan was to force Princess Mary aside and install Lady Jane Grey as queen. He was relying on his control over the council and the Protestant fear of installing Mary, a firm Catholic, on the throne.

Edward VI died on July 6, 1553, at the age of sixteen. In the days preceding his death, John Dudley used his influence to have the king declare his sisters, Mary and Elizabeth, bastards and to pass the succession to Lady Jane Grey. The weakened young king agreed. Dudley kept Edward's death secret and sent his son Robert to arrest Princess Mary Tudor, the successor to the throne according to Henry VIII's will. However, Princess Mary Tudor had been warned not to come to London to visit her sick brother because it was a trap to imprison her. William Cecil may have been one of those who passed on that warning. Mary retreated to Framingham Castle in Norfolk and avoided capture. John Dudley pressured his daughter-in-law to take the throne of England; she reluctantly agreed but reigned for a short nine days.

> To Roger Ascham.
>
> I will tell you, and tell you a truth which perchance you will marvel at. One of the greatest benefits that God ever gave me is that He sent me, with sharp and severe parents, so gentle a schoolmaster. When I am in the presence either of father or mother, whether I sit, stand, or go, eat, drink, be merry or sad, be sewing, playing, dancing, or doing any thing else, I must do it as it were, in such weight, measure, and number, even as perfectly as God made the earth, or else I am so sharply taunted, so cruelly threatened, yea presented sometimes with pinches, nippes, and blows, and other things, (which I will not name for the honour I bear them), so without measure misordered, that I think myself in hell.
>
> Lady Jane Grey [18]

The number of supporters for John Dudley had begun to dwindle quickly. When he departed the council, it reversed its support for Lady Jane Grey. Dudley became increasingly isolated. Whatever the reservations the council and the populace had about placing a Catholic on the throne, were less important than having a legitimate heir more directly descended from Henry VIII. Nor was the Council particularly receptive to having John Dudley rule England through his daughter-in-law, and in a few days, Dudley's support evaporated. John Dudley was, like his predecessor Edward Seymour, a man who far overreached himself in his quest for power. Dudley had created many enemies both among the council and among the common people. He paid for his mistakes with his life. On August 23, 1553, John Dudley, Duke of Northumberland and formerly Lord Protector to Edward VI, was executed.

While Princess Mary was in flight to avoid capture, the 16th Earl of Oxford declared for and received commission papers to raise men in Essex on her behalf. Hedingham, Oxford's principal dwelling, was located strategically north of London. Oxford's declaring for Mary was a pivotal event in the decline of support for John Dudley. Because of his early and key efforts, the 16th Earl bore the sword of state at Mary's coronation and resumed his right to officiate as the Lord Great Chamberlain. That honorary title had been in the family for generations, but his family had lost the honorary position, so the grounds for his acting in this capacity is somewhat dubious except that he had Queen Mary's support. After that, he played virtually no role in Queen Mary's government.

Princess Elizabeth quickly became the hope of the suppressed Protestants during the reign of Queen Mary, whether or not she wanted such attention. She was brought to court and put under virtual room arrest by her sister Mary. She was later allowed to leave and establish her own household, and she retired to Hatfield, but Mary placed many spies there to watch her. Elizabeth attended Catholic services regularly, but was quickly embroiled in politics again with a rebellion led by Thomas Wyatt.

Thomas Wyatt, a Protestant noble, had raised an army or mob (depending on a person's point of view) and had reached the gates of London. He had roused the populace over the issue of Queen Mary's marriage to Prince Philip of Spain. Twenty years of Protestantism had removed many of the people's ties to Catholicism and the Pope. However, the people of London were not dissatisfied enough to rebel against the authority of the monarch. When the citizens of London did not open the gates to the city, Wyatt's army soon dissipated and the rebellion was over. Thomas Wyatt was headed for executioner's block, and Princess Elizabeth was placed in the Tower to join Robert Dudley, son of the infamous John Dudley. The meeting of Elizabeth and Robert in the Tower was the source of much romantic conjecture. What later becomes evident is that Elizabeth was obviously struck by the handsome young Robert Dudley. Eventually, Elizabeth was released to remain under house arrest for the rest of Mary's reign.

After Wyatt's Rebellion, Mary had Lady Jane Grey executed, not for any direct involvement on her part, but more as a means of eliminating a Protestant rival for the throne. Lady Jane Grey's surviving letter gives some indication of the way aristocratic children were treated by their parents. The implication of her letter is that her parents beat her in "some ways which I will not name." Her parents had forced her to take the throne after Edward VI's death against her better judgment. She abdicated when it was apparent Mary had the popular support. She was queen for a mere nine days. Her execution was a precaution against her becoming a focal point for dissatisfaction. There was scant evidence that she had participated in any treasonous plots. When informed of her fate, she almost welcomed death as a relief from an unhappy and tortured life. Elizabeth knew Lady Jane Grey well as they had both lived in the household of Katherine Parr and Thomas Seymour. Death by the executioner's axe was not an abstraction for young Elizabeth.

Queen Mary's pro-Catholic policies soon antagonized everyone. In her short reign, she burned over 300 "heretics" at the stake, for which she derived the sobriquet Bloody Mary. Much of the aristocracy was spared such pain, and the burden fell largely on the common people. Some aristocrats who were firm Protestants, such as Francis Walsingham, fled the country, while others, such as William Cecil, went into a state of dormancy. The church bells tolled throughout England when Mary died on November 17, 1558, and Elizabeth ascended the throne of England. The first appointments that Elizabeth made were William Cecil as her Secretary of State and Robert Dudley as Master of the Horse.

Sir William Cecil and Sir Thomas Gresham should also be credited with assisting in creating the economic vitality of the Elizabethan reign. During the reign of Henry VIII, Edward VI, and Mary I, the currency had been debased by continually re-minting coins with less than their stated amount of gold or silver. Sir Thomas Gresham, Sir William Cecil, and Queen Elizabeth secretly planned and then quickly executed a re-coinage in which old coins were replaced by new. While the Crown profited by this replacement, the overall result was a stable currency. The stable currency led to increased trade within the country and with foreign trading partners. Gresham's Law of economics has its origins in this period; the law states that when two currencies are in circulation, one debased and the other of value, individuals will tend to hoard the valued currency and trade the devalued currency, or bad money drives out good money.

Elizabeth's parsimony regarding public expenditures and the avoidance of wasteful military adventures was another contributing factor to economic and political stability. Elizabeth also did not go on a grandiose building spree, as did her father, Henry VIII. England's economic resurgence provided fertile ground for the Elizabethan Renaissance in the arts, just as an economic resurgence of the Italian city-states had provided fertile ground for the artists, sculptors, and painters of the Italian Renaissance.

THE RISE AND QUICK DEMISE OF JOHN DE VERE

John de Vere was one of the noblemen chosen to accompany Elizabeth from her seclusion at Hatfield House to her coronation. There, the Countess of Oxford,[c] Margery Golding, was named a maid of honor to the new queen. The 16th Earl of Oxford officiated as Lord Great Chamberlain at the Queen's coronation in London. When the second son to the king of Sweden was sent to negotiate a marriage with the new queen, Robert Dudley and John de Vere were present to greet him and escort him to London. John de Vere's star was on the rise, and he was soon invited to live at court. It was not recorded whether his son, Edward, also came to court but this might be very likely. Very little else is known of Edward de Vere's childhood or youth beyond what can be inferred from a few fragmentary records, by his position in society, and by the tutors assigned to him.

It is doubtful that John de Vere ever knew the identity of the child or children that had been placed in his care, and there is no reason for William Cecil to have told him. There is further evidence that John did not know who his foster son was when, in 1559, he began to arrange a marriage for his ostensible son, Edward de Vere, to either of two sisters, Mary or Elizabeth Hastings. This arrangement involved two possible brides; in case one of them died, the contract would still be valid. Arranging such a marriage would be perfectly proper for John de Vere if Edward de Vere was in fact his legitimate son, or if he was treating Edward de Vere as his foster son. However, it makes no sense for John de Vere to be arranging such a marriage if he was aware of the true identity of Edward de Vere. If this was the case, John de Vere would be

---

[c]King and Earl are the two titles in England descended from German-English, whereas the rest are imported from French, such as dukes and barons, but there are no counts in England. The feminine of a duke is a duchess, of a baron, a baroness, and of a count, a countess. However, applying these French feminine endings to an earl would produce an "earl-ess", or pronounced another way, an "ear-less." To avoid this pronunciation problem, the wife of an earl is a countess, despite the absence of actual counts.

overstepping his bounds by arranging such a marriage that tread on royal prerogatives. Under the wardship system, the Oxford-Hastings marriage contract would be invalid if the 16th Earl of Oxford had not ratified the agreement after Edward reached the age of fourteen. It would have been senseless for the Earl to make such a marriage contract if he did not expect to live for at least five years.

From August 14 to August 19, 1561, in the third year of her reign, Elizabeth went on a progress to visit Hedingham Castle in Essex. The usual pattern of these stays was that the host would be responsible for entertaining the Queen with outdoor amusements such as riding and hunting and indoor amusements and theatrical productions. The 16th Earl of Oxford had maintained a company of players for many years. It would be likely and logical that the young Edward de Vere would have been in close company with the reigning queen during such a visit.

In 1561, William Cecil was made Master of the Wards. The wards were aristocratic males whose fathers had died before their sons reached their majority of twenty-one years. The Master of the Wards and the Queen thus gained financial control over their estates, and most important, they gained the right to arrange the marriage of the underage wards. The wardship system allowed the Crown to manage the affairs of the ward in ways that would be favorable only to the guardian and leave the ward with virtually nothing. The system was revived by Henry VII to produce revenue for the Crown; as a by-product, it crippled the old aristocracy. As one gentleman of the times put it, by the time a ward received his inheritance, it was reduced to woods, decayed old houses, and land ploughed to bare ground. Further, the heir rarely received his inheritance automatically when he became of age; rather, he had to engage in a costly legal process of suing for "livery."

The orphaned heir of an aristocrat rarely stayed a royal ward except in name for very long. The Crown soon sold the rights to his guardianship, sometimes to his mother but more often to a complete stranger. The Crown then made an immediate profit on the transaction (an inheritance tax, if you wish), and the administration of the wardship passed into other hands. The purchaser of the wardship then made a profit by exploiting the lands of the youthful heir and selling the marriage rights. With his guardianship would go the right to manage the lands, and the heir was obligated to marry whomever the guardian chose or be forced to pay an often enormous fine to the guardian.

In the year after William Cecil becomes Master of the Wards, John de Vere, apparently in good health, or at least with no reference to ill health, made a new will during July 1562. In this will, he gives several favorable and loving references to those close to him, including his horse. He includes phrases such as:

> ... my loving and well beloved wife ... my loving son-in-law the Lord Wyndsor ... my three loving systers the Lady Darcy, the Ladye Surrey, and the Ladye Sheffeilde ... my very good lord Sir Nicholas Bacon knight, Lord Keeper of the Great Seal of England ... my right trusty and loving friend Sir William Cecil knight ... my singular good lord the Duke of Norfolk ... one of my great horses ...[19]

When he mentions his one and only son, the inheritor of his great estates and the title of the 17th Earl in a line that extends back to William the Conqueror, he simply calls him "Edward" three times, "my son Edward" once, and "Edward, Lord Bulbeck" once. He mentions his daughter Mary once as "my daughter the Lady Mary" and once as "Lady Mary my daughter." This unemotional farewell shows no affection toward either Edward or Mary, hardly what one would expect, especially toward an only son. This was also the first appearance in the historical record of Mary Seymour after her disappearance.

John de Vere's will specifies that Edward de Vere was to be one of the executors of the will, but this was legally impossible because Edward was a minor, ostensibly twelve years of age. This indicates that John expected to live at least nine years, until Edward became of age. There is nothing in the will that indicates that the 16th Earl was in ill health, nor is there anything in the historical record to indicate such. Up to this point, the making of a will was proper and prudent for a man of John de Vere's position to complete.

When viewed more closely, the will has some unexpected executors. The first executor of the will was Robert Dudley, Earl of Leicester [pronounced Lester], son of the treacherous John Dudley, and, at the time, the Queen's favorite. John de Vere's refusal to aid John Dudley, Robert's father, was one of the events that resulted in John Dudley's execution. Further, there appears to have been no previous known connection between Robert Dudley and John de Vere. In addition, John de Vere includes "my right trusty and loving friend Sir William Cecil knight" as an executor to his will. The implication is that the Crown and William Cecil were forcing John de Vere into making this new will, which left both Robert Dudley and William Cecil in very favorable positions in the event of the Earl's death. William Cecil, as Master of the Wards, was in a position to control the future of Edward de Vere, while Robert Dudley stood to control many of John de Vere's lands.

John de Vere signed his will on July 28, 1562, and by the end of August 1562, he was dead. There was no account if his hair and fingernails fell out.

Among the criteria for guilt in a crime are motive, opportunity, and means. While the murder of John de Vere cannot be proved beyond any reasonable doubt, the circumstances of his death indicate that there were motives, opportunity, and means for the Queen, Robert Dudley, and William Cecil to murder the Earl. Robert Dudley would gain control over John de Vere's properties and the accruing financial rewards. The Queen and William Cecil would gain control over Edward de Vere, and it hardly was likely that an astute politician like William Cecil would spend such effort over this young child unless he had some ulterior motive.

Elizabeth, in putting Robert Dudley as executor of John de Vere's will, was in effect beggaring her own son for years to come. Edward de Vere's finances were never good, and much of that should be laid at the doorstep of Robert Dudley. From the perspective of Elizabethan times, parents put their interests far ahead of their children, and given Elizabeth's intense fascination with Dudley, it is only logical that she would take care of Robert Dudley's welfare first. Robert Dudley was as rapacious as any other person in England was. As Gwynneth Bowen puts it:

> So it was not Cecil; not Charles Tyrrell; but Robert Dudley who succeeded Edward's father (for the time being) as Lord of the Manors of Castle Hedingham, Earls Colne etc. The spoils were divided: Tyrrell married the late Earl's widow; Cecil obtained the custody of his son; but Dudley got the lands.[20]

The young Earl was now a ward of the Crown. In the normal course of events, his wardship would have been sold by the Crown for cash. However, one of the peculiarities of Oxford's wardship was that the Queen never sold it. In a more strict sense, it was not William Cecil but the Queen who was the guardian of Oxford with William Cecil as the administrator, and the Queen had the right to determine whom Oxford would marry:

> Perhaps Shakespeare, through the mouthpiece of Bertram and his mother, the Countess of Roussillon, strikes the keynote of the feudal relationship. "In delivering my son from me," says the mother, "Bury a second husband." "And I, in going madam," Bertram replies, "weep o'er my father's death anew—but I must attend His Majesty's command, to whom I am now in ward, evermore in subjection." But if Bertram was, as some critics believe, Shakespeare's version of Burghley's ward, the Earl of Oxford, then there is another side of the story; and we shall meet him again in a different context. Yet guardianship, as everyone in Tudor England well knew, was a means to an end: marriage.[21]

Joel Hurstfield makes these astute observations about William Cecil and his wardships. He points out that William Cecil was playing the wardship game not simply for money, but rather for political power, and several of the wards he chose were acknowledged by historians to have a special relationship with the Queen (Essex and Southampton). In regard to the Authorship issue, Hurstfield is making a connection between Oxford the man from Stratford and assuming the man from Stratford had detailed knowledge of Oxford's wardship. How this might be possible, Hurstfield never explains. In spite of this, Hurstfield is dead-on about the Author reflecting on his wardship in the plays, and the comments of Bertram do reflect Oxford's situation. Someone well versed in Shakespeare and knowledgeable about Oxford's situation cannot but trip over references to Oxford in Shakespeare's work.

Historians have never considered that William Cecil had inside knowledge and ulterior motives:

> It is from these sources that we can build up a significant list of wards to whom he stood guardian. It will include Lord Wharton, the seventeenth Earl of Oxford, Philip Howard, Earl of Surrey, the third and fifth Earls of Rutland, the Earl of Essex, and the Earl of Southampton. To these we may add Lord Zouche, purchased in the name of Thomas Cecil, the elder son of Burghley, but brought up in Burghley's household. In all, he gained the wardships of eight noblemen, an unique achievement in Tudor England. But it is still significant that, in his thirty-seven years as Master [of the Wards], he took for himself only nine wards. In short, Burghley was interested in quality—not quantity.[22]

Edward de Vere, as the 17th Earl of Oxford, was done a great injustice by Robert Dudley's usurping his inheritance. However, in another sense, if he was the son of Queen Elizabeth and Thomas Seymour, he really had no right to any inheritance from John de Vere. In this version of reality, he was not Edward de Vere, 17th Earl of Oxford, but Edward Seymour, bastard son of Elizabeth Tudor and Thomas Seymour. Edward de Vere was the cuckoo placed in the household nest of John de Vere. If he was the bastard son of the Queen, then he deserved nothing from John de Vere. Yet, from another point of view, the only person who clearly owned title to any land in England was the Queen; everyone was, in some respect, a tenant of the Crown, and she could do what she saw fit with such lands. She was doing just that by manipulating the inheritance through William Cecil. She assigned Oxford's inheritance to her paramour, Robert Dudley, who received the income from it for nine years. Oxford finally acquired his lands back when he was in his thirties. The Queen more than anyone else kept Oxford in constant financial difficulties. From an financial point of view, the ever-controlling Queen could keep control of Oxford.

Robert Dudley had to be implacably opposed to the very existence of Edward de Vere. Robert clearly had designs to marry Elizabeth, but Edward de Vere was the first male child of Elizabeth and stood between Robert and the throne. That Edward de Vere survived at all can only be thought of as a miracle engineered by William Cecil. Edward de Vere, the Queen's son, provided a pawn or a prince for William Cecil to hold against Robert Dudley. As long as Edward de Vere remained alive and William Cecil knew the secret of his birth, he was in a powerful position against the unscrupulous Dudley. William Cecil had less a financial motive and more a political one to have John de Vere murdered.

After John de Vere's death, Margery Golding married Charles Tyrrell, the comptroller for John de Vere and a retainer of Robert Dudley. This was within months after the death of her husband, but the exact date of the marriage is not certain. In a letter to Cecil in October after the death of John de Vere, she pleads with William Cecil that Robert Dudley has intimidated the tenants of the land to make them not supply her with her rent corn and that she is in desperate straits. She also writes to William Cecil apologizing for her delay in processing "my Lord's late will":

> *I confess that a great trust hath been committed to me of those things which, in my Lord's lifetime, were kept most secret from me.* And since that time the doubtful declaration of my Lord's debts hath so uncertainly fallen out that … I had rather leave up the whole doings thereof to my son (if by your good advice I may so deal honorably) than to venture further, and certainly altogether, with the will …. And what my further determination is touching the will, yet loth to determine without your good advice, for that I mean the honour or gain (if any be) might come wholly to my son, who is under your charge.[23] *[Italics* added]

The particularly interesting sentence in this letter is "I confess that a great trust hath been committed to me of those things which, in my Lord's lifetime, were kept most secret from me." This sentence points in the direction that Margery Golding was put in trust of the young child, but that she had no idea who the child was. In the letter, she also addresses the child as "my son," but this in itself does not establish that Edward de Vere was Margery's natural son.

Both Tyrrell and Margery Golding died a few years later and were buried at Earls Colne, the countess in 1568 and Tyrrell in 1571. Whether they lived at Hedingham, Earls Colne after the 16th Earl's death is uncertain but probable.

Once John de Vere began to act as if his presumed foster son was actually his own by negotiating a marriage contract for Edward, he was stepping on the plans of William Cecil. This marriage arrangement directly conflicted with William Cecil's interests. If Edward was the son of Elizabeth (even illegitimate), he still had an imperfect claim as heir to the throne. In an era when death was often quick and unexpected from either natural or unnatural causes, Edward de Vere was an important link to power. If Edward was contracted to marry, that would preclude any other family from marrying into the royal Tudor line. William Cecil had other marriage plans for Edward de Vere, the young 17th Earl of Oxford.

WHO MURDERED AMY ROBSART?

Legend has it that Elizabeth first met the handsome Robert Dudley when she was imprisoned in the Tower by her sister, Queen Mary. While they may have met there, it would have been to renew an old acquaintance. Elizabeth and Robert knew each other from her childhood days at the court of Henry VIII, where she was the young princess and Robert Dudley was the son of John Dudley, then the Earl of Warwick. He was unscrupulous and exceedingly handsome. Many regarded him as a truly evil influence on the Queen. Whatever his faults, the Queen loved Robert Dudley from the first days of her reign until Dudley's death in 1588, the year of the defeat of the Spanish Armada.

Figure 11. Robert Dudley, Earl of Leicester

In 1550, Robert Dudley married Amy Robsart, daughter of Sir John Robsart of Synderstone in Norfolk. This made Robert a wealthy landowner in Norfolk. It is likely, but unrecorded, that she attended his wedding, but it is virtually impossible that she would not have known of his marriage in the small circle of English aristocracy.

When Elizabeth became queen in 1558, her first appointment was William Cecil to be her Secretary of State. Kat Ashley was made Chief Lady of the Bedchamber and her husband Keeper of the Jewel House. Thomas Parry was knighted, appointed to the post of Controller of the

Household and made a member of the Privy Council. Robert Dudley was appointed Master of the Horse with an annual salary of £1,500, a stupendous sum of money. Dudley organized royal processions and tournaments, masques and banquets, and his duties required constant attendance on Elizabeth. There was probably not a day during her adult life, at least until her very old age, that she did not go riding, and in the early years of her reign, her companion was Robert Dudley. Money and honors soon were bestowed upon the handsome Robert, and Elizabeth later made him Earl of Leicester. John Nichols, in his *Progresses of Queen Elizabeth,* reports on Robert Dudley:

> Immediately after Queen Mary's death, in 1558, this young Nobleman went to the Princess Elizabeth (who was then at Hatfield), mounted on a snow-white steed, being well skilled in riding a managed horse; and paid homage to her on his knees. His beauty, stature, and florid youth, were such powerful recommendations, that she made him Master of the Horse, and conferred on him titles and estates. [24]

He quotes Camden's *Complete History of England* to further describe the relationship between Elizabeth and Robert Dudley:

> He was high in the favour of Queen Elizabeth, who out of royal and princely clemency heaped honours upon him, and saved his life whose father would have destroyed her's. Whether this was from any real virtues in him, whereof he gave some appearances; or in regard of the common lot of their imprisonment in Queen Mary's days; or that there was something in his birth, or the planets that ruled it, which occasioned a mysterious sympathy between their souls," says Camden, "I cannot determine: but most certain it is, that the favour or disfavour of Princes to several persons is governed by a secret kind of fatality. For the Queen having made him Master of the Horse, as the first token of her friendship and esteem, she made him Knight of the Garter (to the amazement of all) in the first year of her reign.
>
> In 1564, he was created Baron of Denbigh and Earl of Leicester. [25]

The movie *Elizabeth* has the princess deeply in love with Robert Dudley, but not know he was married; the historical facts belie this.

> Edward noted the marriage (at which Elizabeth was present) in his diary, "Lord Robert Dudley, third son of the Earl of Warwick, married Sir John Robsart's daughter, after whose marriage there were certain gentlemen that did strive who should take away a goose's head which was hanged alive on two cross-posts." As he was thirteen, his greater interest in the goose was natural enough. [26]

Elizabeth and Robert Dudley lived together as man and wife with separate but adjoining apartments at court. It was well recognized that Robert Dudley wished to marry the Queen and that she wished to marry him. In addition, rumors of the time were that she had children by Robert, rumors that would persist to the end of her reign. In 1581, Henry Hawkins said:

> my Lord Robert hath had five children by the Queen, and she never goeth in progress but to be delivered.[27]

Several other men and women were pilloried or imprisoned for saying that Elizabeth had children by Dudley, including Anne Dow, Thomas Playfair, Robert Gardner, and Dionysia Deryck.

> In August 1570, several persons were tried and some executed at Norwich, for treasonable speeches and designs. "They had set out four proclamations: one was touching the wantonness of the Court;" and one of the conspirators called Marsham, having said that "my Lord of Leicester had two children by the Queen," was sentenced to lose both his ears, or pay a fine of one hundred pounds.[28]

It cannot be expected that there would be any candid printed record of the Queen's affairs. There were no newspapers at the time, and the press was controlled by the Crown. The few comments that do survive are often in legal records showing where someone was tried for slandering the Queen and the record of that slander still exists. One difficulty in finding such records is that the legal language was Latin with a number of peculiar legal abbreviations. Therefore, not all the material of the period is readily available and much might not be translated. Continued primary search of records from the Elizabethan period still might yield some historical gems.

In addition, the myth of the Virgin Queen has incapacitated historical researchers from looking at the letters and other correspondence from the point of view that Elizabeth had children. Such correspondence might reveal familiarities and connections with the Queen that have been heretofore undiscovered and point to her having more than one child. The appendix contains a list of candidates and raises the possibility that Elizabeth had seven children during her lifetime, all raised by foster parents.

The legend of the Virgin Queen is one that is defended by practically every historian of the period. It is the assumption that every biographer of Elizabeth starts with and defends, in one way or the other, to the last page. The involvement of Elizabeth with Robert Dudley is played down despite the fact that the Queen and her handsome Master of the Horse had adjoining apartments in various castles and could freely see each other day and night. Facts and incidents that disturb the rosy picture of the

Virgin Queen, dedicated to her people, are quickly put aside or diminished to the role of insignificance.

Robert Dudley, as Earl of Leicester, became the most unpopular man in England. He was not supported by any political or religious faction because of his relation with the Queen. If he would have married Elizabeth, he would have been regarded, given the male chauvinism of the time, as the de facto King of England, with Elizabeth a proper wife obeying her husband's wishes. Another impediment to the marriage of Robert Dudley and Elizabeth was his wife, Amy, who was alive and well.

Robert Dudley's crafty foe was William Cecil, who did not want to see Robert Dudley on the throne. Cecil, with spies in many corners, must have gotten wind that a plot was afoot, for he confided to the Spanish ambassador that he might have to withdraw from Elizabeth's service because of her strange behavior. The Spanish ambassador reported the following back to his king in the spring of 1559:

> Lord Robert has come so much into favour that he does whatever he likes with affairs, and it is even said that Her Majesty visits him in his chamber night and day. People talk of this so freely that they go so far as to say that his wife has a malady in one of her breasts and the Queen is only waiting for her to die to marry Lord Robert.[29]

This raises the issue of Amy Robsart, and it raises the possibility that Robert Dudley was in contact with the Spaniards. The feeling throughout Europe is reflected in the following:

> she is in love with Lord Robert and never lets him leave her.[30]

Alvaro De Quadra, Bishop of Aquila, came to England that summer as the new Spanish ambassador, and he reported:

> I have heard from a certain person [William Cecil] who is accustomed to give veracious news that Lord Robert has sent to poison his wife. Certainly all the Queen has done in the matter of her marriage is only keeping Lord Robert's enemies and the country engaged with words until this wicked deed is consummated.[31]

Of course, Cecil knew that the minister would immediately write a letter and send it in a diplomatic pouch back to Spain or the Netherlands where it would be kept safe in the files of the Spanish government. Thus, Cecil had recorded for posterity his noninvolvement in this plot to kill Amy Robsart, and he had ingratiated himself with the Spanish ambassador. Cecil also realized that the minister, while reporting to his king, could not reveal such information to Elizabeth or the English court. If he did reveal such information, Cecil would simply deny he was the source and say that many lies were circulating about Elizabeth and Robert.

Dispatches from foreign diplomats back to their home countries are often invaluable sources of information. While they may be biased by the particular foreign interpretation of events, these dispatches do have advantages. They are often observations of non-participants who had no interest the outcome of events, but perhaps more importantly, the documents are safely stored away from those who might have an interest in destroying an accurate record of events. A difficulty is that they require a great deal of tedious reading of handwritten dispatches in a foreign language; nevertheless, valuable insights into the Elizabethan period exist in foreign dispatches and nowhere else.

Court was at Windsor Palace September 6, 1560, a Friday. De Quadra had a conversation with William Cecil. Following his audience with the Queen, he wrote in his dispatch:

> After my conversation with the Queen, I met the Secretary Cecil, whom I knew to be in disgrace. Lord Robert, I was aware, was endeavoring to deprive him of his place. He said that the Queen was conducting herself in such a way that he thought of retiring. He said it was a bad sailor who did not enter a port if he saw a storm coming on, and he clearly foresaw the ruin of the realm through Robert's intimacy with the Queen, who surrendered all affairs to him and meant to marry him. He said he should ask leave to go home, though he thought they would cast him into the Tower first. He ended by begging me in God's name to point out to the Queen the effect of her misconduct and to persuade her not to abandon business entirely, but to look to her realm; and then he repeated to me twice over that Lord Robert would be better in paradise than here.

> Last of all he said that *they were thinking of destroying Lord Robert's wife.* They had given out that she was ill, but she was not ill at all; *she was very well and taking care not to be poisoned.*[32] [*Italics* added]

The next day, Saturday, September 7, was the Queen's birthday, and the ambassador spoke with the Queen when she returned from hunting:

> The Queen told me on her return from hunting that Lord Robert's wife was dead, or nearly so, and begged me to say nothing about it.[33]

On September 8, the day after the Queen's conversation foretelling the death, Amy Robsart was found dead at Cumnor Hall at the foot of a staircase. In a postscript, the ambassador adds to his previous note:

> Since this was written the Queen has published the death of Lord Robert's wife and has said in Italian, *Si ba rotto il collo*. She must have fallen down a staircase.[34]

The implication is that Elizabeth knew of plans to murder Amy Robsart in advance. She intimated that something was going to happen, and then the next day, despite the travel times in Elizabethan England, she knew the cause of death. As the building had only a ground floor and one story above, Amy Robsart would have had to fall down the entire flight and land in such a way as to break her neck. Amy was a youthful twenty-seven at the time of the incident, and falling down one flight of stairs so severely that she would break her neck was unlikely.

The whole matter is lost in a fog of euphemisms and evasions. For example, one historian calls the circumstances of Amy Robsart's death "mysterious," when everyone in the country at the time believed Dudley wanted to poison his wife, and the ambassador's reports directly implicate the Queen and Dudley. Another historian invents evidence that Amy had cancer that made her bones very brittle. The Spanish ambassador's reports are very hard evidence that the Queen knew in advance of the impending death of Amy Robsart. One English historian, Mary M. Luke, in her book, *Gloriana, The Years of Elizabeth I,* deals with it by denial:

> The Spanish ambassador's letter is misleading. In the phrases "after my conversation with the Queen, I met with the Secretary Cecil" and "the day after his conversation" his chronology becomes blurred. If De Quadra meant to imply—as it appears—that he spoke with Elizabeth on the sixth, with Cecil immediately afterward and again on the following day—which would have been Saturday, the seventh—then Elizabeth told him that Amy "was dead or nearly so" *before the accident had even occurred*—a fact so incredibly unbelievable as to negate itself.[35]

In other words, the direct written record of a foreign ambassador *cannot be true.* The author gives no reason why it *cannot be true* because she cannot express the hidden assumption of English history: *"If it casts doubt on the morality of Queen Elizabeth, it is automatically untrue."*

Further, the passage refers to the death as an "accident" when De Quadra and Cecil were talking about Robert Dudley's plan to murder his wife, Amy Robsart. This is an incident of dissembling if there ever was one, yet Luke follows a much-traveled route in denying the actual historical record. The myth of the Virgin Queen has been built up over the years. When evidence appears to contradict it, that evidence is simply denied. This author later discusses the possibility that the Queen was referring to Amy Robsart being ill. In her book, the passages in De Quadra's report that state reports of Amy Robsart's illness were false ("but she was not ill at all") are omitted. This would appear to be a case of Luke misleading the reader by knowingly withholding vital information and then making a conclusion that would be seen as plainly false if full information was available. Typical of a defense attorney, the author blames the victim for her own tragic end:

> In the words of modern usage, they might have meant that Amy was an emotionally unbalanced person, a 'social misfit' as she might be called today, one who was 'her own worst enemy.'[36]

Using "unblinkered historical imagination," she then proposes the notion that Amy Robsart committed suicide by throwing herself down a flight of stairs:

> But a fall downstairs is no way to kill anyone, and a professional murderer would have sought a method more certain. Yet Amy, if bent on suicide, might have thought it a very good method indeed—and had succeeded beyond her wildest and warped expectations.[37]

Yes, one would conclude that a professional murderer would not try to kill someone by throwing them down a flight of stairs, but for the same reason, one would conclude that someone bent on suicide would not use this as a method of ending a life either. Most likely, Amy Robsart was strangled and then thrown down the stairs to give some cover to the murder. Simply being found strangled with no possibility of an accidental death would lead straight to Robert Dudley with no other explanation. In an unblinkered denial of all the relevant facts of the case, Mary Luke concludes:

> Whatever the reason for the death of poor, misguided Amy Dudley, there is no verifiable conclusion other than the jury's ultimate decision of accidental death.[38]

This historian simply gives more elaborate explanations and excuses. In a deliberate twisting of the available evidence, the victim becomes responsible for her own death because the Queen and her lover cannot be responsible.[d]

A pamphlet of the time gives a view of what the population thought at the time of the murder, and most likely, believed to be the truth:

> When he [Dudley] was in full hope to marry the Queen, he did but send his wife aside to the house of his servant, Forster of Cumnor, where shortly after she had the chance to fall from a pair of stairs and break her neck, but yet without hurting of the hood that stood upon her head.[39]

Dudley acted little like a grieved husband. He went to the trouble only to write to one of his retainers ordering him to investigate the rumors.

---

[d] In fairness to historians of the period, Hugh Ross Williamson, in his book, *Historical Enigmas*, candidly points out the difficulties and implications of the Amy Robsart affair, but his book is not a biography of Elizabeth.

Dudley also did what most prominent suspects do in such cases: He called for an inquest to find the perpetrator of the crime, excluding himself. Amy was buried at Cumnor Hall. In spite of himself, the Earl's chaplain had a hard time keeping the story straight:

> The Queen was once desirous of making him her husband; yet submitted the gratifying her passion for him to prevailing reasons against it: at one time he so far flattered himself in these ambitious views (to which his brother Lord Guildford Dudley, having been near the Crown, [the husband of the unfortunate Lady Jane Grey], might not a little conduce) as to procure his first Lady to be got out of the way, by having her neck broke in a fall down stairs: but this accident raising some suspicion, the Earl caused her to be buried a second time in the University Church at Oxford, with great pomp and solemnity, and her funeral Sermon to be made by his chaplain Dr. Babington, who unhappily tript twice in his Speech by recommending to their memories that virtuous Lady "so pitifully murdered," instead of "so pitifully slain."[40]

Later, there was an inquest that ruled the death was by mischance. Many years later, one of the jurors claimed that he and other jurors had been coerced and bribed into their verdict. At the time there was a furor and uproar in England and abroad over the death of Amy Robsart:

> What religion is this that a subject shall kill his wife and the Prince not only bear withal, but marry with him?[40]

The English pulpits rang with words of admonition for the Queen, and few believed that Amy Robsart's death was accidental. The Queen took reluctant action against Dudley by banishing him from court for a period of months. Nevertheless, Elizabeth and Robert Dudley were firm on their intent to marry.

Dudley's brother-in-law, Sir Henry Sidney, came to De Quadra with a proposal. If Spain would support the marriage of Elizabeth and Dudley, then Dudley would personally lead a delegation to the Council of Trent and thus bring England back into the Catholic fold. While this may not have meant a full return to Catholicism and the rule of the Pope, it was nevertheless a significant step away from the reform religion and religious supremacy of the Crown. One of the conditions of the proposal was better treatment of Catholics in England. A few days after the proposal had been made, Elizabeth broached the subject and acknowledged that Sidney had made his proposal with her knowledge and approval. A delegate from the Pope was on his way to England, and the marriage was to be announced on April 23, 1561, St. George's Day, the proposed marriage having received the blessing of the Papal delegate.

William Cecil quickly fabricated one of his "Catholic plots." He first arrested a priest at Gravesend who, under torture, or the threat thereof, admitted that he was chaplain of Sir Edward Waldgrave and that he had said Mass daily at Waldgrave's house. At the same time, he intercepted a letter from an imprisoned Catholic bishop who wrote of the expectation that the Pope's delegate might effect their release. Cecil then arrested Waldgrave and other prominent Catholics throughout the country. William Cecil created a general alarm and enflamed Protestant fears of a Catholic conspiracy. The delegate from the Pope coming to England could only arouse the suspicions and mistrust of the population, especially the largely Protestant London population. Sir Edward Waldgrave had been one of Queen Mary's Privy Councilors, and the many burnings of Protestant martyrs under Mary's reign were fresh in the minds of the Protestants. When Elizabeth's council met to discuss the reception of the Papal delegate, the council declared that anyone who voted for the delegate's reception would be guilty of treason. This effectively squashed the arrival of the Pope's delegate and Dudley's plan to marry the Queen and ally England more firmly with Catholic Spain.

Cecil had prevented Elizabeth from marrying the man she loved. While Sir William Cecil has been portrayed as the very loyal councilor to Elizabeth, in this case he clearly acted to prevent her from marrying Dudley. The thought of Robert Dudley as king and a closer alliance with the Catholic Spain was too much for even this loyal councilor. The idea that Elizabeth never had any true intention of marrying anyone is yet another myth. She loved Robert Dudley, made him a wealthy man, elevated him to the peerage, engaged in a conspiracy to murder his wife, slept with him, most likely had children by him, and maintained a relationship with him throughout her life. Only the actions of William Cecil prevented her from marrying him and making him the de facto king. All of which somehow leaves a sad thought of the unfulfilled love of an unmarried Queen Elizabeth.

During the height of the Princess Diana craze, the princess was covered by every possible news media in London, Europe, and the world. The media reported on every possible detail of the lives of the princess, her husband, and other royalty. Yet there was hardly ever a negative word said about Queen Elizabeth II, her behavior toward Diana, or the raising of the Queen's children. The Queen in the British press and for the rest of the world was simply above reproach or censure. When dealing with a person's individual mother or an icon that represents the national mother, very deep, powerful feelings are evoked. It is difficult, if not impossible, to be objective. Similarly, it is very difficult for the press or historians to criticize someone who represents a version of the national, historical mother.

Queen Elizabeth I realized that she represented a national icon to the English nation during her lifetime, and she capitalized on her sex and maternal role in her politics. In an address to Parliament in 1559, she said, as reported by the contemporary historian of the period, William Camden, in his *Annals of Queen Elizabeth*:

> But not that the publick Care of governing the Kingdom is laid upon me, to draw upon me also the Cares of Marriage may seem a point of inconsiderate Folly. Yea, to satisfie you, I have already joyned my self in Marriage to an Husband, namely, the Kingdom of England. And behold (said she, which I marvell ye have forgotten,) the Pledge of this my Wedlock and Marriage with my Kingdom.
>
> (And therewith she drew the Ring from her Finger, and shewed it, wherewith at her Coronation she had in a set form of words solemnly given her self in Marriage to her Kingdom.)[42]

It is worth pointing out that William Camden was directly influenced and most likely financed by William Cecil:

> Above eighteen Years since William Cecyll, Baron of Burghley, Lord High Treasurer of England, (when full little I thought of any such Business) imparted to me, first his own, and then the Queen's Rolls, Memorials and Records, willing me to compile from thence an Historical Account of the first Beginnings of the Reign of Queen Elizabeth: with what Intent I know not, unless, while he had a desire to eternize the Memory of that Renowned Queen.[43]

In other words, the history of the period was under the direction, or at least influence, of the chief architect of Tudor chicanery and deception, William Cecil. Camden goes on to record Elizabeth as saying:

> And to me it shall be a full satisfaction, both for the memorial of my Name, and for my Glory also, if when I shall let my last breath, it be ingraven upon my marble Tomb, *"Here lieth Elizabeth, which Reigned a Virgin, and died a Virgin."*[44]

It does not seem possible that it can be made any clearer that the Virgin Queen myth was a deliberate piece of political propaganda, created by William Cecil to establish and strengthen the Tudor reign. As with most political propaganda, the historical facts are irrelevant.

When Elizabeth was stricken with smallpox in 1562 and close to death, she named Robert Dudley as Lord Protector, in effect the King of England, as there was no clear heir to the throne. In 1564, she made him Earl of Leicester and awarded huge land grants to the earl. In 1580, he went to the Netherlands to head English forces against the Spanish, and when threatened with the invasion of the Armada, she made him general of the English land forces that prepared for the invasion.

Elizabeth was furious when she found out he had married the beautiful and very pregnant Lettice Knollys and threw him into a stockade at the Greenwich Palace. The only reason that Robert Dudley publicly married was the action of Lettice's father. Her father knew that Robert Dudley had previously secretly married a lady who had born his child and then declared the marriage to have never taken place. He foiled any possibility of this repeating itself by forcing Robert Dudley to marry his daughter in a public ceremony.

Robert Dudley died in September 1588 shortly after the defeat of Spanish Armada in July of that year.[e] He had written a letter to the Queen a few months before his death, which she kept in a box at her bedside. It was labeled "his last letter." Elizabeth forced his widow, Lettice Knollys, whom she despised, to sell most of her property to repay the debts owed the Crown, but she did not take into account the jewels, which he gave to Elizabeth in his will. William Camden chronicles the relationship in his epitaph for Robert Dudley:

> ... under Queen Elizabeth, (to whom by reason of a certain Conjunction and Affinity of their Minds, and that haply through a hidden Conspiracy and Consent of their stars, [which the Greek Astrologers term *Synastria*] he was most dear,) ...

> In a word, people talked openly in his Commendation, but privately he was ill spoken of by the greater part. But whereas he was in the Queen's Debt, his Goods were sold a publick Outcry: for the Queen, though in other things

---

[e] Americans celebrate Thanksgiving in commemoration of the Pilgrims on the third Thursday of November. American history portrays the event as originating with a spontaneous display of gratitude to their Native American benefactors by the Pilgrims in 1621. American history does not ask the unsettling question of why the Pilgrims waited three months from the end of the harvest in late August or early September until the cold winds were blowing at the end of November.

The Spanish Armada was defeated in July 1588. Robert Dudley, the Queen's favorite died in September and Elizabeth had a religious service in St. Paul's Cathedral on November 28, 1588. It was a Thanksgiving for defeat of the Spanish Armada. However, this Thanksgiving custom goes back even earlier. When Henry VIII was delayed from his return from Calais due to bad weather, England celebrated his return on November 24, 1532. The Queen built upon this date for her celebration. The Pilgrims were celebrating this Thanksgiving in the New World. In addition, their celebration coincided with the Pequot winter festival at the end of November. Thus, the American Thanksgiving's origins had little to do with a spontaneous show of gratitude to the Native Americans.

The point of this factoid is that each country's history is a collection of facts and omissions to fit the socio-political-emotional needs of the country. It would be hardly fitting or appropriately patriotic to celebrate the defeat of the Spanish Armada in homes throughout the United States. Elizabethan history, the history of Shakespeare, and in fact, all history is written within a cultural and historical construct that determines what is acceptable and what is not. Facts that contradict that view are either minimized or simply ignored.

she were favorable enough, yet seldom or never did she remit the Debts owing to her treasury.[45] [brackets as in original]

PRINCE OF THE REALM

Several strands of evidence point to the fact that Edward de Vere was placed in the foster home of John de Vere and raised as Edward de Vere, 17th Earl of Oxford. This evidence includes the forced circumstances of John de Vere's marriage to Margery Golding; the lack of any birth records for Edward; the coincidental appearance of a "sister," Mary; the interest of Sir William Cecil in the affairs of John de Vere; and the circumstances of John de Vere's death. John de Vere was murdered when he was no longer needed to serve as a foster parent for Edward de Vere. By then, William Cecil's position as Master of the Wards gave him firm control over the young man's future. The Queen, in contrast to her selling all other wardships, retained control of Edward's wardship. The Queen would determine whom the young man would marry.

The third criterion mentioned in the introduction for evidence of Edward de Vere as Elizabeth's child is whether a changeling child was raised differently within that small circle close to the mother that indicated a maternal relationship with the parent. Were any special privileges given to the child? Did the child seem to obtain special treatment from a possible parent? Was there a special interest taken in the child beyond what might be normally expected? Was there a deference given to the child that cannot be explained?

This criterion is satisfied by the events in the childhood of Edward de Vere and, as will be shown in the next chapter, Oxford was not raised as an orphaned son of an earl; instead, he was raised as a Prince of the Realm.

A Not So Brief Chronicle

Horses Seven Score[a]

> The iij day of September cam rydyng owt of Essex from [the funeral] of the
> yerle of Oxford ys father the yonge yerle of Oxford, with vij-skore horse all
> in blake throughe London and Chepe and Ludgatt, and so to Tempulle bare,
> and so to *(blank)*, be-twyn v and vj of the cloke at after-none.[1]

As the sun set over the Thames on September 3, 1562, the greatest
literary mind the world would ever know rode into London accompanied
by 140 men on horse wearing the Blue Boar insignia. Edward de Vere,
17th Earl of Oxford, was fourteen years old.

Crowds lined the streets to watch the dramatic entry of the young lord
who was now the 17th Earl of Oxford after the death of John de Vere. Was
this the entrance of an earl's son or was it the entrance of a Prince of the
Realm? One hundred and forty men was a sizeable number considering
only a small number of palace guards protected the Queen. When
Elizabeth entered the city of London as a princess to become Queen, 200
men accompanied her. By any standard of the day, Londoners knew that a
person of considerable importance had entered. His final destination in
London was the large house with the imposing gardens of Sir William
Cecil, where he would live as a ward of the Crown.

It is not certain exactly where Oxford was raised before moving to
London. While it might be that he lived with John de Vere and Margery
Golding at Hedingham Castle in his early years, Oxford may have stayed
in Sir Thomas's home in 1554 when he was six years old. There was a
letter from Sir Thomas Smith to William Cecil concerning Oxford, which
indicates Cecil's oversight of Edward de Vere. One biographer reports
that Oxford lived at the home of Sir Thomas Smith until the death of John
de Vere in 1562, but this does not appear to be certain. When John de
Vere died and Oxford moved to William Cecil's house in London, Sir
Thomas Smith's educational relationship with Edward de Vere ended, and
Sir Thomas Smith went to France as a diplomatic envoy.

---

[a] This chapter covers a period of over forty years, an inadequate amount of space to fully
detail Oxford's life. A much fuller description of the events and life of Edward de Vere is
contained in *The Mysterious William Shakespeare* by Charlton Ogburn, which can only be
recommended. In addition, *This Star of England* by Charlton Ogburn Sr. and his wife, Dorothy
Ogburn, gives 1,200 pages of admirable detail about the relation between the man and his works.

Oxford had studied the classics of Greece and Rome and had matriculated at Queen's College, Cambridge, when he was eleven years old, and there are indications Oxford knew Sir Thomas's son at Queen's College. Exactly how long Edward was at Cambridge is uncertain. It is certain that one of his tutors was Sir Thomas Smith, who was a fellow of Queen's College and at one time held the Chair in Civil Law at Cambridge University. In his early twenties, he was a lecturer in Greek, and a professor of Civil Law at twenty-seven. He later became Vice

Burghley's Record of Oxford's Instruction	
7 to 7:30	Dancing
7:30 to 8	Breakfast
8 to 9	French
9 to 10	Latin
10 to 10:30	Writing and drawing
Then common prayers, and so to dinner.	
1 to 2	Cosmography
2 to 3	Latin
3 to 4	French
4 to 4:30	Penmanship
All the rest of the day to be spent in riding, shooting, dancing, walking, and other commendable exercises, saving the time for Prayer.[2]	

Chancellor of the University. Smith had spent a year and a half studying law in Padua, Italy, the center for Italian law. It can only be imagined that an intellect and scholar such as Sir Thomas Smith would have a great impact on the young Oxford and serve as an intellectual and scholarly inspiration for the young man.

Sir Thomas Smith was also the individual who was secretary to Edward Seymour, and he was the one who interrogated Kat Ashley. Both Sir Thomas Smith and William Cecil served as advisors to Edward Seymour (Lord Protector during Edward VI's reign). Smith and Cecil had a long relationship that began when Cecil was a student of Smith's at Cambridge. Sir Thomas was the Principal Secretary under the Protectorship of Edward Seymour, and Smith fell from influence upon Seymour's fall from power and execution. At that point, his former pupil William Cecil was able to align himself with the new Protectorship, and Cecil eclipsed Sir Thomas forevermore. Smith later became one of Elizabeth's councilors along with Sir William Cecil, but he never regained his former influential positions.

The early participation of Sir Thomas Smith in Oxford's education confirms the involvement of William Cecil in the young earl's education and the fact that Oxford's education was overseen by people in very high places. William Cecil was a consummate politician and master strategist. He would not have wasted his time on the son of an earl of the old aristocracy unless there were greater implications. In addition, John de Vere, the 16th Earl of Oxford, had no intellectual accomplishments and few political or religious connections to the Protestant university scholars. He would seem an unlikely person to so educate Edward de Vere.

STUDY AT THE CECIL HOUSE

William Cecil's house on the Strand was no simple house by any standard definition of a domestic dwelling. The sheer size of the house obviously indicates there was plenty of room for another ward or two. William Cecil had some eighty servants in the household, not including those who attended him at court. His expenses were estimated between £30 and £50 per week, depending on whether or not Cecil was in residence. It is difficult to translate money into current values, but roughly, it might be said that his residence was costing, in current value, at the low side of £10,000 per week, or about $15,000. This expense sounds enormous, and it was, but the Cecil House was much more than a private residence. It was a political center of power, authority, and learning. A multitude of servants, retainers, and scholars who served Cecil in some capacity resided at the Cecil House.

Other wards of the Queen later joined Oxford to live at Cecil's residence. Financially, this made little difference to Sir William Cecil, especially when he charged his wards for their maintenance and upkeep. In addition, Sir William had a direct influence in this position on the education and upbringing of many of the future nobility that would govern England. The education was rigorous and Protestant. Whatever William Cecil's faults were in administering his wards' estates, he must be credited with establishing one of the best private schools in Europe. The record is uncertain, but William Cecil was more interested in the political influence he might acquire by his association with his young wards than in financial gain. Other young nobles, not under the wardship system, frequently sought admission to Cecil's school:

> There can be no doubt that, at Cecil House in the Strand, there existed the best school for statesmen in Elizabethan England, perhaps in all Europe ... It was a highly selective school to which only very fortunate young men gained admission.[3]

William Cecil was dedicated to the Protestant notions of gaining education and knowledge through study; this was shared by his second wife, Mildred Cooke, who was the young woman who exceeded Elizabeth in her knowledge of Greek. Roger Ascham said that Mildred could speak Greek as fluently as she could speak English:

If the Cecil House could attract the flower of English youth, it could also attract some of the best scholars of the day. Lawrence Nowell, Dean of Litchfield, was a tutor there; so was Robert Ramsden, Archdeacon of York and chaplain to Burghley; the scholar Sylvius Frisius likewise joined the staff. John Harte, the Chester Herald, one of the earliest spelling reformers and a pioneer of shorthand in this country, exercised a general supervision of the wards. Roger Ascham [the former tutor of Elizabeth] came and stayed with Cecil.[4]

In Cecil's school, Oxford continued to receive a classical education in Greek and Latin as well as learning the contemporary languages Italian and French. Dancing, drawing, and other studies were also part of the curriculum. This is not to say that Oxford's education started at this school. By thirteen, he had written a letter in contemporary French that survives today in the British Library. The Author, later known as William Shakespeare, received this educational foundation under the guidance of William Cecil. Without this classical foundation and education, Shakespeare would obviously not be the Shakespeare that is known today. The wide range of classical knowledge, the study of the law, and the knowledge of botany, astronomy, and medicine would not have been in the Author's grasp without his rigorous studies under Cecil. William Cecil's library was one of the finest in England, if not the finest, and the young Edward de Vere had access to it:

Central to the question of what Oxford might have learned while with Burghley is the size and nature of his [Burghley's] library. What can be gleaned from the records about this library? Martin Hume tells us, for example, that Burghley was an insatiable book buyer and eagerly purchased any new books from France sent him by Sir William Pickering and Sir John Mason (48 et seq.). Eventually Burghley's library came to include books published in many different European cities: Rome, Vienna, Hamburg, Antwerp, Hanover, London, Paris, Florence, Venice, Oxford, Geneva, Edinburgh, Wittenberg and many more. This brings Oxford from the age of twelve into contact with upwards of 1700 titles (some in multi-volumes) and approximately 249 manuscripts.[5]

Dean Keith Simonton stresses in *Greatness: Who Makes History and Why* that those making their mark on the world are omnivorous readers:

For achievers in general, self–education often assumes the form of omnivorous reading. In Terman's study, gifted children read much, read widely, and read hard. By elementary school, they would read a half dozen books per month. The volumes would span challenging topics, such as science, history, biography, poetry, drama, and travel. One study of contemporary luminaries found that at least half were voracious readers from childhood. In fact, early omnivorous reading is associated positively with later eminence. To have read widely is a hallmark of those who become widely read about.[6]

The knowledge the Author exhibits in the works of William Shakespeare has not been an academic area of interest in the past several decades. Pressured by a growing inconsistency between the knowledge of the Author and the known biography of the man from Stratford-upon-Avon, Stratfordian scholars and authors began dumbing Shakespeare down to make the Author fit the biography. While genius may be from an innate set of traits and personal characteristics, knowledge comes from experience and study. The relevant knowledge either from experience or from a superb classical education is not in the biography of the man from Stratford-upon-Avon. To accommodate this, Stratfordian scholars have changed the Author, a genius in intellect with a superb understanding of language and a variety of other subjects, into an untutored artist who was primarily a borrower of other people's ideas. Oxford was the first person of the English Renaissance, and perhaps the last person in the world who knew everything there was to know. There simply does not seem to be another person on the planet, past or present, other than the Earl of Oxford who had the opportunity to acquire the knowledge and education shown in the works of William Shakespeare:

> Specialists in various fields have documented Shakespeare's detailed knowledge of ancient history, archery, art, astrology, astronomy, the Bible, botany, the classics, court politics, coursing, dancing, falconry, fencing, France, heraldry, horsemanship, hunting, Italy, languages, law, literature, medicine, music, ornithology, politics, seamanship, royal tennis, and tournaments.[7]

It was the Protestant strivers for upward mobility who saw education as a means of gaining access to the higher echelons of feudal society. This orientation provided Oxford an education that went far beyond that typically given to most young nobles. However, while one can have a library or leave books on the table, that does not ensure that a child will be a conscientious student, nor a student with the motivation of the young Edward de Vere. There must have been some innate drive in the youth to engage in the most rigorous intellectual activity. Perhaps Albert Einstein's youthful interest in physics or Mozart's dedication to music might serve as comparisons for Edward de Vere's youthful interest and dedication to learning. To give an idea of Edward de Vere's youthful dedication, today we feel that students are accomplished if they learn one foreign language: Edward de Vere by the time he was a young man had mastered at least four: French, Greek, Latin, and Italian. The youthful scholar simply had to devour books in every possible subject, in a variety of languages, to have the residual background knowledge that he easily brings to bear as the mature Author. Sir William Cecil, in his role as advisor to the child, believed that the future monarch should be well educated, and well educated Oxford was, but Oxford's life took a direction that not anyone, even one as wise and crafty as William Cecil, could foretell.

In August 1564, the young Earl received a master's degree at Cambridge University at the age of sixteen.[b] Aristocrats received only masters' degrees as their first degree because a bachelor's degree was considered beneath them. The Queen attended the ceremony. This was the first time she had attended the ceremonies of a university. Robert Dudley and William Cecil also attended. At the ceremony, the Queen addressed the audience in Latin. She again attended such a ceremony when Oxford received a master's of arts degree at Oxford in 1566. The Queen only attended three university commencement ceremonies in her lifetime. The final time was when Henry Wriothesley, 3rd Earl of Southampton was lauded at Oxford University in 1592. The Queen gave orations in Latin at these proceedings.

Stephanie Caruana and Elisabeth Sears perceptively remarked over a decade ago of the motherly interest that Elizabeth took in the young Earl of Oxford:

> When Oxford arrived in London at the age of twelve, Queen Elizabeth was twenty-nine—at the height of her beauty and personal powers. She was old enough to be his mother, and she took delight in his personal talents and achievements, almost as though he were her son.[8]

In 1567, Oxford enrolled in Gray's Inn, which was one of the prominent legal schools of the time. It was a combination of a young gentleman's club and law school. Among those who received this legal training were the young lords who would later need to administer their estates and the affairs of the Crown. Areas of study included estates, heraldry, and inheritance law along with other more common subjects such as tort and criminal law. Ironically, the man who has one of his characters say "Kill all the lawyers" was in fact a lawyer, or at least trained as one. However, this famous saying is generally taken out of context and consequently the irony of the statement is lost. The context is that the words are spoken to the demagogue rebel Jack Cade, who claims to be heir to the throne. Cade wants to replace a civilized society ruled by laws with his own rule of tyranny or rule of the mob. Shakespeare's writings had little sympathy for this point of view, and his sophisticated

---

[b] When referring to Oxford's age, this book will use the year 1548 as his birth date as opposed to the traditional date of 1550 recorded by William Cecil. Obviously, the point of this book is to establish Oxford as the son of Elizabeth who was born in 1548.

legal mind dealt with the problems inherent in the conflict between law (the established rules) and equity (the concept of fairness).

THE COOK IS DEAD

At the age of sixteen, Oxford killed a cook employed by William Cecil. The detractors of the Earl of Oxford have maintained for many years that this showed the fecklessness of the young nobleman, who only averted punishment because of the influence of the powerful William Cecil. The fact that the jury ruled the death a suicide by the man running upon Oxford's sword could only seem the gravest insult and most tortured reasoning. On the other side of the coin, supporters of the Earl of Oxford as William Shakespeare say that the cook might have been a spy of William Cecil's hiding behind the arras and then run through by the young earl, in a scene reminiscent of *Hamlet*.

The facts of the matter seem much more prosaic. The coroner's inquest reads as follows:

> A legally constituted enquiry held at St. Martin's in the Fields in the aforesaid county on the 22nd day of July in the ninth year of the reign of Elizabeth, by the grace of God Queen of England, France, and Ireland, Defender of the Faith etc., before Richard Vale Coroner of the aforesaid Lady Queen in the aforesaid county concerning the appearance of the body of Thomas Brinckenell, yeoman lately of the city of Westminster in the aforesaid county who was found lying dead in that same place, with statements given under oath by John Martin, William Waters, Anthony Harris, John Whitehead, William Besely, Humphrey Mote, John Toyber, John Baves, William Fletcher, Randolph Holinshed, John Bagleyne, Thomas Sedon, George Hedges, James Seward, William Wakefield, James Pykes and Robert Bottell, upright and law-abiding men from the aforesaid county, who say under oath that on the 23rd day of July in the aforesaid ninth year between the hours of one and two o'clock in the afternoon of the same day Edward Duke of Oxford and a certain Edward Baynam, a taylor from the aforesaid city, were together in a certain place called the backyard south of the town house of William Cecil, a soldier, in the parish of St.Clement Danes in the aforesaid county, and had no intention or plan to harm any person then in the same place. One of these, who had a sword made from iron and brass called a foil, was at that time and in the same place sporting with the other who had a similar sword, called a foil, and defending himself in a knowledgeable way. To this same place came the aforesaid Thomas Brinckenell and then in that same place the same Thomas, who was drunk and having difficulty in seeing properly, was led on and tricked by some deceit of the Devil and charged in desperately and fell on the point of the aforesaid sword called a foil, which was worth 11 pence, which the aforesaid Edward Duke of Oxford then and in that same place had in his right hand

and was holding with the intention of sporting, as he alleges, with Rove Cinus.

Then and in the same place the aforesaid Thomas struck himself criminally with the same sword called a foil in the back of his left thigh, stabbed himself, and there and then gave himself a mortal blow with the aforesaid sword four inches deep and one inch wide. The aforesaid Thomas then and there at once died of this mortal blow. The aforesaid witnesses likewise state under oath that the aforesaid Thomas Brickenell killed himself criminally and voluntarily in the aforesaid parish of St. Clements Danes in the aforesaid county and murdered himself to the detriment of the peace, crown and dignity of the aforesaid Lady Queen. Likewise they state that the same Thomas Brinckenell came to his own death neither differently nor in any other way than is stated above. To testify to this matter both the aforesaid Coroner and the aforesaid witnesses have placed their signatures one after the other on this document. Drawn up by me, Richard Vale the Coroner, on the day and year first mentioned above, concerning a self-inflicted injury.[9] [translation by Professor Tom Holland]

Critics and supporters of Oxford seem to have interpreted this incident in light of their own views. The matter was much more mundane, that the cook was drunk, stumbled into the fencing practice and received a fatal wound in his leg. But how he was tricked by 'the deceit of the Devil' or why he stabbed himself in the back of his leg remains difficult to understand. The incident also points out the difficulty of doing historical research of the Elizabethan period. The legal record of this event was in legal Latin, which was usually in the older English-German handwriting and contained legal abbreviations; these documents require special expertise to read and translate.

TO THE JOUSTS!

In 1571, at the age of twenty-three, Oxford came to the attention of the court by winning a tournament. This was a surprising triumph considering that his opponents were older and much more experienced. As reported by the historian John Stow,:

> The first, second, and third of May 1571, was holden at Westminster, before the Queen's Majesty, a solmn joust at the tilt, tournay, and barriers. The challengers were Edward Earl of Oxford, Charles Howard, Sir Henry Lee, and Christopher Hatton, Esq., who all did very valiantly; but the chief honour was given to the Earl of Oxford.[10]

In a letter to Edward Manners, 3rd Earl of Rutland, in June 1571, George Delves describes Oxford at the tournament:

> The Earl of Oxford's livery was crimson velvet, very costly; he himself, and the furniture, was in some more colours, yet he was the Red Knight.[11]

George Delves further reports:

> Lord Oxford performed his challenge at tilt, tourney and barriers, far above expectation of the world....There is no man of life and agility in every respect in the Court but the Earl of Oxford.[12] [c]

Oxford was given the prize of a "tablet of diamonds."[13] There were a number of meanings for the word "tablet," but the most likely is a small notebook with its cover encrusted with diamonds. Oxford would win another such tournament on January 22, 1581. A description of the gaudy display of the Earl of Oxford in this later tournament gives some idea of the ostentatious young earl:

> By the Tilt stoode a stately tent of Orenge tawny Taffeta, curiously imbroidered with Silver and pendents on the Pinacles very sightly to behold. From forth this Tent came the noble Earl of Oxenford in rich gilt Armour, and sat down under a great high Bay tree, the whole stocke branches, and leaves whereof, were all gilded over, that nothing but Gold could be discerned. By the tree stood twelve tilting staves, all which likewise were gilded clean over. After a solemn sound of more sweet music, he mounts his courser, very richly caparisoned. In the window high above stands her Highness, all to see.[14]

Christopher Hatton was an opponent of Oxford's in the first tournament. In 1573, Hatton became Captain of the Gentlemen's Pensioners; it was said:

---

[c] In Spenser's *Faerie Queen,* the Red Cross Knight represents St. George, the patron saint of England.

Mr. Hatton had more recourse unto Her Majesty in her Privy Chamber than reason would suffer, if she were so virtuous and well inclined as some noiseth her.[15]

Elizabeth always called Hatton her "Mutton" for his "modest sweetness of manner." Judging from the foregoing portraits and Elizabeth's relation with Thomas Seymour and later Sir Walter Raleigh, there was a certain type of handsome, au courant, swashbuckling man who appealed to her feminine senses. Hatton was devoted to the Queen and never married. Elizabeth had nicknames for many at court: Oxford she called her "boar," and Hatton advised Elizabeth to beware of Oxford when he wrote her:

God bless you for ever; the branch of the sweetest bush I will wear and bear to my life's end: God witness I feign not. It is a gracious favour most dear and welcome unto me: reserve it to the Sheep: he hath no tooth to bite, where the Boar's tusk may both rase and tear."[16]

Hatton had also written the Queen a note expressing his undying affection and signed it with an "x" covered with an ^ for "Hat-ten."

One can only imagine what a mind like Oxford's must have thought about this schoolboy drivel, but it was endearing to the Queen, so Hatton must have had his charms. Hatton was perhaps the only consort of the Queen's to have never married; whatever his faults, he was loyal only to her. At this 1571 tournament, Hatton won a bell and chain, which he often wears in his portraits. In a meaningless little piece of dialogue, Oxford mocks Hatton, with a reference to Hatton's ball and chain that would be clearly recognized by all members of the Court. This was a small chuckle at the expense of Christopher Hatton:

DROMIO OF SYRACUSE
Not on a band, but on a stronger thing;
A chain, a chain! Do you not hear it ring?

ADRIANA
What, the chain?

DROMIO OF SYRACUSE
No, no, the bell: 'tis time that I were gone:
It was two ere I left him, and now the clock strikes one.
The Comedy of Errors, Act 4, Sc. 2

In 1578, Oxford invested in a scheme to explore the northwest portion of the New World. He was apparently defrauded the amount of his investment, some £3,000. In this sense, the debtor was short or "shy" in gambling terms of his repayment. The speculator to whom Oxford lent the money was Michael Lok. Hence, the name "Shylock" for the usurious moneylender. There is no other record in literature or in fact of this being the name of a character, or a family name. Oxford lost this money about the same time his rival, Christopher Hatton, made a fortune from the exploits of Sir Francis Drake. This was a painful financial blow to Oxford, indeed; for Christopher Hatton, it was a very large chuckle.

MARRY MY DAUGHTER

William Cecil was a formidable power in this real life game of political chess because he could see deeper and plan ahead more moves. Where others saw only a jumble of human emotions, errors, misdeeds, and confusion, he saw patterns of behavior and opportunities. He was intelligent and ruthless in acting for England's and the Cecils' interests, which he saw as virtually the same. Seeing this far into the game, Cecil often made small moves that years later would have large consequences. His guardianship of Edward de Vere shows how far ahead Cecil would plan and how he could find a route to advance himself and his family. Whereas others might have seen an illegitimate son of Elizabeth as a personal and political disaster, William Cecil made it into an opportunity to have Elizabeth always indebted to him. Cecil became the keeper of the hidden secret, and he used this knowledge to keep a hold over Elizabeth throughout his life. The strategic planning in this era of political alliances through marriage involved planning for children's marriages before they were in their teens as parents today might plan for the college education of their offspring.

Cecil's brilliant political strategy was due in great part to his ruthless self-interest. He could see so far ahead because he was dispassionate about the personalities and lives that he was dealing with. Cecil had no more qualms about murdering someone to advance his goals (as with John de Vere) than a chess player has over knocking a knight off the board. As long as people were useful to him for his political game, he maintained relationships and friendships. However, if someone was no longer useful to his and his family's ends, he could and would dispose of them. Human kindness, attachments, and the needs of others were not considerations for him. His relationship with Edward de Vere was solely and only for the advancement of himself and his family. There was never a personal or paternal relationship between himself and the young man despite his life-long association with Oxford. When it finally became obvious that William Cecil would not gain the royal status for his family that he so avidly sought, he would turn on Oxford and attempt to ruin him financially.

In 1544, Henry VIII's Parliament passed the Act of Succession, which declared that in the event that Edward died without an heir and Mary Tudor likewise, then the crown would fall to Elizabeth and then to her children. The key clause in this following excerpt is "laufully begotten." This explicitly excludes any illegitimate children Elizabeth might have:

> The said Imperiall Crowne and other the pmisses shal be to the Ladye Elizabeth the Kings seconde daughter and to the ***heires of the bodie of the saide Lady Elizabeth laufully begotten***.[17] [*Italics* added]

In 1571, an Act of Treason was passed by Parliament (*Statutes Made in Parliament, begun to be holden at Westminster, on the Second Day of April, In the THIRTEENTH Year of the Reign of Q. Elizabeth, An Acte whereby certayne Offences bee made Treason*), which declared various and sundry things to be treason against the Queen. For example, discussing the Queen's death became a treasonous offense. This act is listed first in *The Statues of the Realm* without a date. It may have been passed in April at the beginning of the session, or it could have been past later. It may be listed first because it touched directly on the Queen, not because it was chronologically first.

This act in its convoluted language and logic specifically reversed the previous Act of Succession. The key phrase "laufully begotten" was dropped. Instead, heirs to the throne could now be "the naturall yssue of her Ma'j body." Paragraph five is the crucial change in succession:

> And for the avoydyng of contentious and seditious spreading abrode of Tytles to the Succession of the Crowne of this Realme to the dysturbyng of the comon quiet of the Realme; Bee yt enacted by the aucthoritie aforesaid, That whosoever shall hereafter duryng the Lyef of o' said Sovaigne Ladye, by any Booke or Worke prynted or written, dyrectly & expresly declare and affyrme at any tyme before the same be by Acte of Parlyament of this Realme established and affyrmed, that any one pticul' pson whosoever it be, is our ought to be the ryght Heire & Successor to the Queenes Matie [majesty] that nowe is (whome God longe preserve) ***except the same be the naturall yssue of her Ma'j Body*** or shall willfully set upp in open place publishe or spreade any Bookes or Scrowles to that effect, or shall print bynde or put to sale, or utter or cause to be prynted bounde or put to sale or uttered any such Booke or Wrytynge wittinglye, that he or they theire Abbetto's and Counselors, & evy of them, shall for the fyrste Offence suffer ymprysoment of one whole yere, and forfayet halfe his Goodes.[18] [*Italics* added]

The summary explanation on the side of the document states:

> Punishment on printing or publishing that any particular Person, not so declared by Act of Parliament, is Heir & Successor to the Queen, except her issue; 1st Offence, One Year's Imprisonment, &c. 2d Offence, Premunire.[19]

In other words, it was unlawful for anyone to publish or declare that anyone was the legitimate heir to Elizabeth, "*except the same be the naturall yssue of her Ma'j Body.*" Someone who was, or someone who might be in the future, the natural issue of the Queen's body can publish the fact that he or she is the "*ryght Heire & Successor to the Queenes Majestie.*" This person or persons were given specific exemptions by this act of Parliament, which on the face of it was absurd. Elizabeth had no recognized children, lawful or unlawful, and she was reaching an age where marriage and children were unlikely.

The act was convoluted legal language, but it was obscure for a purpose. The complexity of the language hides the momentous change in succession and opens up the possibility for an heir to the throne from Elizabeth, even an illegitimate one. This law was passed even though there had never been an acknowledged illegitimate child from Elizabeth, and it would hardly seem that Parliament was writing this law for the possibility that the Queen might have an illegitimate child in the future.

The more important point is that the act in one stroke made Edward de Vere, 17th Earl of Oxford, the heir to the throne, legitimate offspring of Elizabeth or not. Before this, even if Oxford was her son, he was still not the heir to the thrown according to Henry's Act of Succession of 1544 because he was not "laufully begotten." If Elizabeth had given birth to other illegitimate children, they too would have become legal heirs to the throne by this act.

As Elizabeth's most powerful minister, only William Cecil had both the motive and the power to influence Parliament to change the succession to the throne. He changed the line of succession in a way that was not immediately apparent, and this act of Parliament does not have this stated as its intent. Rather, it was in a clever wording of an act ostensibly written to protect the Queen's security that Oxford becomes an heir to the throne. William Cecil had marriage plans for Edward de Vere.

On Christmas Day 1571, Edward de Vere, 17th Earl of Oxford, was married in Westminster Cathedral under the watchful eye of Queen Elizabeth and First Secretary William Cecil. Within a year, Cecil had changed the order of succession to the throne to make Oxford heir, and completed the marriage of his daughter, Anne Cecil, to Oxford, placing her directly in line to be Queen of England. As reported in a letter by Lord St. John to the Earl of Rutland:

> The Earl of Oxford hath gotten him a wife—or at the least a wife hath caught him; this is Mistress Anne Cecil; whereto the Queen hath given her consent, and the which hath caused great weeping, wailing, and sorrowful cheer of those that had hope to have that golden day. Thus you may see

whilst that some triumph with olive branches, others follow the chariot with willow garlands.[20]

Queen Elizabeth made Sir William Cecil a noble, Baron Burghley, so that the disparity in rank between the Earl of Oxford and the daughter of a mere knight would not be so great. William Cecil was the only commoner raised to the peerage in Elizabeth's forty-five year reign.

A STAR-CROSSED DISASTER

The marriage was a star-crossed disaster that provided untold grief to all parties involved: Anne, Oxford, William Cecil, and the Queen. Oxford resisted the marriage, or at least the first ceremony was scheduled for September 21st at William Cecil's residence but the bridegroom fled to the Continent. The powerful incentive to the marriage must have been that Oxford would be the legitimate heir. The date of the Act of Treason is uncertain, but appears likely to have been after September and used as an inducement for Oxford to marry Anne Cecil. It appears doubtful that Oxford would have trusted William Cecil to pass such a law after the marriage.

A written record of the events surrounding the marriage comes from William Cecil in a letter to Edward Manners,[d] 3rd Earl of Rutland. (Edward Manners and Edward de Vere were both wards of the Queen in William Cecil's household.) The letter is so transparently self-serving that one can hardly read it with a straight face. William Cecil claims that he had no aspirations for his daughter and it was Oxford who insisted on the marriage. The ponderous speech doubles back on itself and mires itself in its own redundancies, can only remind one of the verbose Polonius, in whose mouth Oxford puts the ironic quip "Brevity is the soul of wit." Neither Polonius nor William Cecil was brief:

> I think it doth seem strange to your Lordship to hear of a purposed determination in my Lord of Oxford to marry with my daughter; and so before his Lordship moved it to me I might have thought it, if any other had moved it to me himself. For at his own motion I could not well imagine what to think, considering I never meant to seek it nor hoped of it. And yet reason

---

[d] Some Oxfordians have entertained the idea that Edward Manners was the twin brother of Edward de Vere (that is, Elizabeth had given birth to twins in 1548), but that is beyond the scope of this book. This author does not have any factual evidence to indicate this could be true. It is only because Edward de Vere is of historical interest as William Shakespeare that sufficient historical evidence has been uncovered to indicate the true circumstances of his birth and life. Whether there were twin Edwards is a question that can be left for future historians to explore. It might be pointed out that changeling children and separated twins are a motif of William Shakespeare.

moved me to think well of my Lord, and to acknowledge myself greatly beholden to him, as indeed I do. Truly, my Lord, after I was acquainted of the former intention of a marriage with Master Philip Sidney, whom always I loved and esteemed, I was fully determined to have of myself moved no marriage for my daughter until she should have been near sixteen, that with moving I might also conclude. And yet I thought it not inconvenient in the meantime, being free to hearken to any motion made by such others as I should have cause to like. Truly, my Lord, my goodwill serves me to have moved such a matter as this in another direction than this is, but having more occasion to doubt of the issue of the matter, I did forbear, and in mine own conceit I could have as well liked there as in any other place in England. Percase your Lordship may guess where I mean, and so shall I, for I will name nobody. Now that the matter is determined betwixt my Lord of Oxford and me, I confess to your Lordship I do honour him so dearly from my heart as I do my own son, and in any case that may touch him for his honour and weal, I shall think him mine own interest therein. And surely, my Lord, by dealing with him I find that which I often heard of your Lordship, that there is much more in him of understanding than any stranger to him would think. And for my own part I find that whereof I take comfort in his wit and knowledge grown by good observation.[21]

The marriage joined the second oldest English title to the emerging Protestant class that William Cecil represented. Given all the Queen's thoughts about nobility and the importance of rank, it is more likely that William Cecil had to persuade the Queen to force this marriage. It is less likely that the marriage would have been her inspiration or that she would be the driving force behind it. The marriage united in a devil's bond perhaps the two most opposite personalities in England, that of the artistic, arrogant, agnostic, flamboyant, spendthrift nobleman and the conservative, power-hungry, dour Protestant. In was a relationship born in hell and played out on the theatrical stages of the world in the relationships of Hamlet, Gertrude, Polonius, and Ophelia.

One difficulty of ordinary minds observing truly brilliant ones is the tendency to reduce the problem to an ordinary level of understanding and knowledge of the situation and then to attribute an error or mistake to the brilliant mind. The majority of historians of the period agree that William Cecil was the most astute statesman of the time and that his personal intelligence made England a world power. Yet, in the same breath, they uniformly regard William Cecil's promotion of the marriage of his daughter, Anne Cecil, to the Earl of Oxford, as a "mistake." Here they reduce the complexity of Cecil's thinking to their own understanding and do not search for deeper motives. According to conventional history, Cecil married his daughter to the headstrong 17th Earl of Oxford for no good reason, and the marriage proved to be a disaster. In a time when daughters were ways to enhance the power and property of a family, this would have been an unthinkable mistake for William Cecil and not a very likely one for him to make. Traditional historical interpretation of the marriage misses the point:

> It was an ill-starred match. Burghley, for once, allowed his uncanny ability for judging character to be blinded by social ambition. The Earl of Oxford was mercurial, eccentric, extravagant, and violent. He took an extreme dislike to both his wife and his father-in-law and remained a thorn in the flesh of the older man all his lifetime. Burghley had hoped that his son-in-law would mature in a worthy representative of the ancient aristocracy. Oxford had hope for office and power far in excess of his deserts, or what Burghley as a responsible statesman could offer. Both were disappointed but the fault lay in Oxford.[22]

It is ironic that William Cecil recognized the importance of a good marriage to the fortunes of a man, but still forced such a marriage on his daughter and Oxford. In his precepts to his son, he writes:

> When it shall please God to bring thee to man's estate, use great providence and circumspection in the choice of thy wife, for from thence may spring all thy future good or ill; and it is an action like a stratagem in war where man can err but once.[23]

Despite his solid advice to his son, Thomas, he arranged a political marriage that was unwanted by the prospective bridegroom and could only be agreed to by the prospective bride. Their interests or desires in the matter were simply not considered relevant. Marriage among the aristocrats was not a personal matter but a political matter to increase fortunes and strengthen political alliances.

One line of thinking to explain why Oxford would agree to marry someone so beneath his station is that he would not consummate the marriage nor produce any heirs. Under these circumstances, he might later annul the marriage on the legal grounds that the marriage had never been consummated. If the portrayal of Anne Cecil as Ophelia in *Hamlet* is a correct interpretation, the brilliant, flamboyant Earl would have had little in common with the sweet girl who was totally dominated by her father. Yet without William Cecil, Oxford had no real support for the argument that he was the son of Elizabeth. If Elizabeth died suddenly (which was always a possibility) and William Cecil did not support him as heir to the throne, his position was untenable. Without William Cecil's support, Oxford had no chance for the throne. The Queen and William Cecil were very successful in hiding the identity of Edward de Vere, so without William Cecil's support, any claims made solely by Oxford would have been regarded as sheer fabrications of a power-hungry artist-courtier.

Oxford regarded his own marriage for exactly what it was, a political marriage. He lived at court apart from his wife, while she stayed with her father:

> PLAYER (BERTRAM)
> Although before the solemn priest I have sworn,
> I will not bed her.
>
> PLAYER (PAROLLES)
> What? What, sweetheart?
>
> PLAYER (BERTRAM)
> O my Parooles, they have married me!
> I'll to the Tuscan wars, and never bed her.

Oxford's position as heir to the throne was further weakened by the St. Bartholomew's Massacre in France in 1572. It may have ended Oxford's hopes of being named heir to the throne. The massacre of the French Protestants significantly changed the political landscape. It indicated to English Protestants what might happen to them if Catholics were to rule England. It became imperative for Elizabeth to engage in diplomatic courtship with France to provide England a friend and ally against Catholic Spain. If Elizabeth took a militant Protestant stance, she would further antagonize Spain and eliminate France as a potential ally and, given France's Catholic leanings, even tilt it toward being an enemy of England. Oxford was in the public position of supporting the French alliance, but it is not likely that he would have privately supported such a marriage. Within this context, Oxford could not be named as an heir to the throne because it would negate any marriage opportunities for Elizabeth. Oxford was to wait in vain for the rest of his life to be recognized by Elizabeth as the legitimate heir to the throne.

In the summer of 1574, Oxford fled to Europe without permission and shortly thereafter was brought back by order of the Queen. (The reasons for his abrupt departure will be covered later.) Then in January of 1575, Oxford departed for a Continental tour with permission of the Queen. Before leaving, he entailed his lands to his cousin, Horatio Vere. This preparation before traveling abroad was consistent with Oxford's legal training and his recognition of foreign travel as perilous adventure. Yet, when Oxford died in 1604, no will was found. It is hard to explain why a man would be so careful in his youth and yet care nothing about how his property and effects would be disposed of in his old age, when death was not an event on some far distant horizon. This is a small point to be revisited later.

He first visited Paris and then traveled to Germany where he stayed with the noted scholar Johannes Sturm until late April. He then proceeded to Italy where he visited Venice, Palermo and Florence. While in Venice he leased a villa and consorted with the most expensive courtesan in the City. It was possible that on a sea trip he may have visited Sicily, gone to Rome and perhaps visited the Greek isles, but none of this is certain. In total, he was gone fifteen months. When he returned he brought the Queen a pair of perfumed gloves. The perfume was called the Earl of Oxford's perfume for many years, but more important, Oxford single-handedly brought the Italian Renaissance to England.

Oxford received a letter from William Cecil on March 17, 1575, while he was in Paris on the outbound leg of his journey that informed him that his wife, Anne Cecil, was pregnant. Oxford took the news with good cheer and wrote back to his father-in-law that he hoped the child would be a son, but that he was going on with his travels to Italy. He sent a Bible to his wife as a present. This indicates that he admitted the fact that he had slept with Anne and thought that the child was his. Exactly when and how this might have occurred is subject to speculation because Oxford had not lived with his wife. One possibility is that he slept with Anne in October after a meeting had been arranged by his father-in-law. There are no records of what happened, but one particular plot device of Shakespeare's is particularly apt. That device is the "bed trick," the tale of an unwilling groom who goes to bed with a woman he thinks is his mistress, but in fact is his wife. At any rate, Oxford did not object to the news of his wife's conception nor attempt to deny his paternity. From Wright's *History of Essex*:

> He (Oxford) forsook his lady's bed, the father of Lady Anne by stratagem, contrived that her husband should unknowingly sleep with her, believing her to be another woman, and she bore a son to him in consequence of this meeting.[24] [Note that the strategy and events seem plausible, but Anne bore Oxford a daughter not a son.]

Upon his return to Paris in March of 1576, his friend, Rowland Yorke, greeted him and informed him that the birth was not in July as Oxford had been informed, but was in September. This date would have made it impossible for Oxford to be the father. The situation of whether Anne Cecil had been unfaithful and if so with whom is very unclear. If one takes the *Hamlet* plot as a literary representation of Oxford's life (with Anne Cecil as Ophelia), there is a reference of Oxford's feelings about this matter. The passage is somewhat ambiguous. Is it a remark directed toward Anne Cecil and possible infidelity, or at William Cecil?

HAMLET
For if the sun breed maggots in a dead dog, being a god kissing carrion—
Have you a daughter?

LORD POLONIUS
I have, my lord.

HAMLET
Let her not walk i' the sun: conception is a blessing: but not as your
daughter   may   conceive.
Friend, look to 't.

After receiving this news, Oxford returned from France to England in
April 1576, and on his return voyage, pirates attacked his ship but he
escaped with his life. He may have to have bribed one of the pirates, who
recognized him, not to kill him; he returned to England minus his
possessions. On one hand, this could be a random act of piracy, for there
had been pirates operating in the English Channel for centuries. On the
other, could it be that this was an event set up by the one man capable of
having information on when and how Oxford would cross the channel and
also capable of orchestrating a cooperating band of pirates to stage the
attack to kill Oxford? William Cecil was the only man in England with the
extensive spy network and foreign operatives to carry out such a plot. He
was also the only one who would have a motive to kill Oxford. The
newborn heir, Oxford's child and William Cecil's grandchild, would
inherit Oxford's estates and would be heir to the throne.

When Oxford returned safely, he would meet neither with his wife nor
with William Cecil. He made arrangements whereby Anne would not be
in court when he was there; he refused to see the child. Oxford
considerably outranked William Cecil (Lord Burghley), in the British
hierarchy; in addition, Cecil always wanted to be in the good graces of
Oxford. Edward de Vere was Burghley's route to bring his family into the
nobility.

The unresolved question is "Who fathered the child?" Here there is a
division of opinion among those knowledgeable about Oxford. One group
believes that the father was Robert Dudley, Earl of Leicester, who, to spite
Oxford, raped Anne Cecil. However, the probability of this scenario has
the drawback that to get to Anne Cecil, Robert Dudley would either have
had to have the consent of William Cecil or reach Anne without his
knowledge. Both seem to be unlikely scenarios.

The other candidate for fatherhood is unspeakable, Anne Cecil's father,
William Cecil. He had the most to lose if Oxford died abroad without an
heir. If Oxford died on his European tour without an heir, his properties
and titles would revert to others in the Vere family. Conversely, Cecil had

the most to gain if Anne Cecil had a child. The child would be the legitimate heir of Oxford, and no one would be the wiser. As to some other father for the child, if anyone else was to impregnate Anne, there would be the possibility that the information could leak out and the paternity of the child would be legally questioned. This is what makes the attack on Oxford in the channel that much more suspicious. It may have been a gamble to eliminate Oxford, but William Cecil was a ruthless man who had resorted to murder before (John de Vere) to advance the Cecil family.

Whatever the biological paternity of Oxford's daughter, Elizabeth Vere, Oxford fully recognized her as his child.[e] From 1571 when they married until 1582, the couple had only this one child, Elizabeth, whose paternity was an issue. In 1582, Oxford returned to live with his wife, and from then until his wife's death in 1588, they had four children: a son, who died at birth in 1583; Bridget, born in 1584; Frances, born in 1585, who died at the age of two or three; and Susan, born in 1587. These were all grandchildren of William Cecil, but none of Oxford's children by Anne Cecil were males. This must have been a deep disappointment to grandfather William Cecil. There was no legitimate male line of nobility from his daughter and Oxford. The number of children indicates that Oxford did not regard Anne as a wife before 1582, nor did he sleep with her (with the exception of one possible dalliance) for eleven years, until they began living together as man and wife in 1582. (Perhaps as a coincidence, Oxford had three surviving daughters. The same number as Lear, an anagram of earl.)

In *Hamlet,* the mismatch between the temperamental, aristocratic prince and the sweet Ophelia could not be plainer. It may be because of a guilty conscience that several plays by Shakespeare have the themes of women wrongly accused of infidelity. Desdemona in *Othello* is the most poignant example.

---

[e] Under English and American law, a child of a married couple is legally the child of the married father, no matter who the natural father might be. A husband could not absolve himself of responsibilities by claiming that a child born to his wife was the product of another man. With the advent of modern DNA testing, this legal assumption has been challenged in cases wherein the child, through DNA testing, is shown to have a father other than the husband.

OXFORD IN THE TOWER

Thomas Knyvet, a Gentleman of the Chamber and Keeper of Westminster Palace, introduced his niece, Anne Vavasor, to the court when she was about sixteen. William Cecil considered her a woman of easy virtue and at one time called her a drab, that is, a prostitute. The one portrait of her shows a thin, not very attractive woman with a rather stern countenance, but this painting cannot do justice to her attractiveness and feminine charms. If the poetry left by Edward de Vere is any indication, she was a woman of great wit, and she definitely fascinated the young earl. She eventually had two illegitimate sons, both of whom became distinguished members of the English aristocracy. She also had three husbands, apparently two at one time, and many other flirtations and lovers. She lived into her nineties.[f]

She became a Gentlewoman of the Royal Bedchamber in 1580, as her mother had been. While the selection to be such a handmaiden of the Queen brought a young woman into the circles of the highest ranks of nobility, it brought her under the Queen's almost complete control. The Queen both protected and resented the young women around her. They were required to have the Queen's permission to marry. The women were to be comely and courteous, but not outshine the Virgin Queen.

There can be little doubt that Oxford was deeply in love with Anne Vavasor, as is reflected in his poetry. Anne Vavasor is not mentioned in these poems, but several scholars see her as the subject of Oxford's poetry. The following is a poem of the period signed by Oxford:

Echo Verses
Sitting alone I upon my thought in melancholy mood,
In sight of sea, and at my back and ancient hoary wood,
I saw a fair young lady come, her secret fears to wail,
Clad all in colour of a nun, and covered with a veil;
Yet (for the day was calm and clear) I might discern her face,
As one might see a damask rose hid under crystal glass.
Three times, with her soft hand, full hard on her left side she knocks,
And sign'd so sore as might have mov'd some pity in the rocks;
From sighs and shedding amber tears into sweet song she brake,
When thus the echo answered her to every word she spake:
Oh, heavens! Who was the first that bred in me this fever? Vere.

---

[f] Anne Vavasor may have been the woman Edmund Spenser drew on for Rosalind, and also that Oxford drew on for Rosaline in *Love's Labours Lost.* (This could be a footnote that spawns a thousand doctoral dissertations.) Additionally, Eva Turner Clark dates *Romeo and Juliet* shortly after the Vavasor affair, and there are parallels between events of Oxford's life and those in the play.

Who was the first that gave the wound whose fear I wear forever? Vere.
What tyrant, Cupid, to my harm usurps thy golden quiver? Vere?
What wight first cauth this heart and can from bondage it deliver? Vere.
Yet who doth most adore this wight, oh hollow caves tell true? You.
What nymph deserves his liking best, yet doth in sorrow rue? You.
What makes him not reward good will with some reward or ruth? Youth.
What makes him show besides his birth, such pride and such untruth?
Youth.
May I his favour match with love, if he my love will try? Ay.
May I requite his birth with faith? Then faithful will I die? Ay.
    And I, that knew his lady well,
        Said, Lord how great a miracle,
    To her how Echo told the truth,
        As true as Phoebus' oracle.
                The Earle of Oxforde

J. Thomas Looney in his epic work *Shakespeare Identified* lists one of the distinguishing characteristics of the Author as "doubtful and somewhat conflicting in his attitude to woman."[26] Given his experiences, this attitude is understandable:

Woman's Changeableness
If women could be fair and yet not fond, [foolish]
    Or that their love were firm not fickle, still,
I would not marvel that they make men bond,
    By service long to purchase their good will;
But when I see how frail those creatures are,
I muse that men forget themselves so far.

To mark the choice they make, and how they change,
    How oft from Phoebus do they flee to Pan,
Unsettled still like haggards wild they range,
    These gentle birds that fly from man to man;
Who would not scorn and shake them from the first
And let them fly fair fools which way they list.

Yet for disport we fawn and flatter both,
    To pass the time when nothing else can please,
And train them to our lure with subtle oath,
    Till, weary of their wiles, ourselves we ease;
And then we say when we their fancy try,
To play with fools, O what a fool was I.
              Earle of Oxenforde

Whatever he found with Anne Vavasor was soon gone forever. Sir Francis Walsingham reports to the Earl of Huntington in a letter dated March 23, 1581:

> On Tuesday at night Anne Vavysor was brought to bed of a son in the maiden's chamber. The E. of Oxford is vowed to be the father, who hath withdrawn himself with intent, as it is thought, to pass the seas. The ports are laid for him and therefore if he have any such determination it is not likely that he will escape. The gentlewoman the selfsame night she was delivered was conveyed out of the house and the next day committed to the Tower. Others that have been found in any ways party to the cause have also been committed. Her Majesty is greatly grieved with the accident, and therefore I hope there will be some order taken as the like inconvenience will be avoided.[25]

This letter shows the Queen's vindictiveness. Taking a mother the day after a birth and committing her to prison is cruelty in the extreme, but the Queen could be and would be cruel to anyone she felt had betrayed her. Oxford did not flee the country but was sent to the Tower shortly thereafter:

> The Earl of Oxford, also arrested but soon set at liberty, is again in the Tower for forgetting himself with one of the Queen's Maids of Honour [Anne Vavasor], who is in the Tower likewise. This in spite of his having a pretty wife, daughter of the Treasurer. But he will not live with her.[26]

On June 8, Oxford was released from the Tower. The story behind Oxford's original arrest is long and complicated. Oxford had accused Henry Howard and Charles Arundel of treason, specifically of plotting to murder the Queen. This pro-Catholic faction made equally grievous charges against Oxford, including the charge of homosexuality with the musicians he had brought back from Italy. Subsequent events eventually proved Oxford correct. Charles Arundel fled to the Continent, and Henry Howard was imprisoned. Howard was released and then arrested and imprisoned again after Francis Throckmorton was arrested, tortured and revealed a plot for the invasion of England by a French force led by the Duke of Guise or by a Spanish and Italian force sent by Philip II. The Spanish ambassador, Mendoza, was well aware of these plots, and he was expelled from England.

Upon his release from the Tower, Oxford was placed under house arrest when his charges against Howard and Arundel were proved true, yet he was still not allowed to return to court. Anne Vavasor's and Oxford's son was named Edward Vere, and she received some £2,000 and estates from Oxford. Edward Vere would later have a distinguished military career fighting in the Low Countries and also gain a seat in Parliament.

William Cecil gives a precise definition to Oxford's use of the word "disgrace" in a typically long-winded, tedious, and sanctimonious letter to Christopher Hatton:

Say what they will against my Lord of Oxford, and have presence to utter their humours, and my Lord of Oxford is neither heard nor hath presence either to complain or defend himself. And so long as he shall be subject to the disgrace of her Majesty (from which God deliver him) I see it apparently that, innocent soever he shall be, the advantages will fall out with his adversaries; and so, I hear, they do prognosticate.

But I submit all these things to God's will, who knoweth best why it pleaseth Him to afflict my Lord of Oxford in this sort, who hath, I confess, forgotten his duty to God, and yet I hope he may be made a good servant to her Majesty, if it please her of her clemency to remit her displeasure; for his fall in her court, which is now twice yeared, and he punished as far or farther than any like crime hath been, first by her Majesty, and then by the drab's friend in revenge to peril of his life.[27]

The Queen's fury against Oxford did not stop with his release from the Tower. Anne Vavasor's uncle, Thomas Knyvet, soon engaged Oxford in a duel. Such a duel could only have taken place with either the consent or encouragement of the Queen, who would have been accepting the possibility of Oxford's injury or death. Her behavior was contrary to her direct intervention to prevent a duel in 1576, when Oxford had been involved in a quarrel over a tennis court with Sir Philip Sidney. Philip challenged Oxford to a duel after Oxford called him a "puppy." The duel would have proceeded except that the Queen intervened because there could not be a duel between two nobles of such unequal rank. According to Fulke Greville, a friend of Philip Sidney's:

...the Queen, who saw that by loss or disgrace of either could gain nothing, presently undertakes Sir Philip, and (like an excellent Monarch) lays before him the difference in degree between Earls and Gentlemen, the respect inferiors owed to their superiors, and the necessity in Princes to maintain their own creations, as degrees descending between the people's licentiousness and the anointed sovereignty of Crowns; how the Gentleman's neglect of the Nobility taught the peasant to insult both.[28]

Thomas Knyvet and Oxford were of most unequal rank but soon engaged in a bloody encounter:

In England of later, there hath been a fray between my Lord of Oxford and Master Thomas Knevet of the Privy Chamber, who are both hurt, but my Lord of Oxford more dangerously. You know Master Knevet is not meanly beloved in Court, and therefore he is not likely to speed ill whatsoever the quarrel be.[29]

Further, an entry in Rev. Richard Madox's diary notes both the duel and the fact that Oxford was living with his wife Anne Cecil:

My Lord of Oxford fought with Master Knyvet about the quarrel of Bessie Vavasor, and was hurt, which grieved the Lord Treasurer so much the more for that the Earl hath company with his wife since Christmas. But through this mishap, and through the pains he took at the marriage of another daughter to my Lord Wentworth on Shroveday, my Lord Treasurer was sick.[30]

Oxford was gravely wounded in the duel, and many believe this is what is referred to in the sonnets when the Author states, "So I, made lame by fortune's dearest spite" (fortune being the Queen, not luck). Additionally there were several sword fights in the streets of London, which resulted in deaths of men in both Oxford's faction and among Vavasor's relatives. Thomas Knyvet appears to have personally killed one of Oxford's men. Elizabeth subsequently made Thomas Knyvet a knight.

When Elizabeth was visiting Theobalds in June 1583, she summoned Oxford, after "bitter tears and speeches" fully pardoned him, and permitted his return to court. Oxford and his wife had a son the month before, but the child died shortly after birth and was buried on May 9, 1583. This may have had something to do with the Queen's forgiveness. Sir Walter Raleigh had an influence on the Queen that William Cecil could not. Roger Manners wrote in a letter to his brother:

> Her Majesty came yesterday to Greenwich from the Lord Treasurer's ... The day she came away, which was yesterday, the Earl of Oxford came to her presence, and after some bitter words and speeches, in the end all sins are forgiven, and he may repair to the Court at his pleasure. Master Raleigh was a great mean herein, whereat Pondus [William Cecil] is angry for that he could not do so much.[31]

The tumultuous events of the Anne Vavasor affair proved to be a psychological turning point for Oxford. His haughty pride was leveled when the Queen imprisoned him once on charges of treason and again for having a child with Anne Vavasor. He was no longer the high-flying court poet and darling of the court who was able to do no wrong. His ideal of the noble court-poet who embodied Castiglione's courtier qualities was given a rude shake-up by the temperamental and vindictive nature of his sovereign and mother. His invulnerability as a Prince of the Realm must have been shattered.

At a romantic level, the loss of Anne Vavasor must have proved equally devastating. This was Oxford's first and only recorded romance, and it had proved disastrous. The Queen's vindictiveness meant that romantic love, even of an illicit nature, would be impossible for Oxford. Eva Turner Clark dates the rewriting of Oxford's poem *Romulus and Juliet* into the play *Romeo and Juliet* as being in the year 1581. Oxford turned his disastrous misfortune in an immortal tragedy of passionate but doomed lovers. Artistic works are for posterity, but their creation may be driven by the need to bring order and meaning to a disrupted, chaotic, and uncontrollable existence.

THE SPANISH ARMADA

Oxford had never been financially solvent and had often sold lands to pay his expenses, and he never gained full control over the lands inherited from John de Vere. On June 26, 1586, Oxford's financial troubles ended when the Queen granted him a yearly stipend of £1,000 paid in four equal installments. Oxford was thirty-eight at the time. This was extraordinary indeed, given the frugal nature of the Queen. There were no stipulations that Oxford had to do anything in return for these payments. This was an enormous amount of money per year, perhaps equivalent to £4,000,000 in today's money:

> We will and command you of Our treasure being and remaining from time to time within the receipt of Our Exchequer, to deliver and pay, or cause to be delivered and paid, unto Our right trusty and well beloved Cousin the Earl of Oxford, or to his assigns sufficiently authorised by him, the sum of One Thousand Pounds good and lawful money of England. The same to be yearly delivered and paid unto Our said Cousin at four terms of the year by even portions: and so to be continued unto him during Our pleasure, or until such time as he shall be by Us otherwise provided for to be in some manner relieved; at what time Our pleasure is that this payment of One Thousand Pounds yearly to Our said Cousin in manner above specified shall cease. And for the same or any part thereof, Our further will and commandment is that neither the said Earl nor his assigns nor his or their executors nor any of them shall by way of account, impest, or any other way whatsoever be charged toward Us, Our heirs or successors. And these Our letters shall be your sufficient warrant and discharge in that behalf.

> Given under Our Privy Seal at Our Manor of Greenwich, the six and twentieth day of June in the eight and twentieth year of Our reign. [1586].[32]

B.M. Ward in his biography of the Earl of Oxford, *The Seventeenth Earl of Oxford,* discusses the grant in some detail.[34] Elizabeth's grants for personal reasons were in the neighborhood of ten to twenty pounds, so the amount given Oxford was quite extraordinary. Ward concludes that the money did not come from Elizabeth's purse and that the form of the grant was the same used to provide secret service money such as that given to Sir Francis Walsingham. He also compares the amount of this grant to other grants to other persons for their personal use. In addition, Roger Stritmatter has pointed out that the grant came three days after a June 23, 1586, Star Chamber decree concerning the reorganization of printing. In summary, the grant appears to have been made to Oxford for whatever unofficial position he held with the Queen. Most likely, this was the production of plays as propaganda for the legitimacy of the Tudor regime, but one cannot be certain.

Spain's empire consisted of the New World from Florida to the Straits of Magellan, lands in the Pacific, and alliances with or domination over the rest of Catholic Europe. England was small, poor, and isolated in comparison. England was, if not a pawn, perhaps a rook in the ongoing contest between France and Spain for hegemony in Europe. Elizabeth attempted to pursue a course of moderation in her religious policies. Put another way, she continually vacillated, which has been interpreted as a policy of moderation. She needed Protestant support as Queen, but to go too far in that direction would weaken the basic notion of monarchy. At the far extreme of the Protestant cause stood the Calvinists, who recognized no divine right of kings to rule, and in Holland, the monarch had been replaced by an elected ruler. At the other extreme stood the fanatical Catholics who believed that Elizabeth was the bastard daughter of a whore and a heretic who should burn at the stake. The road down the middle was a very narrow one.

The French government was a weak ally to England. The government was generally unfavorable toward the Protestants and only reluctantly recognized the right of the Protestant Huguenots to practice their faith. The French were allies to England only as far as it weakened Spain, but no further. St. Bartholomew's Day in 1572, when mobs in Paris murdered thousands of Huguenots, was never out of the minds of English Protestants. Elizabeth had supported both the French Huguenots and later the Dutch Protestants as a political maneuver against Catholic Spain and Catholic France, but also somewhat as a matter of religious principle. Her support for the Protestant cause in Europe was never wholehearted or financially adequate. It was enough to keep the rebel Protestants from losing completely, but never enough to ensure a victory. While Elizabeth may have seen the Protestants as an ally or at least an irritant against Catholic Spain, she also had great reservations against supporting any rebellion against a legitimate monarch.

The most implacable foe of Elizabeth was King Philip II of Spain. The motivation for Philip's hatred was a combination of religion, political determinations, and personal revenge. Elizabeth's half-sister, Queen Mary I, had been married to Philip, and Elizabeth knew him personally from her days in the Tower. Philip may have been instrumental in convincing Mary not to send Elizabeth to the block for treason. Elizabeth had cordially rejected Philip's offer of marriage after the death of her half-sister.

By 1584, English spies were monitoring the Spanish preparations. Elizabeth had a country filled with its own internal religious strife between Catholics and Protestants. Catholic propaganda harped on the circumstances surrounding Elizabeth's birth and the basic right of Elizabeth to rule. The ability of Elizabeth's government to influence public opinion was limited. Only five percent of the population was literate, and there were no newspapers to report events and opinions. The clergy through their weekly preaching could reach the illiterate population. For this reason, they were tightly controlled. However, the clergy were often divided on religious and political issues, and thus were unreliable. One direct avenue to the population was the popular theater. From this point of view, Oxford's works[g] were propaganda for the legitimacy of the Tudor regime and for the rights of monarchs in general. Consistently, the plays portrayed chaos and bloody disaster resulting from the toppling of a monarch.

The Queen was notoriously tightfisted with her funds, and she took little personal pity on anyone in terms of relieving their financial distress. Whether Oxford was at that time distressed for funds or not, the amount granted to him was still astronomical. Therefore, the question arises, "What did Oxford do with the money?" He did not acquire property, wine, or women, and song was not that expensive—and he did not seem to gamble. Without a sufficient number of vices, it would be impossible to spend money at the rate he did, unless one considers the theater a vice. Oxford once referred to the matter as his "office." The most plausible explanation is the Queen gave money to Oxford to produce plays for the English public as Tudor propaganda.

His banishment from court from 1581 to 1583, combined with the importance of the plays for propaganda, may have turned him more toward public productions. When looked at from this point of view, it becomes apparent that even non-historical plays have a political subtext that would easily have been seen by the Elizabethan audience. The hero of *Othello*, in contemporary times, is often played as an African-American,

---

[g] Another interesting facet of the histories is that they play up or down Oxford's ancestors according to whatever gives the best view. For example, the 15th Earl of Oxford is nowhere mentioned although he was a loyal supporter of Richard III, and the 14th Earl of Oxford is placed at the battle of Agincourt although he in fact had little to do there. Some Oxfordian scholars have taken this to mean that the 17th Earl of Oxford was in fact the 17th Earl of Oxford. Yet the total picture is much more psychologically complex. Edward de Vere (Tudor-Seymour) characterizes himself in his work with both a false identity (Earl of Oxford) and a true identity (Prince of the Realm).

The current rehabilitation of Richard III and Shakespeare's (Oxford's) slanders against him are attempts to right the historical record. One view is that Henry VII had most to fear from the young princes and he was the murderer of the two boys in the Tower, not Richard III.

but the character Othello is a Moor. That is, he was a Spaniard and would have been regarded as such by the Elizabethans. In the play, the Spanish Moor cruelly and unjustly murders his innocent wife. The political subtext would have been taken to heart by the English population as a forewarning of what would happen to them if Spain invaded and controlled England.

When war finally did erupt with the Spanish Armada in 1588, Oxford attempted to be at the forefront of the action. He outfitted a ship, *Edward Bonaventure,* and then proceeded to the fray. Accounts differ as to Oxford's taking part in the action. After the defeat of the Armada, William Camden described the action in his *Annales* as follows:

> The English came within ken of the Spanish Armada, built high like towers and castles ... The Queen forwith commands more ships to the sea, whereupon, in voluntary manner, the Earls of Oxford, Northumberland and Cumberland, Sir Thomas Cecil, Sir Robert Cecil, Sir Walter Raleigh ... and many other honorable personages were suddenly embarked, committing themselves to the sudden chance of war.[33]

However, Elizabeth would have none of it. Robert Dudley, the Earl of Leicester, assumed the head of the English land forces. Oxford was recalled from the Channel and given the defense of a town. He refused that as beneath him and sought the command of a ship. Whether the recall of Oxford was due to the Queen's or Robert Dudley's intervention is uncertain; however, Oxford missed the main English action against the Armada.

In 1588, Oxford's unhappy marriage ended when Anne Cecil died of complications from childbirth. Some of Shakespeare's work portrays women who were slandered or wronged by a passionate husband. Perhaps these plays in some ways attempt to atone for his treatment of her. Yet, if Ophelia of *Hamlet* represents Oxford's wife, the mismatch was as great as between Anne Cecil and Oxford. Anne Cecil was never a suitable match for the headstrong and impetuous young courtier and artist. Three years later, in 1591, Oxford married Elizabeth Trentham and retired from court life. He occupied King's Place in the borough of Hackney, north of London. His residence in this area put him close to the north London theater district.

However, his retirement from the court did not end Oxford's involvement in court politics. In 1593, Henry Wriothesley, the 3rd Earl of Southampton, was nineteen years old, and the question of his marriage grew in importance. Both Oxford and William Cecil favored a match between Oxford's daughter Elizabeth Vere (William Cecil's grand-daughter) and the young lord. Here Oxford appears to have given up any thought of occupying the throne and instead turned his attention to Southampton.

The publication of *Venus and Adonis* and *Lucrece* put him in a position of deference to the young lord. He was concentrating on placing Southampton in a position to become king. *Venus and Adonis* and *Lucrece* were not simply literary works, but were also political works that show his dedication to Southampton. In the end, Southampton refused to marry Elizabeth Vere and paid an enormous fine of £2,000 to his guardian. This effectively ended any interest of William Cecil in either Oxford or the young Southampton because the way to royalty was effectively denied to the Cecil family.

THE ESSEX REBELLION

In 1599, Robert Devereux, 2nd Earl of Essex, was commander of the English troops in Ireland. Without orders or notifying the Queen, he left Ireland for England. After traveling by boat to England, he rode horseback across England and arrived with muddied boots for an audience with the Queen. He entered her chamber room while she was still in her bedclothes without wig or make-up to cover her smallpox-scarred face. Such impertinence was not only the most unimaginable breach of royal protocol, it was also a personal slight and perhaps a threat to the Queen's person. Once before, he had laid his hand on the hilt of his sword when the enraged Queen had slapped him during an interview. This time, he incurred the Queen's wrath by his failure to follow her instructions in Ireland, and then this impetuous trip to confront her.

Robert Devereux, 2nd Earl of Essex, was allegedly the son of Walter Devereux and Lettice Knollys Devereux. While this author has not done any thorough investigation of the birth of Robert Devereux, the most plausible conclusion is that he was the son of Elizabeth and Robert Dudley and was born in 1566. When Walter Devereux died (probably poisoned by Robert Dudley), Lettice married Robert Dudley, in 1578, and she became the Countess of Leicester. From her portraits, Lettice Knollys was a redheaded beauty, and the Queen was always jealous of her. With this marriage, Robert Dudley became legal stepfather to his own natural son. Years later, Robert Dudley championed him for Order of the Garter and as a result, Robert Devereux was made a member of the most prestigious association of the Queen's favorites at the unheard of age of eighteen. When Robert Dudley died in 1588, Robert Devereux, 2nd Earl of Essex, became even more prominent in Elizabethan politics. Elizabeth's treatment of the rash young Earl has always been portrayed as her platonic flirtations with the younger courtier, but the endless recklessness of the young man with the Queen and her tolerant responses seem best explained by the fact that he was her son.

Robert Cecil, who replaced his father as the Secretary of State after his father's death in 1598, masterfully cut the aging Elizabeth off from the outside world and especially from the faction that consisted of Robert Devereux and the younger Henry Wriothesley, Earl of Southampton. If Elizabeth declared a successor from this strong Protestant camp, then Robert Cecil would be outside the circle of power. Robert Cecil had started secret communications with James of Scotland to become King of England before Elizabeth's death. James would need to rely on Robert Cecil for counsel and support, whereas any Protestant claimant would have his own counselors and supporters.

Robert Devereux, 2nd Earl of Essex, was growing increasingly desperate at the turn of the century. The Queen had not renewed one of his valuable monopolies at he was facing financial ruin. He had no access to the Queen because Robert Cecil (William Cecil's son) was effectively in control of the government and he monopolized communication with the Queen. The Essex Rebellion took place under these conditions, although rebellion is a misnomer. The events might more accurately be described as an armed attempt to gain an audience with the Queen. Before the rebellion, Essex had been attacked in the streets of London and several men were killed in the melee. Further, the play *Richard II* had been staged in London.

Orthodox historians have said that the staging of the play was at the instigation of Essex, but this is hardly likely. More likely, Robert Cecil staged the play and had his men attack Essex's followers. This would have created both panic and paranoia in Essex. Having done that, Robert Cecil then probably told the Queen that Essex was proceeding with supporters to overthrow the monarch. The evidence Cecil had created would support this view. Essex's men were armed, and there was in progress the production of a play featuring the overthrow of a regent. However, Elizabeth's knowledge of what was happening in London had to have been provided by Robert Cecil. The Queen was not walking about the streets of London inquiring what plays were being shown, and this scenario has all the earmarks of a classic Cecil plot to set up Essex for his eventual downfall (where the stone was thrown, but the hand was not seen).

The Queen or Robert Cecil acting on her behalf (or even without her knowledge) ordered Essex to come to court. He refused to do so, fearing that this was a plot to murder, arrest, or imprison him. Essex detained the delegation sent to bring him back to court, and Robert Cecil had trapped Essex into disobeying an apparent order of the Queen. Essex in the heat of the moment decided to go to court with an armed contingent. However, leaving Essex House, he did not head west to the court, but rather he headed east toward the city of London. He had previously received unsubstantiated information that the sheriff of London had men waiting to join with him. Essex's supporters were probably confused about why they were going in the opposite direction from their supposed objective. Henry Wriothesley, 3rd Earl of Southampton, was with him and his supporters. Arriving in London, Essex found no such contingent waiting for them, and his supporters soon began to melt into the crowd.

If Essex had proceeded directly to the palace, no doubt they could have gained access and had an audience with the Queen. The palace guard did not number more than fifty men. Whether or not gaining an audience with the Queen would have done any good is an interesting question. The Queen was justifiably suspicious of others and had seen enough death and betrayal in her lifetime to be suspicious of even those closest to her. Essex's delay and roundabout route in moving toward the Queen proved disastrous. Essex's supporters vanished with the growing opposition. Both the Earl of Essex and the Earl of Southampton surrendered and were in the Tower forthwith.

Historical accounts of the Essex Rebellion state that Essex was attempting to overthrow the Queen and become king. This does not answer the question of why Essex should be perceived by himself or any of his supporters as having any claim on the throne, nor does it explain why he had such a special relationship with the Queen. These thorny historical problems are resolved if Essex was the oldest son (other than Oxford) of the Queen. This is the hidden subtext of the whole Essex Rebellion. Essex thought himself special and that he could treat the Queen so imperiously because he was her son. He gained stature as a member of the Order of the Garter because the Queen's favorite, Robert Dudley, had supported him. Robert Dudley supported him because he was his son. He gained supporters because the hidden, unwritten and unspoken assumption was that he was the son of the Queen and therefore had a claim on the throne.

The Earl of Oxford sat at the trial the young earls and the foregone conclusion of guilty was soon pronounced. The question was what sentence would the Queen impose. Essex was executed on February 25, 1601, only six days after his trial. It is not certain whether the Queen signed the death warrant or gave her permission for the execution. Given her reluctance to sign Mary Queen of Scots' death warrant, it appears that

that Robert Cecil maneuvered to quickly execute Essex, with or without the permission of the Queen. The Queen was grief stricken and never recovered her composure after the death of Essex.

From Cecil's point of view, Essex had no political value and he posed a threat to Cecil. Even though in the Tower, both earls were well liked by the population, and if the Queen died as she eventually had to, both Essex and Southampton would be more of a threat. Personal popularity meant the ability to raise men, arms, and political supporters to oppose whatever the ruling faction was at the time. Essex had already shown his willingness to take such actions, and he was hotheaded and unpredictable. Southampton, on the other hand, had the firm support of the Earl of Oxford. One can easily understand why Robert Cecil would have them both executed, but not why he executed one but not the other is an unanswered question. This question has never been broached by conventional historians. Both were equally guilty of treason, but only one was executed.

Robert Cecil used Southampton as a hostage to checkmate Oxford. Robert Cecil knew all the secrets of the Tudor monarchy from William Cecil. With Southampton in the Tower under Cecil's control, Robert Cecil had a blackmail card to use against Oxford. If Southampton were dead, there would be nothing to prevent Oxford from taking firm action with both his pen and his political influence to usurp Robert Cecil's influence with the Queen. The Queen at this time was in declining health, ever closer to death, and totally under the thumb of Robert Cecil. It was the Queen's lifelong reluctance to name a successor, or a Lord Protector, that precipitated Robert Cecil's move to gain power and install a foreign sovereign on the nation. Robert Cecil kept Southampton alive as a way of fending off the aristocratic and Protestant faction. Oxford was helpless. A wrong move on his part meant the death of Southampton. The most likely bargain between Oxford and Robert Cecil was that Southampton would be allowed to live if Oxford would make no claims to the throne for Southampton upon the death of Elizabeth. Oxford might also have been in direct communication with James in Scotland as Agent 40, but this would be only speculation.

The Queen died on March 24, 1603. The new king, James, sent the order from Edinburgh, Scotland, on April 5, 1603; Southampton was released from the Tower on April 10, 1603.

OXFORD'S SIGNATURE: "EDWARD VII"

Elizabethan society was socially stratified in a way that is hard to imagine. Signs of heraldry were regulated, and there were dress codes to regulate the relative ranks of society. Impingement on royal or aristocratic prerogatives by someone of a lower social class was not to be taken lightly. Given this, Oxford's signature goes beyond all bounds of audacity. His signature had a crown above it and seven slashes below it. In brief, he signed his name as Edward VII, and this was what he would have been if he had become king. Edward VI was the boy king who died in his youth.

William Fowler comments on the change in signatures in his book *Shakespeare Revealed in Oxford's Letters*, written in 1984, and his comments were made, therefore, without knowledge of the later research into Oxford's birth:

> The signature, "E. Oxenforde," is underscored with the same looped trefoil design as in his immediately preceding letter of May 7, 1603. These last two underscorings differ radically from the spear-like line with the seven crossmarks which underscore his signatures in all his earlier letters subsequent to his 1563 French one. These last two signatures lack also the wavy line topped by four dots occurring above his prior signatures. This abrupt signature change, following his letter at the end of April, 1603, may have some significance connected with his turning his attention to the new monarch, King James, after paying his final tribute to Queen Elizabeth; or it may be connected with his relief upon Southampton's release from life imprisonment in the Tower.[34]

Oxford began using the Edward VII signature in 1569, which would have been the year he reached his actual majority age of twenty-one. This signature is a direct claim to a place in line the throne. Why the Queen did not stop him is also a reasonable question, which remains unanswered. Edward de Vere found covert ways to claim his identity both in his life and in his artistic creations.

Figure 12. Signature, August 23, 1563
Letter to William Cecil (in French)

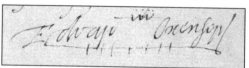

Figure 13. Signature, November 24, 1569
Crown Signature in Letter to William Cecil

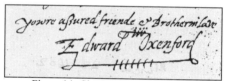

Figure 14. Signature, March 22, 1602
Crown Signature in Letter to Robert Cecil

Queen Elizabeth dies—March 24, 1603

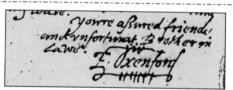

Figure 15. Signature, April 25, 1603
Crown Signature in Letter to Robert Cecil

Queen Elizabeth interred in Westminster—April 28, 1603

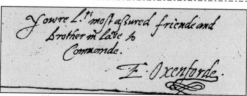

Figure 16. Signature, May 7, 1603
No Crown Signature in Letter to Robert Cecil

Some critics maintain that the crown was an earl's crown and Oxford was merely signing himself as the 17 Earl of Oxford. For them, the long line indicates a ten and the seven slashes make it seventeen. Such critics have never shown another example where this as a convention. (The usual convention is four slashes and a line through signifies five.) Further, they fail to address the fact that Edward de Vere was the Earl of Oxford from the age of fourteen until his death, yet he stopped using this signature only after Queen Elizabeth was buried. The significance of the burial date, not the date of death, is that, by English custom, the new monarch did not reign until the previous monarch was buried. In Elizabeth's case, it was thirty-one days from the day of her death to the day of interment. The day that she was interred in her tomb in Westminster Cathedral, James V of Scotland became King of England and Edward (Tudor-Seymour) de Vere was no longer heir to the throne. He ceased using the signature of Edward VII because he would not be king.

OXFORD DISAPPEARS

As with his life, Oxford's end was mysterious, uncertain, and shrouded. Charlton Ogburn writes in *The Mysterious William Shakespeare:*

> On 24 June 1604 he died, leaving no will, as far as is known. An entry in the old Register of the Church of St. Augustine in Hackney reads: "Edward de Vere, Erle of Oxenford, was buried the 6th day of July, anno 1604." In the margin of the page is the annotation "The plague." Perhaps, already weakened in health, he was one of its victims.[35]

Ogburn goes on to say that Oxford's last wife, Elizabeth Trentham, left in her will that she should be buried next to her husband in the graveyard of the church in Hackney. Ogburn also mentions that Percival Golding (cousin of Arthur Golding) wrote that Oxford was buried in Westminster, but Ogburn says there is no evidence for this.

Given the circumstances described by Ogburn, one would expect that Oxford's death would be recognized by both the court and by the literary world. Oxford was the Lord Great Chamberlain of England and was on good terms with King James. He held one of the oldest titles in England and was Lord Great Chamberlain at James I's coronation. Why there is no mention of his death in aristocratic records and letters is difficult to explain.

As far as literary recognition of his death, even excluding Oxford as William Shakespeare, he was a recognized figure as a producer, musician, poet, writer, and literary patron. In spite of this, there was no public recognition of Oxford's death or funeral ceremony. In the years following

1604, there are no known references, in letters or other public or private communication, concerning the Earl of Oxford. It was as if he vanished off the planet, and no one either noticed or commented.

In January 1604, Oxford wrote a personal letter to King James concerning his rights to the Forest of Waltham. The letter is in an almost perfect hand, and it shows no wavering lines, as is usually the case with an elderly person or a person in ill health. This contradicts the notion that Oxford was in ill health. Second, the notion that Oxford died of the plague is suspect. The plague usually occurred in London in the summer, and it was a result of drinking water contaminated by human and animal waste. During periods of the plague, the nobility and aristocrats fled out of the city to their country estates. Oxford lived well north of London proper, and the plague was less likely in Hackney than in London proper. Murder, poisoning, complications of childbirth, and the executioner's axe seem to be frequent causes of aristocratic deaths; deaths due to the plague are far rarer.

Finally, there were these strange happenings: On the day that Oxford supposedly died, Henry Wriothesley, 3rd Earl of Southampton, and his supporters were remanded to the Tower. There was no English record of these arrests and imprisonment; the only record was in the account of a foreign diplomat. G.P.V. Akrigg in *Shakespeare and the Earl of Southampton* reports:

> Suddenly the even happy flow of Southampton's career came to a halt. Late on the evening of June 24th he was arrested, along with Lord Danvers (his old friend Sir Henry), Sir Henry Neville (the Essex sympathizer who had shared his imprisonment in the Tower), Sir Maurice Berkeley (a fellow member of Queen Anne's council) and Sir William Lee. Southampton's papers were seized and scrutinized. He himself was interrogated. According to the French Ambassador, King James had gone into a complete panic and could not sleep that night even though he had a guard of his Scots posted around his quarters. Presumably to protect his heir, he sent orders to Prince Henry that he must not stir out of his chamber ...
>
> Southampton was quickly found innocent of whatever charges had been brought against him. According to the Venetian and French ambassadors, he was released on June 25th, the day after his arrest. No documents that relate to this episode survive in either the Public Record Office or in that other great repository of state papers of the period, the Cecil Papers at Hatfield.[36]

Some Oxfordians have maintained that Oxford died on June 24, 1604, and King James and Robert Cecil feared that Oxford had left a will or other documents that disclosed that Henry Wriothesley was the son of the Queen. The popular young Earl would be favored as a Prince Tudor, the descendant of the popular Tudor monarchs. If this fact was made public, even if it was not completely believed, then James I would have faced an instant and very credible threat to his reign. A son of the beloved Elizabeth would have been far more appealing to the English public than James I. Personal appeal in those days meant political support, money, and arms to take the throne. Under this scenario, when Oxford died, James and Robert Cecil put Southampton in the Tower for safekeeping until they could destroy any Oxford will or other documents. When that was accomplished, Southampton was released. This would explain the lack of a legal will by Oxford.

However, it does not seem possible that Oxford died and Southampton was arrested the same day unless it was according to some prearranged plan. Oxford's home was in Hackney, to the northeast of the city of London. If Southampton was put in the Tower after the news of Oxford's death, this means that the news had to travel to the Court, a delegation had to be assembled by the King and the delegation had to travel to wherever Southampton might be and bring him to the Tower. This assumes a speed of communication and transportation that was unlikely in the Elizabethan era.

In addition, the arrest of Southampton was perplexing to say the least. He was in the good graces of King James I, and there was no obvious reason why he or his supporters would be sent to the Tower. The death of Oxford and the subsequent arrest of Southampton is a complicated scenario, yet it does not explain why King James would immediately take Southampton back into his good graces if he had suspected a plot against his throne.

A plausible explanation of this set of circumstance is that Oxford did not die in June of 1604. Rather, of his own volition, he simply disappeared and left Elizabethan England. The Elizabethan era was over, and a new king—who was completely disconnected from the long tradition of Tudor monarchs—was on the throne. Oxford may have felt it was simply time to leave. Oxford could no longer, for better or worse, catch the conscience of the king; he was no longer the image of Castiglione's courtier-poet. This scenario would explain

1) why Oxford left no will (he was not in contemplation of death);

2) why there were no eulogies or other recognitions of his death as either a literary figure or as an aristocrat (he was not dead, he had just disappeared);

3) why Southampton was immediately released (King James knew Oxford was gone, and that Southampton posed no threat);

4) why no Oxford library has been found (he took it with him);

5) the plot of *The Tempest* (the king left to set up his kingdom on an island);

6) the dating of *The Tempest* (it could refer to dates after 1604, if Oxford was alive and writing on the Isle of Man or some other island); and

7) "ever-living poet" in *Shake-speares Sonnets,* dated 1609, signifies his death to the world (note the usage of *e-ver* and, also, other than the date on the title page, there is no contemporaneous evidence that *Shake-speares Sonnets* was published at this 1609 date).

The evidence that contradicts this theory is the record of Oxford buried in Hackney (it could have been forged), but more importantly, the will of his last wife, Elizabeth Trentham Vere, in 1612, asks that she be buried next to her husband in the graveyard in the church in Hackney. Perhaps Oxford disappeared, then whenever and wherever he died, he was buried in Hackney; yet is unlikely. But then again, this whole story, although true, is so wildly improbable that a dramatic and mysterious end is only fitting.

Despite this substantive contrary evidence, the disappearance theory as to the final end of Oxford answers the questions as to why Oxford had no burial with aristocratic fanfare or literary tributes to him. Oxford's works may yield some tempting literary clues about his disappearance. *The Tempest* has been recognized as one of the last plays of William Shakespeare, and Prospero gives tantalizing descriptions as to what may have happened:

> In few, they hurried us aboard a bark,
> Bore us some leagues to sea, where they prepar'd
> A rotten carcass of a butt, not rigg'd,
> Nor tackle, sail, nor mast; the very rats
> Instinctively have quit it.

If Oxford is Prospero, perhaps he fled his England to an island. Where did he go? Possibly, it was to the Isle of Man, an independent kingdom off the eastern shore of England. It was beyond the jurisdiction of the English government. Moreover, it was ruled by the Earls of Derby, who were kings of the Isle of Man, and Elizabeth Vere, Oxford's oldest daughter, was married to William Spencer, 6th Earl of Derby. If Oxford did flee to the Isle of Man, he was safely beyond the reach of either Robert Cecil or King James. There he could have continued his writings, including the sonnets and other unfinished plays, or plays still meant for publication.

However, perhaps his journey took him further. Oxford had always been a literary and physical adventurer. He participated in a military campaign in his youth, had fought a duel with Knyvet and had outfitted a ship to participate in the fight against the Spanish. It hardly seems that a man of this sort would retire to an idle or contemplative life. If *The Tempest* is a record of Oxford's life perhaps he did experience a wreck on "the still-vexed Bermoothes," that is Bermuda. Could this have been the shipwreck of Sir George Somers on a voyage to Virginia in July 1609? Could it be that Oxford later returned to England and then wrote his last play which was recorded as being first performed in 1611?

Does *The Tempest* record what Oxford took with him?

> Knowing I loved my books, he furnish'd me
> From mine own library with volumes that
> I prize above my dukedom.

A LITERARY AND THEATRICAL LIFE

OVID'S METAMORPHOSES

HOLOFERNES:
You find not the apostraphas, and so miss the accent: let me supervise the canzonet. Here are only numbers ratified; but, for the elegancy, facility, and golden cadence of poesy, caret. Ovidius Naso was the man: and why, indeed, Naso, but for smelling out the odouriferous flowers of fancy, the jerks of invention? *Love's Labour's Lost*, Act 4, 2, 118

Publius Ovidius Naso was born on the outskirts of Rome in 43 B.C. After he offended the emperor for some reason unrecorded, Caesar Augustus banished him in A.D. 8 to live among the Goths until his death. In fifteen books titled *Metamorphoses*, he recounted all the legends of classical mythology in a single story with the full range of heroes and heroines, who often behaved as gods and just as often as scoundrels. Rape, death, and mutilation were but a few of the themes portrayed in these works. The title stems from the changes that the characters undergo as humans metamorphose into animals or plants, or change from gods to mortals.

In 1565, an anonymous English translation appeared titled *The Fable of Ovid Treating Narcissus,* printed by Thomas Hackett. There is now only one surviving copy, owned by the Huntington Library. A second translation, the first five books of *Metamorphoses,* appeared under the name of Arthur Golding in 1565. The complete translation appeared in 1567, again with Arthur Golding's name on it. This very successful publication went through many reprints.

Arthur Golding was the brother of Margery Golding, wife of John de Vere, 16th Earl of Oxford. Hence, Arthur Golding was Edward de Vere's putative uncle; he was the half-brother of Margery Golding, and served as a receiver in the Cecil household. Arthur Golding was to do several translations over the course of his life; most notably, he translated the sermons of John Calvin from French into English. He was also credited with several original works: *A Brief Discourse of the Later Murther of Master G. Suanders, 1573, A Discourse upon the earthquake that happened through this realme of Englande and other places of Christendom, the sixt of Aprill, 1580*; and *Arthur Golding to the Reader* in *An Aluearie or Triple dictionarie, in Englishe, Latin and French* by John Baret 1580. Only one original poem was credited to him, printed in a commendatory introduction to *Barrels Alvearie [1580]* In addition to the previously mentioned works, Golding was credited with translating verse-to-verse works of Beza's *Trajedie of Abraham's Sacrifice* and with translating two works concerned with Caesar and the Romans, *The eyght bookes of Caius Iulius Caesar* and *The historie of Leonard Aretine.*

There is no doubt that there was an Arthur Golding and that he did translations while he was alive. In 1566, Thomas Blundeville praised "Goldinge ... which Ovid dyd translate." In 1586, William Webbe honored "Master Arthur Golding, for hys labour in Englishing Ovid's *Metamorphoses.*" Thomas Nashe in 1589 said "Arthur Golding for his industrious toile in Englishing *Ovid's Metamorphoses* besides many other exquisite editions of Divinity, turned by him out of the French tongue into our own," and George Puttenham (John Lumley) "Maister *Arthure Golding*, who with no less commendation turned into English meetre the Metamorphosis of *Ovide.*" The substantial number of credits to Arthur Golding by his contemporaries makes a solid prima facie case that the translation of *Metamorphoses* attributed to Arthur Golding was, in fact, translated by Arthur Golding.

However, a number of anomalies raise questions about his authorship. The first suspicion is that the translation of *Metamorphoses* is so different from Golding's other translations. The religious spirit of the large body of Golding's work can be seen in this descriptive subtitle of one such work:

> A worke concerning the trewnesse of the Christian religion, written in French: against atheists, Epicures, Paynims, Iewes, Mahumetists, and other infidels, by Philip of Mornay Lord of Plessie Marlie; begunne to be translated into English by Sir Philip Sidney Knight, and at his request finished by Arthur Golding. Imprinted at London: (By George Robinson) for Thomas Cadman, 1587.

Orthodox Shakespearean scholars have noticed the paradox of a Puritan such as Golding translating Ovid, an author of obvious decadence and depravity:

> An odd collaboration, that between the sophisticated darling of a dissolute society, the author of a scandalous handbook of seduction, and the respectable country gentleman and convinced Puritan who spent much of his life translating the sermons and commentaries of John Calvin. Hardly less striking than the metamorphoses the work dealt with.[1]

The differences in point of view are so extreme that one wonders how a man so inventive in "translating" Ovid's *Metamorphoses* could also translate page after page of the didactic moralizing of John Calvin. With a closer look at Arthur Golding's relation to Ovid's *Metamorphoses,* it becomes increasingly distant and his authorship very dubious. Another strange thing about this work is that one introduction is written in poetry while in another edition it is written in prose. The second is an abject apology from the author for such a decadent work, and the expression of hope that the reader may gain some moral lesson by reading it. In addition, for a man who had translated Ovid from Latin to English verse, it is astonishing that Golding published no body of original verse. Strangely, Arthur Golding never attempted or accomplished anything of this magnitude again. Other works of Golding should be suspect: for example, his histories of Caesar and several prose works attributed to him such as *A Discourse upon the earthquake that happened through this realme of Englande and other places of Christendom, the sixt of Aprill, 1580.*

Orthodox scholars use the word "translation" to describe Golding's *Metamorphoses.* This implies that the writer merely substituted one language for another, which makes ascribing the works to Golding plausible. However, this rendition of *Metamorphoses* is anything but a simple translation. It is a complex, creative effort to rewrite the work in the course of the translation. It might be more properly titled *Metamorphoses Based on the Writings of Ovid.*

Ovid's version in Latin is about 12,000 lines while the "Golding translation" is over 14,000 lines. While the Latin is sparse and to the point, the Golding version is florid and detailed with flights of fancy and imagination that go far beyond translating one language into another. Here are the first four lines of a standard translation of Ovid:

> My purpose is to tell of bodies changed
> To different forms; the gods who made the changes,
> I hope will help me with a poem
> That runs from the earth's beginning to our times.

This is Golding:

> Of shapes transformde to bodies straunge, I purpose to entreate,
> Ye gods vouchsafe (for you are they ywrought this wondrous feate)
> To further this mine enterprise. And from the world begunne,
> Graunt that my verse may to my time, his course directly runne.

The additional words per line of Golding version plus the additional number of lines makes the translation about thirty percent longer than Ovid's original, a remarkable increase. Perhaps one could argue that the choice of the poetic meter requires longer lines, and that may be so. Yet the author-translator has chosen a poetic meter that requires substantial verbal additions to the underlying work. The work itself has metamorphosed.

In his translation of *Th' Abridgement of the histories of Trogus Pomeius*, Golding wrote a dedication to Oxford, then fourteen, which is a quite remarkable description of Oxford's potential:

> It is not unknown to others, and I have had experience thereof myself, how earnest a desire your honour hath naturally graffed in you to read, peruse, and communicate with others as well as the histories of ancient times, and things done long ago, as also of the present estate of things in our days, and that not without a certain pregnancy of wit and ripeness of understanding. The which do not only now rejoice the hearts of all such as bear faithful affection to the honourable house of your ancestors, but also stir up a great hope and expectation of such wisdom and experience in you in times to come, as is meet and beseeming for so noble a race.[2]

Dean Keith Simonton in his book *Greatness: Who Makes History and Why* estimates that it takes ten years to acquire a body of knowledge sufficient to contribute to art or science. For example, the Beatles appear to emerge from nowhere in their early twenties. One assumes they had some innate talent that simply emerged without much preceding effort. The truth is far different: The Beatles were expert musicians who had spent many years learning their craft. Paul and John had played musical instruments since they were youngsters, and both had played in bands since their pre-teens. By the time they reached stardom, they had worked as musicians for over fourteen years. This amount of time is needed to chunk together enough information to produce work at the highest levels:

> When Mozart was only 14 years old, he attended a service in the Sistine Chapel during which he heard Allegri's *Miserere*. This was an elaborate work in four and five parts, with a finale in nine. Because the piece was a state secret of the Pontiff, no scores were available outside the Vatican. Mozart therefore wrote down the composition from memory. Obviously, the teenager had already gained an impressive ability to chunk compositional information. Even more critically, the young musician was already an accomplished composer by then. His name was attached to operas, masses, symphonies, sonatas and dozens of lesser compositions. Does Mozart disprove the 10-year rule? ... By consulting a standard guide to records and tapes, the investigator defined a masterpiece as a composition for which there were five distinct recordings. Given this criterion, Mozart was 12 years into his career before he penned his first master-work. Hence, if anything, Mozart's artistic development was slightly retarded when weighed against the 10-year rule of thumb.[3]

The Beatles' knowledge of music was acquired from both teachers (Paul's father was a musician) and from the experience gained as working musicians. More important, they avidly studied all the popular music that was around them. They knew the tunes, the lyrics, and the structure of the songs of every pop artist from Chuck Berry and Elvis to Little Richard and the Beach Boys. The homemade tapes of the Beatles at the Star Club in Hamburg, Germany, indicate that they had developed a wide repertoire of music and that they had begun to play it with their own personal style. In this tape, the Beatles give a rock and roll rendition of an old American folk tune, "Red River Valley," that shows how they had absorbed the song and recreated it in their own fashion, with their own personality, and with their own musical inspiration. While they may have been untutored in the classical fashion, they were far from unlearned in their own area of musical expertise. In fact, they were experts in the popular music of the time.

From this perspective, Ovid's *Metamorphoses* is not the translation of a devoted religious man. Rather, it is one of the first works of a budding genius, Edward de Vere. Given a venue, a place to stand, and a microphone to the world, he began to place his own particular spin on the words of Ovid. Yet, the work is flawed and unpolished in comparison to his later *Venus and Adonis*. Often, *Metamorphoses* is turgid to the point of being unintelligible. One does not know who is doing what to whom or why. Characters seem to drift in and out again in a page. Oxford subordinates everything to the meter and rhyme, which often makes the narrative difficult to follow. Yet, despite these difficulties, the work is wonderfully creative with new additions to the English language. As with the Beatles, Oxford had no compunction to make up words or use old words in a new manner, as when he describes one woman as a "frizzle topped wench." The Beatles had no reservation about turning *Red River Valley* into a crashing rock and roll arrangement, and Oxford had no reservations about turning Ovid into his unique vision of the world.

Oxford was particularly equipped for verbal inventiveness. He was so schooled in Greek, Latin, French, and Italian that if he could not find an English word that suited his purpose, then he would just make one up based on a similarity in another language. To continue the Beatles analogy, imagine if the Beatles decided to give *Red River Valley* the chords and melodic influences from the "California Sound" of a Beach Boys tune. Fluidity of this sort requires a long period of apprenticeship to bring appropriate chunks of knowledge to bear at exactly the right moment

Ezra Pound remarked that Arthur Golding's translation of Ovid's *Metamorphoses* was one of the most beautiful poems in the English language. According to orthodox history, Golding wrote this one stunning work and then disappeared into almost total obscurity. The fact that he never published a body of original poetry nor had any dramatic career is left as a mystery of literary history. This mystery is solved by the explanation that Arthur Golding had little to do with the translation of Ovid's *Metamorphoses* and, instead, it was translated and transformed by the young Edward de Vere.

ROMEUS AND JULIET

A number of poems, plays, and translations appear in the 1560s and 1570s that orthodox scholars say influenced Shakespeare. These works have a variety of authors and many are anonymous. Some seem to prefigure later works of Shakespeare. The authors attached to the works seem to have produced only one or two works and then disappeared from the literary world or sometimes from history itself. Stephanie Caruana and Betty Sears describe the situation:

> From the mid-1560s through 1588, a series of strikingly original plays, translations, ballads, poems, poetic miscellanies, novels, histories, and essay and short story collections appeared in London, more than a decade before Shaksper of Stratford (1564–1616) could possibly have written them. Many of these works are recognized by scholars as "source material" for the Shakespeare plays. But they are either anonymous, or attributed to a whole troop of shadowy "geniuses," each of whom supposedly produced one or a few important literary works, and then sank back into oblivion. Some are signed with enigmatic initials, "posies," and pen names. The "authors" are literary ghosts who seem to exist only on the fragile pages which bear their "names"; yet each is mentioned repeatedly by scholars as an important "source" for stylistic or plot elements of one or the other of the Shakespeare plays.

> There is also an astonishing crowd of one-shot "geniuses" who appear to have served as *alonymous* authors. These were real people behind who we believe the true author, Oxford, hid his identity, beginning at the age of about twelve. They are now given credit for writing various "orphan" literary works of genius.[4]

The first of these works is *Romeus and Juliet,* published in English in 1562. It was based on a story that only existed in Italian, and the "translation" was credited to Arthur Brooke. Interestingly, neither the title page nor the body of the work lists an Arthur Brooke. Rather only initials are in the title:

> THE TRAGICAL HISTORY of Romeus and Juliet, written first in Italian by Bandell, and nowe in Englishe by Ar. Br.

"A rose by any other name"

The following attempts to list Oxford's pen names. Some of these names are obvious pseudonyms, others are Latin phrases, and finally there are living people. Many of these living people had literary histories that are highly suspect. Many produced only one or two works that orthodox scholars say "influenced" Shakespeare, and then the authors disappeared from history. One such case is John Lyly, the longtime secretary for the Earl of Oxford. Lyly is credited with several works, including the earliest novel *Euphues*. Strangely, although he lived another ten years after leaving Oxford's service (perhaps for being a spy for William Cecil), John Lyly never wrote another literary work.

A True English Man
Arthur Brooke—*Romeus and Juliette*
Arthur Golding—Ovid's *Metamorphoses*
The Auchthour
Christopher Marlowe
Clement Robinson—*Handful of Pleasant Delights*
Dan Bartholemew of Bathe
Dan Bartholmew His Name I Hide
Deepe Disire
Deere Familyar Friend
Dewe Desert
Geffrey Gates
George Gascoigne
George Pettie—*Pettie's Palace of Pleasure*
The Greene Knight
Ignoto
John Dowland (Music) Oxford author of the song "Green Sleeves"?
John Lyly—*Campaspe, Sapho and Phao,* etc.
John Pykering—*Horestes*
John Studely
Martin Mar-prelate—Political Tracts
Master Eduouardo Donati
Master F. I.
Meritum petere, grave
Nemiesis
The Oke
Philomene
The Reporter
Robert Greene (Ver?)
Sylvanus Mercuire
Thomas Kyd—*The Spanish Tragedy, Arden of Feversham*
William Adlington—*The Golden Asse*
William North—*Lives of the Ancient Greeks and Romans*
William Shakespeare

The author also signs his preface of the book "Ar. Br." Thus, the first assumption was that Ar. Br. was the mysterious Arthur Brooke. J.J. Munro says in his introduction to *Romeus and Juliet* in 1908:

> Of Arthur Brooke himself we know very little: our interest in him must always be principally due to his connexion with Shakspere.[5]

True to his word, Munro provides no details on his birth or his education and credits him with only one other work, a translation out of French by an "Arthure Broke." Munro uses the following as confirmation that Brooke died in a shipwreck the year after publication of the poem:

> In a letter from Henry Cobham to Challoner, dated May 14, 1563, the writer says: "Sir Thomas Finch was drowned going over to Newhaven (i.e., Le Havre) as knightmarshall in Sir Adrian Poinings' place, who is come over. James Wentworth and his brother John were cast away in the same vessel, on the sands near Rye, and little Brook and some other petty gentlemen." In view of the parallel circumstances and the dates, we are justified in believing that "little Brook" is our own Arthur Brooke, the poet.[7]

This is hardly overwhelming evidence that Arthur Brooke existed, was a poet, or wrote *Romeus and Juliet*. Munro provides no information where Arthur Brooke might have acquired Italian to read any original accounts of the story in that language and to translate them into English. There was a poem by George Turberville in 1570, *An Epitaph on the death of Master Arthur Brooke, drowned in passing to Newhaven*, that confirms the existence of Brooke. On the other hand, perhaps Turberville was creating a false tale to dispose of a nonexistent person or perhaps he was simply using his literary license to create a poem. In summary, the evidence that Arthur Brooke existed is scant, and there is no evidence that he was the author of *Romeus and Juliet*, except the initials "Ar. Br." on the title page and introduction.

It is far more likely that the youthful Oxford was the translator of the Italian story. Again, as with Ovid's *Metamorphoses,* the word "translation" does not adequately describe the creative endeavor at work in *Romeus and Juliet*, a poem of 3,000 lines of rhymed couplets. Here are the opening lines:

> There is beyond the Alps, a town of ancient fame,
> Whose bright renown yet shineth clear: Verona men it name;
> Built in a happy time, built on fertile soil.
> Maintainéd by the heavenly fates, and by the townish toil.

Romeus and Juliet is more than a source for Shakespeare's. Rather, the poem is a template for the play. Munro gives over a hundred correspondences between the text of *Romeus and Juliet* and the text of *Romeo and Juliet.* There are exact parallels between the action of the poem and the action of the play. The most sensible interpretation of this is that Edward de Vere translated *Romeus and Juliet* from the original Italian in his youth. When he decided to write the play *Romeo and Juliet,* he turned to his translation and dramatized the action and characters in another art form using the same plot line and characters without much modification.

Another work mentioned as a source for Shakespeare is *Agamemnon* by Seneca. It was published in 1566, and the translation credited to a "John Studley," who apparently attended Cambridge and graduated with a bachelor's of arts in 1566 and a master's of arts in 1570. He is credited with translating four plays while at Cambridge: *Agamemnon, Media, Hippolytus,* and *Hercules Oeteus.* Again, the word "translation" does not completely describe these works because the translator added various re-narrations, a prologue, and other verses. *Agamemnon* is dedicated to Sir William Cecil. In 1572, John Studley was charged with nonconformity at Cambridge, and he vacated his fellowship. From there, he disappears from the historical record. This suggests that Oxford knew him at the university, and as with others, Oxford used Studley's name to publish his own work. Studley was never again credited with any published work.

The Historye of Horestes with the cruell revengment of his Fathers death, upon his unnatural Mother, published in 1567, foreshadows the writing of *Hamlet.* This was credited to a John Pikering. After searching for over a hundred years, scholars have never been able to locate Pikering. This was an original play based on Greek mythology. A play "of Orestes" was one of a group of plays presented at court between Christmas and Shrovetide 1567. This suggests that this play might be one of Oxford's first court productions.

Palaemon and Arcite was performed at Oxford University when the Queen attended the graduation ceremonies of the young Earl of Oxford. The two main characters of this play, Palaemon and Arcite, are the two main characters of a later play, *The Two Noble Kinsman,* which was not included in the *First Folio* but which has been considered by many to be a Shakespeare play. It was first published in 1634 and credited to John Fletcher and William Shakespeare. Again, this is one of those plays of the period that looks suspiciously like an early Shakespeare play but is not credited to him by orthodox scholars.

The play *Locrine* appears in the *Third Folio* (1664) and *Fourth Folio* (1685), and is identified as a play of William Shakespeare. Orthodox scholars have rejected this attribution because the play was written in a verse style that suggests authorship in the 1560s. Obviously, accepting a play such as this means that the playwright from Stratford-upon-Avon was writing before he was four years old. The orthodox ideology has to reject information that does not fit its theory of authorship rather than question the theory.

The Supposes and *Jocasta* are other examples of works that may have been translated or written by Oxford and then influenced his later works under the name of William Shakespeare. The first is a translation of an Italian comedy, *Gli Suppositi,* written by Ariosto in 1509. The translation was performed at Gray's Inn in 1567 shortly before Oxford became a law student there. The first published version of the play appeared in 1572 and is credited to George Gascoigne. The plot of *Supposes* was used as a subplot in another anonymous play, *Taming of a Shrew,* that precedes Shakespeare's *The Taming of the Shrew.* Gascoigne, an acknowledged poet, was involved in a rather complex literary imbroglio with Sir Christopher Hatton against the Earl of Oxford in 1573. The second was *Jocasta* by Euripides, a translation from Greek to English credited to George Gascoigne and Francis Kinwelmershe. This play was also presented at Gray's Inn in 1567 while Oxford was a student there. While George Gascoigne did publish other works under his own name, he did not become a major poet or playwright of the Elizabethan era. Kinwelmershe was also a real person, despite the opportunity for his name to be an ironic comic pen name.

Beethoven, Bach, Picasso, Jane Austin, and anyone else one can think of show a developmental period wherein they develop and polish their skills with less than sterling works. Such acknowledged geniuses produce many immature works that show promise but lack the consistency and polish of their later efforts. This is also the case for Edward de Vere. Tracking his literary biography is much more difficult because of the aristocratic taboo against a noble actively engaging in a trade such as writing. The number of anonymous plays of this early period and the number of real people that were used to cover his authorship make the task even more difficult. However, it is in these early works that the budding genius of Edward de Vere can be seen. The works mentioned here, and most likely yet to be discovered others, foreshadow the emergence of "William Shakespeare."

SHAKESPEARE AS TRANSLATOR

William Shakespeare is acknowledged as having made the greatest impact on the English language by a single person. He created expressions, coined words, and introduced English versions of words from Latin, Greek, Italian, and Hebrew. Edward de Vere developed his great linguistic skill by translating many works from Latin, Greek, French, and Italian until these languages were as familiar to him as his native English. If a word in English was not adequate to express what he needed, then he drew on other language, or simply made up a word to fit his needs, as does the author of "Golding's" *Metamorphoses.*

Here is a sample of words introduced by Oxford-Shakespeare that have become part of today's English language:[7]

> accommodation, assassination, barefaced, countless, courtship, dislocate, dwindle, eventful, fancy-free, lack-luster, laughable, premeditated, submerged

To be fair, here is a list of words that Shakespeare introduced that have not survived into modern usage:

> abruption, appertainments, exsufflicate, persistive, protractive, questrist, soliure, tortive, ungenitured, unplausive, vastidity

Here are a few of the expressions introduced into the English language by Oxford that survive today:

> play fast and loose; a tower of strength; make a virtue of necessity; cold comfort; at one fell swoop; to the manner born; brevity is the soul of wit; hold the mirror up to nature; I must be cruel only to be kind; all our yesterdays; with bated breath; love is blind; as good luck would have it; milk of human kindness; more sinned against than sinning; salad days; strange bedfellows; loved not wisely but too well

Compounds using a hyphen are also distinguishing characteristics of his writing:

> arch-heretique, baby-eyes, breake-vow, faire-play, giant-world, halfe-blown, ill-tuned, pell-mell, smooth-fac'd, vile-concluded, widow-comfort

The most famous of all these is "Shake-speare," which appears on the first two published plays and on the title page of *Shake-speares Sonnets:*

1598	*Tragedie of King Richard 2nd*	William Shake-speare
1598	*Richard the Third*	William Shake-speare
1609	*Shake-speares Sonnets^a*	*(No author listed)*

The language of Shakespeare alone indicates that the writer was a skilled translator who was fluent in many languages, which has two major implications. First, it eliminates almost every other writer of the Elizabethan period as William Shakespeare, other than perhaps Queen Elizabeth. While some were familiar with Latin or Greek, few, if any, had the knowledge of languages that Oxford possessed. Oxford was fluent in four foreign languages, Latin, Greek, Italian, and French, and one scholar believes he knew some Hebrew. Second, those early translations and original works that are attributed to everybody but Oxford, works of originality, were in fact written by Shakespeare (the Earl of Oxford) in the earlier stages of his career.

Diana Price tells how orthodox scholars handle Shakespeare's fluency in foreign languages and use of sources not translated into English. In *Shakespeare's Unorthodox Biography*, she says:

> When the earliest known English translation postdates the relevant Shakespearean play or poem, scholars often minimize or discredit Shakespeare's reliance on the source, or they divert attention to another favorite catchall solution: The lost intermediary source. The lost sources are hypothetical adaptations or translations into English of foreign-language books on which the dramatist supposedly relied.

> Shakespeare's reliance on books in foreign languages puzzles the experts, so they suppose all sorts of things rather than conclude the obvious. If Shakespeare regularly relied on books not yet translated from Italian, French, and Spanish, then he must have been able to read in Italian, French and Spanish.[8]

Edward de Vere did not emerge from the head of Zeus. The skills he later shows as a playwright and poet developed over years of hard work and a consuming dedication to a literary life from his earliest years to his death.

---

[a] The title page of *Sonnets* reads *Shake-speares Sonnets.* There is a hyphen between "Shake" and "speare," and there is no apostrophe to signal the possessive case. (See the graphic of the title page later in this book.) Orthodox scholars deliberately leave out the unwanted hyphen.

THEN COMES VERONA

Ernesto Grillo, M.A., D.Lit., LL.D., D.C.L., was a professor of Italian language and literature at the University of Glasgow. He was a native of Italy, where he received an LL.D. and a D.C.L. He studied at Bonn University and St. John's College, Cambridge. He was Professor of English and German in the University of Urbino, Italy. He accepted a post before World War II at Glasgow University as Head of the Department of Italian Language and Literature and remained at Glasgow for the remainder of his life. His department at first consisted of one student, but Dr. Grillo is described as a charismatic teacher and soon had well-attended lectures. As his credentials indicate, he was a knowledgeable scholar of Italy, Italian literature, and Shakespeare.

He comments as follows on the relation between Shakespeare and Italy:

> The frequent use that the poet made of Italian *Novelle* and other works and the accuracy with which he introduced proper names and even whole sentences into his dramas are sufficient proof of the poet's knowledge of the Italian language. It has been argued that in Elizabethan England translations of Italian books abounded, but certainly, Shakespeare's knowledge of life and customs in Italy was not entirely derived from them. In his lifetime some of the books to which he was indebted for much of his material had not been translated into English. In the collection of tales by Ser Giovanni Fiorentino entitled *Il Pecorone* we find the whole plot of the *Merchant of Venice*; and in the *Hecatomiti* of Cinthio we may read the story of *Othello*, and that of the adventures of Isabella, which Shakespeare utilized in *Measure for Measure*. Many of Cinthio's *Novelle* had been translated into French, but the tragic tale of Othello was to be found in neither Latin nor English. This collection of short stories—*Il Pecorone*—was only published in Italy in 1558.[9]

> Notwithstanding the fact that his Italian scenes are depicted in colours faithfully reproduced from the originals, the majority of commentators tell us that Shakespeare knew nothing of conditions in northern Italy, and that he was totally ignorant of the geography of these provinces. The well-known passages are quoted in support of their assertion: the first in The Tempest, the second in the Two Gentlemen of Verona and the third in the Taming of the Shrew ... It is erroneously repeated that Shakespeare described Verona as a city on the sea coast, and Bergamo as a place where canvas was woven for the making of sails, without considering that Shakespeare in his allusions to Verona was careful to mention not the sea but the very river—the Adige—which flows through that city.[10]

> Shakespeare's accurate knowledge of the geography of Italy is all the more noteworthy as it contrasts strikingly with his ignorance of other European countries, France, for example.[11]

English critics while seeming to encourage the idea that Shakespeare was an unlearned genius fallen meteor-like from heaven, aver with strange inconsistency that it was easy enough for him to obtain the necessary information by consulting the volumes about travels in Italy which were in circulation at that time. They even go so far a to quote a long list of books in Italian, French, Latin, English and German—books which in all probability the dramatist never either saw or read. Some Italian authors have asserted that Shakespeare must have obtained information relating to Italy at the house of the Earl of Southampton.[12]

This is very straightforward; however, this is coming from a knowledgeable scholar who believes the man from Stratford to be William Shakespeare. Professor Grillo appeared unaware of the existence of Edward de Vere, so he may have been unaware of the literary landmine he stepped on by pointing out the strong Italian influence in Shakespeare's plays. Professor Grillo's solution to the Italian problem within the Stratfordian framework is also rather straightforward:

Here [in the plays] we find such definite characteristics, such vivid colour and such a wealth of precise and vigorous details that we are forced to conclude that Shakespeare must have visited Milan, Verona, Venice, Padua and Mantua. With this in mind we can fix with some certainty the date of his journey between the autumn of 1592 and the summer of 1593.[13]

Italy was the magic land where the joys of life abounded. With even the slenderest of resources it was possible to undertake the pilgrimage, for one could travel at little expense on foot, on horseback, by boat or even in a carriage. Living in those days was very inexpensive.[14]

He continues:

Shakespeare evinces a varied and profound knowledge of the country in general and of our cities in particular. His writings display the breadth of his sympathy for Italy throughout the whole course of his career. The loveliest lyrical passages in his plays are of the purest Italian inspiration. There is no poet, with the exception of Dante, who has loved our land more ardently than the great English dramatist. Innumerable are the passages where he speaks of the special characteristics of our peninsula, of her history and of her customs. He knows that Padua possessed a great university and was the majestic Alma Mater of the arts.

For the great desire I had
To see fair Padua, nursery of the arts,
I am arrived for fruitful Lombardy,
The pleasant garden of great Italy ...

He knew that Padua with all its learning was under the protection of Venice and that Mantua was not. Besides he assigns special and precise attributes to various cities, e.g. Pisa, renowned for her wealth but still more for her 'grave citizens', and expression used by Dante; Milan is 'the fair' and possesses a 'royal court' and the famous St. Gregory Well. Elsewhere he speaks of the Florentines and Neapolitans, and accuses the inhabitants of Pisa of being avaricious. He knew that the Florentines were notable merchants and mathematicians, making frequent use in their commerce of letters of credit and counting their money by ducats; and he was also aware that they were constantly in conflict with the Sienese. And here the poet uses a phrase which is pure Italian—The Florentines and the Sienese are by the ear (*si pigliano per gli orecchi*). Apart from all the references to Italy in general which are about 800, and to Rome which are about 400, we find that the most important Italian cities are mentioned in the following order of frequency—Venice 52 times, Naples 34, Milan 25, Florence 23, Padua 22 and Verona 20. Then follow Genoa, Mantua, Pisa, Ferrara and others.[15]

Today, most authors who have never visited or traveled to New York can describe the Empire State Building and with the aid of a map can determine where it is located. But it would take an extremely diligent researcher to know what park is behind the New York Public Library or that the Greenwich Village's Houston Street is pronounced "House-tun" Street, not "Hew-stun" Street, as in the Texas city. In addition, there were few, if any, illustrated books of the streets of Italian cities during the Elizabethan era. Orthodox scholars assume that Shakespeare is wrong when his descriptions of Italy do not fit their contemporary knowledge. For example, when Shakespeare describes characters travelling by water between two landlocked cities, this is not a mistake. The cities might be landlocked today, but there were numerous canals in Italy and travel via canals was often preferable to the ill-paved roads of the 1500s. It is this level of detail of Italy that baffles traditional orthodox scholars because it leads to the inevitable conclusion that the man from Stratford, who never saw the ocean much less Italy, could not have written the works.

In a similar manner, orthodox scholars assume that Shakespeare was wrong when he describes life in ancient Rome in a way that differs from their conception. According to orthodox scholars, there is an anachronism in *The History of Julius Caesar* because they say there were no clocks that could strike in ancient Rome:

BRUTUS: Peace! Count the clock.
CASSIUS: The clock hath stricken three.

Act 2, 1, 201

However, in *The Ancient* Engineers by L. Sprague de Camp we find this description:

A favorite time-marking mechanism with the early clock markers was a bird that moved and sang on the hour, exactly as does the bird in a modern cuckoo clock. The earliest clocks were designed to mark the hours by noisy alarums, not to subdivide the times between. When Shakespeare's Cassius in

Julius Caesar says: "The clock hath stricken three" (Act 2, sc. 1) he is not anachronistic after all.[16]

It was Edward de Vere's detailed knowledge of Greek and Roman history from his extensive reading and translation that proves Shakespeare correct and modern scholarship wrong. There were clocks in the Greek and Roman era. They had been in existence for almost three centuries before the Romans. These clocks operated by water filling a container. A float in the container was moved upward by the rising water and the float was attached to gears, which operated a clock. They were often equipped with gongs or other noise-making devices to tell the citizens of the city the time. This is also why "clockwise" is a movement from left to right. The clock time mirrors the rising and setting of the sun. As seen from the Northern Hemisphere, the sun moves from east to west or left to right in the course of daylight hours.[b] Ktesibios (285–247 B.C) from Alexandria was a prolific inventor, who invented the water clock.

The literary import of all this is that orthodox Shakespeare scholars have subverted the interpretation and intellectual history of Shakespeare's literary works to remain within what is possible for the man from Stratford to have read and experienced. Shakespeare's canon is directly influenced by Italy, with over a dozen works set in the country, and directly influenced by the classics of Greece and Rome. It was influenced by and an extension of the Italian Renaissance, Protestant Reformation, and English humanism. This intellectual and literary history of the period is almost totally ignored by contemporary scholars much to the impoverishment of the students they teach and our understanding of Shakespeare.

CASTIGLIONE'S *IL CORTEGIANO* (THE COURTIER)

As it is difficult to imagine the Elizabethan psychology, it is equally difficult to imagine the vastly different attitudes toward class and class distinctions that separate this aristocratic, late-medieval society from modern society. There were sumptuary laws that specified how different ranks were to dress so that a nobleman would not be confused with a wealthy gentleman, or a gentleman with an apprentice, and so on. The livery of a nobleman's retainers advertised their social rank. The Queen was exceedingly conscious of these social distinctions and banned Lettice

---

[b] Why clocks repeat two twelve-hour cycles remains somewhat a mystery to this author. If clocks mirrored the movement of the sun, why not start the day at dawn equals zero (at the nine o'clock position) and then have noon at the top and midnight at the bottom?

Knollys from court for wearing a dress that had too many pearls, for it would not do to have some upstart aristocratic parvenu dress beyond her station in life, especially one as attractive as Lettice Knollys. As has been stated before, the Queen forbade a duel between Oxford and Sir Philip Sidney based on unequal rank. She remarked that if a man of lower rank were to challenge one of higher rank, eventually the commoner would challenge the nobleman. This aristocratic caste society was based on birth, not on accomplishment or talent.

The aristocrats separated themselves from those who lived from the product of their labor whether they were carpenters, poets, or playwrights. It was the rule, not the exception, that those within the inner court circle would publish under pen names. Elizabethan writers who published under pen names during their lifetimes included Sir Edward Dyer, John Fletcher, Fulke Greville-Lord Brooke, George Herbert, Alexander Hume, Sir Walter Raleigh, Thomas Sackville, and Sir Philip Sidney, to name but a few. Sometimes an aristocrat's works might be published under his own name, but usually this was after his death. (Later in this book, there will be an explanation of why Oxford's works were not posthumously attributed to him.) This is not to say that those in the inner circle of the small literary world, which consisted at most of a hundred writers and fifty publishers, did not know who was writing what, but the aristocratic taboos kept these names from being publicly revealed. Often publishers would say they had come upon manuscripts, copies of poems, or other works and publish them claiming that they had "come into his hands, accidentally." An offended nobleman could do little: He could not claim authorship and thereby make his authorship even more public. Or perhaps the noble writer might be behind the printing but claim not to be.

Occasionally, someone would reveal in print the names of those involved in this literary circle, but they were generally circumspect about attributing a particular work to a particular author. William Webbe's comments in 1586 about the Earl of Oxford:

> I may not omit the deserved commendations of many honourable and noble Lords and Gentlemen in Her Majesty's court, which, in the rare devices of poetry, have been and yet are most skilful; among whom the right honourable Earl of Oxford may challenge to himself the title of the most excellent among the rest
> — William Webbe, *A discourse of English Poetry,* 1586[17]

Yet more, from the author of *The Arte of English Poesie*:

> So as I know very many notable Gentlemen in the Court that have written commendably, and suppressed it agayne, or els suffred it to be publisht without their owne names to it: as if it were a discredit for a Gentleman, to seeme learned, and to shew him selfe amorous of any good art … (whether it be in prose of in Poesie, if they them selves be able to write, or have written any thing well or of rare invention) be any whit squeamish to let it be publisht under their names, for reason serves it, and modesitie doth not repugne …

> And in her Majestys time that now is are sprong up another crew of Courtly makers [poets], Noble men and Gentlemen of her Majesty's own servauntes, who had written excellently well as it would appeare if their doings could be found out and made publicke with the rest, of which number is first that noble gentleman *Edward* Earl of Oxford …

> For Tragedie the Lord of Buckhurst and Master *Edwards Ferrys* for such doings as I have sene of theirs do deserve the hyest price [praise]: Th'Earle of Oxford and Maister *Edwardes* of her Majesites Chappel for Comedy and Enterlude.
>
> — George Puttenham, *The Arte of English Poesie,* 1589[18]

Francis Meres was not so circumspect about naming Oxford:

> The best for comedy among us be Edward Earl of Oxford.
>
> — Francis Meres, *Palladis Tamia*, 1598[19]

The historical record does not reveal exactly what the Queen thought of her courtier-poets. One can only infer her attitudes from what she allowed to happen during the period. The Queen enjoyed the efforts of her courtier-poets. Elizabeth as much as anyone encouraged the production of plays in her court and, as it has been described before in this book, there were over 200 productions at court of plays, masques, and interludes for the Queen's and her court's enjoyment. The courtier-playwright-poets had a degree of freedom of expression. Oxford used this freedom of expression to burlesque his court opponents such as Christopher Hatton. Oxford was once described as a small man who was dangerous because he had a very large wit, which he used to skewer his less intellectually nimble opponents.

It was then a major break in tradition in 1571 when Edward de Vere, 17th Earl of Oxford, attached a signed preface, written in Latin, to the reader indicating his high praise for Bartholomew Clerke's translation of Baldassare Castiglione's[c] *Il Cortegiano* (The Courtier) from Italian to Latin. Here again the case with Oxford is that nothing is ever quite simple

---

[c] Baldassare Castiglione (1478-1529), Italian statesman and literary figure. *Il Cortegiano* was published in Venice in 1528.

and straightforward. While there was a taboo against aristocrats not attaching their names to literary works, Oxford paid it no mind when he felt the occasion to express himself in print under his own name. The word "pen name" did not come into the English language until a century or so later. The thought that an author could completely hide his identity behind such a name is a modern concept, not an Elizabethan concept. There were only a small number of writers during the Elizabethan period, and there were an even smaller number of printing establishments. In this small world, where everyone knew everyone, it strains plausibility that a new poem or play would appear under an unfamiliar name and be credited to an unknown person. A new pen name or "poesie" did not automatically signal a new writer but, more likely, that some established writer had chosen a new guise. Pen names provided only the fashionably decorous cover that protocol required. This does not mean that there were no erroneous attributions, as is the case with Arthur Golding and the translation of Ovid's *Metamorphoses*. Whether those lauding Golding realized who was behind the translation and kept up the pretense or whether they did not know the true author remains to be determined. Certainly, if any had thought about it at the time, or in any of the four centuries thereafter, Arthur Golding would have been an extremely unlikely candidate for the translation of Ovid.

Oxford's introduction to Bartholomew Clerke's translation of *The Courtier* is mature, confident, and insightful for a man of twenty-three years. Then again, it is not absolute calendar years that give polish and maturity, but rather the number of years and intensity of effort during which the artist has been applying himself, learning his craft, and increasing his knowledge that produces artistic maturity. By the time Oxford wrote the introduction, he had spent almost twelve years of intensive study of literature and the arts.

Scholars have long remarked that Shakespeare's point of view is reflected in *The Courtier,* but the relationship is much stronger than that. The preface written in Latin by Edward de Vere is almost a statement of principles for Shakespeare and an essay on his view of the role of the literary and theatrical arts. It is almost impossible to understand Shakespeare without reading and understanding Oxford's preface to *The Courtier.* The preface shows Oxford's belief in the older principles of honor and duty that were part of the age of chivalry (if only in myth). These are principles that emerge in Oxford's plays and poetry. His preface also indicates Oxford's general attitudes toward literature and his preciseness of mind, aptness of thought, and ability to clearly articulate his point of view. (Unfortunately, Oxford's Latin introduction is absent from many modern printings of the work.) His introduction might be aptly titled *Shakespeare on Shakespeare*:

> Edward Vere, Earl of Oxford, Lord Great Chamberlain of England, Viscount Bulbeck and Baron Scales and Badlesmere to the Reader—Greeting.
>
> A frequent and earnest consideration of the translation of Castiglione's Italian work, which had now for a long time been undertaken and finally carried out by my friend Clerke, has caused me to waver between two opinions: debating in my mind whether I should preface it by some writing and letter of my own, or whether I should do no more than study it with a mind full of gratitude. The first course seemed to demand greater skill and art than I can lay claim to, the second to be a work of no less good-will and application. To do both, however, seemed to combine a task of delightful industry with an indication of special good-will.
>
> I have therefore undertaken the work, and I do so the more willingly, in order that I may lay a laurel wreath of my own on the translation in which I have studied this book, and also to ensure that neither my good-will (which is very great) should remain unexpressed, nor that my skill (which is small) should seem to fear to face the light and the eyes of men.
>
> It is no more than its due that praises of every kind should be rendered to this descriptive of a Courtier. It is indeed in every way right and one may say almost inevitable that with the highest and greatest praises I should address both the author and translator, and even more the great patroness of so great a work, whose name alone on the title-page gives it a right majestic and honourable introduction.[20]

Oxford believes this book is to "lay down principles for guidance of the very Monarch himself." In other words, art or theater is not simply entertainment; rather, it is for the instruction of the most supreme ruler of the state. In *Hamlet,* he repeats the same thoughts in dramatic fashion when "the play is the thing" to "catch the conscience of the King." Oxford is spelling out the philosophy that is evident in his plays; that is, the play for him is a means of moral instruction not for the masses— his courtier-poet-hero is to instruct the monarch:

> For what more difficult, more noble, or more magnificent task has anyone ever undertaken than our author Castiglione, who has drawn for us the figure and model of a courtier, a work to which nothing can be added, in which there is no redundant word, a portrait which we shall recognize as that of the highest and most perfect type of man. And so, although nature herself had made nothing perfect in every detail, yet the manners of men exceed in dignity that with which nature has endowed them; and he who surpasses others has here surpassed himself, and has even outdone nature which by no one has ever been surpassed. Nay more, however elaborate the ceremonial, whatever the magnificence of the Court, the splendour of the Courtiers, and the multitude of spectators, he has been able to lay down principles for guidance of the very Monarch himself.

Again, Castiglione has vividly depicted more and even greater things than these. For who has spoken of Princes with greater gravity? Who has discoursed of illustrious women with a more ample dignity? No one has written of military affairs more eloquently, more aptly about horseracing, and more clearly and admirably about encounters under arms on the field of battle. I will say nothing of the fitness and the excellence with which he has depicted the beauty of chivalry in the noblest persons. Nor will I refer to his delineations in the case of those persons who cannot be Courtiers, when he alludes to some notable defect, or to some ridiculous character, or to some deformity of appearance. Whatever is heard in the mouths of men in casual talk and in society, whether apt and candid, or villainous and shameful, that he has set down in so natural a manner that it seems to be acted before our very eyes.[21]

In the next paragraphs, Oxford's appreciation of language and the craft of writing become evident. It is not simply the thought, but also the use of the right words for the right expression of that thought: *"If weighty matters are under consideration, he unfolds his theme in a solemn and majestic rhythm; if the subject is familiar and facetious, he makes use of words that are witty and amusing."* What could be more true? Oxford's plays employ the right expression, with exactly the right words, at exactly the right time. This is very much a craftsman's approach to the creation of literature and the approach of a man who has given considerable thought to the expression of his ideas:

Again, to the credit of the translator of so great a work, a writer too who is no mean orator, must be added a new glory of language. For although Latin has come down to us from the ancient city of Rome, a city in which the study of eloquence flourished exceedingly, it has now given back its features for use in modern Courts as a polished language of an excellent temper, fitted out with royal pomp, (and possessing admirable dignity.) All this my good friend Clerke has done, combining exceptional genius with wonderful eloquence. For he has resuscitated that dormant quality of fluent discourse. He has recalled those ornaments and lights which he had laid aside, for use in connection with subjects most worthy of them. For this reason he deserves all the more honour, because that to great subjects—and they are indeed great—he has applied the greatest lights and ornaments.

For who is clearer in his use of words? Or richer in the dignity of his sentences? Or who can conform to the variety of circumstances with greater art? If weighty matters are under consideration, he unfolds his theme in a solemn and majestic rhythm; if the subject is familiar and facetious, he makes use of words that are witty and amusing. When therefore he writes with precise and well-chosen words, with skillfully constructed and crystal clear sentences, and with every art of dignified rhetoric, it cannot be but that some noble quality should be felt to proceed from his work. To me indeed it seems, when I read this courtly Latin, that I am listening to Crassus, Antonius, and Hortensius, discoursing on this very theme.[22]

We might add to this the obvious insinuation that Oxford was well versed in classical literature. Oxford concludes with homage to the Queen in the flowery style of the Elizabethan era:

> And, great as all these qualities are, our translator has wisely added one single surpassing title of distinction to recommend his work. For indeed what more effective action could he have taken to make his work fruitful of good results than to dedicate his *Courtier* to our most illustrious and noble Queen, in whom all courtly qualities are personified, together with those diviner and truly celestial virtues? For there is no pen so skilful or powerful, no kind of speech so clear, that is not left behind by her own surpassing virtue. It was therefore an excellent display of wisdom on the part of our translator to seek out as a patroness of his work one who was of surpassing virtue, of wisest mind, of soundest religion, and cultivated in the highest degree in learning and in literary studies.

> Lastly, if the noblest attributes of the wisest Princes, the safest protection of a flourishing commonwealth, the greatest qualities of the best citizens, by her own merit, and in the opinion of all, continually encompass her around; surely to obtain the protection of that authority, to strengthen it with gifts, and to mark it with the superscription of her name, is a work which, while worthy of all Monarchs, is most worthy of our own Queen, to whom alone is due all the praise of all the Muses and all the glory of literature.

> Given at the Royal Court on the 5th of January 1571.[23]

Clerke's translation went through six Latin editions, and all the editions contained Oxford's Latin preface to the reader. This was a very popular work with the educated Elizabethans, and it had to have established the young Earl as a youthful patron of the arts. Oxford had gone beyond the conventions of the day with his open support of the author, the work, and the ideas contained in the work. In the parlance of our time, Oxford made himself a player in the literary scene with his preface to *The Courtier.* This did not go unnoticed. Seven years later, Gabriel Harvey wrote of Oxford's "epistle":

> Pallas striking her shield with her spear shaft will attend thee. For a long time past Phoebus Apollo has cultivated thy mind in the arts. English poetical measures have been sung by thee long enough. Let that Courtly Epistle—more polished even that the writings of Castiglione himself— witness how greatly thou dost excel in letters. I have seen many Latin verses of thine, yea, even more English verses are extant; thou has drunk deep draughts not only of the Muses of France and Italy, but has learned the manners of many men, and the arts of foreign countries ... Thine eyes flash fire, thy countenance shakes spears.

> — Gabriel Harvey, *Gratulationes Validinenses, libri quatutor*, 1578[24]

This translation of Harvey's Latin has been bitterly contested by supporters of the man from Stratford-upon-Avon. The key Latin phrase is "Tela vibrat," which Stratfordians insist means anything but "spear shaker." To test this, the passage was sent to Professor Tom Holland, Head of Classics at Cheltenham Ladies College, England, who is the director of the Latin translation service Quintus. He was unaware of the relevance of this statement to the Shakespeare Authorship issues. Professor Holland translates:

> Martius ardor inest: scintillant lumina: vultus
> Tela vibrat: quis non rediuiuum iuret Achillem?

> A martial blaze lies within you. Your expression brandishes spears.
> Who would not swear that you are a reborn Achilles?

Oxfordians maintain that this is one of the reasons that Oxford later chose the pen name of William Shakespeare, and Holland's translation supports this view.

Literary Lion

Oxford followed with a second break with tradition in the publication of *Cardanus Comforte* in 1573, written by Thomas Bedingfield. The title page of the book reads:

> Cardanus' Comforte, translated into Englishe. And published by comaundement of the right honourable the Earle of Oxenforde. Anno Domini 1573

In other words, Oxford is not simply allowing himself to be a dedicatee of the author, which implies that he provided financial support. Rather, Oxford is using his rank to ensure that the work was published. Taken at its face value, the sentence implies Oxford is "commanding" that the work be published.

As a preface, Oxford included a long letter "To my loving friend Thomas Bedingfield Esquire, one of Her Majesty's Gentlemen Pensioners" explaining why he believed it was better to publish the book even though Bedingfield had objected to its publication. Oxford then followed with a poem, which violated the taboo of aristocrats connecting themselves with published poetry:

THE EARL OF OXFORD TO THE READER OF BEDINGFIELD'S "CARDANUS' COMFORT"

The labouring man that tills the fertile soil,
And reaps the harvest fruit, hath not indeed
The gain but pain; and if for all his toil
He gets the straw, the lord will have the seed.
The manchet fine falls not unto his share;
On coarsest cheat his hungry stomach feeds.
The landlord doth possess the finest fare;
He pulls the flowers, he plucks but weeds.
The mason poor that builds the lordly halls,
Dwells not in them; they are for high degree;
His cottage is compact in paper walls,
And not with brick or stone as others be.
The idle drone that labours not at all,
Sucks up the sweet of honey from the bee;
Who worketh most to their share least doth fall,
With due desert reward will never be.
The swiftest hare unto the mastive [mastiff] slow
Oft-times doth fall, to him as for a prey;
The greyhound thereby doth miss his game we know
For which he made such speedy hast away.
So he that takes the pain to pen the book,
Reaps not the gifts of goodly golden muse;
But those gain that, who on the work shall look,
And from the sour the sweet by skill shall choose;
For he that beats the bush the bird not gets,
But who sits still and holdeth fast the nets.[d]

Many Oxfordian historians have discussed where Oxford spent his money. It was often customary to dedicate the book to the nobleman who financed the publishing. If that is so, the following list of dedications indicates that he spent a good deal of it supporting writers:

---

[d] The reader might make note of the poem's use of opposites (laboring man versus Lord, the one who sows but does not reap the harvest, the bee that gathers honey but does not keep it, etc). We will see this again in a later poem of Oxford's.

Dedications to Oxford[26]

1564[a]	*The Histories of Trogus Pompeius*	trans: Arthur Golding
1569	*An Æthopian History*	trans. Thomas Underdowne
1570	*Peisistratus and Catanea*	by Edmund Elviden
1571	*The Psalms of David trans.*	by Arthur Golding
1573	*Cardanus Comfort*	trans: Thomas Bedingfield
1573	*The Breviary of Britain*	trans: Thomas Twyne
1574	*Oleum Magistrale*	trans: George Baker
1577	*The Staff of Christian Faith*	trans: John Brooke
1579	*The Mirror of Mutability*	by Anthony Munday
1579	*Defense of Military Profession*	by Geoffrey Gates
1580	*Zelauto*	by Anthony Munday
1580	*Euphues and His England*	by John Lyly
1580	*Phioravanti's Short Discourse upon Surgery*	trans: John Hester
1581	*Diverse Sermons of Calvin*	trans: Thomas Stocker
1582	*Hekatompathia*	by Thomas Watson
1584	*Pandora*	by John Southern
1584	*Card of Fancy*	by Robert Greene
1586	*The English Secretary*	by Angel Day
1588	*Palmerin d'Oliva* (part 1)	trans: Anthony Munday
1588	*Palmerin d'Oliva* (part 2)	trans: Anthony Munday
1590	*The Faerie Queene*[e]	by Edmund Spenser
1591	*Plain-song*	by John Farmer
1592	*Strange News*	by Thomas Nashe
1597	*The Book of Ecclesiastes*	by Henry Lok
1599	*The First Set of English Madrigals*	by John Farmer
1599	*The English Secretary*	by Angel Day (revised ed.)
1599	*The Practice of the New and Old Physic*	by George Baker
1603	*Anagrammata*	by F. D. [Francis Davison]
1619	*Primaleon of Greece*	trans: Anthony Munday

---

[e] In the forward to this poem, Spenser writes a poem to Oxford titled "To the right Honourable the Earle of Oxenford, Lord High Chamberlayne of England, &c." Oxford responds by writing a response praising the work "I here pronounce this workmanship is such/As that no pen can set it forth too much." Oxford signs this work "Ignoto." This pen name should be kept in mind for future reference.

THE SKULL OF A LAWYER

While novelists and dramatists are constantly making mistakes as to the laws of marriage, of wills and inheritance, to Shakespeare's law, lavishly as he expounds it, there can neither be demurrer, nor bill of exceptions, nor writ of error.

Lord John Campbell
Shakespeare's Legal Acquirements (1859)

No dramatist of the time ... used legal phrases with Shakespeare's readiness and exactness ... The phrases peculiar to other occupations serve him on rare occasions by way of description, comparison or illustration, generally when something in the scene suggests them, but legal phrases flow from his pen as part of his vocabulary, and parcel of his thought.

Richard Grant White
Memoirs of Shakespeare (1865)

No legal solecisms will be found. The abstrusest elements of the common law are impressed into a disciplined service. Over and over again, where such knowledge is unexampled in writers unlearned in the law, Shakespeare appears in perfect possession of it.

Senator Cushman K. Davis
The Law in Shakespeare (1883)

At every turn and point at which the author required a metaphor, simile, or illustration, his mind ever turned first to the law. He seems almost to have thought in legal phrases, the commonest of legal expressions were ever at the end of his pen in description or illustration.

Lord Penzance
The Bacon-Shakespeare Controversy (1902)

The plays and poems of Shakespeare supply ample evidence that their author not only had a very extensive and accurate knowledge of law, but also that he was well acquainted with the manners and customs of members of the Inns of Court and with legal life generally.

Sir George Greenwood
The Shakespeare Problem Restated (1908)

If I had under my superintendence a controversy appointed to decide whether Shakespeare wrote Shakespeare or not, I believe I would place before the debaters only the one question, WAS SHAKESPEARE EVER A PRACTICING LAWYER? and leave everything else out.

Mark Twain
Is Shakespeare Dead? (1909) [26]

There is a history dating back to the middle of the nineteenth century of authors writing about Shakespeare and the law. Shakespeare's precise use of legal terms has led many to conclude that Shakespeare, whoever he might be, was a lawyer. There were several attempts to find evidence that the man from Stratford-upon-Avon gained his legal expertise by working as a legal clerk, but no such evidence could be found. More recently, orthodox scholars have downplayed Shakespeare's knowledge of the law. Supporters of the man from Stratford-upon-Avon taking this route argue that the Author made many mistakes in the law (he did not), that he could have learned all he needed to know from his minor law suits (sounds impossible) and finally that he learned the law by just being in "legal London" (location undefined). The exquisite knowledge of a trained mind dealing with highly complex matters of law, truth, and justice is reflected in such plays as *Measure for Measure, Julius Caesar,* and *The Merchant of Venice.*

Oxford's tutor, Sir Thomas Smith, was one of the leading legal scholars of his time. Further, Oxford was a juror in major trials, including those of Mary Queen of Scots and the Earl of Southampton. Oxford is documented as having enrolled in the legal school Gray's Inn. He sat in eight of nine sessions of Parliament during Elizabeth's reign. In brief, Oxford was a lawyer, or one wants to quibble with that definition, Oxford was educated in law and had frequent opportunities to participate in legislative and judicial processes. One does not have to scratch the surface of Shakespeare's work too deeply to see the lawyer in Oxford emerge. Oxford uses legal terms with ease and familiarity: fine and recover, statues merchant, purchase, indenture, tenure, double voucher, fee simple, fee farm, remainder, reversion, forfeiture. They are part of his conscious and subconscious thinking. They are not simply examples of abstract legal knowledge. The law is one of the lenses through which he sees life. Here are some legalisms in *Shake-speares Sonnets:*

Sonnet 35
line 6   Authorizing thy trespas with compare
line 10   Thy adverse party is thy Advocate
                And gainst my selfe a lawfull plea commence:

Sonnet 46
line 7   But the defendant doth that plea deny.
line 9   To side this title is impanelled
                A quest of thoughts, all tennants to the heart,
                And by their verdict is determined

Sonnet 49
line 11   And this my hand against myself upreare,
                To guard the lawfull reasons on thy part.
                    To leave poore me, thou hast the strength of lawes,
                    Since why to love, I can alledge no cause.

Sonnet 58
line 8   Without accusing you of injury.
                Be where thou list, your charter is so strong
                That you your selfe may priviledge your time
                To what you will, to you it doth belong
                Yourself to pardon of self-doing crime.

Sonnet 120
Line 13   But that your trespasse now becomes a fee:
                Mine ransoms yours, and yours must ransome mee.

In *Hamlet,* Oxford mocks the lawyers in their language as only a lawyer could:

> There's another; why might not that be the skull of a lawyer? Where be his quiddits now, his quillets [quibbles, subtleties], his cases, his tenures, and his tricks? Why does he suffer this rude knave now to knock him about the sconce with a dirty shovel, and will not tell him of his action of battery? H'm!
>
> This fellow might be in's time a great buyer of land, with his statues, his recognizances, his fines, his double vouchers, his recoveries: is this the fine of his fines and the recovery of his recoveries, to have his fine pate full of fine dirt? Will his vouchers vouch him no more of his purchases, and double ones too, than the length and breadth of a pair of indentures? The very conveyances of his lands will hardly lie in this box; and must th' inheritor himself have no more, ha?

"Ha?" indeed!

POETRY OF EDWARD DE VERE

There are approximately twenty or so poems either written under Oxford's name or attributed to Oxford. Then there are a number of other poems assigned to Oxford but for which the attributions are not as strong. A precise one-to-one comparison of Oxford's poetry to the poetry published under the name of William Shakespeare is very difficult. There are so few of Oxford's poems, but more important, most of Oxford's known poetry is from his early years, while the poetry he published under the name William Shakespeare is from his later years when he was over forty years old. One can hardly compare the work of the early Beatles when they were writing and performing as the four mop-tops to their later, more complicated and enigmatic works. In spite of these difficulties, it is useful to look at some of the themes, language, and styles in Oxford's poetry and make rough comparisons to poetry under the name of William Shakespeare.

Woman's Changeableness is credited to Oxford and is included in most anthologies of his poetry. It is dated approximately 1577:

Woman's Changeableness

If women could be fair and yet not fond, [foolish]
    Or that their love were firm not fickle, still,
I would not marvel though they made men bond,
    By service long to purchase their good will,
But when I see how frail those creatures are,
I must that men forget themselves so far.

To mark the choice they make, and how they change
    How of from Phoebus do they flee to Pan,
Unsettled still like haggards wild they range,
    These gentle birds that fly from man to man,
Who would not scorn and shake them from the fist
And let them fly, fair fools, which way they list? [desire]

Yet for disport, we fawn and flatter both,
    To pass the time when nothing else can please,
And train them to our lure with subtle oath,
    Till, weary of their wiles, ourselves we ease;
And then we say, when we their fancy try,
To play with fools, Oh what a fool was I.

In the poem, Oxford uses legal terminology and phrasing, as has already been discussed. Further, Oxford uses the language of the aristocracy in his creation of a metaphor for the changeableness of women: "Unsettled still like haggards wild they range." This is not a description of anything that is known in most twenty-first century lives. Nor, for that matter, was it a name of anything in the ordinary course of life for a commoner in Elizabethan England. "Haggard" was a specific term from the aristocratic sport of falconry. The sport was so aristocratic that various levels of the nobility were allocated different birds according to their rank. This was also a sport that was forbidden to commoners. In short, the definition of haggard is "an adult hawk caught wild." An obsolete definition that may stem from this poem is "an intractable person." An adult hawk caught in the wild would be far more difficult to train and to keep than one that is raised in captivity.

In Shakespeare, this metaphor for an untamable, intractable person is used five times in a variety of contexts specifically referring to women:

Her spirits were as coy and wild,
As haggards of the rock,
Much Ado About Nothing, III, 1, 35

Another way I have to man my haggard,
To make her come.
Taming of The Shrew, IV, 1, 196

I have loved this proud disdainful haggard.
Taming of The Shrew, IV, 2, 39

Like the haggard, check at every feather
That comes before his eye.
Twelfth Night, III, 1, 71

If I do prove her haggard,
Though that her jesses were my dear heartstrings,
I'd whistle her off.
Othello, III, 3, 260

In the plays, the Author has an easy familiarity with the aristocratic sport of tennis. In the Elizabethan era, it was played outdoors, or indoors as court tennis:[f]

No, but the barber's man hath been seen with him, and the old ornament of his cheek hath already stuffed tennis-balls.
Much Ado About Nothing, III, 2, 42

---

[f] This version of tennis is now played in a very limited number of exclusive clubs. There is one in New York City for anyone who might want to take up this ancient sport. The court is odd-shaped with windows, galleries, and a sloping roof as was the tennis court at Hampton Court in the Middle Ages.

A man whom both the waters and the wind,
In that vast tennis-court, have made the ball
For them to play upon, entreats you pity him:
He asks of you, that never used to beg.

Pericles, Prince of Tyre, II, 2, 1

At "closes in the consequence," ay, marry;
He closes thus: "I know the gentleman;
I saw him yesterday, or t' other day,
Or then, or then; with such, or such; and, as you say,
There was a' gaming; there o'ertook in's rouse;
There falling out at tennis:" or perchance,

Hamlet II, 1, 64

Here is one more of Oxford's poems, which apparently was a best-seller:

Love Compared to a Tennis Play

Whereas the Heart at tennis plays and men to gaming fall,
Love is the Court, Hope is the House, and Favor serves the ball.
The ball itself is True Desert, the line which measure shows
Is Reason, whereon Judgment looks how players win or lose.
The getty is deceitful Guile, the stopper, Jealousy,
Which hath Sir Argoes' hundred eyes, wherewith to watch and pry.
The fault wherewith fifteen is lost is want of Wit and Sense,
And he that brings the racket in, is Double Diligence.
And lo the racket is Freewill, which makes the ball rebound,
And noble Beauty is the chase, of every game the ground.
But rashness strikes the ball awry, and where is Oversight?
"A Bandy ho!" the people cry, and so the ball takes flight.
Now in the end good-liking proves
Content the game and gain.
Thus in a tennis knit I love,
A pleasure mix's with pain.

Made by the Earl of Oxenforde

"A Bandy ho!" perhaps was a forerunner of "Tennis anyone?".

Most of Oxford's surviving letters were in the library of William Cecil, Lord Burghley, who kept meticulous records. Lord Burghley was very concerned with the record he left history and often he wrote memos of record that portrayed himself in a flattering light. No letters to Lord Burghley survive that show Oxford's interest in the theater, poetry, or the arts. Given Oxford's well-acknowledged and public activities in these areas, this is strange indeed. Equally strange is that no letters survive that were sent to Oxford. One would expect voluminous correspondence from authors, poets, and publishers seeking this powerful and wealthy lord's favor. However, none survive. One can only assume that William Cecil and later his son, Robert Cecil, destroyed the correspondence to Oxford. Further, given the powerful secret service of these two men, it is doubtful that any author or publisher of the time kept any secret letters or diaries recording the activities of the Earl of Oxford. Alternatively, if they did, they could have been found and destroyed by the Cecils' army of spies and double agents. It was common for William Cecil to employ cooks or servants in a noble's household to serve as spies for the Crown and Cecil's personal interests.

Nevertheless, in some of the few surviving letters to William Cecil, there are parallels between the ideas expressed and the ideas in the plays by Oxford-Shakespeare:

I serve Her Majesty, and I am that I am.	I am that I am.
(Letter to Lord Burghley, June 20, 1593)	(Sonnet 121)
That never am less idle, lo! than when I am alone.	That most are busied when they're most alone.
(Oxford Poem, *Care and Disappointment*)	*(Romeo and Juliet)*
For truth is truth, though never so old, and time cannot make that false which was once true.	Truth is truth, to the end of the reckoning. *(Measure for Measure)*
(Letter to Sir Robert Cecil, May, 7, 1603)	Nay, it is ten times true; for truth is truth. *(Measure for Measure)*

Authors reveal themselves in their works in many ways: in the themes they choose, in their characters, and in their similes and metaphors. Tracing Oxford's use of the bee as a metaphor gives an insight into the Author's personality by his characterization and admiration for this "humble bee":

Arthur Golding to the Reader

The plesant juice that Prime of yeere doth yeeld,
In here, in flower, in leafe, in plant or tree,
By natures gift abroad in frith and feeld,
Or mans deuice in gardens not so free
As faire and finelie kept, the busie Bee[g]

---

[g] The Internet has greatly contributed to the research on Shakespeare by providing several concordances online where all the works are stored with search engines to find any word or set of words. Type in "bee" and "bees," and the Shakespeare text pops up for the twenty or so listings. This enables the scholar and Shakespeare lovers to see how the Author uses certain words or phrases.

As a footnote to Shakespeare's literary use of bees, he uses six references to the "humble-bee" but never to a "bumble bee," and twice he refers specifically to the "red-tailed" or "red-hipped humble bee." It seems that somewhere in the course of four centuries, the more alliterative

With restlesse trauell gathereth to his Hyue, [hive]
To how great use, they know that knowe to thryue. [thrive]

The virtues of the humble bee are found in the introduction to *Romeus and Juliet*, allegedly written by Arthur Brooke:

And as each flower yieldeth honey to the bee, so every example ministereth good lessons to the well-disposed mind.[4]

Here is another observation on the bees from Oxford in a signed poem:

THE EARL OF OXFORD TO THE READER OF BEDINGFIELD'S "CARDANUS' COMFORT"

The idle drone that labours not at all,
Sucks up the sweet of honey from the bee;
Who worketh most to their share least doth fall,
With due desert reward will never be.

There are more than twenty references to bees in the plays alone. Here is one in *Henry IV*:

When, like the bee, culling from every flower
The virtuous sweets,
Our thighs pack'd with wax, our mouths with honey,
We bring it to the hive, and, like the bees,
Are murdered for our pains.

King Henry IV, Part 2, IV, 5, 88

Oxford's sharp eye for nature precisely describes the bee's pollen gathering efforts: "Our thighs pack'd with wax." There is more than one book on Shakespeare's knowledge of botany and nature and his precise definitions of flowers, plants, and animals. During the time that Oxford was at Cecil's home, the head gardener was John Gerard, who had written a major book on botany, *Herbal, or General History of Plants*, in 1567. He may have been helpful in developing Oxford's appreciation for botany and nature as well as developing the vocabulary to express his appreciation.

Oxford is providing an important insight into his own character by his consistent, lifelong admiration for the humble but "busie bee." In addition, he is reflecting on his own position in recognizing that the bee, for all his industrious efforts, does not always enjoy the fruits, in this case honey, from those efforts. This melancholy thought may resonate from Oxford's study of the Bible:

---

and easier to pronounce "bumble" bee replaced the industrious but "humble" bee. Also, he may have coined that familiar term "busy bee."

I returned, and saw under the sun, that the race is not to the swift, nor the battle to the strong, neither yet bread to the wise, nor yet riches to men of understanding, nor yet favour to men of skill; but time and chance happeneth to them all.

For man also knoweth not his time: as the fishes that are taken in an evil net, and as the birds that are caught in the snare; so are the sons of men snared in an evil time, when it falleth suddenly upon them.

This wisdom have I seen also under the sun, and it seemed great unto me:

Ecclesiastes 9:11–13

COURT PLAYWRIGHT AND IMPRESARIO

Orthodox Shakespearean scholars give the impression that the main theatrical activities of the Elizabethan Renaissance took place in the public theaters, especially the Globe, which was rebuilt in 1599 on the south bank of the Thames from the timbers of a disassembled theater named the Theatre. This date conveniently coincides with the first plays published under the name William Shakespeare and gives the impression that Shakespeare and the Globe were closely intertwined. As the following list shows, the theaters on the south bank of the Thames were built rather late in the century and were not the center of London's Elizabethan theater for the bulk of Elizabeth's reign. The more prominent earlier theaters were those north of the city walls and the inn theaters located within the city walls proper. The building of the theaters outside of the city walls was required because the theaters drew noisy, boisterous crowds to which the city fathers objected:

Outside/North of the City
1567: Red Lion, Whitechapel
1576: The Theatre, Finsbury Fields, Shoreditch
1577: The Curtain, Finsbury Fields, Shoreditch
1600: The Fortune, Golding Lane, Clerkenwell
1600: The Boar's Head, Whitechapel
1604: The Red Bull, Clerkenwell
1616: The Cockpit, Drury Lane, Westminster
1629: Salisbury Court, Westminster

Within the City of London
1576: Paul's, Cathedral precinct
1576: The (first) Blackfriars, Blackfriars
1596: The (second) Blackfriars, Blackfriars

City inns used for plays between 1576 and 1594 either in yards or indoors
The Bel Savage Inn
The Bull's Inn
The Bell Inn
The Cross Keys Inn

South of the Thames
1576: Newington Butts, Southwark, Surrey
1587: The Rose, Bankside, Surrey
1595: The Swan, Paris Garden, Surrey
1599: The Globe, Bankside, Surrey
1614: The Hope (the Bear Garden), Bankside, Surrey

In addition to the public theaters, there were the legal Inns of Court. As has already been described, Oxford had entered Gray's Inn, which was one of the prominent legal schools in 1567. Students there frequently put on dramas, masques, and entertainments for their own amusement. It was a law school, a social club, and a literary meeting place for the men who would later rule the country. The interior of Gray's Inn is anything but an low-ceilinged English pub. Gray's Inn was (and still is) almost an auditorium, with a high ceiling perfectly suited for a stage production. Further, many pubs in England even today have theaters within the structure; one such is the Water Rats at King's Cross. To this day, the fringe theater of London carries forth its tradition with legitimate theater productions in pubs and inns.

In the Elizabethan era and later, such inn-theaters were often the rehearsal space for Oxford's productions at court, and there was constant conflict between the Puritan authorities of London who wished to restrict their theatrical use and the court (Oxford) who desired them as rehearsal space for productions.

One can read fifty texts on the man from Stratford-upon-Avon and Elizabethan theater and not read one word about the hundreds of productions that were performed at Elizabeth's court. This is despite extant records of the court productions that were kept by the Court Revels (appropriately named). In these records, expenditures were noted for the performances, but unfortunately, the authors of the particular plays were not recorded. This is expected, given the reservations about attaching an aristocrat's name to a play. It is also most unfortunate that the records for the Court Revels for the period 1589 to 1604 have been lost. This is the key period in the emergence of William Shakespeare. To complicate matters further, there is no definitive listing of plays performed in London during the period. The records of individual companies for payment are scarce, and historians have often relied on diaries or letters of individuals who said they attended a particular performance. Consequently, public or court performance dates of most of Shakespeare's most popular plays during the Elizabethan era cannot be verified.

Eva Turner Clark did groundbreaking work in her *Shakespeare's Plays in the Order of their Writing, A Study Based on Records of the Court Revels and Historic Allusions.* Clark first looked for the titles of all the plays recorded by the Court Revels. She then compared them to the titles of the Shakespeare canon. Finally, she examined the plays for the historical allusions that might date the plays earlier than the 1590s. This required knowledge of the plays, knowledge of English history on a year-by-year basis, and knowledge of the biographies of the principal persons at court year by year.

One of the greatest falsehoods of the entire orthodox position on Shakespeare is the dating of the plays. The supporters of the man from Stratford-upon-Avon are forced to date the plays between 1593, the date of the publishing of *Venus and Adonis* and 1616, the date of the death of the man from Stratford. To recognize any plays earlier than 1593 as being by Shakespeare would in effect acknowledge that the man from Stratford did not write the plays. A further difficulty is that the man from Stratford returned to his hometown around 1600 with little evidence of residence in London thereafter. Presumably, he faxed his scripts into the Globe. The orthodox dating of the plays shoehorns the plays into the period between 1593 and 1616, using whatever topical references can be found or imagined as a rationale for their dating.

After having made their conjectural analysis, the orthodox scholars then claim this to be proof that Oxford could not have written the plays because they claim some to have been written after 1604, the year of Oxford's disappearance. As will later be shown, there were very few plays published between 1604 and 1623, which is inexplicable if one believes the man from Stratford wrote them. Certain orthodox scholars attempted to date *Hamlet* earlier than is recognized, which would make authorship by the Stratford man impossible, but academic careers have foundered on such treacherous shores, and after brief voyages, such excursions into heresy were ended.

The whole process of conventional naming and dating of plays by conventional scholars has been accomplished by retrofitting Elizabethan plays onto known, acceptable candidates of the era. This is particularly true with the romantic figure of Christopher Marlowe. There are plays of the period that had on the title page the name Christopher Marlowe. Other anonymous plays of the period were later attributed to Marlowe. Whether the plays with Marlowe's name on them are written by someone named

Marlowe is one question. The second independent question is whether the plays later attributed to Marlowe are in fact his or whether he is just a convenient dumping ground for some otherwise anonymous plays that look very Shakespearean. The different plays attributed to Marlowe vary so greatly in style and polish that it is hardly likely that the same man wrote them, no matter who the author was.

Despite, or perhaps because of, the scanty historical record on Christopher Marlowe (Marley or Marlo), an entire literary mini-industry has formed around him. He has become a romantic figure among Elizabethan scholars just as Elvis Presley, James Dean, and John Lennon have become in modern times. Marlowe's early death, or romantic disappearance, has created a host of unverifiable scenarios, such as that Marlowe was a secret agent who wrote his works in Paris or Istanbul and sent them via secret courier to be staged in London. The beauty of being a "secret agent" for a biographer is that one can concoct almost any story and claim it cannot be verified because the authorities have kept all the records top secret. The theory of Marlowe as Shakespeare (excluding the possibility of him faxing in his scripts from Istanbul) runs afoul of one important historical fact: Shakespeare-like plays were presented at court as early as the 1570s, which predates Marlowe by two decades. Biographical connections between Marlowe and the works are as numerous as biographical connections to the man from Stratford: that is, there are none.

Orthodox scholarship has completely ignored Eva Turner Clark's findings. Looking at the list of plays, it becomes obvious that the plays uncovered by Clark throw authorship by the man from Stratford into the dustbin. *The Historie of Error* was performed at Hampton Court on January 1, 1577. Orthodox scholars cannot attribute it to any author. This is despite the fact that, as it has been previously shown, Oxford was a playwright known for comedy. In other words, a number of plays suspiciously sounding like Shakespeare's work supposedly have no author, while a known playwright, Oxford, has no plays:

The Historie of Error	Hampton Court, Jan. 1, 1577
The Historie of the Solitarie Knight	Whitehall, Feb. 17, 1577
The Historye of Titus and Gisippus	Whitehall, Feb. 19, 1577
A Pastorell or Historie of a Greeke Maide	At court, Dec. 29, 1577
An History of the Crueltie of a Stepmother	Richmond, Dec. 28, 1578
A Morall of the Marryage of Mynde and Measure	Richmond, Jan. 1, 1579
The Historie the Rape of the Second Helene	At Court Jan. 6, 1578
The History of Murderous Mychaell	Whitehall, Mar. 3, 1579

A History of the Duke of Millayn	
and the Marquis of Mantus	Whitehall, Dec. 26, 1579
The Jew	The Bull, 1579
Portio and Demonrates	At court, Feb. 2, 1580
Ptolome	The Bull, 1579; At court, Feb. 1580
The History of Serpedon	Whitehall, Nov. 21, 1581
The History of fferrar	At court, Jan. 6, 1583
A History of Ariodante and Geneuora	Richmond, Feb. 12, 1583
A Pastorall of Phillyda & Choryn	Greenwich, Dec. 26, 1584
Agamemnon and Ulisse	Greenwich, Dec. 27, 1584
Felix and Philomela (Ur-Hamlet)	Greenwich, Jan. 3, 1585
An Antick Play and Comodye	Somerset, Feb. 23, 1585

Most titles do not provide much of a clue as to the Shakespearean title, but others seem obviously related to Shakespeare:

A History of the Duke of Millayn		
and the Marquis of Mantus	is	*Two Gentlemen of Verona*
The Jew	is	*The Merchant of Venice*
Portio and Demonrates	is	*The Merchant of Venice*
Ptolome	is	*Antony and Cleopatra*

Clark believes *The History of fferrar* to be a mistranscription or misspelling by the Elizabethan clerk. She believes the initial "f" should be a "c." With the second "f" interpreted as a modern "s," the play's title would be *The History of Cserrar*, which is much closer to what would be recognized as Shakespeare's *The History of Caesar*.

Other problems arise for orthodox scholars when they start to examine plays performed at Elizabeth's court. For example, the play *Arden of Feversham* appears to be written by Shakespeare given its style and content, but orthodox scholars have been reluctant to attribute it to Shakespeare. This play departs from most Shakespearean plays in that it is set in a non-aristocratic setting (Shakespeare only wrote one other play in such a setting, *The Merry Wives of Windsor*). The plot concerns a woman who has her servant murder her husband, Arden of Feversham. This play was based on a well-known contemporary event of the period, which was published in Holinshed's *Chronicle* a few months before the performance. (This same Holinshed was a juror on the inquest concerning the death of the cook killed by Oxford.) The name of the husband's murderer was, of course, Michael. Putting this play in the Shakespeare canon would link *Arden of Feversham* back to *The history of murderous mychaell,* which was performed when the lad from Stratford-upon-Avon was fifteen. That would be very unacceptable to orthodox Shakespearean theology, so this line of investigation is never pursued.

Further, in a letter of the period, Gilbert Talbot reports to his father about the doings of the court. In it, he reveals Oxford as a writer and presenter at court:

> At Shrovetide, according, as it seemed, customary at the season, were shows presented at Court before her Majesty at night. The chiefest was a device presented by the persons of the Earl of Oxford, the Earl of Surrey, and the Lords Thomas and Windsor. But the devices prettier than it hap to be performed; but the best of it, and I think the best liked, was two jewels which were presented to her Majesty by the two Earls.[27]

Further, there is this entry in the account of the Master of Revels for the year 1584 that indicates that Oxford was presenting works by his players before the Queen. In this case, the translation of a play

> The history of Agamemnon and Ulisses presented and enacted before her Ma[tie] [majesty] by the Earle of Oxenford his boyes on St. Johns daie at night at Grenewich.[28]

This is the work that Eva Turner Clark believes to be *Troilus and Cressida,* and it is unlikely that Oxford would be simply presenting a translation at this late date. At any rate, this entry firmly connects Oxford and his players to presentations before the Queen.

Many scenes in Shakespeare's work almost defy interpretation or understanding. They seem to be out of context to the play and to be almost talking to an audience with a purpose beyond the script. These insider jokes and commentaries only baffle present-day sensibilities. Richard Whalen[29] directs our attention to the odd scene before Cleopatra's death in *Antony and Cleopatra,* a scene that makes little sense according to orthodox interpretations. A clown brings in the instrument of death, which is never referred to as a snake or asp; it is always referred to as a "worm." The clown then goes on to pun and joke about the "worm." This is an odd scene to say the least.

Imagine the scene presented at court, where all the audience is fluent in French. Then it becomes apparent that Oxford engages in self-mockery at a most surprising moment. "Ver" in French means "worm." The audience has simultaneously the extreme emotions of the expectation of death and a humorous self-parody of the Author. The educated court audience would know both French and the identity of the Author (or at least the Queen would know, and she was an audience of one for Oxford).

With this in mind, read the following scene recognizing that the audience, especially the Queen, in her multilingual world, can easily hear the word "ver" in French and translate it simultaneously into "worm" and "Edward de Vere."

Guard	This is the man.
CLEOPATRA	Avoid, and leave him. (Exit Guardsman) Hast thou the *pretty worm* of Nilus there, That kills and pains not?
Clown	Truly, I have him: but I would not be the party that should desire you to touch him, for his biting is immortal; those that do die of it do seldom or never recover.
CLEOPATRA	Rememberest thou any that have died on't?
Clown	Very many, men and women too. I heard of one of them no longer than yesterday: a very honest woman, but something given to lie; as a woman should not do, but in the way of honesty: how she died of the biting of it, what pain she felt: truly, *she makes a very good report o' the worm*; but he that will believe all that they say, shall never be saved by half that they do: but this is most fallible, *the worm's an odd worm.*
CLEOPATRA	Get thee hence; farewell.
Clown	I wish you all *joy of the worm.* (Setting down his basket.)
CLEOPATRA	Farewell.
Clown	You must think this, look you, that *the worm will do his kind.*
CLEOPATRA	Ay, ay; farewell.
Clown	Look you, *the worm is not to be trusted* but in the keeping of wise people; for, indeed, *there is no goodness in worm.*
CLEOPATRA	Take thou no care; it shall be heeded.
Clown	Very good. Give it nothing, I pray you, for it is not worth the feeding.
CLEOPATRA	Will it eat me?
Clown	You must not think I am so simple but I know the devil himself will not eat a woman: I know that a woman is a dish for the gods, if the devil dress her not. But, truly, these same whoreson devils do the gods great harm in their women; for in every ten that they make, the devils mar five.
CLEOPATRA	Well, get thee gone; farewell.
Clown	Yes, forsooth: I wish you *joy o' the worm.* Exit

OXFORD AS HAMLET

Conventional Oxfordians have made much of the fact that Oxford's purported mother, Margery Golding, married quickly after the death of the 16th Earl, John de Vere. Therefore, they argue, the relations between Hamlet, Claudius, and Gertrude can be interpreted as a fairly straightforward autobiography of Edward de Vere, wherein the plot of the play mirrors the behavior of Oxford's hastily married mother. In fact, Oxford had quite a bit less to do with the 16th Earl of Oxford and Margery Golding than many imagine. Lord John de Vere did not seem to be especially close to his ostensible eldest son. Finally, Oxford had no apparent or recorded relationship with Margery Golding in the five years after the death of John de Vere.

However, these conventional Oxfordians do not extend the logic of Thomas Looney, which proposes that the works of Shakespeare should reveal the biography of the writer. If this is true, then the most obvious biographical play is *Hamlet*. What Oxfordians more or less ignore in this play is that Hamlet is the son of the Queen. The evidence assembled in this book indicates that this is the actual biographical relationship of Oxford and Elizabeth Tudor. The characters in *Hamlet* compared to the figures in Oxford's life are as follows:

Hamlet	Earl of Oxford
Claudius	Robert Dudley, Earl of Leicester (Queen's lover)
Gertrude	Elizabeth I
Polonius	William Cecil, Lord Burghley
Ophelia	Anne Cecil, Oxford's wife
Horatio	Horace de Vere, Oxford's cousin

The broad biographical interpretation mirrors Oxford's actual life circumstances. Oxford was the son of the Queen denied his rightful inheritance of the throne of England because of her actions, just as Hamlet is denied his rightful inheritance of the throne because of Gertrude's actions. In addition, Oxford's true father, Thomas Seymour, was executed by his brother, Edward Seymour. If Thomas Seymour had lived, there is little doubt that he would have pursued Elizabeth to be his wife. If Thomas Seymour had married Elizabeth, then there was the possibility that he could have become king—and Oxford could have been the recognized heir to the throne.

Claudius in *Hamlet* may represent a combination of Thomas Seymour and Robert Dudley, murderer of Oxford's foster father, John de Vere, most likely through poisoning. Was it a historical reality that poison in the ear caused of death of John de Vere? More importantly, Dudley usurped

Thomas Seymour's place in Elizabeth's bed. Freud had this to say about *Hamlet*:

> Another of the great creations of tragic poetry, Shakespeare's *Hamlet*, has its roots in the same soil as *Oedipus Rex.*
>
> In the *Oedipus* the child's wishful phantasy that underlies it is brought into the open and realized as it would be in a dream. In *Hamlet* it remains repressed; and—just as in the case of a neurosis—we only learn of its existence from its inhibiting consequences. Strangely enough, the overwhelming effect produced by the more modern tragedy has turned out to be compatible with the fact that people have remained completely in the dark as to the hero's character. The play is built up on Hamlet's hesitations over fulfilling the task of revenge that is assigned to him; but its text offers no reasons or motives for these hesitations and an immense variety of attempts at interpreting them have failed to produce a result....
>
> What is it, then, that inhibits him in fulfilling the task set him by his father's ghost? The answer, once again, is that it is the peculiar nature of the task. Hamlet is able to do anything—except take vengeance on the man who did away with his father and took that father's place with his mother, the man who shows him the repressed wishes of his own childhood realized. Thus the loathing which should drive him on to revenge is replaced in him by self-reproaches, by scruples of conscience, which remind him that he himself is literally no better than the sinner whom he is to punish.[30]

Some theatrical directors have chosen to direct the play with Hamlet and Gertrude as almost lovers; their interpretations were more on the mark than they knew.

To further assess the parallels between the people in Oxford's life and the characters in Hamlet, consider the Shakespearean scholar who first wrote about the similarities between William Cecil and the stage character Polonius. William Cecil had written to his somewhat dissolute son in Paris. In this letter, he wrote down his precepts of conduct for his son, who probably paid no attention. By now, the reader is familiar with William Cecil's long-winded and pompous prose. Oxford satirizes this letter of William Cecil in *Hamlet* when Polonius gives his farewell speech to Laertes. It is also inconceivable that any person could have access or knowledge of such a letter who did not have access to the good lord's personal papers, and it is equally inconceivable that anyone not of high aristocratic rank would dare mock the all-powerful William Cecil:

Burghley's Precepts[31]

When it shall please god to bring thee to man's estate, use great providence and circumspection in the choice of thy wife, for from thence may spring al thy future good or ill; and it is an action like a stratagem in war where man can err but once. If thy estate be good, match near home and at leisure; if weak, then far off and quickly. Inquire diligently of her disposition and how her parents have been inclined in their youth. Let her not be poor how generous soever, for a man can buy nothing in the market with gentility. Neither choose a base and uncomely creature altogether for wealth, for it will cause contempt in others and loathing in thee. Make not choice of a dwarf or a fool, for from the one thou mayest beget a race of pygmies, the other may be thy daily disgrace; for it will irk thee to have her talk, for then thou shalt find to thy great grief that there is nothing more fulsome than a she-fool.

LORD POLONIUS

Yet here, Laertes! aboard, aboard, for shame!
The wind sits in the shoulder of your sail,
And you are stay'd for. There; my blessing with thee!
And these few precepts in thy memory
See thou character. Give thy thoughts no tongue,
Nor any unproportioned thought his act.
Be thou familiar, but by no means vulgar.
Those friends thou hast, and their adoption tried,
Grapple them to thy soul with hoops of steel;
But do not dull thy palm with entertainment
Of each new-hatch'd, unfledged comrade. Beware
Of entrance to a quarrel, but being in,
Bear't that the opposed may beware of thee.
Give every man thy ear, but few thy voice;
Take each man's censure, but reserve thy judgment.
Costly thy habit as thy purse can buy,
But not express'd in fancy; rich, not gaudy;
For the apparel oft proclaims the man,
And they in France of the best rank and station
Are of a most select and generous chief in that.
Neither a borrower nor a lender be;
For loan oft loses both itself and friend,
And borrowing dulls the edge of husbandry.
This above all: to thine ownself be true,
And it must follow, as the night the day,
Thou canst not then be false to any man.
Farewell: my blessing season this in thee!

Hamlet mirrors Oxford. The Queen is his mother, he is prevented from ascending to the throne by her, and he cannot to do anything about it.

THEATRICAL PRODUCER

There were two Lord Chamberlains in English society. The Lord Chamberlain was responsible for maintenance and running of the court household. This title was held by a number of different men during Elizabeth's reign. The second, the Lord Great Chamberlain, had duties that were only ceremonial, such as carrying the sword of state in coronations, processions, and the opening of Parliament. This honorary title was held by John de Vere, 16th Earl of Oxford, who officiated at the coronation of Queen Mary and Queen Elizabeth. Additionally, confusion exists because both titles were often referred to as "Lord Chamberlain" and both were often abbreviated "Lrd Chm."

Orthodox scholars have always assumed that the theatrical company called the Lord Chamberlain's Men was operated by the series of men responsible for running the court household. However, few if any of these men had any particular affiliation with the theater or with the arts. However, from the death of John de Vere, 16th Earl of Oxford, in 1562 until Oxford's supposed death in 1604 there was only one Lord Great Chamberlain, Edward de Vere, 17th Earl of Oxford, who was always actively involved in the theater. Given Oxford's involvement in the theater and his known accolades as a playwright, it is a reasonable assumption that Oxford was the aristocrat responsible for the court productions of the Lord Chamberlain's Men, regardless of who had the occupation of Lord Chamberlain.

In addition to the Lord Chamberlain's Men, it is undisputed that Oxford had a touring theater company known as the Children of St. Paul's and another company referred to as Oxford's Boys. These theater companies performed both at court and in public theaters such as the Globe. Orthodox Shakespeare scholars studiously ignore the connections between Oxford and his theater companies. Otherwise, they would be in the uncomfortable position of acknowledging that Shakespeare's or Shakespeare sounding plays were being performed by Oxford's theater companies:

The Historie of Error	Children of St. Paul's
The Historie of The Solitarie Knight	Lord Chamberlain's Men
The Historye of Titus and Gisippus	Children of St. Paul's
A Pastorell or Historie of a Greeke Maide	Lord Chamberlain's Men
An History of the Crueltie of a Stepmother	Children of St. Paul's
A Morall of the Marryage of Mynde and Measure	Lord Chamberlain's Men
The Historie of the Rape of the Second Helene	Lord Chamberlain's Men
The History of Murderous Mychaell	Lord Chamberlain's Men
A History of The Duke of Millayn	
and the Marquis of Mantus	Lord Chamberlain's Men
Agamemnon and Ulisses	Oxford's Boys

In support of this contention, that the Lord Chamberlain's Men was in fact a company run by Oxford, there is this interesting title-page description of the performance of *The Weakest goeth to the Wall,* with a publication date of 1600: (Note that the spellings, italics, capitalization and layout are as on the title page.)

The Weakest goeth to the Wall

As it hath bene sundry times plaide by the right ho-
nourable Earle of Oxenford, Lord great
Chamberlaine of England
His servants[32]

This title connects Oxford in an irrefutable way to an acting company and proves that such actors were "His servants." They were servants to the only Lord Great Chamberlain of England from 1562 until his disappearance in 1604. By extension, this means that other works performed by the Chamberlain's Men were performed by a theatrical company under the control of the Earl of Oxford, such as the following. (Spellings, italics, and capitalization are as on the title page.):

A
Midsommer nights
Dreame.

As it hath bene sundry times pub-
lickely acted, by the Right honourabla-
ble, the Lord Chamberlain his
Servants
Written by William Shakespeare.[33]

This is the theatrical company that had performed such Shakespeare-like plays (*A Morall Of The Marryage Of Mynde And Measure*) in the court as early as 1577. It appears impossible that there would be any doubt in any Elizabethan mind, that William Shakespeare and the Earl of Oxford were one and the same. The inescapable conclusion is that Oxford was writing his own plays and performing them with a theatrical companies that he financed and directed, one of which was the Lord (Great) Chamberlain's Men.

THE OXFORD BIBLE

In October 1536, William Tyndale was burned at the stake by Henry VIII for translating the Bible into English. Henry did not think it socially or politically correct for commoners to debate with the Pope over the meaning of God's word. Three years later, Henry divorced his wife and married Anne Boleyn, who brought from France her well-worn copy of her French Bible. Reading of the Bible was restricted to aristocrats and clergy, but one of the exempted groups was the ladies of the court. Queen Katherine Parr was one of the close students of the Bible and a political-religious reformer. There were five translations of the Bible into English during the 1500s, one of which was the Geneva Bible, translated in

Geneva by Protestant dissidents. In 1539, the first authorized English Bible, the Bishop's Bible, was printed just three years after Tyndale's burning:

> The authority of the written word, inscribed in an alien Latin tongue to be read and interpreted by the priest, began to give way before the impulse for vernacular comprehension which placed the communicant's own knowledge and perspective at the center of an expanding universe of subjectivity.[34]

In 1925, Henry Clay Folger, founder and patron of the Folger Shakespeare Library, purchased a Bible owned by Edward de Vere. The invoice of purchase identifies it, as does the crest of the Earl of Oxford. At the end of his life, Folger began to show some interest in the man a few believed to be William Shakespeare, or at least that is what the purchase of the Ashbourne Portrait and the Geneva Bible would indicate. It is ironic that the institution Folger funded became the main institution of repression for the debate and discussion of the Authorship issue, even though its founder appears to have been well aware of the significance of the Earl of Oxford. In 1993, a Folger Library exhibit, *Roasting the Swan of Avon,* displayed documents espousing various candidates (some absurd) for the Author. The exhibition did not include the Oxford Bible. The institutional Stratfordian ideology could not recognize its existence, its content, or the fact that it was purchased by the library's founder.

A record of the Bible's original purchase in 1570 is by John Hart, Chester Herald of the Court of Wards:

> To William Seres, stationer, for a Geneva Bible gilt, a Chaucer, Plutarch's works in French, and other books and papers...............2-7-10.[35]

In 1990, Paul Nelson first noticed that the Folger Shakespeare Library had the Bible with the Vere crest. He wrote about its significance in his dissertation. This was followed by Roger Stritmatter in 2000, who received his doctorate from the University of Massachusetts at Amherst in Comparative Literature on the basis of his dissertation, which is titled *Edward de Vere's Geneva Bible, the Marginalia of Edward de Vere's Geneva Bible: Providential Discovery, Literary Reasoning, and Historical Consequence.* It is both beyond the scope of this book and beyond the capabilities of this writer to do justice to Stritmatter's work. Therefore, brevity will be the soul of prudence in describing Stritmatter's insights, and this brief summary will err on being too short rather than too long.

Stritmatter finds two types of evidence indicating that the annotator of this Bible was in fact the Author known as William Shakespeare. The first direction of the evidence flows from the Shakespeare canon to the de Vere Bible. There are over 2,000 references in the works to the Bible that have been collected by scholars over the years, including additions by Stritmatter. These specific references are not evenly distributed throughout the Bible, but they are concentrated in certain verses. Approximately eighty verses account for a quarter of the Shakespeare references. Of these eighty verses, thirty-two are directly marked in the de Vere Bible. This is confirmation that what appears in Shakespeare is also in the notations of the Oxford Bible.

The other way of examining the issue is to look at the most frequent annotations in the de Vere Bible and see whether they form any meaningful relationship to the ideas and themes expressed in the Shakespeare canon. Stritmatter points out that the annotator was a close student of this Bible. He used a number of different colors of ink and made his annotations by underlining, by drawing a small hand pointing to particular passages, and by using a fleur-de-lys icon. Stritmatter shows that these underlined passages point to the Shakespeare canon. In addition, he points out that many of the pages seem well worn, and this indicates Oxford-Shakespeare knew many of the Biblical passages by heart. Some of his areas of interest are:

charity toward orphans, widows and strangers;
mercy toward the lame (may reflect Oxford's lame condition from his duel);
cleansing of the sins through water;
hidden works; and
the folly of seeking recognition for hidden good deeds.

Shakespeare was concerned with good and evil, truth and lies, appearances and reality, justice and understanding. Yet current literary criticism has studiously avoided the ethics of Shakespeare in its *deconstruction* of the Author until nothing lies about except a pile of words such as gender, textuality, intertextuality, homologous, cross-cultural, encounters, and popular culture. A smattering of the titles of recent articles in the Folger's *Shakespeare Quarterly* indicates the puerile nature of current Shakespeare literary criticism:

"The Romance of the New World: Gender and the Literary Formations of English Colonialism"

"Renewing Modernity: Changing Contexts and Contents of a Nearly Invisible Concept"

"The Bankruptcy of Homoerotic Amity in Shakespeare's *Merchant of Venice*"

It would be remiss not to mention:

"Unspeakable ShaXXXspeare: Queer Theory and American Kiddie Culture"

Reconstruction should be the effort emphasized for the next century of Shakespearean literary criticism. This starts with understanding the life of the true Author and the literary and intellectual world in which he lived. Connecting Shakespeare back to that most moral and inspired literary work, the Bible, would be a good starting point. Portraying Shakespeare as an atheist or agnostic is to dramatically understate the important influence that the Bible had on his work. To ignore the Bible and its influence on Shakespeare is to ignore the greater moral and intellectual concerns of the Author. These have been replaced by puerile concerns, couched in the cant and jargon of the current academic trade. Certainly, Oxford-Shakespeare was not religious in the sense of proscribing to a set of doctrines, but he was religious or moral in his investigation of moral issues contained in the Bible, and that is reflected in the works of Shakespeare.

Stritmatter's work has produced the closest thing to a "smoking gun" in the entire authorship issue because it links the works of William Shakespeare to the known hand and handwriting of Edward de Vere, 17th Earl of Oxford.

JOHN LYLY AND *SILLY BEES*

John Lyly matriculated at Magdalen College, Oxford, in 1571. He obtained a bachelor's degree in 1573 at the age of seventeen and a master's two years later from Cambridge. About 1577, he made acquaintance with Gabriel Harvey at the Savoy in London, and Lyly took up residence there. The Savoy was a building in which quarters were rented by the Earl of Oxford although it is uncertain whether Oxford ever stayed here, or more likely that he rented quarters for others. For over two decades a number of writers lived, including Anthony Munday, John Lyly, Gabriel Harvey, and others. In 1579, John Lyly became secretary to the Earl of Oxford, and later, he became manager of St. Paul's Boys, one of the theater companies sponsored by the Earl.

John Lyly is best known for two novels, *Euphues: The Anatomy of Wit* and its sequel *Euphues and his England.* The former was dedicated to the Earl of Oxford. The identity of the author of these books has not been questioned, but the main character Euphues was delayed because he "loytered, tarying many a month in Italy viewing the Ladyes in a Painter's shop", implies that the novels were influenced by Oxford or are about him. No record exists of John Lyly traveling to the Continent. Both books were successful publications that enjoyed several reprintings, yet these printings did not make John Lyly a wealthy man. Authors at that time might receive payment from the printer once, but there was no concept of author royalties.

A literary career was not one of direct commercial rewards, as is often the case in modern times, but of indirect rewards of preferment by the aristocrats and royals from whom all benefits flowed. This was accomplished by the author dedicating the work to a famous and important personage, and if the work was well received, it would throw a favorable light on both the patron and the author. Such a favor might mean assignment to a government position, and in fact, John Lyly was considered, but turned down, for the office of Master of the Revels. He is also credited with eight plays performed before the Queen, seven of which were performed by St. Paul's Boys, Oxford's theater company. With one exception, these plays are all in prose, not in the blank verse that was written by Oxford.

From 1588, there were "theater wars" in which the Crown (William Cecil) wanted to limit public performances. In 1591, St. Paul's Boys was dissolved as continuing tension between various literary and government factions continued. In 1595, John Lyly stopped functioning as Oxford's secretary and, thereafter, his literary career plummeted. Exactly what happened to Lyly is only speculation, but one hypothesis is that Lyly was also serving as an informant to William Cecil about the Earl's activities. When this was found out, Lyly may have been dismissed by Oxford, but William Cecil would not take him into his camp and, therefore, John Lyly ended up with no political or financial support. He died in poverty in 1606.

In 1905, R. Warwick Bond wrote three volumes titled *The Complete Works of John Lily.* In this work, Bond views Lyly as a precursor to the Stratfordian author, and he shows many correspondences between the novels of Lyly and the works of Shakespeare. In addition, Bond does a good deal of digging through Elizabethan literature and assigns a number of unattributed songs, plays, and political pamphlets to John Lyly. While doing this, Bond seeks to diminish the role of Oxford as a playwright, musician, or financial benefactor to John Lyly, although he does describe Lyly's residence at the Savoy and employment by Oxford. He attributes many songs of the period to John Lyly:

> In the Music-Books the names of the authors of the words are hardly ever given, partly because the composer was pre-occupied with his own art, partly owing to the modesty of the authors or their fashionable reluctance to

> appear in public as poets; in the Anthologies, while much work is signed, much is anonymous, appearing either without subscription or else with various signatures such as "Ignoto," "Incerto," "Anonimus," and a large proportion is subscribed with initials merely.[36]

However, nowhere in his biography of John Lyly does he provide any evidence that Lyly had any accomplishments as a musician. In contrast, Oxford was known to be an accomplished musician. John Farmer said of him in his dedication of *The First Set of English Madrigals* in 1599:

> For without flattery be it spoke, those that know your Lordship know this, that using this science [music] as recreation, your Lordship have overgone most of them that make it a profession.[37]

There is one known composition by Oxford that still exists, *The Earl of Oxford's March,* and one is known to have been written but is now lost, *The Earl of Oxford's Galliard.* Orthodox scholars ignore the importance and use of music in Shakespeare's plays for three reasons. The first is that literary scholars are generally not musicians. Second, nothing has ever been advanced showing that the man from Stratford had any musical training or accomplishments. Finally, it is one more of Oxford's known accomplishments that Shakspere lacked, giving further credence to Oxford as the Author of the works.

As has been mentioned, the European astronomers of the Middle Ages could did not see any of the supernovas recorded by Chinese astronomers because the European notion of a fixed, unchanging universe precluded them from recognizing any new celestial objects. In a similar fashion, orthodox scholars, such as Bond, simply did not see the very evidence before them that led down any path other than the one to Stratford-upon-Avon. In the case of Bond's work, it even goes beyond that. Bond deliberately downplays Oxford's known reputation as a playwright, theatrical producer, poet, and musician. As Hank Whittemore commented, Bond was "standing on the toe of the giant, but he was unable to see him."

Bond ignores the fact that in the *Faire Queen,* Spenser includes Oxford in one of his dedicatory poems. Another poem in the work lauds Spenser's accomplishment, and it is signed "Ignoto." It is hardly likely that John Lyly, fresh from the university, would be included in such an important work, nor is there any reason why he should be using the pen name Ignoto. Any Elizabethan literary scholar worth his salt would more likely attribute this pen name to the Earl of Oxford, but this is studiously avoided because this would open up a number of unpleasant lines of inquiry. For example, there was a poem by the mysterious Ignoto in a collection of poems published in 1601, which included *The Phoenix and the Turtle,* signed by Shakespeare. Further, Bond is well aware that

Oxford was an acknowledged playwright whose plays mysteriously "disappeared."

After ascribing songs to a man not known for musical accomplishments, Bond goes on to ascribe a number of poems to John Lyly. While they are possibly Lyly's, it is highly unlikely. John Lyly's most successful works were two novels of considerable length and verbosity, and never does he show the poetical impulses of Oxford. There is no clear body of work nor any poems directly credited to John Lyly. Bond describes the allegory behind one poem:

> It laments under a thin allegorical veil the author's lack of all reward for his service; the last stanza in particular speaks of his having been sustained by false hopes and promises for ten years, and specifies money as the object of his dreams; while the third and fourth stanzas allude to the Queen's rejection with rebuke of some special application he had made to her.[38]

These words apply to John Lyly, who had petitioned the Queen in 1598 for favor and complained "nothing applied thes ten yeres to my wantes but promises."[39] In this regard, Lyly could join many others, including Oxford. While the Queen promised much, she delivered very little. The poem is some eighty lines long and might be titled *When Silly Bees Could Speake*:

> It was a tyme when silly Bees could speake
> And in that time I was a silly Bee
> Who suckt on time, untill the hart [be]gan [to] breake
> Yet never founde that tyme would favour me
>   Of all the swarme I onely could not thrive
>   Yet brought I wax & honey to ye hive
>   [See appendix for this new poem.]

Says Bond, "bees furnish probably his [Lyly's] most frequent image in *Euphues* and elsewhere."[40] He continues:

> When a writer is perpetually harping on a particular sentiment, such as the unreliability of women; when he is for ever citing special proverbs like that about smoke and fire, or using certain imagery, e.g. baits and hooks, nettles and roses, storms and anchors, hearts and tongues, double or single, & c., the circumstance gives him a preferential claim to unsigned work in which such sentiments or imagery appear.[41]

One can only add, that bees are metaphors present in the works of Arthur Golding, Arthur Brooke, Oxford, and William Shakespeare. This book has shown that Oxford began by using bees as metaphor for industriousness, but in his later years he changed the metaphor to show the fitful relationship between work expended and rewards received. In summary, Bond, constrained by his orthodox belief that the man from Stratford was

William Shakespeare, has misassigned to John Lyly a poem of the Earl of Oxford.

Importantly, Ward has done a yeoman's job in his research in the Bodleian Library and provided tantalizing clues that yet more of Oxford's work exists, some of it perhaps in Oxford's handwriting:

> *Harleian* MS. 6910 is a very large collection (190) leaves of poems all copied in the same fine small hand; those occupying ff. 1-74 being all by Spenser, and followed in the MS. by "finis 1596" so that the succeeding ones, nearly all of them unsigned, were at least transcribed after that date. Its contents, which are of every shade of merit, range over the whole of Elizabeth's reign, and include poems in the old fourteener, though most are in stanzas of six or seven decasyllabic lines, e.g. there are long transcripts from Sackville's *Induction.*[42]

Are some of these transcriptions in a "fine small hand" by the Earl of Oxford, or put another way, are these undiscovered poems of William Shakespeare?

THE OXFORD CANON

From the youngest age, Edward de Vere poured out a stream of works of the highest literary level, starting with *Metamorphoses* and *Romeus and Juliet*. However, his literary career is difficult to track because he wrote under a variety of pen names, often masking his name with that of a living person. Many of the writers to whom these works were attributed were simply beards for the Earl of Oxford, or perhaps they were simply un-persons to whom a set of facts were later attached to justify attribution. Arthur Brooke and John Studley spring to mind as people of the latter type. Both Marlowe and Brooke seem to have sprung out of the ground fully formed, to have written several works that "influenced Shakespeare" and then disappeared.

In addition, as opposed to the work of later authors, his early works were intended for an audience of one (the Queen, and Oxford had no need to publish, categorize, or organize his works after they had been seen at court. It was not until his later years that he began to publish for the public and to ensure the preservation of some his literary outpourings. Even then, he did not complete the task, and it was not until nineteen years after his death that the *First Folio* was published, containing thirteen plays that had never been published before. To further complicate the matter, many of his plays were revised or later rewritten. Dating the plays in any chronological order is therefore that much more daunting. Some plays seem to be in collaboration with others, yet it may be that other writers finished or reworked partial manuscripts that survived.

Given these considerations, it is a daunting task to produce a list of Oxford's works, but to make no effort at all would be a serious omission. This list is provided as a best estimate of Oxford's total literary output. Although a few works may not be his and others should be added, the length of the list is indicative of the enormous literary output of this singular man.

The Oxford Canon

Dates for the following works are the first date of writing. At best, this is only a preliminary effort at establishing the full canon of Oxford's works. Eva Turner Clark's work is the source for Shakespeare's plays. Plays first published in the *First Folio* are so noted.

Date of Writing	Title (Earlier Title in Parentheses)	Attribution
1562	*Jack the Juggler*, Play	Anonymous
1562	*Romeus and Juliet*, Poem	Arthur Brooke
1562	*Spinning Wheel Poem*, found in Cecil papers to Anne Cecil	No attribution
1563	*The Fable of Ovid Treating of Narcissus*, Translation	Anonymous
1563	*The historie of Leonard Aretine*, Leonardo Bruni, 1369–1444, Translation	Arthur Golding
1564	*The abridgment of the histories of Trogvs Pompeius*, Marcus Junianus, Translation	Arthur Golding
1564	*Palamon & Arcyte, Damon & Pythias*	Richard Edwards
1564	*The eyght bookes of Caius Iulius Caesar*, Julius Caesar, Translation	Arthur Golding
1565-7	*Ovid's Metamorphoses, P. Ouidius Naso*, Translation	Arthur Golding
	Ralph Roister Doister, Play	Nicholas Udall
	Doleful Ditty of Lord Darnleigh	Henry Chettle
1566	*Agamemnon, Medea, Hippolytus*, and *Hercules Oeteus*, Seneca, Translations	John Studley
1566	*Palaemon and Areite*, Play[h]	Anonymous
1566	*Jocasta, Euripides*, Translation	George Gascoigne and Francis Kinwelmershe
1566	*Gli Supposit, The Supposes*, Ariosto, Translation	George Gascoigne
1567	*Horestes*, Translation	John Pikering
1571	*The Courtier*, Balthasar Castiglione: Translation by Bartholomew Clerke	preface by Edward de Vere
1573	*100 Sundrie Flowers*, Various poems, The first English novel, *The Adventures of Master F.I.*,	Meritum petere grave
1573	*Cardanus Comforte*, Introductory Poem	by E. Oxenford
1576	*A Paradise of Dainty Devices*, 7 Poems	by E.O.
1577	*The Famous Victories of Henry V*[i]	Anonymous

---

[h] Performed before Queen Elizabeth at Oxford in 1566; survives as *The Two Noble Kinsmen*, published in 1634.

[i] Play contains a robbery at Gravesend based on one perpetrated by Oxford's men on May 20, 1573. This is an event not related in the actual history of the play, but one perpetrated by Oxford

1577	*The Comedy Of Errors, (The Historie of Error),* Hampton Court, Jan. 1, 1577	Folio 1623
1577	*Timeon Of Athens, (The Historie Of The Solitarie Knight),* Whitehall, Feb. 17, 1577	Folio 1623
1577	*Titus Andronicus, (The historye of Titus and Gisippus),* Whitehall, Feb. 19, 1577	
1577	*Pericles, (A pastorell or historie of a Greeke Maide),* Court, Dec. 29, 1577	
1577	*Woman's Changeableness,* Poem	Anonymous
1577	*Verses Made by the Earl of Oxford,* Poems	Earl of Oxford
1578	*Cymbeline, (An History Of The Crueltie Of A Stepmother),* Richmond, Dec. 28, 1578	Folio 1623
1579	*The Taming Of The Shrew (A Morall Of The Marryage Of Mynde And Measur)* Richmond, Jan. 1, 1579	Folio 1623
1578	*All's Well That Ends Well, (The Historie Of The Rape Of The Second Helene),* Court, Jan. 6, 1578	Folio 1623
1579	*Love's Labours Lost, (Double Maske),* Court, Jan. 11, 1579	
1579	*The Two Gentlemen of Verona, (A History Of The Duke Of Millayn And* *The Marquis Of Mantus),* Whitehall, Dec. 26, 1579	Folio 1623
1579	*Henry VI, Part II*	
1579	The Defense of the Military Profession	
1579	*The Merchant of Venice, (Portio and Demonrates),* Court, Feb. 2, 1580	
1579	*Antony and Cleopatra, (Ptolome, The History of Serpedon),* The Bull and at Court, Feb. 1580, Whitehall, Nov. 21, 1581	Folio 1623
1579	*Thomas of Woodstock,* Play	Anonymous
1579	*Arden of Feversham, (Murderous Michael),* Play	Anonymous
1580 ?	*Lover's Complaint,* Poem	William Shakespeare
1580	*A Discourse upon the earthquake that happened through* *this realme of Englande and other places of Christendom,* *the sixt of Aprill, 1580,* Pamphlet	Arthur Golding
1580	*Twelfth Night*	Folio 1623
1580	*Henry VI, Part III*	
1580	*Richard III*	
1580	*Coriolanus*	Folio 1623
1581	*Measure for Measure*	Folio 1623
1581	*Romeo and Juliet*	
1581	*The Troublesome Reign of King John*	Folio 1623
1581	*Richard II*	
1581	*As You Like It*	Folio 1623
1583	*Julius Caesar, (The History of fferrar),* Court, Jan. 6, 1583	Folio 1623
1583	*Much Ado About Nothing, (A History of Ariodante and Geneuora),* Richmond, Feb. 12, 1583	
1583	*Othello*	
1583	*4 Epitahs to Oxford's Son,* Poems, published in John Soowthern's *Pandora*	Countess Oxford
1584	*Midsummer Night's Dream, (A Pastorall of Phillyda & Choryn),* Greenwich, Dec. 26, 1584	

---

and Oxford's men on servants of Sir William Cecil, the circumstances of which are described in a
letter to William Cecil.

1584	*Triolus and Cressida, (Agamemnon and Ulisses)*, Greenwich, Dec 27, 1584	
1584	*Sapho and Phao*, Play, Translation	John Lyly
1584	*Campaspe*, Play, Translation	John Lyly
1584	*Greene's Card of Fancy*, Book	John Lyly
1584	*Anne Vavasor's Echo*, Poem	Anonymous
1584	*Spanish Trajedgy*, Play	Anonymous, Thomas Kyd
1585	*Hamlet, (Felix and Philomela)* (Ur-Hamlet), Greenwich, Jan. 3, 1585	
1585	*Henry IV, Part I*	Folio 1623
1585	*Merry Wives of Windsor*, (*An Antick Play and Comodye*), Somerset, Feb. 23, 1585	
1584-5	*Campaspe, Sapho and Phao, Galathea, Love's Metamorphosis, Endimion, Midas, Mother Bombie, Woman in the Moon,* Court Comedies	John Lyly
1586	*The Winter's Tale*, (*The Winter's Night's Tale*), Court, Nov. 6, 1611	Folio 1623
1586	*Henry V*	
1586	*Henry VI, Part II*	Folio 1623
1586	*Henry IV, Part II*	
1588	*Macbeth*	Folio 1623
1590	*King Lear*	
1591	*King John*	
1591	*Forty Several ways of two parts in one made upon a plain song*, Song Book Dedication to Oxford;(songs by Oxford?)	John Farmer
1593	*Tears of Fancy, Who taught thee first to sigh?* Poems	Earl of Oxenforde
1593	*Venus and Adonis*, Narrative Poem	William Shakespeare
1594	*Willobie His Avisa*, Narrative Poem	M. Henry Willobie
1594	*The Rape of Lucrece*, Narrative Poem	William Shakespeare
1594	*Edward the Second*	Anonymous, attrb. to Marlowe
1595	*Locrine*, Play	By W.S.
1597	*Isle of Dogs, Play*	Thomas Nashe
1599	*The First Set of English Madrigals,* Dedication to Oxford; songs by Oxford may be included	John Farmer
1599	*THE/Passionate/Pilgrime./by W. Shakespeare*	William Shakespeare
1601	*Shake-speares Sonnets*, Narrative Poems	Anonymous
1601	*Phoenix and the Turtle*, Narrative Poem	William Shakespeare
1603	*Henry VIII*	Folio 1623
1610	*The Tempest*	Folio 1623

For Consideration:

1566	*Patient Grissel*	John Philips
1566	*Heroical Epistles of Ovid*	George Turberville
1569	*A Marveous Strange Fish*	C.R.
1576	*Book of Falconrie*	George Turberville
1576	*A Petite Palace of Pettie His Pleasure*	George Pettie
1576	*The Noble Art of Venerie*	Anonymous
1579	*A Special Remedie Against the Furious Foce of Lawless Love*	Anonymous
1580	*Plutarch's Lives*	Thomas North
1581	*A Farewell to the Military Profession*	Barnaby Rich
1603	*Montaigne's Essays*	John Florio

1594	*Friar Bacon and Friar Bungay*	Robert Greene
1600	*The Weakest goeth to the Wall*	Anonymous
No Date	*A Choice of Emblems*	John Whitney
No Date	*The Golden Ass,* Translation of Apuleius	William Addington
No Date	*Idylls of Theocritus,* Translation	E.D.
No Date	*Gammer Gurton's Needle*	Anonymous
	Sir Thomas More	Anonymous
	Greenes Groats-worth of Wit	Robert Greene (Ver?)
	The Troublesome Raign of King John	Anonymous
	The Taming of a Shrew	Anonymous
	The True Tragedy of Richard Duke of York	Anonymous
	The Contention Betwixt The Two Famous Houses of Yorke and Lancaster	Anonymous

Geniuses not only produce significantly higher-level work, they also produce significantly more higher-level work. The Beatles had twenty-seven number one hits during their existence, not to mention many more tunes that reached the top ten. Mozart and Beethoven not only produced more striking works, they produced more than many of the lesser-ranked composers combined. Picasso was continuously productive from his teen years until old age, often producing one or more canvases a week. Faulkner wrote a significant number of memorable novels. Dickens produced a stream of memorable works from the beginning of his life until the end. While there are exceptions, artists who produced only one or two great works (Herman Melville wrote but a few), generally the fountain of creativity flows strongest among those of the first rank. Their creativity is an unending, bountiful spring.

Edward de Vere produced an almost unimaginable stream of poems, translations, essays, songs, and plays of the highest literary quality throughout every year of his life. During this same lifetime, he was married twice, had a mistress and five acknowledged children. He was a favorite of the Queen, then was thrown into the Tower by her. He lived a full life as a courtier, participated in a military campaign against the Scots, and sat in sessions of Parliament. He won two jousting tournaments, was wounded in a duel, and provisioned a ship against the Spanish Armada. He was a juror in the trial of Mary Queen of Scots and a juror in the trial of Essex and Southampton.

He was a very *busie Bee.*

FIRST HEIR OF MY INVENTION

William Shakespeare emerged for the first time in this world in November 1593. The name was the signature in a dedicatory to Henry Wriothesley, 3rd Earl of Southampton, in the long narrative poem *Venus and Adonis*.

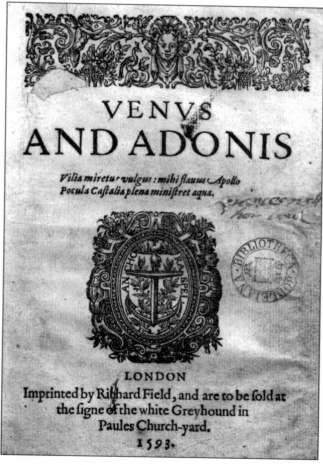

Figure 17. *Venus and Adonis* Title page

Oxford

The publication was a success, with over a dozen printings between its first printing and 1623, when the *First Folio* of plays appeared. *Venus and Adonis* is the salacious story of the seduction of the young Adonis by the older Venus.

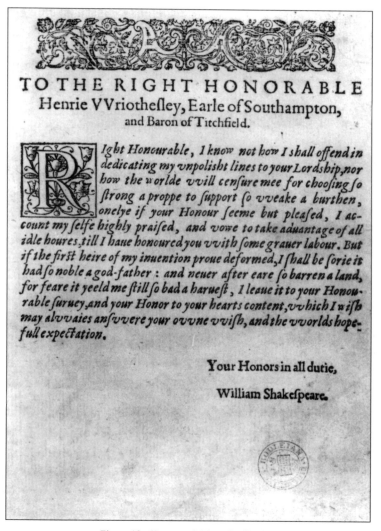

Figure 18. *Venus and Adonis* Dedication

The dedication reads:

TO THE RIGHT HONOURABLE
Henry VVriothesley, Earle of Southampton
And Baron of Titchfield.

Right Honourable, I know not how I shall offend in dedicating my unpolisht lines to your Lordship, nor how the worlde will censure me for choosing so strong a proppe to support so weake a burthen, onelye, if your Honour seeme but pleased, I account myself highly praised, and vowe to take advantage of all idle houres, till I have honoured you with some graver labour. But if the *first heire of my invention* prove deformed, I shall be sorie it had so noble a god-father: and never after eare so barren a land, for fear it yield me still so bad a harvest, I leave it to your honourable survey, and your Honor to your hearts content, which I wish may always answere your own wish, and the world's hopeful expectation.

Your honours in all dutie,
WILLIAM SHAKESPEARE.   [*Italics* added]

There have been about a million gallons of ink spilled by Stratfordian defenders trying to explain that the word "invention" applies to anything but the name William Shakespeare. The particular phrase is "But if the first heire [heir] of my invention should prove deformed ..." The most logical reading of this phrase is that the "first heire" is the poem (which may be deformed because the poem is not well written) and the "invention" is the name that the poem inherited. However, this leads to the name Shakespeare as an invention of the poet. This is clearly an unacceptable interpretation by defenders of the man from Stratford, so if one wishes to read a dozen Stratfordian treatises on the subject, one can find a dozen different reasons why the Author is not signifying that William Shakespeare is a creation of the poet.

At another level, using a little poetic license, Oxford created a statement that is pregnant with meaning. "Invention" is almost synonymous with or certainly highly similar to the word "creation." If one places "creation" in place of "invention," the entire phrase takes on a biological meaning, "the first heir of my creation." The first heir of my creation, apart from a poetic meaning, would mean "my first son." While not referring specifically to the dedicatee of the poem, it creates a powerful sense that Oxford is referring to something beyond dedicating a poem. It is difficult to believe that an Elizabethan audience familiar with allegory and hidden allusions could miss this possible interpretation.[a]

---

[a] Thanks to Hank Whittemore for this insight.

There has been considerable discussion among Oxfordians over Oxford's choice of the name William Shakespeare. Some have posited that Oxford had some relation or knowledge of the man from Stratford-upon-Avon and chose to use his name and persona as a cover for his writings. However, no known direct connection between the two men has surfaced. Others have maintained that Oxford chose this name because it had artistic connections with the Greek goddess Pallas Athene, who with her sword and helmet, was the patron goddess of Athens and the arts. Others doubt this connection, yet the image of Pallas Athene carrying a spear was a common one during the Elizabethan era. One of the most famous of these is the portrait of Elizabeth in *The Judgment of Paris* by Hans Eworth. Queen Elizabeth is judging the beauty of three goddesses: Juno, Minerva (the Greek Pallas Athene), and Venus. The conceit behind this is, "Who could be the judge?" It could only be the most beautiful of all, the Queen. Relevant to the name issue, the portrait shows the image of Minerva (Pallas Athene) in the helmet that made her invisible, and she has her trademark spear.

Figure 19. *Judgment of Paris,* Hans Eworth

On the other hand, Oxford might have chosen Shakespeare as a reference to his success at two jousting tournaments or from the references to Oxford as "shaking spears" in the July 1578 address that Gabriel Harvey, a fellow at Trinity College, gave to dignitaries of the court, Oxford among them, as discussed in the previous chapter.[b]

However, this discussion of the name Shakespeare is ex post facto. It is only relevant because of the misidentification by literary scholars of the man from Stratford-upon-Avon as the Author for some 400 years. As shown in the previous chapter, Oxford simply dominated the theatrical and literary life of Elizabethan England for thirty years as a playwright, poet, man of letters, and patron of theatrical companies. His personal history was well known and his relation with the Queen was openly gossiped about. The references to the Boar and the Queen in *Venus and Adonis* would make it clear to any Elizabethan reader that the two protagonists were Oxford and Elizabeth.

There was no large conspiracy to bury Oxford's name; rather, it was a unique set of customs, taboos, events, and personalities that led to his name being buried. William Cecil undoubtedly destroyed any personal letters Oxford sent to him that mention any theater activities, and perhaps Robert Cecil destroyed other correspondence to Oxford after 1604. What happened to Oxford's library and personal correspondence remains a substantial mystery. However, the lack of Oxford's name in the written record is largely a case of aristocratic protocol. In the first years, Oxford published under a variety of names of living persons and pen names, as well as his own. His plays were not intended for publication but were produced solely for the court. It was not until rather late, 1594, that his plays (other than a few translations) were published, and these were first published anonymously. (The circumstances of the *First Folio* will be covered below.)

Those in literary and theatrical circles were very circumspect about committing to print or to personal correspondence the connection between this high-ranking aristocrat and the theatrical world. Everyone knew, but nobody was openly connecting Oxford to the world of literature and the theater. The pen name was really an irrelevant issue in that period, and it only became an issue in later centuries with the assignment of the works

---

b Harvey acknowledges that he personally knew Oxford; he also mentions Master Thomas Smith, who is the son of Sir Thomas Smith, the noted academic and lawyer, who was Oxford's tutor. "In the prime of his gallantest youth he bestowed Angles (gold coins) upon me in Christ's College in Cambridge, and otherwise vouchsafed me many gracious favours at the affectionate commendation of my cousin, Master Sir Thomas Smith, the son of Sir Thomas."

to the man from Stratford-upon-Avon. Whatever name was on the poems and plays, it was as transparent as glass to the Elizabethans that the man standing behind the works was Edward de Vere, 17th Earl of Oxford.

SHAKESPEARE OR SHAKSPERE?

Contrary to popular belief, William Shakespeare was not born on April 24, 1564, in Stratford-upon-Avon. The man born on that date was named Gulielmus Shakspere.

In the 1800s, biographies of William Shakespeare began to name Shakspere as the man behind the Author's name and to use the family name of the man from Stratford-upon-Avon. They had found their working-class hero and wanted to strengthen the ties by connecting him further to his Stratford-upon-Avon roots. After J. Thomas Looney's *Shakespeare's Identity Revealed,* supporters of the man from Stratford stopped using the Shakspere name. They went in the opposite direction and tried to create a seamless connection between the man born Shakspere and the Author known as Shakespeare.

Stratfordian defenders of Shakspere's authorship try to minimize the significance of the name difference by saying that the variations of spelling are to be expected given the variances in spelling in Elizabethan times or that variations do not make any difference because Shakespeare and Shakspere would be pronounced the same. Neither of these arguments holds up to scrutiny. There were many variations in spelling in Elizabethan times, but in the case of this family name, there are few variations, and they all indicate a "Shak" pronunciation:

		Family Name
1558 Sept. 15	Christening	"Ione Shakspere daughter to Iohn Shakspere"
1562 Dec. 2	Christening	"Margareta filia Iohannis Shakspere"
1563 April 30	Burial	"Margareta filia Iohannis Shakspere"
1564 April 26	Christening	"Gulielmus filius Iohannes Shakspere"
		(William son of John)
1566 Oct. 13	Christening	"Gibertus filius Iohannis Shakspere"
1569 April 15	Christening	"Ione the daughter of Iohn Shakspere"
1571 Sept 28	Christening	"Anna filia magistri Shakspere"
1580 May 3	Christening	"Edmund sonne to Mr. Iohn Shakspere"
1582 Nov. 17	Marriage license	"Wm Shaxpere et Anna Whateley de Temple Grafton"
1582 Nov. 28	Band of sureties	"willm Shagspere one thone partie and Ann hathwey of Stratford"
1583 May 26	Christening	"Susanna daughter to William Shakspere"
1585 Feb. 2	Christening	"Hamnet & Iudith sonne and daughter to William Shakspere"
1596 Aug 11	Burial	"Hamnet filius William Shakspere"

1596 Oct. 20	Grant of arms	"Iohn Shakespere of Stratford;" motto "Shakespere, non sanz droict"
1601 Sept. 8	Burial	"Mr. Johanes Shakspear(e)"
1607 June 5	Marriage	"Iohn Hall gentlema & Susanna Shaxspere"
1608 Sept. 9	Burial	"Mayry Shaxspere wydowe"
1612 Feb. 3	Burial	"Gilbertus Shakspere adolescens"
1613 Feb. 4	Burial	"Rich: Shakspere"
1616 Mar. 25	Legal will	In title "Willm Shackspeare of Stratford on Avon" with three signatures, William Shakspere, Willm Shakspere and William Shakspeare
1616 April 25	Burial record	"will Shakspere gent"
1616 Nov. 23	Christening	"Shaksper fillius Thomas Quyny gent."
1617 May 8	Burial record	"Shakespere fillius Tho. Quyny, gent."
1623 Aug. 8	Burial record	"Mrs. Shakspeare."

It is not until 1597 that the spelling "Shakespeare" turns up in Stratford-upon-Avon in a legal document. In total, only eight spellings of Shakespeare occur in Stratford-upon-Avon, and even after 1597, the "Shakspere" spelling was the most common one. The man from Stratford-upon-Avon did not change the spelling of his name, as do so many people in theater; instead, he kept the most common spelling, "Shakspere." It should be pointed out that the church record was a recopy and not the original, but it does not seem plausible that the copyist would convert Shakespeare into a variety of spellings indicating a Shakspere pronunciation.

The pronunciation defense falls apart when the last will and testament of William Shakspere is examined. In this legal document, the writer clearly follows the convention of using a final "e" to distinguish between a short vowel sound (rat, hat, mat, wif) and a long vowel (rate, hate, mate, wife), or as my daughter was taught in elementary school, the magic "e." This convention is necessary in English because there are more vowel sounds than there are vowels. This is no small matter of spelling because without this convention, the English language would be unintelligible. "I hit the rat with my bat" could be confused with "I hite the rate with my bate." Here are some of the words that show the writer of Shakspere's will was following this convention:

Long vowel pronunciation with the magic "e":	rate, estate, plate, same, have, like, come, date, place, name, make, lyfe (life), wyfe (wife), here
Short vowel pronunciation lacking the magic "e":	yt (it), ys (is), had, god, bed, in, within, wherein, then, them, amen, tenn (ten), att (at), her
The eight mentions of the man's name indicate a short vowel pronunciation: No reason has ever been advanced why there should be so many different spellings in one will.	Shackspeare, Shakspeare, Shackspeare, Shakspere, Shackspere, Shakspere, Shackspeare, Shackspeare
Pronunciations or the same first syllable with and without a final "e":	her vs. hereunto; her vs. hereof

The church records in the village and the legal will indicate that his name was most frequently spelled and pronounced "Shakspere." Academics who pride themselves on attention to detail woefully overlook these facts because they do not serve their case. This line of defense was necessary because no one has ever advanced a plausible reason why the man from Stratford, if he was the writer, would use a variant and confusing spelling of his name.

PUBLICATION OF THE PLAYS

The orthodox position is that the man from Stratford-upon-Avon came to London and published *Venus and Adonis* in 1593 and then *The Rape of Lucrece* the following year. After that, he supposedly began writing, producing, and publishing his plays as a commercial endeavor. This simply does not hold up.

1593	*Venus and Adonis* (poem)	William Shakespeare
1594	*The Rape of Lucrece* (poem)	William Shakespeare
1594	*Titus Andronicus*	Anonymous
1594	*The Taming of a Shrew*	Anonymous
1594	*First Part of the Contention*	Anonymous
1594	*Second Part of Henry VI*	Anonymous
1597	*Tragedie King Richard 3rd*	Anonymous
1595	*Tragedie Richard Duke of York*	Anonymous
1595	*2nd & 3rd Parts of Henry VI*	Anonymous

1595	*Tragedie of Locrine*	V.V.S.[c]
1597	*Tragedie of Romeo and Juliet*	Anonymous
1597	*Tragedie of King Richard 2nd*	Anonymous
1598	*History of Henrie the 4th, 1st Part*	Anonymous
1598	*Famous Victories (Henry V)*	Anonymous
1598	*Tragedie King Richard 2nd*	William Shake-speare [1]

[Some were published more than once in this period.]

In a period of five years, twelve plays later attributed to William Shakespeare were published anonymously and one with the initials V.V.S., which indicates the initials of William Shakespeare. There is some dispute about who authorized the publication of these plays. It is doubtful that any printer would print such plays without the express consent of the Lord Great Chamberlain (Oxford). Also, a good number of Shakespeare plays continued to be published anonymously after 1598. For example, *Romeo and Juliet* was published anonymously in 1599, 1609, and 1622.[2]

There has been no good reason ever advanced by orthodox scholars to explain why the man from Stratford-upon-Avon should require anonymity after 1593 publications attributed to William Shakespeare. Further, there was a sales value to the name or trademark of William Shakespeare after the commercial success of *Venus and Adonis.* Yet the plays appeared in print for five years afterward with no author's name attached. (Performance records are almost nonexistent, so it is difficult to determine what plays were publicly performed or when.)

The extension of this orthodox Shakespeare myth is that the man from Stratford-upon-Avon was a commercial success through writing and selling his plays and that he wrote plays unrelated to his personal life with the sole intention of making money. This contention is undone by the surprising fact that eighteen of Shakespeare's plays were not published during the lifetime of the man from Stratford. These are not minor plays but are some of the best-known plays in the Shakespeare canon. There is no reason put forth why either the man from Stratford-upon-Avon or any theater company would refrain from putting these plays into print:

---

[c] Scholars have been reluctant to classify *Locrine* as a Shakespeare play, even though it was printed in the same period and has WS attached to it. The style indicates it may have been written much earlier, and thus it would lead away from the man from Stratford as Author.

Plays Not Published until the *First Folio* in 1623

> *The Tempest*
> *Two Gentlemen of Verona*
> *Measure for Measure*
> *The Comedy of Errors*
> *As You Like It*
> *The Taming of the Shrew*
> *All Is Well That Ends Well*
> *Twelfe Night, Or What You Will*
> *The Winters Tale*
> *The Life and death of King John*
> *The First Part of King Henry the Sixth*
> *The Life and Death of King Henry the Eighth*
> *The Tragedy of Coriolanus*
> *Timon of Athens*
> *The Life and Death of Julius Caesar*
> *The Tragedy of Macbeth*
> *Anthony and Cleopatra*
> *Cymbeline King of Britaine*[2][d]

The Stratfordian myth further contends that the man from Stratford-upon-Avon first published plays while living in London and continued to write and publish plays after he moved back to Stratford-upon-Avon about 1600. This is contradicted when one looks at the dates of publication. There was a marked decrease in the number of plays published after the death or disappearance of Oxford in 1604, and there is simply no reason why this should occur if the man from Stratford-upon-Avon was writing the plays and was principally motivated by financial reward.

New Plays Published[4]

1593–1604	17	(From first publication to Oxford's disappearance)
1605–1616	4	(From disappearance to Stratford man's death)
1616–1623	1	(From Stratford man's death to *First Folio*)

In summary, the orthodox position of the young actor-writer coming to London and turning out a stream of works that were written, staged, and then published is simply a myth.

---

[d] *Pericles, King of Tyre* was not published in the *First Folio* although it had been published in 1609.

THOSE VERY STRANGE SONNETS

Shake-speares Sonnets was published in 1609 but without an author identified. The title page does not attribute the authorship to any William Shakespeare; rather, the name Shake-speare is used as a brand name such as Warner Brother's movies. Shown below is a typical title page of the times where the author's name is typeset between the lines, but in *Shake-speares Sonnets,* there is a space between the lines for the author, but no author is given. This is an obvious omission.

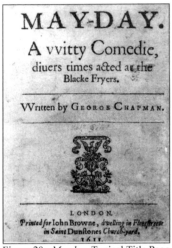

Figure 20. *Mayday*, Typical Title Page

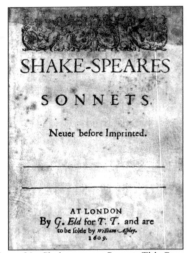

Figure 21. *Shake-speares Sonnets* Title Page

A book twice the length of this one could be written about the publication and mystery of *Shake-speares Sonnets*. However, it is certain that the publication was not a straightforward business arrangement that had anything to do with the man from Stratford-upon-Avon. When of *Shake-speares Sonnets* was published, the man from Stratford-upon-Avon was alive and well in his rural village with seven more years to live. *Venus and Adonis* had been an enormous commercial success involving several reprints. Therefore, it would seem that publishers would be eager to publish and republish the sonnets. But that was not the case.

The sonnets were not published again until 1640 in a misbegotten book containing other works, and the poems were not in the same order as in those with the 1609 date. Only thirteen copies of the first printing have survived. This leads one to wonder if *Shake-speares Sonnets* contained some hidden story that the authorities were anxious to suppress by confiscating existing copies and preventing any further printings. An alternative theory is that it was never printed for commercial distribution; instead, the book may have been printed for a limited distribution. The only clue as to the date of publication is the "1609" on the cover; however, there are no letters or literary references of the time that confirm the book's existence or support that they were actually printed in 1609. They could have been printed at any time, and the date may not signify the printing date at all.

Orthodox Shakespearean scholars have taken three routes to bridge the enormous gap between what was written in the sonnets and the nature of the life of the man from Stratford. (What the sonnets describe will be discussed fully in the next chapter.)

First, they propose that the sonnets are fictional. If the man from Stratford-upon-Avon could make up an entire world of dukes, kings, and Italian princes with which he had no familiarity, why could he not make up an equally fictional persona to be the author of the sonnets? This explanation does not hold up very well in the face of even the most naïve reading of the sonnets.

Second, an opposite approach is to deny that authorship matters. The sonnets from this point of view are only poetry and should not be read as giving any insight into the poet's life. One academic tells his class that these poems were written by Lucy Negro, a prominent London prostitute of the times. This begs the question to avoid the Authorship issues.

The third position is to find indications of the life of rural England in the sonnets. However, as imaginative as their interpretations may be, they fail to explain how he could have had knowledge of life at court:

Sonnet 125

Were 't aught to me I bore *the canopy*,   [*Italics* added]
With my extern the outward honouring,
Or laid great bases for eternity,
Which prove more short than waste or ruining?
Have I not seen dwellers on form and favour
Lose all, and more, by paying too much rent,
For compound sweet forgoing simple savour,
Pitiful thrivers, in their gazing spent?
No, let me be obsequious in thy heart,
And take thou my oblation, poor but free,
Which is not mix'd with seconds, knows no art,
But mutual render, only me for thee.
      Hence, thou suborn'd informer! a true soul
      When most impeach'd stands least in thy control.

What is the canopy? It is the canopy that was carried over the monarch.:

Figure 22. *Queen Elizabeth in Progress to Hunsdon House*

The portrait is of Elizabeth under a canopy in a wedding procession. The portrait is known by various titles, one of which is *Queen Elizabeth in Progress to Hunsdon House.* The Queen is being transported on a cart, followed by the bride in a silver dress. Over the Queen's head is the canopy that always covers the monarch to shield her from the elements outdoors (and one supposes to shield the monarch from leaky roofs indoors). Such a canopy was also carried over the monarch during funeral processions. Most likely, the particular canopy that Oxford is referring to in the sonnet is the funeral canopy, which fits within the context of "laid great basis for eternity."

In B.M. Ward's biography of Oxford, he gives the verses to a song titled "A Joyful Ballad of the Royal entrance of queen Elizabeth into the City of London, the 24th of November in the thirty-first year of Her Majesty's reign, to give God praise for the overthrow of the Spaniards."[5] The Earl of Oxford is mentioned in one of the verses:

The Lord Marquess of Winchester bare-headed there was seen,
Who bare the sword in comely sort before our noble Queen;
The noble Earl of Oxford then High Chamberlain of England
Rode right before Her Majesty his bonnet in his hand.[6]

B.M. Ward further gives a diagram of the procession and has Oxford to the front left of the Queen. Assuming the dignitaries at the 1588 procession were in designated positions for all such events, then the man to the front left of the Queen in the canopy painting would be Oxford.

M.H. Spielmann refers to this man in his 1910 article in *Connoisseur Magazine* in his discussion of the Ashbourne Portrait. The figure in this painting, he says, is similar to the man depicted in the Ashbourne Portrait. From other full-length portraits of Oxford and from the description of him as being a short man with a large wit, it is very likely that this, indeed, is Oxford. The face of the Queen is less realistic than the faces of the other participants in the procession, for it portrays her as years younger than she was at the time of the procession.

There is no evidence that the man from Stratford-upon-Avon ever came within a thousand yards of the Queen or ever carried any canopy, much less the canopy carried over the monarch. Thus, the claim of orthodox scholars that the writer of the sonnets is the man from Stratford-upon-Avon is based almost solely on wishful thinking, with no internal literary evidence that relates the world of the sonnets to the world of Stratford-upon-Avon.

THE FIRST FOLIO 1623

Does the *First Folio* give off a strange and fishy smell? First, look closely at the famous engraved portrait of the title page. Do you see anything wrong?

Martin Droeshout engraved the figure on the title page. He also engraved a likeness of the Duke of Buckingham (James I's lover) and the Prince of Sweden, so by no means was he an unaccomplished artist. He also did a number of caricatures and satirical engravings for publications of the time. When this engraving was done, Droeshout was twenty-two years old and the man from Stratford-upon-Avon had been dead for seven years. It is impossible that Droeshout would have ever seen his subject in his forties, which seems to be about the age of the subject of the engraving. Further, of all the engravers in England, why did the publishers pick someone who was unlikely to have known this famous person? The foul-ups and distortions of the engraving are deliberate and intentional and are not the result of any inadequacies on the part of the engraver. He was picked because he could do stylized caricatures as well as realistic portraits. This engraving has the appearance of a portrait with enough amiss to be noticeable to anyone who halfway examines the face on the cover. The "fishiness" of the First Folio starts on the title page.

Have you found what is wrong with the engraving? First, you can start with the man's forehead, which looks something like a Beluga Whale with its bulbous protrusion. A human skull slopes back above the eyebrows. The human forehead does not go up like a cylinder and then have a bulbous protrusion. Second, the entire head is somewhat distended from the body. Third, there is a line running down the left side of the man's face from his ear to his jaw. A line that has no corresponding line in a human face, but this line gives the impression that the man is wearing a mask.

Finally, there is something so obvious that it is invisible. Notice that the lapels of the doublet do not match. The sitter's right shoulder (to the reader's left) is correct, with the flat breastplate in front. However, the sitter's left shoulder is a right shoulder viewed from the rear. Notice the cut of the garment is rounded to give the shoulder room to move, as it would be seen from the rear. Clearly, the producers of this publication did not intend to give a faithful representation of whoever the author was, and "Honest" Ben Jonson says as much when he warns the reader "look not on his picture, but his book."

Figure 23. *First Folio* Title Page

Another mention of William Shakespeare in the *First Folio* is equally ridiculous. The *First Folio* clearly says:

> The Names of the Principall Actors in all these playes,
> William Shakespeare
> Richard Burbadge
> John Hemmings
> Augustine Phillips
> William Kempt
> Thomas Poope
> George Bryan
> Henry Condell
> [26 actors listed]

If William Shakespeare was a prominent actor in London, it would have been news to the Elizabethans. He is not listed on any playbills nor mentioned in any letters. When the man from Stratford-upon-Avon died in

1616, there were no eulogies at his death, no one commented on it, and no one connected him to the poems or plays of anybody. The only place he is undisputedly mentioned as an actor is after the fact in the works of "Honest" Ben Jonson. Orthodox historians have combed every theatrical record in every village and town, not to mention London, and only two or three records indicate that anyone named Shakespeare was an actor. If he was an actor, he was not a prominent one. Certainly, William Shakespeare was not an actor who would be listed ahead of the most prominent thespians of the Elizabethan stage: Richard Burbage, John Hemmings, Augustine Phillips, and William Kempt.

INCOMPARABLE BRETHREN

While there is a fishy smell about the playwright-actor William Shakespeare, there is no such aroma about the men behind the *First Folio*. The dedicatees are "the incomparable brethren" Philip and William Herbert who were, respectively, the Earl of Montgomery and the Earl of Pembroke. This fact is usually glossed over by orthodox historians for some very good reasons. Philip was married to Susan Vere, Oxford's daughter, and William Herbert had been considered as a husband for Bridget Vere, also a daughter of Oxford's, but they did not marry. Further, that trustworthy soul Ben Jonson had a definite relation with the Herbert brothers. He was on their payroll. He received an annuity of £20, which was an enormous sum of money, and it was raised after the publication of the *First Folio.* Ben Jonson's comments are deliberately vague and misleading because he is being paid to write an ambiguous and misleading cover story.

Far from being a literary-commercial publication, as the Stratfordians have argued, the publication of the *First Folio* was mired in the politics of the Stuart monarchy. In the spring of 1623, Henry de Vere, 18th Earl of Oxford (Edward de Vere's son by Elizabeth Trentham), was in the Tower on charges of treason against King James I and his homosexual lover George Villiers, the Duke of Buckingham. James was raised as a Protestant in Scotland, and he occupied the throne of England by promising freedom of conscience to all—and he largely delivered on that promise. His mother, however, was Mary Queen of Scots, who had been the Catholic hope for Queen of England but was executed by Elizabeth.

In 1622, the King's son was attempting to marry a Spanish princess. This marriage would bring England back into the Catholic Spanish orbit with the possibility of a future king with Spanish blood. This was obviously a very serious situation to the Protestants of England.

Objections to the marriage were strenuous, with Henry de Vere as one of the leaders of the Protestant faction.

In a somewhat ludicrous bit of history, Prince Charles (Stuart) and George Villiers went to Spain in disguise to meet the Spanish princess, but they were found out and the diplomatic marriage mission ended as a disaster. Tensions were high in the spring of 1623. Below is the letter from Count Gondomar known to the English as the Spanish Machiavelli, that resulted in imprisoning the 18th Earl of Oxford. Count Gondomar also played a significant role in the execution of Sir Walter Raleigh by convincing King James that Raleigh's death was necessary to preserve the peace between Spain and England. The 18th Earl's life was in great danger:

> In the letter of April 1, I said to your Majesty how the King removed the Earl of Oxford as commander in chief of the armada in the Strait [channel fleet in 1622] because I told him to, because he [18th Earl of Oxford] was partial to the Dutch, and also because of the way Oxford was bad mouthing the King and me. He spoke even to the point of saying that it was a miserable situation that had reduced England's stature because the people had to tolerate a King who had given the Pope everything spiritual; and everything temporal to the King of Spain. I told King James to arrest this man and put him in the Tower in a narrow cell so that no one can speak to him. I have a strong desire to cut off his head because he is an extremely malicious person and has followers. And he is the second ranking Earl in England, and he and his followers are committed to the Puritan Faction with great passion and to the faction of the Count of the Palatinate against the service of the Emperor and your Majesty.
>
> May 16, 1622 Don Diego Sarmiento de Acuna, Count Gondomar.[7]

The 18th Earl of Oxford was imprisoned in May 1623, and the *First Folio* must have been started about this time in order to be printed in the fall of that year. It was not until November 8, 1623, that sixteen of the eighteen plays that had never been published were registered with the Stationer's Office. This is unusual because the standard procedure was to register before typesetting, not afterward. This indicates that those behind the publication did not want the authorities to know what they were up to until they were about to publish.

There was a meeting in August 1623 on the Earl of Southampton's boat *The Prince* (appropriately titled, some might say). At this meeting were James I, Henry Wriothesley, Horace Vere (Oxford's cousin), and the Herbert brothers. Publication of the *First Folio* occurred the November after this meeting. In the fall of 1623, Buckingham and Prince Charles returned from Spain without a marriage arranged to the Spanish princess.

There were bonfires in the streets of London to celebrate this nonmarriage. The *First Folio* was in the bookstores three months later, in December 1623.

One thing that both Oxfordians and orthodox Shakespearean experts agree on is that the *First Folio* is a literary mess that suffered from a hurried publication. There are hundreds of errors, and each printing is different because the typesetters corrected errors as they went along. What the *First Folio* was not was a strictly commercial and artistic publication attended to with the same care that was given *Venus and Adonis*. It shows more concern with being rushed to press than with spending the year or two that would have been required for a flawless publication. It should be remembered that *Venus and Adonis* and the *Rape of Lucrece* were flawless printings. Neither can the publication of the *First Folio* be connected in any way to anyone from Stratford-upon-Avon. There is no indication in the will of the Stratford-upon-Avon man nor in the actions of his daughter or his literate son-in-law that they had any interest in the matter—and they did not. Orthodox scholarship has regarded the *First Folio* as a literary event that dropped out of the sky, completely disconnected from the political events of its time. Clearly, this is not the case.

The *First Folio* was not simply a literary effort, but a political statement on the part of the Protestant faction. The publication of the *First Folio* was a statement by the Protestant faction that recalled the glory years of Elizabeth and her historical and artistic legacy, which was reflected within the plays of Shakespeare. The works of Shakespeare were being used as political propaganda to remind the English nation of their glory and their independence from Spain, from Catholicism, and perhaps from King James.

One of the greatest mysteries of the publication of the *First Folio* is who was in possession of the manuscripts so that they were "published according to the True Original Copies." Who had the true original copies? The most likely suspects are Susan Vere, Oxford's daughter, and her husband, Philip Herbert, the Earl of Montgomery. There might be others who would have had access to them, but Susan was the most active theatrically and thus the most likely candidate. Therefore, the intriguing question and Holy Grail of the Oxfordian movement is, "Where are the True Original Copies?" Are they still in existence and, if so, where are they? Is a pile of papers sitting unnoticed in some ancient hallway, hidden behind a movable bookshelf, buried in some vault in a stately home, or hidden among manuscripts in a vast library? Are they buried in the tunnel on Oak Island, Nova Scotia?[e] Will the long lost and undiscovered treasure of the original manuscripts of Shakespeare written in the hand of Edward de Vere ever be found?

One can only hope.

CREATION OF THE STRATFORD MYTH

On March 27, 1625, James I died, and his son Charles became king (and was a disastrous monarch for England). He married a French Catholic princess, which alienated the Protestant faction. An invasion by Scotland and the King's authoritarian attitude toward Parliament led to open rebellion and war between the Roundheads (Puritans) and the Cavaliers (Royalists). Finally, Charles was deposed and executed on January 30, 1649. In 1653, Cromwell, leader of the Puritans, declared himself Lord Protector and effectively become the dictator of England. His rule ended with his death on September 3, 1658. Charles II returned to England from France, and the monarchy was restored.

In the years of Cromwell's rule, the theaters were closed. Most of those who had firsthand experience of the English Renaissance were dead by that time. The true stories and identities behind the pseudonyms and elaborate allegories became more impossible to untangle. By the time interest in Shakespeare rekindled in the 1700s, there was no written history of the period and no biography of the man listed on the title page of the *First Folio* as William Shakespeare. There was no corporal body attached to the name on the title page of the *First Folio.*

At the start of the 1700s, George Vertue, an antiquarian, discovered the statue of a man holding a grain sack in a small village west of London. Below the man's statue was inscribed "William Shakspeare." This was the only physical evidence that pointed toward who the Author might be. However, such The conclusion can only be that the foul-ups and distortions of the engraving are deliberate; they are not the result of any inadequacies on the part of the engraver. He was picked because he could

---

[e] Oak Island, Nova Scotia, has a pit or tunnel that was very carefully constructed, and it is assumed that pirates buried treasure in it. However, the pit is an elaborate feat of engineering, complete with a second tunnel leading to the ocean, which floods the tunnel. It seems beyond the skills of an average group of seamen and pirates to construct such a tunnel. Why they would conceal treasure in a way that makes it almost impossible to retrieve it is difficult to explain. Artifacts have been found there from the 1600s, including bottles and traces of mercury. Papers stored in bottles filled with mercury could withstand the ravages of time. This island and sea passage is connected to Oxford because he was an investor in the Frobischer expedition in the 1580s to explore a Northwest Passage via this route. A Mount Oxford on one of the islands is named after him.

do stylized caricatures as well as realistic portraits. This engraving has the appearance of a portrait with enough amiss to be noticeable to anyone who halfway examines the face on the cover. The "fishiness" of the *First Folio* starts on the title page.statues were not uncommon in churches of the area,[f] and nothing about the statue at the time indicated that this was a writer, for the statue was of a man holding a grain or wool sack. Yet without any other reasonable line of investigation, the myth began to grow. In 1709, Nicholas Rowe, a playwright, wrote the first biography of William Shakespeare in the introduction to a collection of Shakespeare's plays. This thin biography was largely conjecture about the life of the man from Stratford-upon-Avon as Author. There was no overwhelming agreement about who wrote the plays.

In 1769, a prominent actor named David Garrick staged a Shakespeare festival in Stratford-upon-Avon much to the amazement of the community and the literary world. This event forever crystallized in the mind of the public and of the literary world that the Author known as William Shakespeare was the man from Stratford-upon-Avon. If nature abhors a vacuum, then literary history abhors one even more. The English nation and the world at large had found a local hero who filled the vacuum and their emotional-historical needs. The "common man as literary giant" myth was born. Little of substance was added to the original biography, and despite centuries of investigation, not one single word has ever been turned up in the Stratford man's handwriting. It is doubtful whether the signatures ascribed to him are genuine. They are all spelled differently with different handwriting, and in an age of illiteracy, legal clerks were allowed to sign a man's name.

Much ink would later be used to define the authorship of the man from Stratford-upon-Avon with qualifying words such as "undoubtedly," "must be the case," or "with certainty we can say" despite the enormous amount of doubt and uncertainty surrounding the case. Reverend Dr. James Wilmot from a small parish church near Stratford-upon-Avon searched around 1785 for evidence of him as the Author in the surrounding countryside: letters, personal stories, books owned by Shakspere, etc. His diligent labors produced nothing that connected the grain dealer born Gulielmus Shakspere with the famous literary author. Since then, only a few pieces of evidence have ever indicated that the man had anything to do with the theater (perhaps an actor, perhaps an owner of shares in the

---

[f] An English lady at a lecture volunteered this information when she saw the illustration of the original statue. She said these statues of sixteenth century merchants were common in churches of the midlands. This could be a subject of further investigation.

Globe), but nothing to indicate that he had ever written anything so much as a letter.

The statue in the church in Stratford-upon-Avon graphically illustrates the metamorphosis of this myth. The first illustration is an engraving of the original monument from a sketch by Sir William Dugdale in 1656; the second is a picture of the current monument with the figure holding a pen, yet writing on the strange surface of a cushion. The grain merchant metamorphosed into the playwright over the centuries.

Figure 24. Shakspere Monument 1656

Figure 25. Current Shakspere Monument

Dr. Merliee Karr gives a lucid interpretation about the rise and continuing durability of the immortal Bard-of-Avon:

> English literature was first taught, not in the universities, but in the Mechanics Institutes and working men's colleges. English literature was the poor man's classical education. The expected social and political benefits of literature justified giving it a budget.
>
> Literature during this time began to produce a lot of larger-than-life characters. The Three Musketeers, Sherlock Holmes and a whole host of others—the ancestors of our super-heroes—overcame superhuman obstacles with superhuman abilities …
>
> This was also the period when Bardolatry was born. Scholars turned a handful of dry facts about the Stratford entrepreneur into the larger-than-life image of the native English literary genius who came from the working classes himself. England sold the new industrial working class a bill of goods to sweeten the Industrial Revolution—"Be our wage slaves and we'll make the national poet a working-class hero"—and their descendants, both biological and ideological still buy it. The historical context also help to

explain why the adherents of the myth of Shakespeare are so resistant to rational, evidence-based analysis: like D'Artagnan and Sherlock Holmes, the Bard has superpowers.[8]

Stratford-upon-Avon is the second most visited city in Great Britain. It is a tourist mecca and a commercial bonanza. It is a wonderful example of an English town. Yet, unfortunately, it lauds the wrong man in the wrong city.

To visit the world of the true Author of the works, one must travel north from London to Hedingham and Earls Colne, the ancient Norman keep of the de Vere family. Or visit the elegant royal castles of Greenwich, Whitehall, or Richmond. Or visit the stately home at Hatfield of Lord Burghley. Or visit the legal inns of London. Or travel down the canals of Venice. Or see the art of the Italian Renaissance in Florence. Or spend a few days in a cell in the Tower of London. Or visit the fringe theater of London where the actors ply their craft to imbibing audiences. This is where the noble Earl lost his reputation and violated the code of his aristocratic caste by associating with those "brief chroniclers of our time," those vagabonds known as actors.

WHO WAS SHAKSPERE?

With one exception, the more than a hundred biographies plus innumerable journal articles and essays of the man from Stratford-upon-Avon start with the premise that this man was the Author known to the world as William Shakespeare. The few facts surrounding the man are stretched, pulled, twisted, contracted, or expanded to make it somewhat plausible that the man was indeed the Author. Various biographers at various times have offered diverse theories to explain how the man from Stratford acquired the knowledge to be the Author of the works. Some authors maintain that Shakespeare went to Italy and that accounted for his intimate knowledge of Italy and its geography, while others maintain that he acquired his knowledge of Italy from an Italian living in England, while others maintain that his knowledge of Italy was not so extensive. Others maintain that Shakespeare was able to use works in Italian not yet translated into English because such translations existed but were lost.

Some biographers maintain that the man from Stratford-upon-Avon worked as a legal clerk to attain his in-depth knowledge of the law, while others maintain that he acquired his knowledge of the law by osmosis because he lived in "legal London." Various implausible scenarios are manufactured to explain how the man from Stratford-upon-Avon crossed the wide social gulf to have detailed knowledge of aristocratic society, such as falconry, tennis, jousting, fencing, and coursing. (You win points for a vocabulary merit badge if you know the meaning of the last word, or you were born in aristocratic circles that most do not inhabit.) In summary, in the history of Western civilization, never has so much historical imagination been put into such dubious, if not outright fraudulent, biographies.

Yet the man from Stratford-upon-Avon did have a theatrical presence in London. There are records that a man named Shakespeare or variants on the spelling lived in different sections of London at different periods. There are records that the man became a successful businessman in Stratford-upon-Avon. There are recorded payments to someone named Shakespeare as an actor, and there are records of someone named Shakespeare owning shares in the Globe Theater.

There are literary references to a Shakspere-like character in the plays of Ben Jonson. There is a famous comment in *Greenes Groats-worth of Wyt* that Shakspere was "well able to bombast out a blank verse as the best of you ... the only Shake-scene in a country," which appears to refer to the man from Stratford as an actor. His family was granted a coat of arms, most likely by bribing officials, with the motto "Not Without Merit," which Ben Jonson mocked when one of his characters is granted a coat of arms with the motto "Not Without Mustard." Orthodox biographers have clutched at these straws and used them to build a bridge to the man as a writer. However, if all these historical findings are true (and most are not too flattering), then the man was a bombastic actor, a businessman, and an owner of shares in a theater; none establish that he was a writer of anything.

Biographies of the Earl of Oxford cover the man from Stratford-upon-Avon in so far as to discredit Shakspere as the Author and are effective in doing so. The main concern of these biographies is to convince readers that Oxford is the Author known as William Shakespeare, and they leave many mysteries still uncovered about the man from Stratford-upon-Avon.

Diana Price, in her marvelous *Shakespeare's Unorthodox Biography: New Evidence of an Authorship Problem*, approaches the question of the man from Stratford-upon-Avon from a very different perspective. She examines all the evidence in detail, not to prove or disprove that he was the Author, but to find out exactly what he was and what he did:

> Price spends next to no time or space on who the poet and playwright actually was except to indicate the likelihood that he was "a gentleman of rank." She instead tackles the question of who William Shakspere of Stratford actually was—a subject that has been too frequently ignored by Stratfordians and anti-Stratfordians alike.

Stratfordians don't deal at length with the subject because they inevitably run into facts that are contrary to their view of the author. Anti-Stratfordians don't deal at length with the subject because they are less interested in what used to be called "the negative argument," that is, the case against the Stratford citizen's claims to authorship, than in making a case for their pet candidate for Shakespearean honors. The result is the neglect of a vital but virtually untouched field of study. Price works that field admirably and the harvest is abundant.[9]

Price's work is especially strong in explaining the writings of Ben Jonson in relation to William Shakespeare. In addition to writing the introduction to the *First Folio,* Ben Jonson wrote plays wherein a Shakspere-like character is parodied. Price points out that such parody is inconsistent with the great William Shakespeare, but is very consistent with the actor-businessman William Shakspere.

Diana Price's *Unorthodox Biography* is indeed unorthodox. It is unorthodox in that it is the first biography of the man from Stratford-upon-Avon that paints a truthful and insightful portrait of the man's existence. It is the first biography that starts with the facts, then examines them and builds its conclusions on those facts. This is in opposition with all previous biographies of the man, which assume that the man from Stratford was the Author and arrange facts and circumstances accordingly. Price's biography might be more aptly subtitled, *The First True and Complete Biography of the Man Known as William Shakespeare*:

> Shakspere is an entrepreneur who exploits anyone and everyone, including writers. He brokers plays and clothes, cuts all kinds of business deals, and arranges loans at interest. He patches together plays, produces corrupt or vulgarized texts, and pilfers others. Shakspere is also a Battillus to a few courtier writers who sell their written works to him, provided they remain anonymous. Despite some of his shady dealings, he is able to operate successfully for many years because it suits those who need his services, whether as a Battillus [someone who claims others work as his], paymaster, broker, or moneylender.[10]

YET ANOTHER CHANGELING

ALL THESE LOVE MATTERS

In 1573, rumors began to surface at the court that Elizabeth had a new favorite, and that person was, surprisingly, Edward de Vere, 17th Earl of Oxford. Oxford had replaced, in the eyes of the court, Elizabeth's previous favorite, Robert Dudley. In a letter from Gilbert Talbot to his father, he writes:

> My Lord of Oxford is lately grown into great credit, for the Queen's majesty delighteth more in his personage and his dancing and valiantness than any other. I think Sussex doth back him all he can. If it were not for this fickle head he would pass any of them shortly. My Lady Burghley, unwisely, has declared herself, as it were, jealous, which is come to the Queen's ear, wherat she has been not a little offended with her, but now she is reconciled again. At all these love matters my Lord Treasurer winketh and will not meddle in any way.

Letter from Gilbert Talbot, May 1573.[1]

Mary Queen of Scots, in a letter to Elizabeth, is not so discreet in her accusations against the Queen and she explicitly states that Elizabeth and Oxford were lovers. Mary was obviously no fan of Elizabeth, and as a Queen felt she was Elizabeth's equal. She writes the letter in an "it can't be true, but here is what the gossip is" style that allows her to make the most slanderous accusations and yet pass them off as unfounded gossip:

The Letter of Scandal from Mary, Queen of Scots to Elizabeth I, 1584

> ...the Countess of Shrewsbury said to me about you what follows as nearly as possible in these terms to the greater part of which I protest I answered rebuking the said lady for believing or speaking so licentiously of you as a thing which I did not at all believe and do not now believe knowing the disposition of the Countess and by what spirit she was then urged on against you: Firstly that one to whom she said you had made a promise of marriage before of your chamber had lain many times with you with all the licence and familiarity which husband and wife can use to one another. But that undoubtedly you were not as other women and for this reason all those who desired your marriage with the duke of anjou, considering that it could not be consummated were foolish and that you would never wish to lose the liberty of making love and gratifying yourself with master haton and another of this Kingdom but on account of the honour of the country that which vexed her the most that you had not only compromised your honour with a foreigner named Simier going to find him at night in the chamber of a lady who the said Countess greatly blamed in this affair, where you kissed him and indulged in divers unseemly familiarities with him. That you had

disported yourself with the same dissoluteness with the Duke his master who had been to find you one night at the door of your chamber where you had met him with only your nightdress and dressing gown on and that afterwards you had let him enter and that he had remained with you nearly three hours.

... that even the count of Oxford dared not reconcile himself or cohabit with his wife for fear of losing the favour, which he hoped to receive, by becoming your lover. That you were lavish towards all such people and those who lent themselves to such practices....

Marie R[2]

Even a traditional Elizabethan scholar cannot but note that the Queen was far less virginal in her life than in her Tudor propaganda:

Elizbeth it was said, was seducing handsome young men and keeping them under surveillance by her well-paid spies when they were not in amourous attendence on her. Prominent among these favorites was Edward de Vere, earl of Oxford, a boyish, hazel-eyed young courtier (who) whose expression combined poetic languour and aristocratic superciliousness. Oxford excelled at the courtly graces Elizabeth admired. He was athletic and acquitted himself brilliantly in the tiltyard, dashing fearlessly, lance lowered, against any and all comers and retiring the victor despite his youth and slight build. He was an agile and energetic dancer, the ideal partner for the Queen, and had a refined ear for music and was a dexterous performer on the virginals. His poetry was unmistakably accomplished, and his education had given him a cultivated mind, at home with the antique authors Elizabeth knew so well.[3]

Historians have written that Elizabeth had fancied young courtiers, but this is always put in the context of a chaste queen flirting with younger men. There is no record or even any suspicions before the arguments presented in this book that Oxford was the son of the Queen. The letter of Mary Queen of Scots implies that Elizabeth would use her royal power as queen for sexual domination over men and that she was not too shy about doing so. It indicates that the Queen's relations with men were hardly chaste and further points toward the Queen being romantically and sexually involved with the Earl of Oxford who was, as this text has pointed out, her son.

Any sexual relation between the Queen and the Earl of Oxford would be as Hamlet declares "incest that abomination." There were only a half dozen souls or so still living that knew of Oxford's true origins (the Queen, William Cecil, Kat Ashley, Thomas Parry and perhaps Sir Anthony Denny). The most important of those was William Cecil, Lord Burghley. In the event of the Queen's death, he would be the only one credible and powerful enough to put Edward de Vere on the throne. In an age when the average life span might be less than forty, neither William

Cecil nor anyone else expected the Queen to live to the ripe age of seventy.

Because Elizabeth was queen, she had control of the events and there could not be an accumulation of circumstantial evidence as there was in the case of the summer of 1548 with the birth of Oxford. The Queen could sequester herself away in one of her castles or go on a progress in the countryside and be unseen for months. Of course, the same principles of tight-lipped loyalty to the Queen would be in operation and it would hardly be likely that any insider would either talk or write about a pregnant Queen. The startling question to be confronted is "Did Elizabeth have a child whose father was her son, Edward de Vere?"

In May 1574, Elizabeth started her summer royal progress to Woodstock, but instead went to Havering-attre-Bowre on the Thames. This was an ancestral estate of the de Vere family comprised of about a thousand acres. In another letter to his father, Gilbert Talbot reports on the Queen's behavior:

> As also that the Lord Treasurer Lord Burghley intending to wait upon the Queen when she came to Woodstock, as she had appointed him, Secretary Walsingham signified to him, that he with the Lord Keeper, should tarry at London; the cause whereof was unknown to the Lord Treasurer, but seemed to surprise him; but he said he would do as he was commanded. The Queen seemed apprehensive of some danger in her absence (which might give occasion to her melancholy), and thereof thought it advisable for these staid counsellors to remain behind.[4]

Shortly after she resumed her progress in July, Oxford fled to Europe:

> The Earl of Oxford departed into Flanders without the Q licence [Queens], and was revoqued by the Queen sending the Ge. Pensionerss for hym.[5]

If a child was born to Elizabeth in this year, this may have been the period for it to happen. In the sonnets, we find these references to the months of April-May:

	Sonnet	Line
Calls backe the lovely Aprill of her prime:	3	10
With Aprills first-borne flowers, and all things rare	21	7
When proud-pide April (dress'd in all his trim)	98	2
Three Aprill perfumes in three hot Junes burn'd	104	7

And there are forty-one uses of the word "may." Here are a few of them:

	Sonnet	Line
Rough windes do shake the darling buds of Maie	18	3
May make seeme bare, in wanting words to shew it	26	6
Then may I dare to boast how I do love thee;	26	13

Oxford had the largest vocabulary in the history of the English language. Yet, in the sonnets he uses a few words repeatedly. This appears to be an indication that he means these words to convey a message outside the poetry, that message would be that Southampton was born in this period.

If that is what happened, where would such a child be placed? Who might this child be? The Queen was in a position of almost absolute power and coercing an aristocratic family to take such a child would not be an impossible task. She could both reward anyone who agreed and punish anyone who refused. Here it should be said that fostering a child did not particularly require the personal involvement of the foster parents because the intimate care of the child would be delegated to a series of governesses and tutors. As with the case of Edward de Vere, the question is, "Where did the child go?"

HIDDEN IDENTITY

One likely foster father for any child by the Queen was Henry Wriothesley, 2nd Earl of Southampton. He was a devout Catholic, often in trouble with the Crown because of his religious convictions. He was apprehended seeking advice from a Jesuit priest at a secret rendezvous. His question to the priest was whether he owed greater loyalty to the monarch or to his religion. This was simply an unthinkable question and treason of the highest sort. He was tried for treason and condemned to death. However, his sentence was commuted, and he was placed under house arrest in May 1573 under the custody of Sir William More.

On October 6, 1573, he reported:

Figure 26. Henry Wriothesley, 3rd Earl of Southampton[a]

Yt has so hapned by the sudden seizing of my wife today, we could not by possibility have your wife present, as we desired. Yet have I thought goode to imparte unto you such comforte as God hath sente me after all my

---

[a] The cat with the quizzical expression was named Trixie. The legend was that the cat searched London until it found its master imprisoned in the Tower and there it remained until Southampton was released.

longe troubles, which is that this present morning at three of the clock, my wife was delivered of a goodly boy (God bless him.)[6]

Henry Wriothesley's child was delivered at his mother's family estate, Cowdrey, a short distance from his father's. In July of 1574, the 2nd Earl of Southampton fled to Spain for reasons unknown. However, he was convinced to return by the Earl of Sussex, and he went back to his estate at Titchfield. There he was joined by a new member of the household, a gentleman of the bedchamber named Thomas Dymocke. The Dymocke family had longtime connections with the Tudor family. Dymocke's great uncle, Sir Thomas Dymocke, had been the Queen's challenger at her coronation in 1558. The younger Thomas in the household had also been educated at Gray's Inn, and would later inherit a barony and become Sir Thomas. The Queen rewarded Thomas Dymocke with several small offices after he was installed with Southampton. He was appointed to the Commission of the Peace for the Hampshires and in 1579, he served on a commission for the suppression of piracy.

In 1577, the 2nd Earl and his wife began falling out when, according to G.P.V. Akrigg:

> ...the Earl, upset at the intimacy of her friendship with a man named Donsame, "a common person," forbade her ever to see him again.[7]

In 1580, the Earl found his wife again at Dogmersfield where Donsame resided, and the Earl broke with her completely. The Countess was removed from Titchfield and sent to another of the Earl's estates. The Earl also broke off his relations with her family. A biography of Southampton by Charlotte Stopes reports the events as follows:

> The Earl of Southampton was taken into favour again and was given certain county offices to perform, which, with his own interests in house-building and farming, seem to have placidly filled his time. He and his wife seem to have continued on affectionate terms until about 1577, and then some misunderstanding arose, fostered by constant mischief making through the Earl's gentleman servants, the chief of whom was Thomas Dymock. The Earl secluded himself more and more among his followers and estranged himself from his wife; he would have no communication with her, except verbally through the servants who had been the cause of the continuance, if not the initiation, of the Earl's bad feeling.[8]

> By later correspondence we learn that she never saw her boy again during the life-time of his father, who kept him with himself and his servants.[9]

The countess is left to communicate with her husband through Dymocke. Akrigg reports:

> The Countess is vehement against Dymock whom she views as "the begynner & contynnuer of the dissentions betwene us" ... this howse is not for them that will not honor Dymocke as a god." The Earl himself, she reports, stands "so doubtful and perplexed betwene hate and dread, as what to do he knoweth nott well."[10]

The Countess attempted to bring her case to the Privy Council through her father, Lord Montague, but she was rebuffed.

It did not help the Earl's situation that he sent messages to the Catholic Jesuit martyr Edmund Campion, who was later to be convicted, hanged, drawn, and quartered. This communication was reported to London, and the Earl was arrested in August 1581. Most likely, Dymocke reported to the Crown on the Earl's behavior. The Earl was soon released, and he returned to Titchfield, where he made a will dated June 24, 1581, stating that he was in "health and perfect memory." Despite this statement, he died four months later, on October 4, 1581. The question remains as to whether he was poisoned by Dymocke. In his will, Thomas Dymocke was named as one of the executors of the will, the one who would decide if there were any disagreements, and he was rewarded handsomely in the will by the Earl. One clause the Earl managed to place in the will is a mysterious statement that provides for the education until the age of twenty-one for "William, my Beggar Boy," who one would suspect might have been his original son.

The Earl's wife contested the will, and apparently, the Earl of Leicester interceded on her behalf and contacted her father. She regained custody of her daughter Mary, removed Dymocke from control of the estates, and otherwise disposed of the assets in a more favorable way. There is no trace of any William to be found anywhere. Did he die, was he murdered, or did he disappear into the mists of English history like Mary Seymour?

Here again, there was a suspicious set of circumstances that submit to no easy, logical explanation. First, the Earl of Southampton appears to have been under great pressure by someone and fled England to Catholic Spain, but then, given reassurances, he returned. Obviously, these reassurances had to come from the highest level of the government, and that could only be the Queen. Then a gentleman loyal to the Queen, Dymocke, was placed in Southampton's household. Further, this gentleman drove a wedge between the Earl and his wife; Southampton was more afraid of Dymocke than he was loyal to his wife. Most interesting, who was the Earl's beggar boy? Perhaps this can all be explained in some rational fashion. Perhaps this is simply a strange set of historical circumstances. Or perhaps another changeling boy is hidden in this entanglement.

If Elizabeth had a child in the summer of 1574, she would have needed a set of foster parents to raise the child. The 2nd Earl of Southampton was in dire straits with the Queen and, thus, he would have been a likely object of coercion.

It might have gone like this: The Queen through her ministers, which would most likely be William Cecil, forces the Earl to take the child and raise him as his own son or face further persecution for his Catholic leanings and possible death. Rather than do this, he flees to Spain but is convinced to return. He faces either permanent exile or compliance with the Queen's desires, and he chooses the latter. He then takes the young child into his home and with him comes Dymocke as the Queen's watchdog. The true son of the Earl is placed in another household, and when his mother attempts to visit him, she incurs the wrath of Dymocke.

What happens to the displaced child remains uncertain, but the Queen's child is then raised as Henry Wriothesley, 3rd Earl of Southampton. When the 2nd Earl of Southampton is through serving his purpose as a surrogate parent, he is disposed of by poison. His foster son, Henry Wriothesley, becomes the 3rd Earl of Southampton at the age of seven and moves to London to be a ward of the Queen at the house of William Cecil, Lord Burghley.

Henry Wriothesley, 3rd Earl of Southampton, and Robert Devereux, 2nd Earl of Essex, are treated by Elizabethan historians as dashing young men who are the favorites of the Queen, and they were definitely that. However, historians never give any reasons why Henry Wriothesley and Robert Devereux received this special treatment beyond what might be explained by the commingling of a flirtatious Virgin Queen and two handsome young men. For example, the Queen attended a ceremony at Cambridge honoring the young Earl of Southampton, one of the three times she visited the universities. The other two times were visits for Edward de Vere. In addition, the two young men, and especially the headstrong Robert Devereux, seem to have gone beyond all bounds of propriety in their treatment of the Queen.

The most plausible reason for her affections toward both these young men is that they were both sons of the Queen.. It would take a much larger space than this to give a full sense of these men's relations with the Queen, but there are several biographies on each that confirm their relationship with the Queen as extraordinary.

The fourth criterion for the presence of a possible changeling child is a special relationship with the alleged parent, and that appears to be fulfilled.

The circumstantial case for Elizabeth having had a child in 1574 is not as strong as that for her having had a child in the summer of 1548, and this is to be expected. Elizabeth as queen was an adult woman with full powers over the government and her servants. She was able to do as she wished and control both her situation and access to her person. She was able to remove herself from public view as she wished, and her servants and courtiers were bound by a code of silence. If is implausible, it should be recognized that John F. Kennedy, while President, had a string of call girls, a gangster's girlfriend, a purported East German female spy, and an endless stream of young women willing to bed down with him. This was done with the aid and abetment of the Secret Service, appropriately named for these assignments. The entire Washington press corps kept a discreet silence about his flagrant adultery and lionized him as the virtuous husband. The Camelot persona of J.F.K. was a myth concocted by a slavish press corps because it fed the emotional needs of the American people and world public, but it was a myth that was far from the reality of the sexual conduct of the boy-president.

Although the circumstantial evidence is not as strong in the case for a child having been born in 1574 as it is in the case for a child born in 1548, the literary evidence left behind by Elizabeth's poet-playwright son, Edward de Vere, is far more substantial. Let us take a closer look at *Venus and Adonis* and *Shake-speares Sonnets*.

VENUS AND ADONIS

The years 1593 and 1594 produced three fascinating literary works: *Venus and Adonis, The Rape of Lucrece,* and *Willobie His Avisa.* All were long narrative poems. The first is best known as the vehicle that introduced William Shakespeare to the world in 1593. The orthodox interpretation of Shakespeare completely disconnects the poem from the times and requires that *Venus and Adonis* be read as a total creative fantasy, disconnected from living persons, when in fact, in much of Elizabethan poetry (as in *The Fairie Queene*) real people are hidden behind a veil of allegory.

In most modern readings, a story about a dog is about a dog. The Elizabethans, with their courtly rituals and stylized customs of what was fit to print (at least openly) read literature very differently. A story about a dog might be read as being about a duke or earl whose emblem was emblazoned with greyhounds. Yet in *Venus and Adonis,* the allegory is made even clearer than that. Venus is described as "queen" six times in the poem. Not the queen of this country or that imaginative land, but simply as "Queen." What other possible interpretation can there be but that this is the Queen of England, the one and the only, the singular Queen of England? Here are the lines referring to "the queen":

> By this the love-sicke Queene began to sweate
> Poor queen of love, in thine own law forlorn
> And these mine eyes, true leaders to their queen,
> "Fair queen," quoth he, "if any love you owe me,…
> But all in vain; good queen, it will not be:
> Holding their course to Paphos, where their queen

In the same manner, the young Adonis goes off to hunt the dreaded prey. What is it? Of course, it is the dreaded boar symbol of the Earl of Oxford. The vile beast appears seventeen times in the poem. A few listings:

> "The Boar!" quoth she; whereat a sudden pale,
> But that thou told'st me thou wouldst hunt the Boar.
> When thou didst name the Boar, not to dissemble …

In these references in *Venus and Adonis,* Oxford describes the boar as he did in Ovid's (Oxford's) *Metamorphoses.* Here is Oxford's earlier boar:

> His eyes did glister blood and fire, right dreadful for to see
> His brawned neck, right dredful was his hair that grew so thick
> With pricking points, as one of them could well by other stick.
> And like a front of Armed pikes set close in battle ray,
> The sturdy bristles on his back stood staring up alway.
> Book VIII, Line 375

Here is the boar in *Venus and Adonis*:

> On his bow-back he hath a battle set
> Of bristley pikes that ever threat his foes;
> His eyes like glow worms shine when he doth fret.
> His brawny sides with heavy bristles armed,
> Are better proof than thy spear's point can enter.

Unexpectedly, the poem is not a pleasant praise of romantic and courtly love. The poem begins with a certain note of disgust toward Venus's pursuit of Adonis:

> Even as the sun with purple-colour'd face
> Had ta'en his last leave of the weeping morn,
> Rose-cheek'd Adonis hied him to the chase;
> Hunting he loved, but love he laugh'd to scorn;
> Sick-thoughted Venus makes amain unto him,

And like a bold-faced suitor 'gins to woo him.
And begin to woo him she does with her promises saying,

"Thrice-rairer than myself," thus she began,
"The field's chief flower, sweet above compare,
Stain to all nymphs, more lovely than a man,
More white and red than doves or roses are;
Nature that made thee, with herself at strife,
Saith that the world hath ending with thy life.

"Vouchsafe, thou wonder, to alight thy steed,
And rein his proud head to the saddle-bow;
If thou wilt deign this favour, for thy meed
A thousand honey secrets shalt thou know:
Here come and sit, where never serpent hisses,
And being set, I'll smother thee with kisses."

The poem has over a thousand lines of explicitly rendered seduction of the young man. The graphic images are fresh and imaginative and make the reader tingle with lusty descriptions of amorous passion that have sent generations of high school students into titters of embarrassment:

"Fondling," she saith, "since I have hemm'd thee here
Within the circuit of this ivory pale,
I'll be a park, and thou shalt be my deer;
Feed where thou wilt, on mountain or in dale:
Graze on my lips; and if those hills be dry,
Stray lower, where the pleasant fountains lie.

Within this limit is relief enough,
Sweet bottom-grass and high delightful plain,
Round rising hillocks, brakes obscure and rough,
To shelter thee from tempest and from rain
Then be my deer, since I am such a park;
No dog shall rouse thee, though a thousand bark."

Venus and Adonis is not the only instance where Oxford uses the image of the young man seduced by an older woman. Here is *THE/Passionate /Pilgrime/By W. Shakespeare,* published in 1599 by William Jaggard:

Sweet Cytherea, sitting by a brook
With young Adonis, lovely, fresh and green,   [Ver = green]
Did court the lad with many a lovely look,
She looks as none could look but beauty's queen.   [Note: beauty's queen]
She told him stories to delight his ear;
She show'd him favours to allure his eye;
To win his heart, she touched him here and there,—
Touches so soft still conquer chastity.
But whether unripe years did want conceit,

Or he refused to take her figured proffer,
The tender nibbler would not touch the bait,
But smile and jest at every gentle offer:
> Then fell she on her back, fair queen, and toward:
> He rose and ran away: ah, fool too forward!

This poem is most vivid in its description of the attempted seduction:

"Once," quote she, "did I see a fair sweet youth
Here in these brakes deep-wounded with a boar,   [Again, the boar]
Deep in the thigh, a spectacle of ruth!
See, in my thigh," quoth she, "here was the sore."
She showed hers: he saw more wounds than one,
And blushing fled, and left her all alone.

Yet, the Venus of *Venus and Adonis* is not simply concerned with the seduction of Adonis: She is concerned with sexual reproduction. She says:

Torches are made to light, jewels to wear,
Dainties to taste, fresh beauty for the use,
Herbs for the smell, and sappy plants to bear:
Things growing to themselves are growth's abuse:
Seeds spring from seeds and beauty breedeth beauty;   [Again, beauty]
Thou wast begot; to get it is thy duty.

It is improbable that any Englishman of the times could have read this poem without identifying the two main characters as Queen Elizabeth and the Earl of Oxford. Oxford's men had their livery emblazoned with the blue boar, and they were recognizable sights to anyone in London. Whether this poem was signed by Oxford or was anonymous makes little difference. Who else would have the nerve to portray the Queen in such a romantic involvement with one of the most prominent courtiers of the time, except Oxford?

Only someone with Oxford's audacity would dare to publish such a poem. It is unimaginable that any printer would touch such a work without protection of some very high-level aristocrat, and there was no other high-level aristocrat as author in existence at the time, except Oxford. If the author had been any person other than Oxford, there is little doubt that William Cecil, Lord Burghley, the staunch Puritan, would have confiscated every published manuscript and had everyone involved imprisoned, flogged, or both.

The question must have been how the Queen would respond to *Venus and Adonis*. She was the only one who would have the power to stop Oxford and confiscate the published manuscripts. Clearly, she was not so offended, and *Venus and Adonis* enjoyed many printings. Looked at from the Queen's point of view, the poem paints a flattering image of the experienced but ever-attractive woman. It portrays her as sensual and ultimately irresistible to the young Adonis. Hidden behind the courtly mask of classical figures, the Queen was safe from having to publicly acknowledge that this was her, but at the same time, the Queen could enjoy the knowledge that all the courtiers, ladies of the court, and the public would view her as this seductress. No doubt, this played very well to the vanity of a most vain woman. The Queen knew well the importance of preserving secrets, dissembling, and keeping up appearances. While at an elementary, allegorical level, it is not difficult to determine the main characters of the poem, there may be a deeper meaning hidden behind the obvious allegory.

Jonathan Bate is an orthodox Shakespearean and classical scholar with an in-depth knowledge of Ovid and the classics. Bate also insists that the man from Stratford is the Author, and he has written a fair amount stating that the Earl of Oxford could not possibly be the Author. Therefore, his literary analysis is free of any consideration of the biography of the Author. He does not believe Oxford to be the Author; therefore, Oxford's biography is irrelevant. The man from Stratford's biography is also irrelevant because, for Bate, the works are not from a matrix of biography, education, and experience. For Bate, the plays and the poetry are the purest abstractions of the creative genius of Shakespeare:

> It is an adroit variation; where Ovid begins his tale with Adonis as a son issuing from a tree, Shakespeare ends with a flower issuing from Adonis, who thus becomes a father. Shakespeare's Venus acts out an extraordinary family romance. By imaging her lover as a father, she makes herself into the mother and the flower into the fruit of their union. But the logic of the imagery dictates that the flower is her sexual partner as well as her child, for it clearly substitutes for Adonis himself—she comforts herself with the thought that it is a love-token, which she can continually kiss. The fusion of lover and mother in the context of vegetative imagery makes Venus in Myrrha once again. It is as if, having slept with her father, the girl is now sleeping with her son.[11]

The assertions of this book are exactly what Bate discovers in this poem, "having slept with her father (stepfather Thomas Seymour), the girl is now sleeping with her son (Edward de Vere)." If Oxford is Adonis, then Bate is pointing out the fact that he is also Venus's (Elizabeth's) son. Jonathan Bate and Oxford are both close students of Ovid. Bate's knowledge of Ovid allows him to see the changes that Oxford made in the original story to show a deeper level of psychological drama. Bate goes on:

> Venus' problem is that she can't actually rape Adonis, as Jove rapes Danae, Neptune Theophane, and Applo Isse—but in the end the poem shows that a

sexual relationship based on coercion is doomed. The inequality is highlighted by the difference in age of the two characters; one function of the allusions to Adonis' mother is to suggest that the sexual dealings of partners of greatly unequal age are bound at some level to replicate the archetypal relations based on an unequal power-structure, incest between a parent and child.[12]

> *Venus and Adonis* is a disturbing poem in that violent death takes the place of the unfulfilled Salacian/Hermaphroditic potential. But stylistically it is a poem that bubbles along in the manner more of the story it's not telling than of the one that is.[13]

Bate's biographical blinders give him a powerful insight into the meaning of this poem. His position as a Stratfordian means that the biography of the writer, if from Stratford, is irrelevant to the creation of the literary works. He is not looking for literary clues in these works of a man from a rural background with a conventional biography. Neither is he looking for a biography of Edward de Vere in these poems. Also, he is not constrained to a conventional view of Oxford as the son of John de Vere. Free of these constraints, he is able to look at the poem in terms of the classical imagery and draw the implications of the changes the Author made in the story of Venus and Adonis. In doing so, he provides powerful literary confirmation that Henry Wriothesley was a child born of an incestuous relationship between Edward de Vere and his mother Elizabeth Tudor.

In the year following *Venus and Adonis*, the *Rape of Lucrece* was registered with the Stationer's Office, on May 9, 1594. (This marked the second appearance of William Shakespeare in another dedicatory letter to the Earl of Southampton.) From the title, it is obvious that this is the story of a rape. In the dedication to Henry Wriothesley, Oxford throws his full support behind Southampton in the most fawning language. As this book has stated earlier, it is not possible that anyone was fooled for a moment about who was the author. This dedication is another "coming out of the closet" for the Earl of Oxford and forcing the issue of Southampton as son of the Queen. Belonging to one of the senior aristocratic lines of the kingdom, in the introduction to *The Rape of Lucrece* Oxford is addressing the young Earl as if he were his king :

> What I have done is yours; what I have to do is yours; being part in all I have, devoted yours. Were my worth greater, my duty would show greater; meantime, as it is, it is bound to your lordship, to whom I wish long life, still lengthened with happiness.

In the same year, a lesser-known work, *Willobie His Avisa*, was registered, on September 3, 1594. This work has never attracted the attention the other two have because the Shakespeare pen name was not attached to it. The ostensible author is Henry Willobie who is described by a fictitious publisher, Hadrian Dorrell, as "M. Henry Willobie a yong man, and a scholler of very good hope."[15] The book creates a fiction whereby the publisher decides to go ahead and publish without the author's consent because Willobie departed voluntarily to her "Majesties service."

The engraved front title page is a small cartouche with a naked woman bathing. A man with a stag's head and antlers approaches her in the engraving. To a reader of the Elizabethan time, this would evoke the legend of Acteon, in which he sees the naked goddess Diana bathing and for his indiscretion, he is turned into a stag. Then his dogs are set upon him to rip him apart.

Willobie has several marks of an Oxford work. First, there is the deep knowledge of classical literature with detailed description of minor characters of classical literature such as "Placilla, wife to the Emperour Theodosius." Then the familiar metaphors of the haggard appears in *Willobie*:

> My hapless hap, fell much awrie,
> To fix my fancies prime delight,
> In haggard Hauke that mounts so hie,
> That checkes the lure, and Fawkners sight;
> > But sore you hie, or flie you low,
> > Stoupe needs you must, before you goe.

Finally, the poem is signed with a familiar "Ever or Never" (that is, "E-ver or Not-E-ver").

The poem is a long narrative that describes the attempts of various men to have the virtue of the noble heroine Avisa, described as a goodly wife. Various suitors attempt to persuade her out of her chastity in a series of didactic poetic arguments. Avisa's (the Queen's) suitors are disguised by various false identities, and the usual suspects are conjectured to be the Queen's suitors: Avisa in the poem trumps them all, sees through their falsehoods and veniality, and retains her virtue. Whatever the merits of the story or the poetry, *Willobie* went through several reprintings, indicating that there was some popular interest in the poem. That this book even survived is surprising because, in 1599, it was included in a list of books to be banned.

In some ways, this work was dealing with irrelevant issues. In 1594, the Queen was sixty years old and her chastity was hardly a burning issue. She was long past the age of child-bearing and could not use marriage and a possible heir as a diplomatic playing card. B.N. De Luna points to one of the Queen's suitors in *The Queen Declined, An Interpretation of Willobie His Avisa*:

> The "Nobleman" of "riper yeares" who first attempts to win Avisa-Elizabeth before her "marriage" [to her kingdom] is of course Thomas Seymour, Baron Seymour of Sudeley, who, after 1547, was Lord High Admiral of England. Younger brother to the Protector Somerset in the reign of the boy-king Edward VI, this was the 40-year-old nobleman whose intriguing to marry the 15-year-old Lady Elizabeth (without the Privy Council's knowledge or consent) caused him to be executed for treason in 1549.[14]

If this modern scholar makes such a connection, it is difficult to believe that the poem's Elizabethan audience would not have interpreted it in a similar fashion. At a minimum, *Willobie His Avisa* brings to the forefront a lover of Elizabeth who has been dead for forty-four years, Thomas Seymour, Oxford's father.

In a space of two years, Oxford produced three long narrative poems: *Venus and Adonis*, *Willobie His Avisa,* and *The Rape of Lucrece*. The themes of these works are seduction, incest, rape, the necessity to reproduce, and a defense of the Queen's purity. The themes may be a reflection of the inner conflict within the author, or perhaps Oxford is deliberately confusing the literary world with a flood of works on the same theme. He may have hoped that someone in the future would be able to discern the underlying reality and historical truth.

In addition to these literary works, the canon of Shakespeare's work there are nineteen uses of the words incest or incestuous. Here are a few of them:

Guilty of incsest, that abomination.
The Rape of Lucrece, line 920]

With such dexterity to incetuous sheets!
Hamlet Tale II, 2, 160

As with foul incest to abuse your soul;
Where now you're both a father and a son.
Pericles, Prince of Tyre, I, 1, 153

Charles Boyle discusses the incestuous relationships that existed around Elizabeth in his review of Marc Shell's book, *Elizabeth's Glass* [mirror]. He examines why Elizabeth's translation of Marguerite of Navarre's work into *The Glass of a Sinful Soul* has been so steadfastly ignored by her biographers. He maintains that this is because the work concerns itself with incest, if only of a spiritual nature. However, it does start a trail to Marguerite of Navarre's work and the influences it might have had on the Virgin Queen. In Marguerite's *Heptameron,* there is a variety of romantic and sexual unions, including:

> In this work, a young man unknowingly has sexual intercourse with his mother (who does know and initiates it) and then marries the offspring of this union—his sister, daughter, and spouse. These two never learned of their kinship and the tale then ends happily: "… and they (the son and daughter) loved each other so much that never were there husband and wife more loving."[15]

Boyle sagely points out the reasons for ignoring Elizabeth's early translation of Marguerite's work:

> The political consequences of publicly acknowledging such a connection, with the Virgin Mary/Virgin Elizabeth icon at its center, would have been then—and perhaps still is now—too much for a government, a society and a culture to bear.[16]

There has never been a biography of Elizabeth that truthfully examined and reported the known facts of her life, much less a biography that fully explored the inner life of this complicated and enigmatic woman.

SHAKE-SPEARES SONNETS REVISITED

In a previous chapter, this author indicated that the sonnets were intimately related to the Earl of Oxford. The sonnets are hallmarks of his known poetry, his education, and his biography. This is true as far as it goes, yet the sonnets have posed difficult problems for even the most ardent Oxfordian supporters. There is a temptation to interpret the sonnets in the light of Mere's comment that they were "sweet sugared sonnets shared amongst his private friends." However, this interpretation implies that Oxford would spend an enormous amount of time and effort to write 154 sonnets and then only distribute them among friends. This would be very odd behavior for a writer and theatrical personality who played out his life on the public stage. Other Oxfordians have interpreted the sonnets as an indication of a homosexual relation between Oxford and Southampton, the fair youth of the sonnets, but there is nothing in Oxford's biography except a few slanderous charges by his enemies to indicate that Oxford had homosexual leanings. In fact, Oxford was acknowledged to have had five children by three women.

In the previous chapter, it was noted that only thirteen copies of the first printing survive and that *Shake-speares Sonnets* did not go through multiple printings, as did the plays and the major poems such as *Venus and Adonis.* This leads to the conclusion that the *Shake-speares Sonnets* were suppressed by King James because they contained material that was damaging to the interests of the crown. If the hypothesis that Henry Wriothesley was the son of Queen Elizabeth is correct, this could be the reason for confiscating and destroying the work. In 1609, King James I was losing his popularity and the reign of Elizabeth was beginning to be looked on as an era of past glory. The Queen's faults began to be overlooked and her virtues inflated. If it were publicly known that Henry Wriothesley was the son of Queen Elizabeth, he would automatically become a threat to James. Without any overt effort on his part, Henry Wriothesley would attract whatever dissident factions existed and become a challenger to King James. From the populace's point of view, any son of Queen Elizabeth would be the preferred monarch over the Scottish import.

Some Oxfordians maintain that 1609 was the year Oxford's widow sold her home in Hackney and they were pirated by a printer during the move and printed without permission. Others are suspicious that writings as valuable and personal as the sonnets would be so carelessly handled. Perhaps the sonnets heralded to the world that Oxford was deceased in its dedication announcing the "ever-living" poet. This interpretation follows the line that if the poet is still alive, he would not be called "ever-living," but if the poet is dead, then he is ever-living in the sense that the poetry lives.

A.L. Rowse has called the sonnets "the greatest puzzle in the history of English literature." The Author says that he is "tongue-tied by authority" and the sonnets are a "written ambassage." This is a simple change in spelling of the word "embassage," meaning a message entrusted to an ambassador. Often these messages would be put to memory to avoid being intercepted or stolen. In addition, during the period, an ambassador was the representative of one sovereign to another. The Author also refers to the sonnets as a "chronicle of wasted time." In summary, the sonnets are the greatest puzzle because the Author was trying to both communicate and disguise his message at the same time.

Hank Whittemore permanently changed the nature of the sonnets' interpretation with his paper *Shakespeare's Invention, the Royal Story of the Sonnets* by taking a far different tack. Whittemore asserts that to understand the sonnets, one must first understand the language of the sonnets as used by Shakespeare. That is, one must delve into the Shakespeare canon to understand the language and not rely on contemporary meaning or simply poetic interpretation of the language. It is also Whittemore's observation that the language of the sonnets is very compressed. That is, the poet-playwright with the largest vocabulary in the English language restricted himself in the sonnets to repetitively using a few words. "Beauty" is used 83 times, "love" is used 212 times, and "ever" is used sixty-eight times, etc. Often, the words are used in slightly different contexts, and sometimes the meanings seem to either blend together or ambiguously take on several meanings simultaneously. In effect, Whittemore has interpreted the sonnets as a literary Rosetta stone, in which the knowledge of one language makes it possible to interpret the words in the other language. Needless to say, Whittemore's point of view will be controversial. This chapter uses Whittemore's work as a foundation and looks forward to his insights that are destined for his book on the sonnets.

Shakespearean scholars have long noted that the sonnets are divided into three parts. Sonnets 1–126 are concerned with the Fair Youth, 127–152 are concerned with the Dark Lady, and 153 and 154 seem to be tagged on to the very end, or perhaps they are two sonnets that should be regarded as a cover letter. Whittemore illustrates that there is even a more detailed structure to the collection of sonnets. The first twenty-seven correspond to the years of Southampton's life up to the date of his imprisonment for the Essex Rebellion. The sonnets then correspond to the time periods of Southampton's imprisonment, the Queen's death, and James's accession. Then the final group, 127 to 152, portray the Dark Lady (the Queen), and the final two, 153 and 154 are a cover letter. Whittemore gives a precise chronology of how the sonnets are arranged in accordance with different periods of Southampton's and Oxford's lives.

However, let us put the sequence of the sonnets aside and look at the first lines of the first sonnet using Whittemore's insights into the language of the sonnets. Thus, a precise understanding of what is communicated in this "ambassage" can be determined. Here are the opening lines of the sonnets:

Sonnet 1
From fairest creatures we desire increase,
That thereby beauties *Rose* might never die.

> [Italics, capitalizations, and spellings of
> the sonnets in this book are from the 1609
> original.]

Now let us take a close look at some of the particular words of these two lines: "creature," "desire," and "beauty." Shakespeare uses "creature" to mean "child":

Bring me the fairest *creature* northward born.
Merchant of Venice II, I, 7   [*Italics* added]

The majesty of the *creature* in resemblance to the mother.
Winter's Tale V, 2 14

I shall see my boy again; for since the birth of Cain, the first male child, to him that did but yesterday suspire, there was not such a gracious *creature* born.   *King John III, 4 86*

If one looks at Shakespeare's language, "desire" has a very specific meaning. In the context of royal speech, "desire" means to "command," not simply to "wish." When Claudius uses "desire," he is implying that it is a royal wish by his use of the royal plural "our desire." In this sense, the royal desire is a royal command, and the plural is the royal "we":

Richmond:
Good Captain Blunt, bear my good night to him
And by the second hour in the morning
Desire the earl to see me in my tent:
Richard III, V, 3, 39 [*Italics* added]

King Henry V:
Commend me to the princes in our camp;
Do my good morrow to them, and anon
Desire them all to my pavilion.
Henry V, IV, 1, 29

King Claudius:
In going back to school in Wittenberg,
It is most retrograde to our *desire:*
And we beseech you, bend you to remain
Here, in the cheer and comfort of our eye,
Our chiefest courtier, cousin, and our son.
Hamlet, Act 1, 2, 118

"Beauty" was one of the many appellations for the Queen. With Oxford, we see her in the *Passionate Pilgrim* and in the *Phoenix and the Turtle*:

Passionate Pilgrim

Did court the lad with many a lovely look,
Such looks as none could look but *beauty's* queen.

[*Italics* added]

Phoenix and the Turtle

As chorus to their tragic scene.
Beauty, truth, and rarity,
Grace in all simplicity.

Alternatively, in Edmund Spenser's *The Faerie Queen*, which has long been recognized as an allegory about Elizabeth:

And she her selfe of *beautie* soueraigne Queene,
Faire Venus seemde unto his bed to bring   C1 S48   [*Italics* added]

And wonder of her *beautie* soueraigne,
Are woone with pitty and unwonted ruth   C6 S12

In a tournament in 1581, the knights for the Queen's honor were defending:

The Gallery or place at the end of the Tilt-yard adjoing to her Majesties's house at Whitehall, whereat her peson should be placed, was called, and not without cause "The Castle or Fortresse of Perfect Beautie."[17]

If it is "beauty's *Rose*," it is therefore the Queen's rose, or in another sense, it is the Tudor Rose, which was the Rose on the banner that symbolized combining the houses of Lancaster and York. Extending this further, it is Henry Wriothesley. Therefore, Whittemore's interpretation leads one to read the first lines of the sonnets as follows:

From her royal son the Queen commands children,
That thereby her Tudor Rose dynasty might never die.

Using both the historical events of the period and the language of Shakespeare as guides, it becomes evident that the first seventeen sonnets urge the young man to marry and reproduce himself.

The sonnets can be thought of as a literary triple helix. The first strand is the English language as Shakespeare used it with his particular meanings and connotations. The second strand of the helix is the language of poetry which allows metaphorical interpretation of the language. A rose is not simply a rose, but a metaphor for the Tudor dynasty, and so on.

Obviously, this allows latitude for interpretation, but Oxford was certainly not at liberty to write a biographical account of events. And, the third strand is the true history of Oxford, Elizabeth and Southampton.

Therefore, the sonnets are not about an erotic homosexual relationship as some think; rather, the concern in the first sonnets is reproduction and continuation of the Tudor line and in the later sonnets, Oxford's relation to the Queen. Sonnet Three will suffice as an example:

Sonnet 3

Look in thy glass, and tell the face thou viewest
Now is the time that face should form another;
Whose fresh repair if now thou not renewest,
Thou dost beguile the world, unbless some mother.
For where is she so fair whose unear'd womb
Disdains the tillage of thy husbandry?
Or who is he so fond will be the tomb
Of his self-love, to stop posterity?
Thou art thy mother's glass, and she in thee
Calls back the lovely April of her prime:
So thou through windows of thine age shall see
Despite of wrinkles this thy golden time.
    But if thou live, remember'd not to be,
    Die single, and thine image dies with thee.

It was around 1590 that Oxford and William Cecil attempted to convince Southampton to marry Elizabeth Vere (granddaughter of William Cecil). This would have preserved the Tudor line and made Cecil's granddaughter a possible Queen of England. When Southampton refused, he gave up his opportunity to be king because he gave up the political support of Elizabeth's most powerful advisor. The Queen was later furious when, in 1598, Wriothesley married the already pregnant Elizabeth Vernon. These sonnets seem to refer to that period.

If William Cecil would have had his granddaughter married to Southampton, then he had a strong incentive to maneuver the political situation to pave the way for Southampton to become king. It is also interesting to note that Oxford was the one who had resisted marriage to William Cecil's daughter, Anne, when he was a young man of marriageable age, but now he was proposing this alliance of his son to Cecil's granddaughter in his later years. It appears that, by this time, Oxford had given up all hope of becoming king and was more interested in the succession of his son, Henry Wriothesley.

In this complicated tale of royal intrigue, it should be also be noted that if Oxford was making no claim to the throne, then the Queen's oldest male heir would be Robert Devereux, 2nd Earl of Essex. In 1588, his father, Robert Dudley, had died and Devereux became one of the logical heirs to the throne. Oxford could only stymie this effort with the aid of William Cecil. Years later, during the brief Essex Rebellion, there were rumors that Essex wanted to become king. Historians have assumed that Essex was simply acting out of a sense of grandeur and that he had no claims to the throne. However, this is not the case: If Essex was the oldest son of Elizabeth and Robert Dudley, he had a claim to the throne as the eldest male heir (excluding Oxford and Robert Cecil, see discussion in appendix as to the number and identities Elizabeth's children)

Now, let us see if the sonnets shed further light on the two major contentions of this book: first, that Henry Wriothesley was the son of Queen Elizabeth and Edward de Vere and, second, that Edward de Vere was the son of Elizabeth. Using Whittemore's method of interpretation, we find:

Sonnet 153

CUPID laid by his brand and fell a sleepe.
A maid of *Dyan's* this advantage found,
And his love-kindling fire did quickly steepe
In a cold vallie-fountaine of that ground.

The child laid aside his stigma and fell asleep
A subject of the Queen took him (Lady
Southampton)
And buried all trace of him

Sonnet 33

Even so my Sunne one early morne did shine,
With all triumphant splendor on my brow,
But out alack, he was but one houre mine,
The region cloude hath mask'd him from me now.

My son was born one early morning
Giving me feelings of triumph

But in one hour he was gone
Hidden from me by Regina (the Queen)

Sonnet 13

O none but unthrifts, deare my love you know,
You had a Father, let your Son say so.

I was your father, let your son say so.

Sonnet 14

As truth and beauty shal together thrive
If from thy selfe, to store thou wouldst convert:
   Or else of thee this I prognosticate,
   Thy end is Truthes and Beauties doome and date.

Vere and the Queen shall thrive
If you agree to this marriage
Or I predict
It will be the end of the Tudor dynasty.

Sonnet 17

Who will beleeve my verse in time to come
If it were fild with your most high deserts?
Though yet heaven knowes it is but a tombe
Which hides your life, and shewes not halfe your parts.
If I could write the beauty of your eyes,
And in fresh numbers number all your graces,
The age to come would say this Poet lies,
Such heavenly touches nere toucht earthly faces.

Who will believe my verse?
Even though it is filled with your royalty,
Heaven knows this verse will be a tomb,
Which hides your life.

If I could write of your royalty
And in fresh verse number your grace
The ages to come will say this Poet lies,
And such royalty never existed.

The puzzle about the identity of the Dark Lady of the sonnets dissolves when one considers the language of the poet. Oxford uses the word "black" thirteen times and "dark" six times, and this is not simply to signify color and the absence of light, but also to mean evil. As in the Shakespeare plays: [***Italics*** added in the examples below]

What scourge for perjury
Can this *dark* monarchy afford false Clarence?
    Richard III I, iv

Dark-working sorcerers that change the mind,
Soul-killing witches that deform the body,
Disguised cheaters, prating mountebanks
    Comedy of Errors I, ii

Wilt thou conceal this *dark* conspiracy?
    Richard II V, ii

To **dark** dishonour's use thou shalt not have.
I am disgraced, impeach d, and baffled here..
    Richard II I, i

And will to France, hoping the consequence
Will prove as bitter, ***black***, and tragical.
    Richard III....IV, iv

What *black* magician conjures up this fiend,
To stop devoted charitable deeds?
    Richard III I, ii

Stars, hide your fires!
Let not light see my ***black*** and deep desires,
    Macbeth I, iv

Her face was to mine eye beyond all wonder;
The rest, hark in thine ear, as **black** as incest;
    Pericles I, ii

Shakespeare/Oxford wrote about truth and justice, hope and disparity, reality and illusion, he was less concerned about the color of a woman's hair. The dark lady of the sonnets refers to the Queen and her misdeeds.

He expresses his despair.

Sonnet 66

Tyr'd with all these, for restful death I cry
As to behold desert a beggar borne,
And needie Nothing trimd in jollitie,
And purest faith unhappily forsworne,
And gilded honour shamefully misplast, [misplaced]
And maiden vertue rudely strumpeted,
And right perfection wrongfully disgrac'd,
And strength by limping sway disabled,
And art made tongue-tied by authoritie,
And Folly (Doctor-like) controuling skill,
And simple-Truth miscalde Simplicitie,
And captive-good attending Captaine ill:
   Ty'd with all these, from these would I be gone;
   Save that to die, I leave my love alone.

My faith in you was forsworn,
My honour doubted when you
imprisoned me
My virginity taken by you,

Wounded in a duel permitted by you,
And my art suppressed by your
authorities
The skill of the Cecils

If I die, I leave Southampton alone.

He begins his rage at the Queen in Sonnet 127 and it lasts through Sonnet 152:

Sonnet 127

In the ould age blacke was not counted faire,
Or if weare, it bore not beauties name:
But now is blacke beauties successive heire,
And Beauty slander'd with a bastard shame:
For since each hand hath put on Natures power,
Fairing the foule with Arts faulse borrow'd face,
Sweet beauty hath no name, no holy boure,
[bower]
But is profan'd, if not lives in disgrace.
Therefore my Mistresse brows are Raven black,
Her eyes so suted, and they mourners seeme
At such who, not born faire, no beauty lack,
Sland'ring Creation with a false esteeme,
   Yet so they mourne, becomming of their woe,
   That every toung saies beauty should look so.

Before evil was not considered good
Or if it was, it was not the Queen

And Southampton is slandered with
a bastard's shame

You are evil.

Was Oxford the son of Elizabeth? Sonnet 143 says so:

Sonnet 143
Loe as a carefull huswife [housewife]runnes to catch
One of her fethered creatures broake away,
Sets downe her babe, and makes all quick dispatch
In pursuit of the thing she would have stay:
Whilst her neglected child holds her in chase,
Cries to catch her whose busie care is bent
To follow that which flies before her face,
Not prizing her poor infants discontent:
So runst thou after that which flies from thee,
Whilst I thy babe chace [chase] thee a farre behind;
But if thou catch thy hope, turne back to me:
And play the mothers part, kiss me, be kind;
    So will I pray that thou maist have thy *Will,*
    If thou turne back and my loude crying still.

You have neglected me.

Cared nothing for your child.

I am your child.

THE PERSIAN PORTRAIT

In Hampton Court, there are several hundred paintings on display, and many of them are of Queen Elizabeth I. After looking at a number of them, one begins to recognize certain features of the Queen's face regardless of the artist's skill, the realism adhered to in portraying the Queen, or the age of the Queen. Elizabeth is painted as a red-headed woman with a broad forehead and a heart-shaped face with a pointed chin. These general features of Elizabeth are revealed in painting after painting, and each painting is dutifully labeled as being of the Queen. Going down the long hallways of portraits, one comes upon a portrait that has the now-familiar face of Elizabeth,[b] but there are several very odd features of this painting. The woman is in a long, flowing robe with a strange, tall headdress. On the portrait, there is a cartouche with a Shakespearean sonnet. Yet with all the similarities to Queen Elizabeth, the painting is labeled as "anonymous."

When an elderly guard once was asked who the subject of the portrait was, he replied that before the World War II, the painting was labeled as "Elizabeth," but after the war, it was changed to "anonymous." The reason for such a change is self-evident when one looks at the painting for even a minute. The subject of the painting is pregnant.

---

[b] The portrait might not still be on display as of this writing.

273

Figure 27. Queen Elizabeth, Persian Portrait

Vertue states (Notebooks, vol. IV, p. 77) that "Sir John (Stanley), some time ago recovered to the Crown the picture of Qu. Elisabeth in a strange fantastik habit (when he was deputy chamberlain to Qu. Anne. which had K. Ch. I Mark behind it." It had been "bought as rubbish in Moor fields by a Painter." It was placed at St. James's (Queen Anne, St., James's, note by Thomas Coke: *In the Blew Room ... over ye Doors ... Queen Elizabeth in fancy dress ...*) and later at Kensington in the Queen's Gallery of full-length portraits of sovereigns (Vertue inv., Kensington, f. 22) moved to Hampton Court, 12 September 1838).

As listed in the *Catalogue of Tudor, Stuart and Early Georgian Pictures in the Royal Collection*, p. 74.

George Vertue (1684–1756) was an engraver and antiquary who moved in fashionable aristocratic circles. Interestingly, he traveled with Robert Harley (1661–1742), the 1st Earl of Oxford,[c] to Stratford-upon-Avon and there made drawings of the interior of the Stratford parish church. About 1734, Harley gave a huge collection of papers and documents to the British Library (Harleian Manuscripts); he also paid for a "refurbishing" of the bust in Stratford. That a painting seven feet high by four feet wide "was bought as rubbish in Moor fields by a Painter," is a story that is, well, just so much rubbish.

The conclusion that the painting was a portrait of Elizabeth was very clear in early biographies of Elizabeth. In *The Private Character of Queen Elizabeth* by F.C. Chamberlain in London, 1921, there are several portraits of Elizabeth illustrated and one is this portrait. The change in identification of this portrait is one of the subtle ways the English culture continues to protect and foster the image of the Virgin Queen. It is almost at an unconscious level that information contradicting this virgin icon is dissembled, changed, or ignored to continue to perpetrate the image created by the Tudor monarchy some 450 years ago. When facts emerge that are clear evidence of the Queen's sexual activity or possible sexual activity, they are subtly changed or, in this case not so subtly changed, to continue the myth. The portrait is a graphic example of this process. The Tudors were always great propagandists and carefully constructed the images of the monarchy they wanted the world to see, but it was unlikely that they thought they would be successful for over four centuries.

The art historian Roy Strong's article "My Weepinge Stagg I Crowne" in *The Art of the Emblem,* edited by Michael Bath, John Manning, and Alan R. Young is a concrete example of how British historians, in this case art historians, maneuver to come up with answers that avoid contradicting the religious dogma of the Virgin Queen. Roy Strong is so circumspect about the painting that he can never put the word "pregnant" in his article, much less "pregnant" and "Elizabeth" in the same sentence. His article never addresses the central issue of whether or not this is a picture of Elizabeth because this, of course, cannot be true, so therefore the article is a search for anybody but Elizabeth. He never even considers for a moment that this might be a portrait of Elizabeth, even though it is of a redhead with Tudor roses and swallows abounding.

The Virgin Queen is simply a myth that is out of bounds for any levelheaded historian. Strong is so nonplussed by the painting that he goes into a long detailed description of the woman's dress but cannot get the

---

[c] Note: There can be a re-creation of a title if legitimate heirs cease. The numbers start over.

word "pregnant" down on paper. The two ideas simply cannot be said, considered, imagined, or dreamed possible by a conventional Elizabethan historian. It is not until he describes his purported subject of the painting, the Countess Essex, that he comes close to being candid. "The loose robe would have suited the Countess's *enceinte condition* at the close of 1600, for her last child, Dorothy, was born in early December." Again, he cannot get the word "pregnant" out of his mouth, or perhaps this is a vocabulary test for the meaning of *enceinte*.

Roy Strong does admit that the portrait was originally identified as a portrait of Elizabeth. He then says:

> The identity as Queen Elizabeth persisted until Sir Lionel Cust's pioneering article on the Elizabethan painter, Marcus Gheeraearts the Younger, in 1914 when he thought the portrait to be one of the Lady Arabella Stuart.[18]

Strong asserts that the portrait cannot be Arabella Stuart on the grounds of comparison to known portraits of her, but of course, it cannot be Elizabeth. Strong then goes on to discuss other candidates and dismiss them until he finally arrives at the Countess Essex, Frances Walsingham. She was the wife of Robert Devereux, Earl of Essex, whose life ended on the block after the putative Essex Rebellion. Strong believes that the Countess had the painting done to appease the Queen, who had her husband in the Tower in 1600.

When Essex was first put under house arrest in October 1599, Lady Essex had tried to gain the Queen's sympathy by going to her in a humble, black widow's dress, which symbolized that she had, metaphorically speaking anyway, lost her husband. This ploy was stopped cold by the Queen. She was turned away from court and told never to come back. Why Lady Essex would then pose for a portrait showing her as pregnant in the richest of pearls and most ornate of outfits and conclude that this would somehow gain the Queen's sympathy is unfathomable. There are royal symbols all over this picture that would only offend Queen Elizabeth if shown as being worn by anyone but the Queen. There is nothing in the portrait to indicate that the subject is contrite about anything. In short, it is unlikely that any woman could appeal to the Queen by dressing up in a luxurious costume, encrusted with pearls and then sending such a portrait to the Queen.

Strong says the portrait is painted by Marcus Gheeraearts the Younger during the Persian craze of 1600. Here he is correct; the portrait can accurately be dated by the flowing robe costume that came into vogue during that very specific period. This vogue was started by the news of Anthony Sherley's adventure in reaching Persia and having an interview with the Shah that was published in the fall of 1600. The book was immediately suppressed because Sherley was accused of being a Catholic collaborator. This did not stop the Persian craze as women started wearing flowing robes and elaborate headgear. Of the hundreds of female portraits of aristocratic English women, few if any, are in this attire. If the subject was painted in conventional attire of the period, there would be little clue as to when the portrait was done, except within a wide margin of changing fashions. In using this elaborate and unconventional female attire, whoever commissioned the painting is giving very direct clues that he or she wants it known that this was painted at a very specific point in history.

Strong then leads the reader down another false trail by comparing the Persian portrait to the Ditchley portrait of the Queen. In the Ditchley portrait, there is a rather stilted face of Queen Elizabeth similar to the portrait in the canopy painting of the Queen going to a wedding. The Ditchley portrait is almost cartoon-like, whereas the Persian portrait is much more realistic. It should be pointed out that, at some point, the Queen did not frequently sit for portraits and that artists often used the same earlier portraits or miniatures of the Queen as models for their work. When this work was done by unskilled artists, the results were often cartoonish. In the case of the Ditchley portrait and the canopy portrait, both have Elizabeth's head in the exact same position, looking slightly to her left, somewhat out of kilter with her body position.

What Strong does not compare the Persian portrait to is the Rainbow portrait of Elizabeth, one of the more famous portraits of the Queen. If a facial comparison is done between the Persian portrait and the Rainbow portrait, the strong similarities between the two become apparent. This painting is acknowledged as being by Marcus Gheeraearts, and the strong similarity in the way the artist has painted the Queen is easily seen. It should be remembered that the Queen in 1600 was in her late sixties, while the subject of the Rainbow portrait and the Persian portrait is of a woman in her thirties. Thus, Gheeraearts is reconstructing what he imagined the Queen to be like at an earlier age. The similarity, to say the least, is striking.

Marcus Gheeraearts came to London from Bruges in 1568 and lived there until 1577, when he went back to the Continent. His son, also named Marcus Gheeraearts, stayed in England, and continuing the family tradition, he became one of the most renowned of court painters. The name similarity only added to the confusion, plus they both signed their paintings the same way. They are now referred to as "Gheeraearts, the older" and "Gheeraearts, the younger," with a variety of spellings used for the last name. Most likely, not every aristocrat spent hours sitting for his portrait, nor did the master painter do every detail of the portrait. It is more plausible that a costume would be picked out and a suitable pose agreed upon and then the face would be added later. Apprentice painters from the master's workshop would then paint the costume and general pose, and the master would finish the portrait.

The imagery in the painting would have significant meaning for an Elizabethan steeped in classical Greek mythology. The symbolism is of the Tudors with red roses covering the dress and the swallows flying about. The woman has a plain necklace around her neck and on it hangs a simple wedding-like ring. The tree is not a sturdy British oak but a weeping willow as the "Sole Arabian Tree" wherein the mythical Phoenix lives. The tree bearing fruit, as referred to in the poem, would be a reference to the fertility of the tree with its fruit hanging down, and is obviously the subject of the portrait. Most interesting is the stag and the fact that the pearls hang about its head as if they are a crown. The stag is part of the Greek tale of Acteon. As mentioned before, this is a repeated theme of Oxford's poetry: Acteon sees Diana (the Queen) naked while bathing in a stream. His punishment for this transgression is to be turned into a stag and then hunted down and killed by his own dogs. Here the stag is given graphic representation. (Also the graphic on the title page of *Willobie His Avisa* is a naked woman bathing, with deer standing nearby.) Here is the Shakespearean sonnet:

The restles swallow fits my restles minde,
In still revivinge still renewinge wronges;
her Just complaintes of cruelly unkinde,
are all the Musique, that my life prolonges.
With pensive thoughtes my weeping Stagg I crowne
whose Melancholy teares my cares Expresse
hes Teares in sylence, and my sighes unknowne
are all the physicke that my harmes redresse.
My onely hope was in this goodly tree,
which I did plant in love bringe up in care:
but all in vanie, for now to late I see
the shales be mine, the kernels others are.
   My Musique may be plaintes, my physique teares
   If this be all the fruite my love tree beares.

Not recognizing
Southampton.
and then treatening him
with death in the Tower.

The Persian portrait was another way for Oxford to preserve his story and the story of Southampton behind a veil of deceptions, literary allusions, classical symbolism and, in this case, visual representation. The absence of a legal will or any letters to Oxford point toward Robert Cecil destroying his documents. Any direct attempt to leave a diary or other written record would have been found and destroyed by the agents of

William and Robert Cecil. While any literary interpretation is subject to skepticism and misinterpretation, suspecting the worst, there simply was no other way for Oxford to leave any historical record of his life except in his poetry and plays, and in this unusually crafty manner, through a painting of the Queen.

A likely scenario for the portrait may be that Oxford commissioned Marcus Gheeraearts to do the painting. Gheeraearts had painted other portraits of the Queen as a younger woman so portraying her at a younger age and fully pregnant would not be difficult. After the portrait was completed, it was hidden on one of Oxford's estates, and it did not emerge until about 1734 when Robert Harley married a granddaughter of Horatio Vere, Oxford's cousin. Robert Harley gained access to the portrait through his marriage, and he brought the painting into public light again with the ridiculous claim that it was found in a potter's field. The marriage provides the historical link back to Edward de Vere, 17th Earl of Oxford.

THE PHOENIX AND THE TURTLE

The Phoenix and the Turtle was included in a collection of poems published in 1601, wherein a number of the contributors submitted poems on the subject (as in Turtle Dove). Contributors were George Chapman, John Marston, Ben Jonson, Shakespeare, and as *The Yale Shakespeare* puts it, "another person who signed himself *Ignoto.*"[19] As previously mentioned, Edmund Spenser wrote a flattering poem addressed to Oxford in *The Faerie Queene,* which Oxford replied to in the same introduction, signing himself Ignoto. As might be expected, *The Yale Shakespeare* has it exactly backwards as to authorship, but it does capture Oxford's intent:

> Shakespeare alone of all the contributors does not seem to have clearly understood—and he cannot be blamed—the real meaning of the allegory. He evidently did not discover that the Phoenix and the Turtle were consumed, only in a metaphorical sense, in the flames of their own love, and that they lived again in the person of a beautiful offspring. He made the two birds die "leaving no posteritie," and described their obsequies, conducted in the presence of the Eagle, the Swan, and the Crow as mourners.[20]

These are the last lines of the poem:

Beauty, truth, and rarity,	[The Queen, Oxford, Southampton]
Grace in all simplicity,	[Royalty]
Here enclos'd in cinders lie.	

Death is not the phoenix' nest;
And the turtle's loyal breast
To eternity doth rest,

Leaving no posterity:
'Twas not their infirmity,
It was married chastity.

Truth may seem, but cannot be;	[Vere]
Beauty brag, but 'tis not she;	[The Queen]
Truth and beauty buried be.	

To this urn let those repair
That are either true or fair;
For these dead birds, sigh a prayer.

AFTERWORD

OXFORD'S GENIUS

Oxford's artistic works were not simply a product of his environment, his education, his energy, or his artistic skills. Oxford was probably one of the first human beings who operated as a psychological whole, integrated human being. These are rare people at any time and even rarer as one goes back in history. He was able to see and illustrate many sides of any issue and retain his own point of view. He was able to be a leader when necessary or accept a secondary role when necessary. He was able to put the interests of others above his own when the situation called for it.

While power and achievement oriented him, he was sensitive to his own inner needs and the needs of others. While judgmental and able to make moral distinctions of right and wrong, he did not seem to bear grudges, seek revenge, or obsessively dwell in self-pity for the hand fate had dealt him. He was self-assured, self-actualizing, and self-expressive. He was aware of the moral and political issues of his time and aware of the existence of other personalities in the universe besides his own. He had a deep and profound world perspective and a morality imposed not by religion, custom, or code, but imposed by his own thoughtfulness and moral conscience. Immersed in a world of death, betrayal, hidden identities, and corruption, he triumphed over his situation through dedication to his art. He wrote what he wrote because he was what he was. "I am that I am."

Oxford blended his aristocratic outlook and his classical training into an unparalleled literary output. Because of the political situation and the necessity of maintaining the myth of the Virgin Queen, Oxford energies and ambitions could not be directed toward being the heir to the throne and eventually the ruler of England. Instead, he sublimated his interests and identity into the courtier-poet role, and his plays and poems were the product of that reshaped identity. It is a combination of absolutely unique and bizarre circumstances that influenced the genius of Oxford: a hidden identity, education at the highest levels of scholarship, access to the privileged inner world of court life, a passionate identity with the courtier-poet, and an inability to influence events directly.

Heirs to the throne are typically in the dilemma of discovering what to do until they ascend to the throne. How can they avoid antagonizing their parents, who dislike reminders of their own mortality and coming demise.

Many monarchs have refused to let their heirs have any meaningful role in the government, and the heirs turn to be playboy princes. Oxford's dilemma was even worse because he could not be recognized as the son of the Queen. The tension between his apparent role and his hidden role surfaced in Shakespeare's works where the Author admires courtier-playwrights and virtuous bastard sons. Denied an outlet, he channeled his energy into literary works.

His strong identification with the courtier-poet ideal gave Oxford a moral compass, and he would not be swayed by external circumstances nor could he be bought by the promise of material or political advantage. He was a personality that was difficult, if not impossible, to control by the imposition of external sanctions. Oxford would do what he felt was moral and right regardless whether it was the most politically expedient course of action. While these qualities may be sterling in a playwright and poet making moral judgments on the nature of humanity, they often worked to his detriment in a political world dominated by a monarch. Elizabeth frequently browbeat her councilors, humiliated them, threatened them, or banished them from court. In short, she was a ruthless, self-centered tyrant whose first concern was her own vanity and position. Oxford would be in lifelong subjugation to her, and that basic conflict would never be resolved. The Queen would act in her interest first whether through uncompromising ruthlessness or endless vacillation, while Oxford would act through what he perceived to be the courtier's code of honor.

Yet circumstances alone do not explain his accomplishment (as if any list of facts can ever enclose genius), for Oxford truly engaged in his literary calling with a single-minded dedication that is almost beyond comprehension. From his earliest years, his output was enormous, and when the final list of Oxford's works is compiled, it may be most of the literary production of the Elizabethan period. While Oxford had a particular upbringing and education that shaped the works, there can be little doubt that, given half an opportunity and a minimal education, his works would have been at an equally high degree of accomplishment no matter what his rank or class, but perhaps from an entirely different point of view. When one better understands the enormous personal traumas Oxford suffered, his resilience and his ability to function at all, much less function at the level of a literary genius, one can only conclude that whether Oxford was of the nobility or born in a rural village in England, he still would have ended up as the genius William Shakespeare.

In addition, the literary output cannot be divorced from the man himself. With the exception of Oxford and Katherine Parr, the personalities introduced in this book were ones that functioned at a very low emotional level. They were unable to form affectionate relationships with others; they mistrusted others and were mistrusted in turn. They were capable of the most cruel behavior, including murder, if it fit their own needs. They lacked self-control, blamed others for their problems, and were incapable of showing remorse or sorrow. In contrast, Oxford and Katherine Parr functioned at a much higher level of humanity. Despite a childhood that involved one of the most bizarre and unusual set of circumstances imaginable, Oxford was able to turn his inner tortures into artistic creations. He did not act destructively, for he could put others before himself, and he behaved with balanced judgment and maturity throughout his life. Hamlet, Lear, and Prospero were all outer projections of the inner life of Oxford. These were characters, as Oxford, who were capable of human contact, remorse, and self-doubt, qualities that one cannot find in other personalities of the age, or many of in any age. What sets Shakespeare's works apart from all others is not simply the breadth of knowledge shown nor the dramatic and poetic ingenuity: it is that as a person and as an artist, Oxford was so driven to explore the inner reaches of his own soul that he could thus touch ours.

As Oxford matured, his interests changed and the topics he addressed in his plays changed. His early plays might be thought of as being about the practical affairs of politics, courtly manners, and romantic love. His later dramas reflect a more mature sensibility and a profound understanding of the relationships governing the inherent conflicts in human existence. His increased sensibilities show his realization that clear-cut actions are not always possible and that all human problems are not solved by codes of conduct and courtly behavior. In his last play, *The Tempest*, he is to be more tolerant and detached from human frailty and misconduct. His artistic maturity reflects his personal maturity. He has come to a greater acceptance of himself, others and the sins and errors that make up human existence.

At Oxford's death, his world was in ashes. He had failed to become the King of England and the way to the throne for his son, Southampton, was blocked by King James I. His works were never published under his name, as he had been "tongue tied by authority." This would continue with the publication of the *First Folio*, and then his name would be lost in the mists of history for centuries. Yet, if there is one quality that Oxford possessed in abundance, it was optimism, the optimism that, even in the worst of times, his lot as a poet-writer was a noble one and what he was doing was worthwhile. Those with less perseverance and dedication would have crumbled under the weight that Oxford carried throughout his life.

The great wheel of fortune often turns slowly, and that wheel is turning slowly his way. A very active Oxfordian movement grows yearly. Major publications such as *Atlantic, Time, Harper's, History Today* and *U.S. News and World Report* have featured articles on the Authorship issues. Eventually, Oxford will prevail, and he will be recognized as the Author of those magnificent works.

In a great irony, Princess Diana Spencer was the daughter of John Spencer, 8th Earl of Spencer. Her ancestry can be traced through a line of descendents back to both Elizabeth de Vere and Henry Wriothesley (3rd Earl of Southampton). Thus, Prince William Windsor is a descendent of Edward de Vere, 17th Earl of Oxford, otherwise known as William Shakespeare.

A Tudor Rose will again be on the throne of Great Britain.

> I over-tooke, coming from Italie,
> In Germanie, a great and famous Earle
> Of England; the most goodly fashion'd man
> I ever saw: from head to foot in forme
> Rare, and most absolute; hee had a face
> Like one of the most ancient honour'd Romanes,
> From whence his noblest Familie was deriv'd;
> He was beside of spirit passing great,
> Valiant, and learn'd, and liberall as the Sunne,
> Spoke and writ sweetly of publike weales;
> And 'twas the Earle of Oxford[a]

As Thomas Nashe wrote in *Choice of Valentines*:

> The fairest bud the red rose ever bare.

---

[a] From the play *The Revenge of Bussy d'Amois*, 1613, by George Chapman.

APPENDIX

ELIZABETH'S BABYLAND

This book has explicitly dealt with only two possible children of Elizabeth: Edward de Vere and Henry Wriothesley and it has alluded to a third, Robert Devereux. A thorough investigation would involve examining the circumstances of the Queen around each alleged birth, the child's early and adult life. Only in the case of Edward de Vere and Henry Wriothesley have such investigations been done because of their relevance to the Shakespeare Authorship issues. It is within the realm of possibility that substantial evidence might be found for other children of the Queen in the coming decades.

Henry Hawkins said, "That my lord Robert hath had fyve children by the Queene, and she never goeth in progress [tour of the countryside] but to be delivered." The following names are candidates for further historical investigation:

Mary Sidney, October 1561. This would be the first child of Robert Dudley and Elizabeth, possibly born at court on October 27, 1561. She was raised by Mary Dudley Sidney (Robert's sister). Mary Sidney married Henry Herbert and they had four children, two of these children were William Herbert and Philip Herbert. They became the "incomparable brethren." to whom the *First Folio* was dedicated. Philip was married to Susan Vere and thus Edward de Vere, 17th Earl of Oxford (deceased) was his father-in-law. William at one time was considered for marriage to Bridget Vere, Oxford's other daughter.

In *The Private Character of Queen Elizabeth*, (page 184), we find an interesting comment, which would be consistent with Queen Elizabeth having a daughter born in 1562 (a year off Mary Sidney's birth date.)

> "I am assured that he (The English Ambassador—F.C.) has let it be known that the pretended Queen Elizabeth has a daughter thirteen years of age, and that she would bestow her in marriage on some one acceptable to his Catholic Majesty. I have heard talk before of this daughter, but the English here say they know nought of such a matter."—Nicholas Ormanetto, Bishop of Padua, Nuncio in Spain, to Ptolemy Galli, Cardinal of Como, from Madrid 9 Dec., 1575; Vat. Arch. Nunt. Di Spagna, vol. Viii. Fol. 601.

Robert Cecil, December 1562. This would be the second child carried by Elizabeth during October 1562 when she suffered smallpox. He was born crippled from the disease. William Cecil and his wife, Mildred, raised him. The other sons of William Cecil never gained the prominence of Robert. Although physically frail to the point of deformity, Robert Cecil was brilliantly suited for the manipulations of court life. In the later years of Elizabeth's reign, he had almost complete control over access to the Queen. When William Cecil, Lord Burghley, died, Robert Cecil took his position as Elizabeth's secretary.

Robert Devereux, 2nd Earl of Essex, November 19, 1566. He would be raised in the household of Walter Devereux and his wife Lettice Knollys. Upon the death of his ostensible father, Walter Devereux, he became the 2nd Earl of Essex. His ostensible mother Lettice Knollys married Robert Dudley in 1578 and became the Countess of Leicester. At that point, Robert Dudley became the legal stepfather of his secret child. Robert Dudley was instrumental in having Robert Devereux elected to the prestigious Order of the Garter. His support for this young man has been inexplicable; knowledge that he was his natural son provides an explanation. Robert Devereux (2nd Earl of Essex) was executed on February 25, 1601 for his leading the so-called Essex rebellion in 1600.

Elizabeth Leighton, 1568. This would be the final child of Elizabeth and Robert Dudley. Cecilia Knollys (Lettice's sister) and her husband Thomas Leighton would be the child's foster parents.

These four, plus Henry Wriothesley would be the five children Henry Hawkins mentions. In total, it is conceivable that Queen Elizabeth had six children. From this perspective, the Elizabethan era is a struggle between the children of Elizabeth.

OXFORD HISTORY

1548   Edward de Vere born, son of Princess Elizabeth Tudor and Thomas Seymour.

1558   His foster father, John de Vere, officiates at Coronation of Queen Elizabeth. John de Vere lives at court, possibly brings Edward with him.

1559   Oxford matriculates at St. John's College, Cambridge.

1561   Queen Elizabeth visits Hedingham.

1562   John de Vere dies and Oxford's foster mother marries soon thereafter; Edward becomes ward of Crown under William Cecil. Edward moves to London to live at William Cecil's.

1564   Oxford receives Masters from Oxford University.

1566   Oxford receives Masters from Cambridge University.

1567   Oxford kills Lord Burghley's cook with sword.

1567   Oxford admitted to Gray's Inn for legal studies.

1567   Translation of *Metamorphoses* published.

1570   Oxford participates in military campaign with Earl of Sussex in North.

1571   Oxford weds Anne Cecil, William Cecil's daughter; Cecil raised to Baron Burghley.

1572   Bartholomew Clerke's translation into Latin of *Il Cortegiano* (*The Courtier*) published. Preface by Oxford.

1573   Calvin's version of the *Psalms of David* published by Arthur Golding with dedication to Oxford.

1574   Henry Wriothesley, 3rd Earl of Southampton born to Oxford and Elizabeth.

1574   Oxford flees to continent, quickly returns.

1575   Oxford travels to Paris, Venice, Italy. Before he leaves, he makes arrangements leaving property to Horatio Vere.

1575   Daughter, Elizabeth Vere born to Anne Cecil.

1576   Oxford returns to England; stripped of possession by pirates on his return voyage; returns with young Italian male singer; later Oxford accused of homosexuality; singer states de Vere speaks fluent Latin and Italian; Oxford implies Anne's child, Elizabeth, is not his.

1577   *The Historie of Error* performed at court. The first of many court plays.

1578   Oxford singled out as "countenance shakes spears," by Gabriel Harvey.

1578   Oxford loses £3,000 in a sea venture to Michael Lok (hence Lok is shy his debt to Oxford).

1579   Quarrel over tennis court with Philip Sidney; question of duel, until Queen intercedes.

1579   *The Jew* performed at Bull Theater.

1581	Oxford has son, Edward, born to Anne Vavasor, both sent to the Tower; resumes living with his wife.
1582	Wounded in duel with Thomas Knyvet; Knyvet is later knighted.
1583	Reported in poverty with only three servants; buries newborn son.
1584	Daughter Bridget is born.
1585	Public production of plays begins with no attribution.
1585	Daughter Frances born; dies later at age 2 or 3.
1586	Mary Queen of Scots tried and sentenced to death.
1586	Granted £1,000 per year by Elizabeth I; funds from QE's Privy Purse.
1586	Oxford sits at trial of Mary Queen of Scots.
1587	Susan Vere born. In 1605, she marries Philip Herbert (Earl of Montgomery), one of two nobles of dedication to First Folio).
1588	Spanish Armada.
1588	Wife Anne dies.
1588	Robert Dudley (Earl of Leicester) dies.
1591	Marries Elizabeth Trentham, moves to Kings Place, Hackney. Drops from court life.
1593	*Venus and Adonis* dedication to the 3rd Earl of Southampton with first appearance in England of "William Shakespeare" name.
1593	Oxford's wife Elizabeth Trentham gives birth to a son, Henry.
1594	*Henry V, Pt. 2* published, without naming author; begins a series of plays published anonymously.
1594	*Rape of Lucrece* under name of "William Shakespeare." dedicated to 3rd Earl of Southampton
1598	First plays with name "Shakespeare" *Love's Labor's Lost, Henry IV, Pt. 1, Merchant of Venice.*
1599	Robert Devereux, (Earl of Essex) leads campaign against Irish rebels, with him is Henry Wriothesley (3rd Earl of Southampton).
1601	Robert Devereux, (Earl of Essex) leads abortive revolt and is beheaded; Henry Wriothesley (3rd Earl of Southampton) sent to Tower for life.
1603	Queen Elizabeth I dies. James I ascends to throne; Southampton released.
1604	Oxford disappears under mysterious circumstances; no will found.
1609	Date of *Shake-speares Sonnets*.
1616	William Shakspere dies in Stratford-upon-Avon.
1623	Meeting of James I, Horatio Vere, Southampton, Philip and Henry Herbert on Southampton's boat *The Prince*.
1623	First Folio is published.

WHEN SILLY BEES COULD SPEAKE

It was a tyme when silly Bees could speake
and in that time I was a silly Bee
who suckt on time, untill the hart [be]gan [to] breake
yet never founde that tyme would favour me
    Of all the swarme I onely could not thrive
    yet brought I wax & honey to ye hive

Then thus I busd when time no sap would give
Why is this blessed tyme to me so dry
Sith in this tyme, ye lazie Drone doth live
ye waspe, ye worme, ye Gnat, ye butterfly
    Mated with grief I kneeled on my knees
    And thus complain'd unto ye King of Bees

My leige god grant thy time may have no end
and yet vouchsafe to heare my plaint of tyme
Synce every fruitlesse fly hath found a friend
& I cast down while Attomies doe clyme
    The king replide but thus, peace peevish Bee
    Thou art borne to serve the time, ye time not thee.

The time not thee, this word clipt short my wings
And made me worme-like creepe yet once did fly
Awfull regard disputeth not with kings
Recreauethe a Repulse not asking why?
    Then from the tyme, I for a tyme withdrew
    To feed on Henbane, Hemlock, Nettles, Rue,

But from those leves no dram of sweete I drayne
their head strong furry did my head bewitch
The juice disperst black bloud in every veine
for hony gall, for wax I gathered pitch
    My Combe a Rift, my hive a leafe must bee
    so chang'd that Bees scarce took me for a Bee

I work on weedes when Moone is in ye waine
whilst all ye swarme in sunnshine tast ye rose
onn black Roote ferne I sitt & suck my baine
whilst on ye Eglentine the rest repose
    having too much they still repine for more
    & cloyd with fullness surfeit on their store

Swolne fatt with feasts full merrily they passe
In sweetned Clusters falling from ye tree
where finding me to nibble on ye grasse
some scorne, some muse, & some doe pitty me
    And some envy & whipser to the king
    Some must be still & some must have no sting.

Are Bees waxt waspes, or spiders to infect
Doe hony bowells make ye sperit gall
Is this ye juice of flowers to stir suspect
Ist not enough to tread on them that fall
    what sting hath patience but a sighing grief
    That stings nought but itselfe without Relief

True patience ye prouender of fooles
sad patience that waiteth at the doore
Patience yt learnes thus to conclude in schools
Patience I am therefore I must be poore
    Great king of Bees it rightest every wrong
    Listen to patience in her dying song

I cannot feed on fennel like some flyes
nor flye to every flower to gather gaine
myne appetite waites on my prince his eyes
Contented with contempt, & pleased with payne
    and yet expecting of an happy houre
    when he shall say this Bee shall suck a flower

Of all the griefes it must my patience grate
there's one that fretteth in ye high'st degree
To see some Catterpillers bred up of late
cropping the fruit it should sustane the Bee
    yet smiled I, for it the wisest knowes
    that mothes doe frett the Clothe Canker the Rose

Once did I see by flying in the feild
fowle beasts to browse upon the Lilly fayre
Virtue & beauty could noe succour yeild
All's prouender for Asses, but the ayre
    the partiall world of this takes litle heed
    to give them flowers it should on thistles feed

This onely I must draine AEgiptian flowers
having noe sauor, bitter sap they have
& seek out Rotten Tombes & dead mens bowers
and bite on nightshade growing by the grave
    If this I cannot have, as hapless Bee
    witching Tobacco I will fly to thee

What thouge thou dy mens lungs in deepest black
A mourning habitt suites a sable hart
what if thy fumes sound memory doe crack
fforgettfullnes is fittest for my smart
    o vertuous fume let it be graued in oke
    it wordes, hopes, witts & all the worlds but smoke

ffive years twise told with promises perfume
my hope stuft head was cast into a slumber
Sweete dreames of gold, on dreams I then presume
& mongst the Bees thoughe I were in the number
    waking I founde, hives hopes had made me vaine
    Twas not Tobacco stupifyed the braine

Ingenium, studium, nummos, spem, tempus, amicos
    Cum male perdiderim: perdere verba leve est.

Since I have wretchedly lost my talent, zeal, money, hope, time and friends,
it is a trivial matter to waste my words.

Princess Diana Spencer

Princess Elizabeth Tudor & Thomas Seymour

Edward de Vere, 17th Earl of Oxford, [Lord Great, Chamberlain of England] married Anne Cecil, daughter of William Cecil, Lord Burghley, 19 Dec 1571

Elizabeth "Bess" Vere, married: William Stanley, 6th Earl of Derby, 26 Jun 1594

James Stanley, 7th Earl of Derby, Derby

Amelia Sophia Stanley married: John Murray, 1st Marquess of Atholl, 5 May 1659

John Murray, 1st Duke of Atholl

Susan Murray, married: William Gordon, 2nd Earl of Aberdeen, 25 April 1716 as 2nd wife

Catherine Gordon, married: Cosmo George Gordon, 3rd Duke of Gordon, 3 Sept 1741

Alexander Gordon, 4th Duke of Gordon

Georgiana Gordon, married: John Russell, 6th Duke of Bedford, 17 April 1803 as 2nd wife

Louisa Jane Russell, married: James Hamilton, Duke of Abercorn, 25 Oct 1832

James Hamilton, 2nd Duke of Abercorn

James Albert Hamilton 3rd Duke of Abercorn

Cynthia Eleanor Beatrix Hamilton, married: John Spencer, 7th Earl of Spencer, 28 Feb 1919

Edward John Spencer, 8th Earl of Spencer

Princess Elizabeth Tudor & Thomas Seymour

Edward de Vere [Seymour], 17th Earl of Oxford, [Lord Great, Chamberlain of England] & Elizabeth Tudor, Queen of England

Henry Wriothesley, 3rd Earl of Southampton, 1574

Penelope Wriothesley, married William Spencer, 2nd Baron Spencer, 1614

Henry Spencer, 1st Earl of Sunderland

Robert Spencer, 2nd Earl of Sunderland

Charles Spencer, 3rd Earl of Sunderland

John Spencer, 1st Earl of Spencer

George John Spencer, 2nd Earl of Spencer

Frederick Spencer, 4th Earl of Spencer[a]

John Spencer, 5th Earl of Spencer

Charles Spencer, 6th Earl of Spencer

Albert John Spencer, 7th Earl of Spencer

Edward John Spencer, 8th Earl of Spencer

Diana Frances Spencer, Princess of Wales, married: Charles Windsor, Prince of Wales, 29 July 1981

Prince William Windsor, Prince Henry Windsor

---

[a] 3rd Earl, John Charles Spencer, apparently died and title went to his brother Frederick.

ENDNOTES

Introduction
1   J. Thomas Looney, *Shakespeare Identified,* pg. 80.

Chapter 1.   The Ashbourne Portrait
1.   Folger Shakespeare Library website, April 2001.
2.   M.H. Spielmann, "The Ashbourne Portrait, *Connoisseur Magazine,* Jan.-April, 1910, pg. 249.
3.   Ibid., pg. 249.
4.   M.H. Spielmann, "The Ashbourne Portrait," *Connoisseur Magazine,* May-August, 1910, pg. 42.
5.   Charles Wisner Barrell, "Identifying 'Shakespeare," *Scientific American* Vol. 162, January 1940, pg. 45.
6.   Ibid., pg. 45.
7.   Elisabeth Sears, email dated Tuesday, 24 October 2000.
8.   William L. Pressly, "The Ashbourne Portrait of Shakespeare: Through the Looking Glass," *The Shakespeare Quarterly,* vol. 44, Spring 1993, No.1., pg. 61.
9.   Ibid., pg. 61.
10. Ibid., pg. 62.
11. William L. Pressly, *A Catalogue of Paintings in the Folger Shakespeare Library,* pg. vii.
12. Ibid., pg. 263.
13. Ibid., pg. 263.
14. Ibid., pg. 263.
15. Ibid., pg. 340.
16. Gail Kern Paster, "The Ghost of Shakespeare," *Harper's Magazine,* April 1999, pg. 39.
17. Frank J. Sulloway, *Born to Rebel,* pg. 16.
18. Ibid., pg. 16.
19. Thomas S. Kuhn, *The Structure of Scientific Revolutions,* pg. 116.
20. Bacon, Delia, *The Philosophy of the Plays of Shakspere Unfolded,* pg. 309.
21. J. Thomas Looney, *Shakespeare Identified,* pg. 80.
22. Giles Dawson, "Dorothy and Charlton Ogburn's This Star of England," *The Shakespeare Quarterly*, 1953, pg. 165.
23. Ibid., pg. 166.
24. Ibid., pg. 165.
25. Ibid., pg. 165.
26. Ibid., pg. 170.
27. S. Schoenbaum, *Shakespeare's Lives,* pg. 10.
28. G.P.V. Akrigg, *Shakespeare and the Earl of Southampton,* pg. 191.
29. Jonathan Bate, *The Genius of Shakespeare, pg. 188.*
30. Walt Whitman, *November Boughs,* pg. 1148.
31. Ibid., pg. 1152.

32. Harold Bloom, "The Ghost of Shakespeare," *Harper's Magazine,* April 1999, pg. 56.
33. Ibid., pg. 56.
34. Ibid., pg. 56
35. Gail Kern Paster, "The Ghost of Shakespeare," *Harper's Magazine,* April 1999, pg. 39.
36. Harold Bloom, *Shakespeare, the Invention of the Human*, pg. xviii.

Chapter 2. Sex, Murder, Incest and Tudors
1. Jane Resh Thomas, *Behind the Mask, The Life of Queen Elizabeth I*, pg. 34.
2. Mary M. Luke, *A Crown for Elizabeth*, pg.72
3. Bruce Thomas Boeher, *Monarchy and Incest in Renaissance England*, pg. 75, (Stow, sig. 3S4r).
4. Joel Hurstfield, *The Queen's Wards*, pg. xv.
5. Ibid., pg. 339.
6. Japer Ridley, *Henry VIII, The Politics of Tyranny*, pg. 217.
7. Ibid., pg. 158.
8. Ibid., pg. 281.
9. Marc Shell, *Elizabeth's Glass*, pg. 111.
10. Ibid., pg. 111
11. Christopher Haigh, *Elizabeth I*, pg. 4.
12. F.C. Chamberlain, *The Private Character of Queen Elizabeth, pg. 23.*
13. Jane Resh Thomas, *Behind the Mask, The Life of Queen Elizabeth I*, pg. 34.
14. Antony Martienssen, *Queen Katherine Parr*, pg.153.
15. Ibid., pg. 173.
16. Ibid., pg. 217.
17. Ibid., pg. 217.

Chapter 3. The Summer of 1548
1. Mary M. Luke, *A Crown for Elizabeth*, pg. 185.
2. Susan E. James, *Kateryn Parr: The Making of a Queen*, pg. 93.
3. William Seymour, *Ordeal By Ambition*, pg. 221.
4. Anthony Martienssen, *Queen Katherine Parr*, pg. 329.
5. Alison Plowden, *The Young Elizabeth*, pg. 94.
6. Anthony Martienssen, *Queen Katherine Parr*, pg. 237.
7. Alison Plowden, *The Young Elizabeth*, pg. 95.
8. Anthony Martienssen, *Queen Katherine Parr*, pg. 238.
9. William Seymour, *Ordeal By Ambition*, pg. 246.
10. C.S. Knighton, *Calendar of State Papers Domestic Series of the reign of Edward VII 1547-1553*, pg. 127-8.
11. Anthony Martienssen, *Queen Katherine Parr*, pg. 241.
12. Susan E. James, *Kateryn Parr: The Making of a Queen*, pg. 339.
13. Hugh Ross Williamson, *Historical Enigmas*, pg. 91.
14. Frederick Chamberlain, *The Private Character of Queen Elizabeth*, pg. 41.
15. Conyers Read, *Mr. Secretary Cecil and Queen Elizabeth*, pg. 64.
16. Samuel Haynes, *State Papers*, pg. 99.

17. Ibid., pg. 99.
18. Frederick Chamberlain, *The Private Character of Queen Elizabeth,* pg. 11.
19. Alison Plowden, *The Young Elizabeth,* pg. 110.
20. Ibid., pg. 109.
21. Frederick Chamberlain, *The Private Character of Queen Elizabeth,* pg. 6.
22. Ibid., pg.11.
23. Ibid., pg. 13. *From Life of Jane Dormer, Duchess of Feria* (ascribed to Henry Clifford, a member of her household), London, 1887, p. 86.

Chapter 4. A Hasty Marriage and Three Murders
1. Louis Thorn Golding, *An Elizabethan Puritan* pg. 38. Source: the second volume of *The History of Essex.* pg. 293..
2. Ibid., pg. 41.
3. B.M. Ward, *The Seventeenth Earl of Oxford,* pg. 7.
4. Alan H. Nelson, *Depositions re. marriage of 16th Earl to Margery Golding in 1548.*
5. Ibid.
6. Ibid.
7. Ibid.
8. Ibid.
9. Ibid.
10. Ibid.
11. Ibid.
12. Louis Thorn Golding, *The Elizabethan Puritan,* pg. 38.
13. Ibid., pg. 38.
14. Alison Plowden, *The Young Elizabeth,* pg. 122.
15. Frederick Chamberlin, *The Private Character of Queen Elizabeth,* pg. 285.
16. John Nichols, *Progresses of Queen Elizabeth,* Vol. 3, pg. 613.
17. Ibid., pg. 618.
18. Mary M. Luke, *A Crown for Elizabeth,* pg. 191.
19. Alan H. Nelson, ed. Public Record Office, second surviving will of John de Vere 16th Earl of Oxford.
20. Gwynneth Bowen, "What Happened at Hedingham and Earls Colne Part II," *The Shakespearean Authorship Review,* Vol. 25, Sept. 1971, pg. 7.
21. Joel Hurstfield, *The Queens Wards,* pg. 129.
22. Ibid., pg. 249
23. Gwynneth Bowen, "What Happened at Hedingham and Earls Colne Part II," *The Shakespearean Authorship Review,* Vol. 25, Sept. 1971, pg. 5.
24. John Nichols, *Progresses of Queen Elizabeth,* pg. 613.
25. Ibid., pg. 613.
26. Hugh Ross Williamson, *Historical Enigmas,* pg. 87.
27. A.L. Rowse, *The Elizabethan Renaissance,* pg. 162. q. E.K. Chambers, *The Elizabethan Stage,* I., pg.107.
28. Nichols, Harris, *The Life and Times of Sir Christopher Hatton,* pg. 14.
29. Hugh Ross Williamson, *Historical Enigmas,* pg. 89.
30. Ibid., pg. 88.
31. Ibid., pg. 89.
32. Ibid., pg. 91.

33. Ibid., pg. 91.
34. Ibid., pg. 92.
35. Mary M. Luke, *Gloriana, The Years of Elizabeth I*, pg. 109.
36. Ibid., pg. 117.
37. Ibid., pg. 118.
38. Ibid., pg. 118.
39. Hugh Ross Williamson, *Historical Enigmas*, pg. 83.
40. John Nichols, *Progresses of Queen Elizabeth*, pg. 617 from *Leicester's Commonwealth*, pp. 22, 36.
41. Mary M. Luke, *Gloriana, The Years of Elizabeth I*, pg. 122
42. William Camden, *The History of the Most Renowned and Victorious Princess Elizabeth, Late Queen of England*, pg. 29.
43. Ibid., pg. 3.
44. Ibid., pg. 30.
45. Ibid., pg. 329-30.

Chapter 5. A Not So Brief Chronicle

1. Henry Machyn, *The Diary of Henry Machyn*, pg. 291.
2. B.M. Ward, *The Seventeenth Earl of Oxford*, pg. 20.
3. Joel Hurstfield, *The Queens Wards*, pg. 255.
4. Ibid., pg. 256.
5. Eddi Jolly, *"Shakespeare" and Burghley's Library*, The Oxfordian, October, 2000, pg. 6.
6. Dean Keith Simonton, *Greatness, Who Makes History and Why*, pg. 165.
7. Diana Price, *Shakespeare's Unorthodox Biography: New Evidence of an Authorship Problem*, pg. 262.
8. Stephanie Caruana & Elisabeth Sears, *Oxford's Revenge*, pg. 11.
9. Bronson Feldman, *Hamlet Himself*, pg. 123. Translated by Tom Holland, Head of Classics, The Cheltenham Ladies College, England --Qunitus Latin Translation service.
10. B.M. Ward, *The Seventeenth Earl of Oxford*, pg. 56.
11. Charlton Ogburn, *The Mysterious William Shakespeare*, pg. 480.
12. Ibid., pg. 480.
13. Ibid., pg. 479.
14. Alan Young, *Tudor and Jacobean Tournaments*, pg. 93.
15. Charlton Ogburn, *The Mysterious William Shakespeare*, pg. 502.
16. Ibid., pg. 504.
17. Statutes of the Realm, Vol. 3, pg. 955.
18. Statutes of the Realm, Vol. 4, Part I, pg. 527.
19. Ibid., pg. 527.
20. B.M. Ward, *The Seventeenth Earl of Oxford*, pg. 61.
21. Ibid., pg. 62.
22. Joel Hurstfield, *The Queen's Wards*, pg. 253.
23. William Cecil, *Advice to a Son*, Louis B. Wright, ed., pg. 9.
24. J. Thomas Looney, *Shakespeare Identified*, pg. 234; from *Wright's History of Essex*, Vol. I, pg. 517.
25. Dorothy and Charlton Ogburn, Sr., *This Star of England*, pg. 306.

26. Victor Von Klarwill, *The Fugger News-Letters,* pg. 55.
27. Miller, Ruth Loyd, ed., *Shakespeare Identified, Vol. II. Oxfordian Vistas,* pg. 93.
28. Charlton Ogburn, *The Mysterious William Shakespeare,* pg. 621.
29. Thomas Birch, *Memoirs of the Reign of Queen Elizabeth,* pg. 22.
30. B.M. Ward, quot. Cotton MSS., Appendix 47, *The Seventeenth Earl of Oxford,* pg. 227.
31. Charlton Ogburn, *The Mysterious William Shakespeare,* pg. 666.
32. B.M. Ward, *The Seventeenth Earl of Oxford,* pg. 257.
33. Camden, William, *Annales,* Vol. 3, pg. 267.
34. William Plumer Fowler, *Shakespeare Revealed In Oxford's Letters,* pg. 803.
35. Charlton Ogburn, *The Mysterious William Shakespeare,* pg. 440.
36. G.P.V. Akrigg, *Shakespeare and the Earl of Southampton,* pg.140.

Chapter 6. A Literary and Theatrical Life

1. John Frederick Nims ed., *Ovid's Metamorphoses, the Arthur Golding Translation, 1567,* Paul Dry Books, Philadelphia, 2000, pg xiv.
2. Dorothy and Charlton Ogburn, *This Star of England,* pg. 11.
3. B.M. Ward, *The Seventeenth Earl of Oxford,* pg. 23.
4. Dean Keith Simonton, *Greatness, Who Makes History and Why,* pg. 67.
5. Stephanie Caruana and Betty Sears, *Oxford's Revenge,* pg. intro.
6. J.J. Munro, *Brooke's 'Romeus and Juliet' Being The Original of Shakespeare's "Romeo and Juliet' Newly Edited,* pg. xxi.
7. Ibid., Appendix III, pg. 165.
8. Jeffrey McQuain and Stanley Malles, *Coined by Shakespeare;* Michael Macaone, *Brush Up Your Shakespeare.*
9. Diana Price, *Shakespeare's Unorthodox Biography,* pg. 248.
10. Ernesto Grillo, *Shakespeare and Italy,* pg. 126.
11. Ibid., pg. 141.
12. Ibid., pg. 146.
13. Ibid., pg. 134.
14. Ibid., pg. 132.
15. Ibid., pg. 134.
16. Ibid., pg. 97.
17. L. Sprague de Camp, *The Ancient Engineers,* pg. 142.
18. Charlton Ogburn, *The Mysterious William Shakespeare,* pg. 687.
19. George Puttenham, *Arte of Englishe Poetry,* pg. 16,17,49, 51
20. Charlton Ogburn, *The Mysterious William Shakespeare,* pg. 195.
21. B.M. Ward, *The Seventeenth Earl of Oxford,* pg. 80.
22. Ibid., pg. 81.
23. Ibid., pg 81.
24. Ibid., pg. 81.
25. Charlton Ogburn, *The Mysterious William Shakespeare,* pg. 597.
26. Katherine Chiljan, Dedication Letters to the Earl of Oxford.
27. Mark Alexander, *Shakespeare and the Law,* pg. 1-6.
28. Charlton Ogburn, *The Mysterious William Shakespeare,* pg. 617.
29. Richard Whalen, "The Queen's Worm," *Shakespeare Oxford Review* pg. 12.

30. Peter Cunning, *Extracts from the Accounts of the Revels at Court*, pg. 188.
31. Sigmund Freud, *The Interpretation of Dreams*, pg. 264.
32. William Cecil, *Advice to a Son*, Louis B. Wright, ed., pg. 9-13.
33. Robert Brazil, *The True Story of the Shake-speare Publications,* pg. 97.
34. Ibid., pg 71.
35. Roger Stritmatter, *Edward de Vere's Geneva Bible*, pg. 81.
36. Ibid. pg. 48.
37. Vol. 1, pg.434
38. Charlton Ogburn, *The Mysterious William Shakespeare*, pg. 750.
39. Vol.3, pg.446.
40. Vol.3, pg.447.
41. Vol.3, pg.447.
42. Vol.3, pg.437.
43. Vol.3, pg.445.

Chapter 7. Shakespeare Appears

1. Robert Brazil, *The True Story of the Shake-speare Publications,* pg. 57.
2. Ibid., pg. 57.
3. Ibid., pg. 33.
4. Ibid., pg. 33.
5. B.M. Ward, *The Seventeenth Earl of Oxford,* pg. 294.
6. Ibid., pg. 294.
7. William Boyle, "Shakespeare on Death Row," Translation is courtesy of Dr. Juan Manuel Perez of the Hispanic division Of the Library of Congress, *The Shakespeare Oxford Newsletter*, Vol. 34: no 2, Summer 1998.
8. Dr. Merilee Karr, *Semiotics and the Shakespeare Authorship Debate, The Shakespeare Oxford Newsletter, Vol. 36. no 4., Winter 2001.*
9. Warren Hope, "Shakespeare: An Unorthodox Biography," *The Elizabethan Review*, Autumn, 2000.
10. Diana Price, *Shakespeare: An Unorthodox Biography,* pg. 101.

Chapter 8. Yet Another Changeling

1. Charlton Ogburn, The Mysterious William Shakespeare, pg. 510.
2. Frederick Chamberlin, MS. At Hatfield House. From the Private Character of Queen Elizabeth; pg. 166-9.
3. Carolly Erickson, The First Elizabeth, pg. 267.
4. Dorothy and Charlton Ogburn, This Star of England, pg. 834.
5. Ibid, pg. 836.
6. Charlotte Stopes, *The Life of Henry, Third Earl of Southampton, Shakespeare's Patron,* pg 1.
7. G.P.V. Akrigg, *Shakespeare and the Earl of Southampton,* pg. 13.
8. Charlotte Stopes, *The Life of Henry, Third Earl of Southampton, Shakespeare's Patron,* pg 3.
9. Ibid., pg. 4.
10. G.P.V. Akrigg, *Shakespeare and the Earl of Southampton,* pg. 13.
11. Jonathan Bate *Shakespeare and Ovid,* pg. 57.

12. Ibid., 64.
13. Ibid., pg. 64.
14. B.N. De Luna, *The Queen Declined, An Interpretation of Willobie His Avisa*, pg. 47.
15. Boyle, Charles, "Elizabeth's Glass," *The Shakespeare Oxford Newsletter,* Winter 2000, pg. 15.
16. Ibid., pg. 17.
17. John Nichols, *The Progresess and Public Processions of Queen Elizabeth.* Vol. II, pg. 313.
18. Roy Strong, "The Persian Lady Reconsidered" in *The Art of the Emblem*, pg. 106.
19. Wilbur L. Cross and Tucker Brooke, *The Yale Shakespeare*, pg. 1437.
20. Ibid., pg. 1437.

PERMISSIONS

By Permission of the Folger Shakespeare Library:
Ashbourne Shakespeare Portrait
Mayday Title Page by George Chapman
Shake-speares Sonnets Title Page
First Folio, Martin Droeshout Engraving
Shakspere Monument 1656, *Antiquities of Warwickshire*

By permission of The Haberdasher's Company:
Sir Hugh Hamersley

By courtesy of the National Portrait Gallery, London:
Queen Anne Boleyn,
Queen Katherine Parr
Edward de Vere, Paris Portrait (cropping with permission)
Thomas Seymour
William Cecil

By kind permission of His Grace the Duke of Buccleuch and Queensberry, K.T.:
Henry Wriothesley, 3rd Earl of Southampton,

By permission of the Royal Collection © 2000, Her Majesty Queen Elizabeth II:
Princess Elizabeth Tudor
Queen Elizabeth (Portrait of a Woman in Oriental Dress)
Judgment of Paris, Hans Eworth

By permission of Private Collection, Bridgeman Art Library:
Queen Elizabeth I (1533-1603) being carried in Procession, c. 1600 (oil on canvas) by Robert Peake (fl. 1580-1626) (attr. to)

By Permission of the Bodleian Library:
Venus and Adonis Title Page
Venus and Adonis Dedication

By permission of Wallace Collection, London, UK Bridgeman Art Library:
Robert Dudley, Earl of Leicester (oil on oak panel) by Steven van der Meulen (fl. 1543-68) (attr. to)

By permission of the British Library:
Oxford Signatures dated November 24, 1569 (Lansdowne MS 11, f. 121),
August 23, 1563 (Lansdowne MS.6.f. 79)
Letter of Kat Ashley with signature of Princess Elizabeth (Lansdowne MS 1236, ff. 41 r-v)

By permission of the Marquess of Salisbury:
Oxford signatures dated: March 22, 1602; April 25/27 1603; May 7, 1603

BIBLIOGRAPHY

Akrigg, G.P.V., *Shakespeare and the Earl of Southampton,* Harvard University Press, Cambridge Mass., 1968.

Alexander, Mark. K., *Shakespeare and the Law.*

Anderson, Verily, *The de Veres of Castle Hedingham,* Terence Dalton Limited, Lavenham, Suffolk, 1993

Anthony, Katharine, *Queen Elizabeth,* The Literary Guild, New York, 1929.

Arnold, Janet, *Queen Elizabeth's Wardrobe Unlock'd,* W.S. Manley & Son Ltd., Leeds, England, 1988.

Ascham, Roger, *The Scholemaster,* London, 1570, reprinted by Da Capo Theatrum Orbis Terrarum Ltd., Amsterdam, New York, 1968.

Bacon, Delia, *The Philosophy of the Plays of Shakspere Unfolded,* London, Groombridge and Sons, Paternoster, Row, 1857, reprinted by AMS Press, Inc., New York, 1970.

Ballantine, Roberta, *Through Babyland, A Brief for the Maternity of the First Queen Elizabeth,* Sarasota, Florida, 2000.

Bate, Jonathan, *Shakespeare and Ovid,* Clarendon Press, Oxford, 1993.

Bate, Jonathan, *The Genius of Shakespeare,* New York & Oxford, Oxford University Press, 1998.

Belloc, Hilaire, *Elizabeth: creature of circumstance,* New York, London, Harper & Brothers [1942].

Birch, Thomas, *Memoirs of the Reign of Queen Elizabeth,* Reprint of 1754 edition, Vol. 1, 2, AMS Press, New York, 1970.

Bloom, Harold, *Shakespeare, the Invention of the Human,* Riverhead Books, New York, 1998.

Bloom, Harold, "The Ghost of Shakespeare," *Harper's Magazine,* April 1999.

Boehrer, Bruce, Thomas, *Monarchy and Incest in Renaissance England,* University of Pennsylvania Press, 1992.

Bond, R. Warwick, *The Complete Works of John Lyly,* At the Clarendon Press, Oxford, 1902.

Bowen, Gwynneth, "What happened at Hedingham and Earls Colne," *The Shakespearean Authorship Review,* No. 24, Spring, 1971.

Boyle, Charles, "Elizabeth's Glass," *The Shakespeare Oxford Newsletter,* Vol. 36 no. 4, Winter 2000.

Boyle, William, "Shakespeare on Death Row," Translation is courtesy of Dr. Juan Manuel Perez of the Hispanic division of the Library of Congress, *The Shakespeare Oxford Newsletter,* Vol. 34: no 2, Summer 1998.

Brazil, Robert Sean, *The True Story of the Shake-speare Publications,* 1999.

Brewster, Eleanor, *Oxford and his Elizabethan Ladies,* Durance & Company, Philadelphia, 1972.

Burgess, Anthony, *Shakespeare,* Alfred A. Knopf, New York, 1970.

Burris, Barbara, "The Golden Book, Bound Richly Up," Independent Paper, 1999.

Camden, William, *The History of the Most Renowned and Victorious Princess Elizabeth,... Late Queen of England (selected chapters)*, edited by Wallace T. MacCaffrey, University of Chicago Press, Chicago and London, 1970.

Campbell, Susan, "The Last Known Letter of Edward de Vere," *Shakespeare Oxford Newsletter*, Vol. 36. no. 1 Spring, 2000.

Caruana, Stephanie, & Elisabeth Sears, *Oxford's Revenge*, 1989.

Chambers, E.K., *The Elizabethan Stage, Vol. I-IV*, The Clarendon Press, 1923, reprinted by D.R. Hillman & Sons Ltd., Oxford Press, Oxford 1961.

Chamberlain, F.C., *The Private Character of Queen Elizabeth*, John Line The Bodley Head Ltd., London, 1921.

Chamberlain, F.C., *Elizabeth and Leicester*, Dodd, Mead & Company, New York, 1939.

Chidsey, Donald Barr, *Elizabeth I, A Great Life in Brief.* Alfred A. Knopf, New York, 1955.

Chiljan, Katherine, *Dedications & Letters to the Earl of Oxford* 1994.

Clark, Eva Turner, *Axiophilus, or Oxford alias Shakespeare,* The Knickerbocker Press, New York, 1926.

Clark, Eva Turner, *Hidden Allusions in Shakespeare's Plays*, W. F. Payson, New York, 1931.

Clark, Eva Turner, *Shakespeare's Plays in the Order of their Writing, A Study Based on Records of the Court Revels and Historic Allusions*; London, C. Palmer, 1930.

Cross, Wilbur L. and Brooke, Tucker, *The Yale Shakespeare,* Barnes and Noble Books, New York, 1993.

Cunning, Peter, *Extracts from the Accounts of the Revels at Court, in the reigns of Queen Elizabeth and King James I., from the Original Office Books of the Masters and Yeoman,* The Shakespeare Society, London, 1842, reprinted by AMS Press Inc., N.Y. 1971.

Davies, John, *The Poems of Sir John Davies*, Introduction and Notes by Clare Howard, Columbia University Press, New York, 1941.

Dawson, Giles, *Dorothy and Charlton Ogburn's "This Star of England," Shakespeare Quarterly,* 1953.

De Camp, Sprague L., *The Ancient Engineers*, Barnes & Noble, New York, 1960.

De Luna, B.N., *The Queen Declined, An Interpretation of Willobie His Avisa*, Oxford University Press, Oxford 1970.

Dersin, Denise, ed., *What Life Was Like In The Realm of Elizabeth*, Alexandria, Virginia, Time Life Books, 1998.

Dewar, Mary, *Sir Thomas Smith, A Tudor Intellectual in Office*, The Athlone Press, London, 1964.

Erickson, Carolly, *The First Elizabeth,* Summit Books, New York, 1983.

Feldman, Bronson, *Hamlet Himself,* Lovelore Press, Philadelphia, 1977.

Folger Shakespeare Library, website, April 2001.

Fowler, William Plummer, *Shakespeare Revealed In Oxford's Letters,* Peter E. Randal, Portsmouth, New Hampshire, 1986.

Fraser, Antonia, *The Wives of Henry VIII*, Alfred A. Knopf, New York, 1993.

Freud, Sigmund, *Abriss der Psycho-Analyse, 1940.* Published in English as *An Outline of Psychoanalysis.* Translated by James Strachey. W.W. Norton, New York, 1963.

Freud, Sigmund, *The Interpretation of Dreams,* translated from the German and edited by James Strachey, Science Editions, Inc., New York, 1961.

Gelernt, Jules, *World of Many Loves: The Heptameron of Marguerite de Navarre,* The University of North Carolina Press, Chapel Hill, 1966.

Goldberg, Steven, *Why Men Rule,* Open Court Publishing, Chicago & LaSalle, Illinois, 1993.

Golding, Arthur, (John Frederick Nims, ed.), *Ovid's Metamorphoses, the Arthur Golding Translation, 1567,* Paul Dry Books, Philadelphia, 2000.

Golding, Arthur, (Rouse, W.H.D.), *Shakespeare's Ovid Being Arthur Golding's Translation of the Metamorphoses,* De La More Press, London, 1904.

Golding, Arthur, (Rouse, W.H.D., ed.), *Shakespeare's Ovid, being Arthur Golding's Translation of the Metamorphoses,* Southern Illinois University Press, Carbondale, Illinois, 1961.

Golding, Arthur, *Martiall Exploytes in Gallia,* Julius Caesar, translated from the Latin, London 1565. The English Experience (Published in Facsimile), Da Capo Press, Theatrum Orbis Terrarum Ltd., Amsterdam, New York, 1968.

Golding, Arthur, *The Excellent and Plasant Worke of Caisus Julius Solinus,* 1587, translated from the Latin, Scholars' Facsimiles & Reprints, Gainesville, Florida, 1955.

Golding, Louis Thorn, *An Elizabethan Puritan,* Richard R. Smith, New York, 1937.

Green, Nina, email dated March 5, 2001.

Greenwood, Granville George, *The Shakespeare Problem Restated,* John Lane The Bodley Head, London, 1907.

Grillo, Ernesto, *Shakespeare and Italy,* Haskell House Publishers Ltd., New York, 1949.

Hager, Alan, *Understanding Romeo and Juliet,* Greenwood Press, Wesport, CT, 1999.

Haigh, Christopher, *Elizabeth I, Profiles in Power,* Longman, London and New York, 1998.

Hamilton, Charles, *In Search of Shakespeare,* London, Harcourt Brace Jovanovich, San Diego, New York, 1985.

Haynes, Samuel, and Murdin, William, editors, *A Collection of State Papers...left by William Cecill Lord Burghley,* William Bowyer, London, 1740.

Harrison, G.B., ed., *Elizabethan & Jacobean Quartos, Willobie His Avisa, 1594,* Barnes and Noble, New York, 1966.

Harrison, G.B., ed., *The Letters of Queen Elizabeth I.* Funk & Wagnalls, New York, 1935.

Hayden, Ilse, *Symbol and Privilege, the Ritual Context of British Royalty,* University of Arizona Press, Tucson, 1987.

Henry, James, *The Letters of Henry James.* Letter to Miss Violet Hunt, August 26, 1903. Selected and edited by Percy Lubbock, Octagon Books, New York, 1970

Hibbert, Christopher, *The Virgin Queen,* Addison-Wesley Publishing, Reading, Mass., 1991.

Hibbert, Christopher, *The Virgin Queen, Elizabeth I, Genius of the Golden Age,* Addison-Wesley Publishing Company, Inc., Reading, Mass., 1924.

Holland H.H., *Shakespeare, Oxford and Elizabethan Times,* Dennis Archer, London, 1933.

Hope, Warren and Holston, Kim, *The Shakespeare Controversy.* London, McFarland & Company, Inc., Jefferson, North Carolina, 1992.

Hope, Warren, "A Review of *Shakespeare's Unorthodox Biography*", *The Elizabethan Review,* Autumn 2000, Internet Publication.

Hudson, Winthrop S., *The Cambridge Connection and the Elizabethan Settlement,* Duke University Press, Durham, North Carolina, 1980.

Hughes, Stephanie Hopkins, "Shakespeare's Tutor: Sir Thomas Smith" *(1513-1577), The Oxfordian,* Vol. III, October 2000.

Ives, Eric W., *Anne Boleyn,* Basil Blackwell Ltd., Oxford and New York, 1986.

James, Susan E., *Kateryn Parr, The Making of a Queen,* Ashgate, Aldershot U.K., 1999.

Jenkins, Elizabeth, *Elizabeth and Leicester.* Coward-McCann, Inc., New York, 1961.

Johnson, Paul, *Elizabeth I,* Holt, Rinehart and Winston, New York, 1974.

Jolly, Eddi, *"Shakespeare" and Burghley's Library, Biblotheca Ilustris: Sive Catalogus Varioum Librorum,* The Oxfordian, Vol. III, October 2000.

Jordan, W.K., *Edward the Young King,* The Belknap Press of Harvard University Press, Cambridge Mass., 1968.

Kail, Aubrey C., *The Medical Mind of Shakespeare,* Williams & Wilkins Adis Pty Limited, Balgowlah, Australia, 1986.

Kamen, Henry, *Philip of Spain.* Yale University Press, New Haven and London, 1997.

Karr, Merilee "Semiotics and the Shakespeare Authorship Debate," *The Shakespeare Oxford Newsletter, Vol. 36. no 4., Winter 2001.*

Kirsh, James, *Shakespeare's Royal Self.* Longmans, Canada, Ltd., Toronto, 1966.

Knighton, C.S., *Calendar of State Papers Domestic Series of the Reign of Edward VI 1547-1553,* Crown copyright, 1992.

Kornstein, Daniel J., *Kill All the Lawyers? Shakespeare's Legal Appeal.* Princeton University Press, Princeton, 1994.

Kotker, Norman ed., *The Horizon Book of The Elizabethan World,* American Heritage, New York, 1967.

Kuhn, Thomas S., *The Structure of Scientific Revolutions,* The University of Chicago Press, Chicago and London, 1962.

Lofite, William John, *Memorials of the Savoy,* Macmillan and Co., London 1878.

Lofts, Norah, *Anne Boleyn,* Coward, McCann & Geoghegan, Inc., New York, 1979.

Looney, J. Thomas, *"Shakespeare" Identified In Edward de Vere The Seventeenth Earl of Oxford,* Frederick A. Stokes Company, New York, 1920.

Luke, Mary M., *A Crown for Elizabeth,* Coward-McCann, Inc., New York, 1970.

Luke, Mary M., *Gloriana, The Years of Elizabeth I,* Coward, McCann & Geoghegan, Inc., New York, 1973.

Macaone, Michael, *Brush Up Your Shakespeare,* Gramercy Books, New York, 1990.

Machyn, Henry, (John Gough Nichols, ed.) *The Diary of Henry Machyn,* J.B Nichols and Son, London, 1848.

Martienssen, Anthony, *Queen Katherine Parr,* McGraw-Hill Book Company, New York, 1973.

Matus, Irvin Leigh, *Shakespeare and the Living Record,* New York, St. Martin's Press, 1991.

Matus, Irvin Leigh, *Shakespeare In Fact.* New York, Continuum, 1994.

McCabe, Richard A., *Incest, Drama and Nature's Law 1550-1700,* Cambridge University Press, Cambridge, 1993.

McMichael, George & Glenn, Edgar M., *Shakespeare and His Rivals,* The Odyssey Press Inc., New York, 1962.

McQuain, Jeffrey and Malles, Stanley Malles, *Coined by Shakespeare, Meriam-Webster, Springfield, Mass., 1998*

Millar, Oliver, Catalogue of Tudor, Stuart and Early Georgian Pictures in the Royal Collection.

Miller, Ruth Loyd, ed., *Shakespeare Identified, Vol. II. Oxfordian Vistas,* Kennikat Press Corp., Port Washing, New York, Minos Publishing, Jennings, Louisiana, 1975.

Mumby, Frank A., *The Girlhood of Queen Elizabeth,* Houghton Mifflin Company, Boston & New York, 1910.

Munro, J.J., Brooke's *'Romeus and Juliet' Being The Original of Shakespeare's "Romeo and Juliet' Newly Edited,* Duffield and Company, London, 1908.

Nelson, Alan H., transcription, Public Record Office, PRO PROB11/46, ff. 174-6: 28 July 1562, *Second surviving will of John de Vere 16th Earl of Oxford,* posted on http:// socrates.berkeley.edu/~ahnelson/oxdocs.html, February 2000.

Nelson, Alan H., transcription, Huntington Library, MS EL5870: 19-20 January 1585, *Depositions re. The Marriage of 16th earl to Margery Golding in 1548,* posted on http:// Socrates.berkeley.edu/~ ahnelson/oxdocs.html, February 2000; Huntington Library Collection, EL 5870.

Nichols, Harris, *Memoirs of the Life and Times of Sir Christopher Hatton, K.G.,* Richard Bentley, London, 1843.

Nichols, John., *The Progresess and Public Processions of Queen Elizabeth.* Vol. I-III. Reprint of the 1828 edition., Burt Franklin, New York, 1967.

Ogburn, Charlton, *The Man Who Was Shakespeare,* EPM Publications, McLean, Virginia, 1995.

Ogburn, Charlton, *The Mysterious William Shakespeare, the Myth and the Reality,* EPM Publications, McLean, Virginia, 1984.

Ogburn, Dorothy, and Charlton Ogburn, *This Star of England,* Coward-McCann, New York, 1952.

Owen, David, *The Chosen One, The New Yorker*, August 21, 2000.

Palmer, Alan, *Kings and Queens of England*, Octopus Books, London, 1976.

Palmer, Cecil, *The Tragic Story of "Shakespeare,"* Cecil Palmer, London, 1932.

Paster, Gail Kern, "The Ghost of Shakespeare," *Harper's Magazine,* April 1999.

Peachem, Henry, *The Compleat Gentleman,* London, 1622. No. 59, The English Experience, (Published in Facsimile) Da Capo Press, Theatrum Orbis Terrarum Ltd., Amsterdam, New York, 1968.

Peterson, Merrill D., *Thomas Jefferson and the New Nation,* Oxford University Press, New York, 1970.

Phillips, Gerald, *The Tragic Story of "Shakespeare" Disclosed in the Sonnets, and the Life of Edward de Vere, Seventeenth Earl of Oxford*, Cecil Palmer, London, 1932.

Piper, David, *Kings and Queens of England and Scotland*, Faber and Faber, London, 1980.

Plowden, Alison, *Marriage with my Kingdom, The Courtships of Queen Elizabeth I*. Stein and Day, New York, 1977.

Plowden, Alison, *The Elizabethan Renaissance, the Cultural Achievement*, Charles Scribner's Sons, New York, 1972.

Plowden, Alison, *The Young Elizabeth*. Stein and Day, New York, 1971.

Plowden, Alison, *Tudor Women*, Athenaeum, New York, 1979.

Pollard, A.F., *England Under Protector Somerset An Essay*, Russell & Russell, New York, 1966.

Pressly, William L., *A Catalogue of Paintings in the Folger Shakespeare Library*, Yale University Press, New Haven and London, 1993.

Pressly, William L., *The Ashbourne Portrait of Shakespeare: Through The Looking Glass*, Shakespeare Quarterly Vol. 44, Spring, 1993.

Price, Diana, *Shakespeare's Unorthodox Biography*, Greenwood Press, Westport, Connecticut, 2001.

Puttenham, George *The Arte of English Poesie 1589*, The Scholar Press Limited, Menston, England, 1968.

Read, Conyers, *Lord Burghley and Queen Elizabeth*, Alfred A. Knopf, New York, 1960.

Read, Conyers, *Mr. Secretary Cecil and Queen Elizabeth*, New York, Alfred A. Knopf, 1960.

Ridley, Jasper, *Elizabeth I, The Shrewdness of Virtue*, Viking, New York, 1987

Ridley, Jasper, *The Tudor Age*, The Overlook Press, Woodstock, New York, 1988.

Ross, Josephine, *The Monarchy of Britain*, William Morrow and Company, Inc., New York, 1982.

Ross, Josephine, *Suitors to the Queen*. New York, Coward, McCann & Geoghegan, Inc. 1975.

Rowse, A.L., *Eminent Elizabethans*, University of Georgia Press, Athens, 1983.

Rowse, A.L., *The Elizabethan Renaissance*, Charles Scribners's Sons, New York, 1971.

Rowse, A.L., *Shakespeare, The Elizabethan*, G.P. Putnam's Sons, New York, 1977.

Rowse, A.L., *Shakespeare, The Globe and the World*, Folger Shakespeare Library, Oxford University Press, New York, 1979.

Scarisbrick, J.J., *Henry VIII*, University of California Press, Berkeley and Los Angeles, 1968.

Schoenbaum, S., *Shakespeare's Lives*, Clarendon Press, Oxford, 1991.

Schoenbaum, S., *William Shakespeare: A Documentary Life*, Oxford University Press in association with The Scholar Press, New York, 1975.

Sears, Elisabeth, *Shakespeare and the Tudor Rose*, Seattle, Consolidated Press Printing, 1991.

Seymour, William, *Ordeal By Ambition, An English Family in the shadow of the Tudors*, St. Martin's, New York, 1972.

Shakespeare-Oxford Society, web site, http://www.shakespeare-oxford.com/, "Honor Roll of Sceptics, 2001.

Shell, Marc, *The End of Kinship*, Stanford University Press, Stanford, California, 1988.

Shell, Marc, *Elizabeth's Glass*. with *the Glass of the Sinful Soul* by Elizabeth I (1544) and *Epistle Dedicatory & Conclusion* by John Bale (1548), University of Nebraska Press, Lincoln and London, 1993.

Simons, Eric N., *The Queen and the Rebel,* Frederick Muller Limited, London, 1964.

Simonton, Dean Keith, *Greatness, Who Makes History and Why,* The Guilford Press, New York, 1994.

Sitwell, Edith, *The Queens and their Hive,* Toronto, Little Brown and Company, Boston, 1962.

Sobran, Joseph, *Alias Shakespeare: Solving the Greatest Literary Mystery of All Time,* The Free Press, New York, 1997.

Somerset, Anne, *Elizabeth I,* Alfred A. Knopf, New York, 1991.

Spielmann, M.H. "The Ashbourne Portrait," *Connoisseur Magazine,* Jan.-April, and May-August, 1910, pg. 42.

Statutes of the Realm, Vol. 3, Vol. 4, Part I, William S. Hein & Co., Inc., Buffalo, N.Y., 1993.

Stochholm, Johanne Magdalen, *Garrick's Folly; the Shakespeare Jubilee of 1769 at Stratford and Drury Lane,* London, Methuen, 1964.

Stone, Lawrence, *The Family Sex and Marriage,* Harper & Row, Publishers, New York, 1979.

Stopes, Charlotte Carmichael, *The Life of Henry, Third Earl of Southampton, Shakespeare's Patron,* AMS Press, New York, 1922.

Stritmatter, Roger, *Edward de Vere's Geneva Bible,* Oxenford Press, Northampton, MA., 2001.

Strong Roy, *The Persian Lady Reconsidered* in *The Art of the Emblem,* edited by Michael Bath, John Manning, Alan R. Young, AMS Press, Inc., New York, 1993.

Sulloway, Frank J., *Born to Rebel,* Vintage Books, New York, 1997.

Tetel, Marcel, *Marguerite de Navarre's Heptameron: Themes, Language, and Structure,* Duke University Press, Durham, N.C. 1973.

Thane, Elswyth, *The Tudor Wench*. Harcourt, Brace and Company, New York, 1932.

Thomas, Jane Resh, *Behind the Mask, The Life of Queen Elizabeth I,* Clarion Books, New York, 1998.

Thurley, Simon, *The Royal Palaces of Tudor England,* Yale University Press, New Haven and London, 1993.

Twain, Mark, *"Is Shakespeare Dead"* In *The Outrageous Mark Twain,* edited by Charles Neider, 137-89, Doubleday, New York, 1987.

Waldman, Milton, *Elizabeth and Leicester*, Houghton Mifflin Company, Boston, 1945.

Ward, B.M. *A Hundred Sundrie Flowers,* from the original, with pen name of *Meritum Petere, grave*, 1573, Frederick Etch ells and Hugh MacDonald, London, 1926.

Ward, B.M., *The Seventeenth Earl of Oxford,* John Murray, London, 1928.

Watkins, Susan, *The Public and Private Worlds of Elizabeth I,* Thames and Hudson, Inc., New York, 1998.

Weir, Alison, *The Children of Henry VIII,*. New York, Ballantine Books, New York, 1996.

Whalen, Richard, F., *Shakespeare—Who Was He? The Oxford Challenge to the Bard of Avon,* Pager, Westport, Connecticut, 1994.

Whalen, Richard, "The Queen's Worm In *Antony and Cleopatra,*" *Shakespeare Oxford Newsletter,* Vol. 34, No. 2, Summer 1998.

Von Klarwill, Victor, *The Fugger News-Letters, Second Series,* London, John Lane The Bodley Head, Ltd., 1926.

Whitman, Walt, *Complete Poetry and Collected Prose,* The Library of America, New York, 1982.

Whittemore, Hank, *Shakespeare's Invention, The Royal Story of the Sonnets,* 1999.

Williams, Neville, *All the Queens Men,* The Macmillan Co., New York, 1971.

Williams, Neville, *Henry VIII and His Court,* The Macmillan Co., New York, 1971.

Williams, Neville, *The Life and Times of Elizabeth I,* The Doubleday Company, New York, 1972.

Williamson, Hugh Ross, *Historical Enigmas,* St. Martin's Press, New York, 1974.

Wright, Louis B., *Advice to a Son, Precepts of Lord Burghley, Sir Walter Raleigh, and Francis Osborne,* Cornell University Press, Ithaca, New York, 1962.

Young, Alan, *Tudor and Jacobean Tournaments,* Dobbs Ferry, NY, Sheridan House, 1987.

INDEX

ABOUT THE AUTHOR

Paul Streitz has an AB from Hamilton College, was a member of the 82nd Airborne in Vietnam and has an MBA from the University of Chicago. He is co-author of the musicals *Oh, Johnny* and *Madison Avenue, the subliminal musical.*

Mr. Streitz is director of the Oxford Institute which sponsors events and symposiums to promote the awareness of the Earl of Oxford. He is a member of the Shakespeare-Oxford Society, the Shakespeare Fellowship and the Shakespeare Association of America. He frequently lectures about the Earl of Oxford.

He lives contentedly in Darien, CT with his lovely wife, adorable daughter and small dog, Shamrock.